# Syntactic Argumentation and
the Structure of English

# Syntactic Argumentation and the Structure of English

DAVID M. PERLMUTTER
SCOTT SOAMES

UNIVERSITY OF CALIFORNIA PRESS
Berkeley     Los Angeles     London

*Note:* This book is a joint work of the two authors. To emphasize this, we have listed the authors' names in alphabetical order on the title page and in the Library of Congress cataloging data, and in reverse alphabetical order on the cover.

University of California Press
Berkeley and Los Angeles, California

University of California Press, Ltd.
London, England

Library of Congress Catalog Card Number 78-65471

3   4   5   6   7   8   9

# Contents

## PART 3: THE CYCLE

## PART 4: CYCLE-TYPE OF RULES

# PART 5: FURTHER ISSUES IN COMPLEMENTATION

# PART 6: MOVEMENT RULES

# PART 7: ROSS'S CONSTRAINTS

# PART 8: PRONOMINALIZATION

## DISCUSSIONS OF PROBLEMS

## SOME FURTHER ISSUES

## BIBLIOGRAPHY

## ACKNOWLEDGMENTS

The people who contributed to this book in one way or another are too numerous to mention. They include the many students and teaching assistants who used these materials in different stages of development and whose suggestions and questions led to improvements. Special thanks go to Jane Soames for her invaluable work in typing and editing the manuscript and for living with this book over a long period. Without Brian Joseph, the chapter on modern Greek could not have been written. Polly Jacobson read and commented on the manuscript of Part 8. Mark Baltin, Geoffrey Pullum, Ivan Sag, and Annie Zaenen gave valuable advice on the Bibliography. Philip Hubbard, Keiko Otsuka, Gregory Richter, Carol Schwartz, and Kunitoshi Takahashi helped with proof-reading, and Ava Berinstein escorted the edited manuscript from Cardiff-by-the-Sea to Los Angeles.

# Introduction

## 1. THE ROLE OF ARGUMENTATION

The best way to learn syntax is not simply to *study* it, but to *do* it. The purpose of this book is to bring readers to the point where they can "do syntax" themselves. This ability is essential for understanding the field and reading its burgeoning literature.

We have designed the book for students in linguistics, for those in related fields, and for those studying linguistics for what it can contribute to their general education. We have found that focusing on syntactic argumentation is the key to meeting the needs of each of these groups.

The student who learns how to use linguistic data to argue for one hypothesis over another learns the essence of scientific method. An important advantage of linguistics in this respect is that its data is generally much more accessible than data in other sciences and typically can be obtained without time-consuming experiments. In the course of constructing syntactic arguments, the student discovers that each time a set of data leads to the rejection of one hypothesis, another must be formulated and tested against further data. In this way, one is led to investigate language in greater and greater depth and to discover the surprising intricacy of what may initially have seemed to be a familiar and ordinary phenomenon.

Syntactic argumentation is also crucial for the student who wishes to go further in linguistics. For this student, it is as important to learn the reasons for a theory as it is to learn the theory itself. Particular theories and proposals will give way to others in time. What remains most stable are the standards of argumentation and the criteria for choosing among competing hypotheses. In addition, as new theories replace old, each new one is expected to account for the data covered by its predecessors. Thus, in constructing arguments the student not only learns why some hypotheses have been rejected in favor of others, but also becomes familiar with data that has shaped the direction of the field.

Most arguments in syntax use data to show that if one makes certain assumptions, then certain conclusions follow. Examples of various argument forms are the following:

(1)  *Given assumptions A, B, and C, the data requires one to conclude D as well.*
(2)  *Given A, B, and C, the data requires one to reject D in favor of E.*
(3)  *Given A, B, and C, the data is compatible with either D or E.*
(4)  *The data makes it impossible to maintain A, B, and C jointly; at least one of them must be given up.*

In general, arguments are not absolute. They typically do not show that something *must* be the case, independent of other assumptions. Rather, they show that given specific assumptions, certain conclusions follow.

In some cases the arguments we present are quite abstract. For example, after giving an argument of the form (1), we might speak of "freeing conclusion D from assumption B." Doing this involves showing that the data requires D, whether or not one assumes B. Abstract though they may be, arguments of this type are vital for an understanding of the theoretical and empirical bases of linguists' conclusions.

## 2. THEORETICAL ORIENTATION

The advent of generative grammar in the late 1950s brought an increased interest in syntax and many new results in the field. Within generative grammar, there was a period of theoretical consensus extending to the late 1960s, at which point syntacticians began to diverge in various directions. A full understanding of the different trends in syntax in the 1970s requires an understanding of the work done in the previous decade. For this reason, the theoretical orientation of this book is very roughly that of the middle-to-late 1960s. However, we have augmented that orientation in several respects. For example, the book does not assume rule ordering, it includes new arguments for the cycle and certain other principles, and it incorporates a significant number of analyses drawn from the 1970s. The final chapter (part 8), dealing with pronominal anaphora, is used to point the way to some of the most prominent theoretical paradigms that arose in the 1970s.

### 3. TREATMENT OF FORMALISM

This book contains brief discussions of the formalism of transformational generative grammar. However, we do not dwell on it to any great extent. Although we do not discourage interest in formalism, we have found that an excessive emphasis on it at the beginning of one's study of syntax can get in the way of learning how to construct arguments and of assimilating the empirical basis of important results in the field. Those who wish to pursue formal issues in more detail may find it useful to consult other sources in conjunction with this book.

### 4. HOW TO USE THIS BOOK

The book consists of arguments, discussions, and a large number of problems that require the student to construct syntactic arguments. Many of the problems have discussions and sample solutions in the back of the book. In some cases the discussions are relatively complete; in others they amount only to hints for solving the problem in the text. There are also problems for which no discussion is given. A student who wants to become proficient in syntactic argumentation, and who wishes to derive full benefit from the problems, should work through each of them carefully before consulting the discussions. Problems for which complete discussions are not given can be used by teachers for assignments or springboards for class discussion.

At the end of each of the eight parts of the text is a section relating the material in that part to the broader linguistic literature. At the end of the entire book is a section called "Some Further Issues," which discusses issues and questions that may arise when working through various parts of the text. The material in this section is not a prerequisite for understanding and working through the text, but is intended for the reader who is interested in pursuing certain questions in greater detail.

This book developed out of an intensive introductory syntax course and has been classroom-tested at four universities. It assumes no previous background in linguistics and contains sufficient material for a two-semester sequence. It can also be used in intermediate or advanced syntax courses, either alone or in combination with other materials. Courses beyond the introductory level may use the early parts as review and then proceed through the rest of the book, or may use only those portions that deal with topics of particular interest.

In addition to use in courses, the book has been designed as a text for possible self-study and as a source book of important arguments and results that may be useful to both professional linguists and to scholars in other fields who wish to learn more about generative syntax.

# PART 1

## *Introduction and One-Story Rules*

# 1

## *Setting the Stage*

Language pervades almost every aspect of our lives. We talk, think, argue, question, theorize, command, insult, promise, and joke—all with language. An infinitely adaptable system, human language allows speakers to be as specific or general as they wish in communicating on an endless variety of topics. The ability to use language in this way is unique to human beings. It is so important that we can scarcely imagine what our lives would be like without it.

The focus of the study of language is linguistics, which aims at the development of a unified account of all human language. Although linguistics deals with a wide variety of different areas involving many complicated and subtle issues, its central questions can be simply stated:

(1) *In what ways do human languages (English, Chinese, Swahili, etc.) differ from each other, and in what ways are they all alike?*

(2) *What makes natural languages unique? What are the essential properties that distinguish them from animal communication systems and from invented languages like those of logic, mathematics, and computer science?*

In attempting to answer these questions, linguists hope to provide insights into one of our most fundamental human abilities.

An essential aspect of our linguistic competence is our ability to produce and understand sentences that we have never encountered before. For example, a competent speaker of English can recognize that the examples in (3) are grammatical sentences, whereas those in (4) are not;[1] that the sentences in (5) are synonymous; and that (6) is ambiguous.

[1] We use an asterisk to indicate deviant examples that are not well-formed sentences of English.

*3*

(3) a. *Groundhogs are apt to overrun New York unless something is done about joblessness in the burrows.*

    b. *Which subway is it likely that the groundhogs will invade?*

    c. *Groundhogs dig in for a long siege.*

(4) a. *\*The deadline expired the mayor.*

    b. *\*What subway is that the groundhogs will invade likely?*

    c. *\*Of which but then not was never.*

(5) a. *That the mayor will chastise the invaders for undermining his authority is certain.*

    b. *It is certain that the mayor will chastise the invaders for undermining his authority.*

    c. *The mayor is certain to chastise the invaders for undermining his authority.*

(6) *They are amusing groundhogs.*
*(What they are doing is amusing groundhogs.)*
*(Those groundhogs are amusing.)*

In addition, competent speakers can recognize a variety of other facts including what relationships various constituents of a sentence have to one another.

(7) a. *Groundhogs are easy to please.*
*(**Groundhogs** is understood to be the object of **please**—i.e., groundhogs are the ones who will be pleased.)*

    b. *Groundhogs are eager to please.*
*(**Groundhogs** is understood to be the subject of **please**—i.e., groundhogs will do the pleasing.)*

These examples illustrate the open-endedness of the different kinds of knowledge that go into one's understanding of a language. Even though it is unlikely that anyone has ever heard these sentences before, a competent speaker of English can recognize their properties immediately. How is this possible? Speakers do not learn sentences one by one. Rather, they implicitly grasp rules of sentence construction that enable them to produce and understand novel sentences. These rules determine which sequences of words are grammatical sentences and specify how these sentences are understood.

The productivity of natural languages is another indication that they are rule-governed. Although the vocabulary of each language is relatively small, the number of grammatical sentences that can be constructed from that vocabulary is enormous—so many, in fact, that one would not have time to learn them one by one. It has been estimated that the number of possible sentences of English containing twenty words or less greatly exceeds the number of seconds since the

*[handwritten annotation: generative - rule governed 1) can produce & understand novel sentences 2) infinite number of sentences]*

dawn of civilization.[2] Only by implicitly grasping productive principles of sentence construction can speakers achieve a mastery of so much linguistic material.

Since natural languages are rule-governed systems, the next question is, "What are the rules of sentence construction and interpretation in different languages?" Linguists try to answer this question by constructing grammars for individual languages and by forming hypotheses about the similarities inherent in all such grammars. In constructing these grammars, linguists are not attempting to tell people what rules they ought to follow when they speak; rather they are trying to formulate rules that correctly describe how people do speak. Thus, the linguist's grammar is *descriptive* rather than *prescriptive*.

Three aspects of the study of grammar essential to the linguist's investigations are syntax, semantics, and phonology. *Syntax* is the study of sentence construction. In specifying the syntactic component of a grammar, linguists attempt to formulate rules that generate each of the grammatical sentences of the language and none of the ungrammatical ones. *Semantics*, the study of meaning, explains how sentences are understood. It specifies which sentences are synonymous, which are ambiguous, which are logically contradictory, which are true by definition, which logically imply which other sentences, and so on. The semantic component of a grammar provides the basis for these specifications by giving the meanings of individual words and by describing how the meaning of a sentence is determined by the meanings of its parts. *Phonology* is concerned with how expressions are spoken and pronounced. The phonological component of a grammar describes the basic sounds used in the language and gives the

---

[2] Miller, Galanter, and Pribram (1960, pp. 146–147) estimate that the number of English sentences containing twenty words or less is on the order of $10^{30}$. The number of seconds in a century is roughly $3.15 \times 10^9$. These figures are also cited in Postal (1968).

Even this does not exhaust the set of English sentences. Given a sentence of English, we can always make it longer by adding a conjunct, by prefacing it with an expression of the form, "X thinks that . . . " or by using other techniques. Since processes like these can be repeated indefinitely, there are infinitely many English sentences.

Of course, not all grammatical sentences can be used by English speakers. For example, no one will live long enough to produce a sentence one billion words long. However, this is not a fact about English, but a fact about human longevity. Our ability to use language is limited by restrictions on memory, interest, attention span, and so on. As one compensates for these factors, the number of sentences one is able to understand increases accordingly.

This conclusion is analogous to many similar conclusions in mathematics. Although we know that there are infinitely many prime numbers, and although we can specify procedures for locating larger and larger primes, no human being could ever perform the calculations necessary to find and write down the billionth prime. This does not undermine our belief in the infinity of prime numbers, but rather makes us aware of practical limitations on computation. Similarly, we recognize that there are infinitely many sentences formed by the processes of English sentence construction even though practical limitations make it possible for us to use only a finite number of them.

rules specifying how they interact to determine the spoken form of each expression. A complete grammar must produce all and only the grammatical sentences of the language (syntax), correctly describe the meaning(s) of each sentence (semantics), and indicate the spoken form of each expression (phonology).

In addition to constructing grammars of individual languages, linguists also attempt to construct a general linguistic theory that specifies the similarities found in the grammars of all natural languages and the differences that exist among them. In so doing, linguists make explicit hypotheses about syntactic, semantic, and phonological *universals.* The task of formulating and testing these hypotheses is crucial to answering the fundamental questions of linguistics ([1] and [2]).

Linguists' theoretical constructs also bear directly on psychological issues involving language learning and language use. The work of linguists has shown natural languages to be intricate and complex systems. Yet they are mastered almost effortlessly by native speakers. It is the task of psychologists and psycholinguists to explain how this is possible.

These investigators begin with the linguists' rules, testing them with a variety of psycholinguistic techniques to determine whether or not they are unconsciously used by speakers.[3] In this way, they can find out whether or not the linguists' theoretical constructs are psychologically real. Although no one postulates a *complete* correspondence between linguists' rules and the speaker's unconscious mental processes, it is widely agreed that there must be a significant relationship between the two. One of the chief goals of psycholinguists is to discover what this relationship is. Thus, in constructing the simplest and most general set of rules describing human languages, linguists provide the foundation for the psychological investigation of language use.

They also provide a foundation for theories of language acquisition. Here, two issues stand out. First, the complexity of natural languages has led linguists to speculate that they can be learned only on the assumption that many linguistic principles are innate. Second, there is evidence that the grammars of all natural languages contain many common elements (linguistic universals). If these universals are innate, they place sharp restrictions on the form of any possible human language and help to account for the speed and ease with which these languages are acquired by children. On this view, significant aspects of the grammars of natural languages do not have to be learned at all because they are already present in the mind. This means that the mind of the child learning language is not a *tabula rasa,* but rather imposes structure on the sentences

---

[3] Two of the books that provide an introduction to psycholinguistics and useful bibliographies are Fodor, Bever, and Garrett (1974) and Clark and Clark (1977).

encountered in accordance with inborn principles for constructing rules and grammars.[4]

Speculation like this illustrates why speakers' knowledge and use of language is of great interest to psychology. There is no other human mental phenomenon of comparable complexity that is so accessible to study. For this reason, the study of language can offer unparalleled insights into human mental abilities.

Linguistics also has much to contribute to other disciplines. The question of whether or not man's linguistic abilities are innate revives a centuries-old philosophical controversy about the existence of innate mental structure. In addition, many contemporary philosophers are concerned with theories of language and with bringing these theories to bear on traditional philosophical problems. Mathematical linguists study the mathematical properties of different kinds of grammars. Computer scientists investigate the relationship between natural languages and computer languages with an eye to incorporating segments of natural languages into computer programs. Anthropologists study the relation between language and culture. Sociologists and sociolinguists are interested in the interaction between language use and social structures. Educators look for ways to use the linguists' results to improve language teaching.

While linguistics has implications for a number of other disciplines, the study of language is interesting in itself. The familiarity of language makes it altogether too easy for us to take it for granted. When it comes under scientific scrutiny, however, a wealth of intriguing facts come to light. The discovery of such unexplained facts and the attempt to account for them offer challenges that are both fascinating and demanding.

---

[4] It is the task of the psychologist, the biologist, the psycholinguist, and others to find out whether this conception of language acquisition is correct. Among the questions that must be answered are these: Are linguistic universals really innate? Would invented languages violating linguistic universals be learnable by children in the normal way? Are there alternative explanations not involving innateness for the similarities found in existing languages and for the speed and ease with which they are learned? How does the innateness hypothesis square with observed facts of language learning by children? Are the mistakes children make ones that the hypothesis would lead one to expect?

# 2

# *Reflexive and Nonreflexive Pronouns — 1*

## *1. THE DATA*

The discovery of the rules of grammar begins with an examination of linguistic data. Finding consistent patterns in the data leads to the formulation of rules which account for these regularities. Consider the distribution of reflexive and nonreflexive pronouns in the paradigms below. (Asterisks indicate ungrammatical sentences.)

| (1) | a. | *I kicked me. | (2) | a. | I kicked myself. |
| | b. | You kicked me. | | b. | *You kicked myself. |
| | c. | He kicked me. | | c. | *He kicked myself. |
| (3) | a. | I kicked you. | (4) | a. | *I kicked yourself. |
| | b. | *You kicked you. | | b. | You kicked yourself. |
| | c. | He kicked you. | | c. | *He kicked yourself. |

Reflexive pronouns are grammatical as direct objects just in those cases where nonreflexive pronouns are ungrammatical, and nonreflexive pronouns are grammatical just in those cases where reflexive pronouns are ungrammatical. Looking at the pattern of asterisks in (1–4), we see

| (1) | a. | * | (2) | a. | |
| | b. | | | b. | * |
| | c. | | | c. | * |
| (3) | a. | | (4) | a. | * |
| | b. | * | | b. | |
| | c. | | | c. | * |

Here, reflexive and nonreflexive pronouns are in *complementary distribution*.

## 2. ACCOUNTING FOR THE DATA

### 2.1 A Hypothesis

Generative grammarians have accounted for the data in (1–4) by making the following assumptions.

*Assumption 1*

We start out with structures that contain no reflexive pronouns—i.e., with structures like those in (1) and (3).

*Assumption 2*

Reflexive pronouns arise as the result of the following obligatory rule:

*Reflexivization* (Obligatory)

If the direct object of a verb is coreferential[1] with the subject, it becomes a reflexive pronoun.

### 2.2 Definitions

The entities we start out with are called the *underlying structures* of sentences.[2] Rules that apply to these structures (such as Reflexivization) are *transformations*. The entities that we end up with after all transformations have applied are called *surface structures*. Underlying structures to which no transformations apply are also surface structures by this definition.

### 2.3 The Nature of the Hypothesis

The hypothesis predicts that the surface structures it generates are grammatical sentences. Sentences that the hypothesis does not allow to be generated as surface structures are predicted to be ungrammatical. To be adequate, the hypothesis must generate all the grammatical sentences in (1–4) and prevent any ungrammatical sentences from being generated.

---

[1] When the intended referents of two noun phrases are the same, we say that they are *coreferential*.

[2] The question of where the underlying structures come from will be dealt with in section 7—Phrase Structure Rules.

### 2.4   How the Hypothesis Works

To see how assumptions (1–2) work, consider first the underlying structure

(5)   [*I kicked me*]

(We will enclose underlying structures in square brackets.) In (5) the direct object is coreferential with the subject. As a result, the rule of Reflexivization will apply, producing the surface structure

(2a)   *I kicked myself.*

Since Reflexivization is obligatory, it *must* apply to (5). This means that *(1a) will not be generated as a surface structure. Consequently, the hypothesis correctly characterizes (2a) as grammatical and *(1a) as ungrammatical.

Now consider an underlying structure in which the direct object is not coreferential with the subject.

(6)   [*you kicked me*]

Since Reflexivization cannot apply, *(2b) cannot be generated as a surface structure, and we end up with (1b) instead.

(1b)   *You kicked me.*

Here again our hypothesis characterizes the examples correctly. It accounts for the rest of the data in (1–4) in the same way. It also accounts for why (5) is realized as (2a) rather than

(7)   *\*Myself kicked me.*

and why

(8)   [*you kicked you*]

is realized as (4b) rather than

(9)   *\*Yourself kicked you.*

## 3.  CONCLUSIONS

The hypothesis that has been proposed to account for the distribution of reflexive and nonreflexive pronouns in (1–4) leads to the following conclusions:

1.   Underlying a sentence is an *underlying structure* that may be distinct from the actually occurring *surface structure.*
2.   Transformations (in this case, Reflexivization) apply to underlying structures to produce the actually occurring surface structures.

# 3

## *Reflexive and Nonreflexive Pronouns* — 2

### *1. FIRST EXTENSION OF THE DATA: THIRD PERSON REFLEXIVES AND NONREFLEXIVES*

Consider now the following paradigm:

(1)  a.  *I kicked him.*　　(2)  a.  *\*I kicked himself.*
　　 b.  *You kicked him.*　　　　 b.  *\*You kicked himself.*
　　 c.  *He kicked him.*　　　　　 c.  *He kicked himself.*

In (1a–b) the object is not coreferential with the subject. As a result, Reflexivization does not apply, and *(2a–b) are ungrammatical.

Now consider (1c) and (2c). Two facts about these sentences stand out.

(3)  a.  *A third person object can be either reflexive or nonreflexive.*
　　 b.  *(1c) and (2c) differ in meaning. In (2c), the person who kicked and the person who was kicked are the same; in (1c), they are different.*

The Reflexivization hypothesis will account for these facts if this assumption is made:

(4)  *The meaning of a sentence, including coreference information, is represented in its underlying structure.*

From assumption (4) it follows that (1c) and (2c) must have different underlying structures. In the structure underlying (2c), the subject and object are coreferential. In the structure underlying (1c) they are not. Since Reflexivization requires coreferentiality, it applies to the structure underlying (2c), but not to the structure underlying (1c). As a result, each sentence is generated from an underlying structure that correctly represents its meaning.

Since (4) allows us to account for these sentences, we will tentatively adopt this assumption, which has been influential in the development of generative grammar. In part 8 we will test its consequences in greater detail.

For purposes of exposition, we will adopt a standard device that has been used in the literature to represent coreference and noncoreference. Coreferential noun phrases will be marked with identical subscripts and noncoreferential noun phrases will be marked with distinct subscripts. Thus, we will represent the structure underlying (2c) as[1]

(5)    [*he$_i$ kicked him$_i$*]

and the structure underlying (1c) as

(6)    [*he$_i$ kicked him$_j$*]

Note that nonpronominal noun phrases can also trigger reflexivization:

(7)    *Tom kicked himself.*
(8)    *The man who lives next door kicked himself.*

We will assume that subject and object are marked for coreference in the structures underlying (7) and (8).[2]


## 2. SECOND EXTENSION OF THE DATA: NON-OBJECT REFLEXIVES AND NON-SUBJECT TRIGGERS

We formulated the Reflexivization rule as follows:

(9)    **Reflexivization (Obligatory)**

     *If the direct object of a verb is coreferential with the subject, the direct object becomes a reflexive pronoun.*

---

[1] The forms *he* and *him* have been used in underlying forms here simply in order to make underlying forms easy to read. The question of whether these pronouns should be represented in the underlying structure as *he* or *him* is left open here.

[2] Examples like (7) and (8) raise the issue of whether the entities that are reflexivized are full noun phrases or pronouns in underlying structure—i.e., whether the underlying structure for a sentence like (8) is (i) or (ii).

    (i)   *[(The man who lives next door)$_i$ kicked him$_i$]*
   (ii)   *[(The man who lives next door)$_i$ kicked (the man who lives next door)$_i$]*

This question raises fundamental issues about the nature of pronouns and coreference. These issues will be discussed in more detail in part 8. For the present, we leave it open whether (i) or (ii) underlies (8).

However, this formulation is too narrow in two respects. First, NPs[3] that are not direct objects of the verb can undergo Reflexivization:

(10)  *Tom is disgusted with himself.*
(11)  *Tom often thinks about himself.*
(12)  *Tom told Sue about himself.*

Second, NPs other than the subject can trigger Reflexivization:

(13)  *I talked to Bill about himself.*

To account for these facts, we reformulate Reflexivization.

(14)  **Reflexivization (Obligatory)**

>    *A noun phrase that is coreferential with a preceding noun phrase becomes a reflexive pronoun.*

(14) accounts for all the data that (9) does. In addition, it accounts for (10–13), which (9) does not.


## 3. THIRD EXTENSION OF THE DATA: REFLEXIVIZATION OPERATES ONLY WITHIN THE CLAUSE

Now consider the following data:[4]

(15)  a.  *Mark$_i$ says that Sally dislikes him$_i$.*
      b.  *\*Mark$_i$ says that Sally dislikes himself$_i$.*
(16)  a.  *Marie$_i$ wishes that everyone would praise her$_i$.*
      b.  *\*Marie$_i$ wishes that everyone would praise herself$_i$.*
(17)  a.  *Susan$_i$ believes that she$_i$ is brilliant.*
      b.  *\*Susan$_i$ believes that herself$_i$ is brilliant.*

---

[3] We use the abbreviation *NP* for "noun phrase."

[4] Note that (15a), (16a) and (17a) can be understood in two different ways. On one reading, the pronoun is coreferential with the first noun phrase in the sentence. On the other reading, the pronoun refers to someone not mentioned earlier in the sentence. The assumption that the meaning of a sentence is represented in underlying structure requires that each of these sentences be derived from two different underlying structures—one in which the pronoun and the initial NP are marked coreferential and one in which they are marked noncoreferential. The identical subscripts in the example sentences indicate that we are interested only in the coreferential readings.

In (15–17), reflexive pronouns are ungrammatical and nonreflexive pronouns are required. The situation is just the reverse with (18) and (19).

(18) a. *$Mark_i$ dislikes $him_i$.[5]
 b.  $Mark_i$ dislikes $himself_i$.
(19) a. *$Marie_i$ praises $her_i$.
 b.  $Marie_i$ praises $herself_i$.

Here, only reflexive pronouns are grammatical on the intended reading.

There is a clear difference between (15–17) and (18–19). (18–19) consist of a *single clause*, while (15–17) consist of *two clauses*.[6] This suggests that the Reflexivization rule should be reformulated as (20).

(20) *Reflexivization (Obligatory)*

> *A noun phrase that is coreferential with a preceding noun phrase* **in the same clause** *becomes a reflexive pronoun.*

This rule accounts for all the data that has been presented.

---

[5] Although *(18a) is grammatical with the meaning that the person Mark dislikes is someone other than Mark himself, it cannot have the meaning according to which *Mark* and *him* are coreferential. That is why *(18a) is marked with an asterisk. The same applies to *(19a).

[6] In this discussion we are relying on an intuitive notion of *clause*. Later, in section 15, we make explicit what the structures underlying (15–17) are and use these structures to characterize the notion more carefully.

# 4

## *Imperatives*

### 1. THE PHENOMENON

Although other English sentences have subjects, imperatives appear without them.

(1)    *Close the door.*
(2)    *Read the instructions.*

These sentences seem to be counterexamples to the generalization that every English sentence has a subject. How is this to be accounted for?

### 2. TWO HYPOTHESES

In our discussion of reflexive pronouns, we postulated a distinction between underlying and surface structures with a transformational rule relating the two. A similar hypothesis can be used to account for imperatives.

*Hypothesis A*

Imperative sentences are derived from underlying structures with *you* as subject by a rule called *Imperative Deletion* which deletes the subject *you* in imperatives.[1]

---

[1] Hypothesis A requires that there be some way of identifying imperative sentences, so that Imperative Deletion operates only on them (and not on all sentences with *you* as subject). For example, Imperative Deletion does not apply in sentences like

(i)    a.    *You are very tall*
       b.    *You must like Beethoven*
       c.    *You left too soon.*

We will not be concerned here with how imperative sentences are distinguished from non-imperative sentences in underlying structure.

According to this hypothesis, Imperative Deletion applies to the underlying structure

(3)　　[*you close the door*]

to produce (1). Thus, Hypothesis A claims that imperatives have subjects in underlying structure, but not in surface structure.

It is also possible to construct a hypothesis that does not make use of the distinction between underlying and surface structure.

*Hypothesis B*

Imperatives like (1) and (2) lack subjects in both underlying and surface structure. There is no rule of Imperative Deletion.

According to this hypothesis, the underlying structures of (1) and (2) are the same as their surface structures.

To decide between these two hypotheses, we must look for evidence bearing on the underlying structure of imperatives. In what follows we will refer to a grammar incorporating Hypothesis A as "Grammar A" and a grammar incorporating Hypothesis B as "Grammar B."

## 3. TESTING THE HYPOTHESES

### 3.1 The Data

The first set of data we will consider involves the distribution of reflexive and nonreflexive pronouns. Note the parallel between (4) and (5) and between (6) and (7).

| | | | | | |
|---|---|---|---|---|---|
| (4) | a. | *Kick yourself.* | (5) | a. | *You kicked yourself.* |
| | b. | *Kick yourselves.* | | b. | *You kicked yourselves.* |
| | c. | *\*Kick myself.* | | c. | *\*You kicked myself.* |
| | d. | *\*Kick himself.* | | d. | *\*You kicked himself.* |
| | e. | *\*Kick ourselves.* | | e. | *\*You kicked ourselves.* |
| | f. | *\*Kick themselves.* | | f. | *\*You kicked themselves.* |
| (6) | a. | *\*Kick you.* | (7) | a. | *\*You kicked you.* |
| | b. | *Kick me.* | | b. | *You kicked me.* |
| | c. | *Kick him.* | | c. | *You kicked him.* |
| | d. | *Kick us.* | | d. | *You kicked us.* |
| | e. | *Kick them.* | | e. | *You kicked them.* |

*Yourself* and *yourselves* are the only reflexive pronouns that can occur as direct objects of imperatives and nonimperatives with *you* as subject. *You* is the only nonreflexive pronoun that cannot be the direct object of these sentences. Why is this so?

## 3.2 Grammar A: An Answer

First consider the parallel between (4) and (5). The Reflexivization rule accounts for the data in (5). Since *you* is the underlying subject of imperatives, it also accounts for the data in (4). First it applies to the imperative underlying structure

(8)  [*you kicked you*]

producing

(9)  [*you kicked yourself*] .[2]

Then Imperative Deletion applies, yielding

(4a)  *Kick yourself.*

In this way, Grammar A accounts for the fact that imperatives can have *yourself* (or *yourselves*) as direct object.

It also accounts for the fact that these are the only reflexive pronouns that can be objects of imperatives. Since Reflexivization requires coreferentiality, it can apply to a structure of the form

(10)  [*you kick NP*]

only if the object is *you*. Thus, the reflexive pronoun will always be either *yourself* or *yourselves,* never *myself, himself, ourselves* or *themselves.*

The key to this account is its use of the Reflexivization transformation. By making *you* the underlying subject of imperatives, Grammar A allows Reflexivization to apply in imperatives in the same way that it applies in nonimperatives. As a result it correctly accounts for the parallel between (4) and (5).

Now consider the parallel between (6) and (7). The reason that nonimperatives with *you* as subject cannot have *you* as direct object is that Reflexivization is obligatory. Since it must apply to

(11)  [*you kicked you*]

(5a) will be produced and *(7a) will not be derived.

(5a)  *You kicked yourself.*
(7a)  *\*You kicked you.*

---

[2] Until now we have used square brackets to indicate underlying structures. From now on, we will use them to indicate any nonsurface structure, whether underlying or derived.

In the case of imperatives there is a new factor to consider. If

(12)  [*you kick you*]

is the structure underlying an imperative, then both Reflexivization and Imperative Deletion can apply. Further, nothing that we have said so far imposes any condition on the order in which they may apply. If Reflexivization applies first, followed by Imperative Deletion,

(4a) *Kick yourself.*

will be generated. However, if Imperative Deletion applies first,

(6a) *\*Kick you.*

will be produced, and Reflexivization will not be able to operate. Since *(6a) is ungrammatical, Imperative Deletion must be prevented from applying before Reflexivization.[3]

### 3.3 Grammar B: An Alternative

Grammar B posits that imperatives have underlying structures like

(13)  [*kick you*] .

Since these structures contain no antecedent triggering Reflexivization, this rule cannot be used to account for the parallels between (4-5) and (6-7).

Instead, Grammar B would have to adopt a new rule of Reflexivization just for imperative sentences *in addition to* the rule of Reflexivization already posited.

*2nd Person Reflexivization in Imperatives* (Obligatory)

Second person pronouns become reflexive in the main clause of imperatives.

This rule is needed in order to derive (4a) and block *(6a).

---

[3] There are several ways in which this could be accomplished. Some of these will be discussed in part 4. For the present we will not be concerned with the actual mechanism with which the grammar ensures that Imperative Deletion does not apply before Reflexivization. We will simply assume that some such mechanism exists. If this is the case, then Grammar A will not allow sentences like *(6a) to be generated, and the parallel between (6) and (7) will be accounted for.

## 4. THE RESULTS OF OUR TEST: AN ARGUMENT FOR GRAMMAR A

Although both grammars account for the data, Grammar A gives a unified account whereas Grammar B does not. In Grammar A, the rule of Reflexivization that applies in nonimperative sentences is responsible for the reflexive pronouns in imperatives as well. Thus, Grammar A captures the generalization that Reflexivization in imperatives is the same phenomenon as Reflexivization in nonimperatives. Since Grammar B is forced to posit an extra reflexivization rule for imperatives, it fails to capture this generalization. This constitutes an argument against Grammar B in favor of Grammar A.

## 5. THE PATTERN OF ARGUMENT

This result illustrates how to construct more arguments that will decide between the two grammars.

*Step 1*

Look for more parallels between imperatives and nonimperative sentences with *you* as subject.

*Step 2*

Show that Grammar A accounts for these parallels by using the same devices in imperatives that are needed independently for nonimperatives.

*Step 3*

Show that Grammar B can correctly account for the parallels in question only by adopting totally new devices for imperatives *in addition to* the devices that are needed independently for nonimperatives.

If this strategy can be carried through in a variety of cases, we will have strong reasons for selecting Grammar A over Grammar B. Grammar A implicitly claims that imperatives and nonimperatives with *you* as subject are alike. If this claim is correct, them Grammar A gives a simple and unified explanation of this similarity. Grammar B implicitly claims that imperatives and their corresponding nonimperatives are not alike. If this claim is incorrect, then the only way to make Grammar B consistent with the facts would be to adopt a series of unmotivated rules that operate only in imperatives—one additional rule for each new parallel. A grammar that is forced to do this must be rejected in favor of one that automatically makes the right predictions without any extra devices.

## 6. THE PROBLEM

### 6.1 Strategy

Below are three sets of data that illustrate certain sentence properties that depend on the subject. It is possible to use these properties to construct arguments for Grammar A and against Grammar B.[4]

### 6.2 The Data

*First Set of Data*

(19)  *Marge washed her own car.*
(20)  *I washed my own car.*
(21) **Marge washed my own car.*
(22) **I washed her own car.*
(23) **You washed their own car.*
(24)  *You washed your own car.*

*Second Set of Data*

(25)  *I held my breath.*
(26)  *You held your breath.*
(27) **I held your breath.*
(28) **You held my breath.*
(29) **I held her breath.*
(30) **I held their breath.*

*Third Set of Data*

(31)  *I won their cooperation.*
(32)  *I won his cooperation.*
(33)  *I won your cooperation.*
(34) **I won my cooperation.*
(35)  *You won their cooperation.*
(36)  *You won his cooperation.*
(37)  *You won my cooperation.*
(38) **You won your cooperation.*

---

[4] In the sentences that follow, an asterisk indicates that the sentence so marked is in some way deviant. It is irrelevant to this problem whether this deviance is characterized as syntactic or semantic.

## 6.3 The Problem

Use the sets of data above to construct three arguments in favor of Grammar A and against Grammar B. In each case, proceed in the following way: First, state what it is that depends on the subject, showing how the dependency in question is manifested in nonimperative sentences with *you* as subject. Second, show that imperatives have exactly the same properties as their non-imperative counterparts. Third, show that Grammar A automatically accounts for this fact whereas Grammar B does not. Indicate why this constitutes an argument for rejecting Grammar B in favor of Grammar A.

## 6.4 Some Pitfalls to Avoid

It is not obvious whether the dependencies illustrated by some of the sentences in this problem are the result of the application of a transformational rule or whether they are due to constraints on what is a possible underlying structure to begin with. Whichever is the case, an argument can be constructed showing that *you* is the underlying subject of imperatives. To avoid unnecessary complications in working the problem, assume that the dependencies in question are due to constraints on what is a possible underlying structure. Your arguments should show that if Grammar A is adopted, then whatever constraints are needed for nonimperatives will automatically produce the right results for imperatives as well.

In constructing your arguments, it is important to realize that it is not necessary to know *why* the sentences in the three sets of data have the properties that they do. It is enough to state the properties and to show that, however the properties may ultimately be explained, Grammar A allows the same explanation to be given for imperatives as for nonimperatives with *you* as subject, whereas Grammar B does not.

*These rules as well as the Reflexive Tr. are based on subject dependencies, i.e. that there must be a subject to form process several transforma-tions ('own' Tr., hold x's breath Tr., won x's coop. Tr and Refl. Tr.)*

# 5

# *Imperatives: Further Conclusions*

## *1. UNDERLYING STRUCTURE AND MEANING*

In section 4 we considered four different sets of data from English that lead to the conclusion that *you* is the subject of imperatives in underlying structure. Now consider the *meaning* of imperative sentences. It is often said that *you* is "understood" as the subject of imperative sentences. Thus, imperative sentences provide us with a striking correspondence. The element that is needed as subject of imperatives in underlying structure is also the element that is understood as the semantic subject of these sentences.

This correspondence has important consequences for the grammar of English that we are trying to construct. If we constructed a grammar in which the underlying structure of imperatives lacked a subject, or a grammar in which meaning was determined by surface structure, then we would need an additional rule or principle to tell us that *you* (and not *I, Mrs. Jones,* or *the people next door*) is understood as the subject of imperatives. No such additional rule or principle is needed in a grammar in which the underlying structures of sentences represent their meaning. *You* is understood as the subject of imperatives because *you* is the subject of imperatives in underlying structure.

## *2. THE OPTIONALITY OF IMPERATIVE DELETION*

So far we have been concerned with imperative sentences that have no subject in surface structure. However, there are also imperative sentences that have a surface subject.

(1)  a.    *You go home at once!*
     b.    *Go home at once!*
(2)  a.    *Don't you ever do that!*
     b.    *Don't ever do that!*

The two sentences in each pair have the same underlying structure. They differ in that Imperative Deletion has applied in the derivation of the (b)-sentences but not in the derivation of the (a)-sentences. All of these sentences will be accounted for if Imperative Deletion is an optional rule—i.e., a rule that may, but need not, apply to structures to which it is applicable.

# 6

## *Arguments and Conclusions*

So far we have posited two rules and adopted three principles about the form of the grammar of English.

*Reflexivization* (Obligatory)

A noun phrase that is coreferential with a preceding noun phrase in the same clause becomes a reflexive pronoun.

*Imperative Deletion* (Optional)

The subject (*you*) of imperative sentences is deleted.

(1) *Sentences are derived from underlying structures that may be distinct from their surface structures.*
(2) *Transformations apply to underlying structures to produce surface structures.*
(3) *The meaning of a sentence is represented in its underlying structure.*

We have also seen how linguists use data about sentences to test hypotheses and decide among competing analyses. In the case of Reflexivization we started with a small set of data which was the basis for the first formulation of the rule. We gradually expanded the data under consideration, reformulating the rule until it covered all our examples.

In deciding between a grammar with Imperative Deletion and one without it, we were concerned with capturing generalizations. Both grammars could be made to account for the data. However, only the grammar with Imperative Deletion did this automatically, using the same devices in both imperatives and nonimperatives with *you* as subject.

These two examples bring to light two requirements on all grammatical analyses.

*Requirement 1*

Whenever a hypothesis prevents a grammatical sentence from being derived or allows an ungrammatical one to be produced, it must be rejected as incorrect (e.g., the early formulations of Reflexivization).

*Requirement 2*

All other things being equal, we reject a hypothesis that posits unmotivated grammatical devices and thereby misses a generalization, in favor of a hypothesis that makes the facts follow from an independently motivated rule, thereby capturing the relevant generalization.

Requirement 1 ensures that a grammar accounts for the data. Requirement 2 reflects a basic principle of scientific inquiry. Scientists do not settle for just any description of observed facts, but rather strive to explain them by bringing them under ever simpler and more general principles or laws. Similarly, linguists do not settle for just any description of a language. Rather they attempt to explain linguistic data by subsuming it under the simplest and most general set of rules possible. In the case of imperatives, positing *you* as the underlying subject explains why imperatives behave like other sentences with *you* as subject with respect to reflexives and expressions like *Wash X's own car, Hold X's breath,* and *Win X's cooperation.*

# 7

## *Phrase Structure Rules*

We have seen that an adequate grammar of English must posit *underlying structures* for sentences that may be distinct from their surface structures. Nothing has yet been said about where these underlying structures come from.

The devices that have been used by generative grammarians to produce underlying structures are *phrase structure rules.*[1] These rules consist of three parts: an arrow, a single symbol to the left of the arrow, and a symbol or string of symbols to the right of the arrow. For example, the phrase structure rule

(1)   S → NP VP

*expands* S into *NP* and *VP*. Application of (1) to the initial symbol S produces the structure

(2)

in which an *S*-node *dominates* an *NP*-node and a *VP*-node. Suppose the grammar has another phrase structure rule:

(3)   VP → V NP

Application of (3) to (2) produces the structure

---

[1] The phrase structure rules that we present in this book go under the technical name *context-free* phrase structure rules. Although linguists have also studied other types, it has been argued that context-free rules are the only kind of phrase structure rules needed in the grammars of natural languages.

(4)

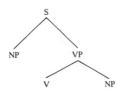

When lexical items are introduced into (4), as in

(5)

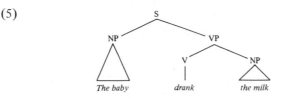

the resulting phrase structure says that the verb and the following noun phrase together constitute a verb phrase, and that the initial noun phrase and the verb phrase together constitute a sentence.[2]

In producing underlying structures like (4), one always begins by applying a phrase structure rule to the initial symbol *S*. The difficulty lies in determining just what the phrase structure rules of a particular language are. For example, (3) cannot be the only rule of English that expands *VP*, for there are also sentences with intransitive verb phrases such as

(6)    *The baby slept.*

To generate the structure underlying (6), we need the phrase structure rule

(7)    VP → V

[2] *S* stands for *sentence*.
*NP* stands for *noun phrase*.
*VP* stands for *verb phrase*.
*V* stands for *verb*.
*PP* stands for *prepositional phrase*.

We italicize the symbols when we wish to refer to the symbols themselves. Thus, to say that (1) expands *S* into *NP* and *VP* is to say that one expands the *the symbol S* into *the symbols NP* and *VP*. Similarly, to talk about the *S*-node in (2) is to talk about the node that is labeled with the symbol *S*.

In other cases we use symbols, not to refer to themselves, but to talk about various phrases in English (or other languages). For example, we might say that the V in (5) is transitive. Here 'V' is used to refer to the verb in (5), namely *drank*. Since 'V' is here being used to refer to something other than itself, it is not italicized. Similarly, when we say that *the baby* is an NP in (5), we are saying that *the baby* is a noun phrase in (5). Since 'NP' is not here being used to refer to itself, it is not italicized.

Application of (7) to (2) produces

    (8)

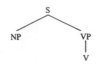

which is the underlying structure of (6).

    Now notice that (3) and (7) are partially identical; each introduces a
*V*-node under the *VP*-node. (3) also introduces an *NP*-node. Thus, (3) and (7)
can be combined to form the phrase structure rule

    (9)   V → V (NP)

Here, parentheses indicate optionality. Consequently, (9) is capable of producing
both structures like (10) and structures like (11).

However, this is still not enough. English also contains sentences like

    (12)  *Marge went to Honolulu.*

whose verb phrase is not generated by (9). In light of this, we can replace (9) by
the rule

    (13)  VP → V (NP) (PP)

which generates the structures

    (14)

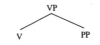

and

    (15)

as well as (10) and (11). Structure (14) underlies the verb phrase in (12).
Structure (15) underlies the verb phrase in

(16) *Helen eats rice with chopsticks.*

We have been assuming here that the underlying structures of (6), (12), and (16) are essentially the same as their surface structures. Under this assumption, (13) will generate the correct underlying structures. This assumption might be questioned, however, and other analyses of these sentences might be proposed. In that case, different phrase structure rules might be needed. We are *not* claiming that (13) is correct and therefore must be included in the grammar of English. Rather, we are using (13) to illustrate how phrase structure rules generate underlying structures.

Although it is often difficult to decide just which phrase structure rules a grammar should include, the purpose of these rules is clear. They are needed to produce underlying structures. The way to justify a particular phrase structure rule is to show that it is needed to generate the underlying structure of some well-formed sentence.[3]

[3] In some cases there may be no major transformations that apply to the underlying structure. In such cases, the underlying structure generated by the phrase structure rules is essentially the same as the surface structure. In other cases the way to justify a phrase structure rule is to show that it produces an underlying structure that is needed in order for transformations to apply correctly.

# 8

# *Actives and Passives*

## *1. THE PHENOMENON*

There are active and passive sentence pairs in English, for example:

(1)  *Columbus discovered America.*
(2)  *America was discovered by Columbus.*

The question arises as to whether these sentences have the same or different underlying structures.

Consider the following two hypotheses:

*Hypothesis A*

Active and passive sentences are derived from different underlying structures. The underlying structure of each is essentially the same as its surface structure.

*Hypothesis B*

Active and passive sentences are derived from the same underlying structures.[1]

In this section we will present an argument that has been used by generative grammarians to decide between these hypotheses. The argument is based on

---

[1] Either there is a transformation that derives passive sentences from active underlying structures, or else there is a transformation that derives active sentences from passive underlying structures. For present purposes, it does not matter which of these alternatives is considered.

restrictions on the possible subjects and objects that certain verbs can take. These restrictions are usually called *selectional restrictions.* We will first illustrate some of these restrictions with active sentences. We will then show that corresponding restrictions hold for passive sentences.

## 2. SELECTIONAL RESTRICTIONS IN ACTIVES AND PASSIVES

Compare the following active sentences.

(3)   a.   *The legislature impeached the President.*
       b.   *The legislature impeached the judge.*
       c.   *The legislature impeached the commissioner.*
       d.   *The legislature impeached the senator.*
(4)   a.   *\*The legislature impeached the artichokes.*
       b.   *\*The legislature impeached the Bible.*
       c.   *\*The legislature impeached the wallpaper.*
       d.   *\*The legislature impeached protein.*
(5)   a.   *George III reapportioned Parliament.*
       b.   *The governor reapportioned the legislature.*
       c.   *The commission reapportioned the Congress.*
       d.   *The Twenty-fifth Amendment to the state constitution reapportioned the state senate.*
(6)   a.   *\*The wallpaper reapportioned Congress.*
       b.   *\*The artichoke reapportioned Congress.*
       c.   *\*The goldfish reapportioned Congress.*
       d.   *\*The explosion reapportioned Congress.*

The sentences in \*(4) violate selectional restrictions that determine what the object of the verb *impeach* may be. The sentences in \*(6) violate selectional restrictions that determine what the subject of *reapportion* may be. Thus, the sentences in \*(4) and \*(6) are strange in a way that the sentences in (3) and (5) are not.

In general, the class of possible subjects that a verb can have in passive sentences is identical with the class of possible objects that it can have in active sentences. For example, an NP can be the subject of *be impeached* in a passive sentence if and only if it can be the object of impeach in the corresponding active. Thus, corresponding to (3) and \*(4) we have

(7)   a.   *The President was impeached by the legislature.*
       b.   *The judge was impeached by the legislature.*
       c.   *The commissioner was impeached by the legislature.*
       d.   *The senator was impeached by the legislature.*

(8)  a.  *\*The artichokes were impeached by the legislature.*
     b.  *\*The Bible was impeached by the legislature.*
     c.  *\*The wallpaper was impeached by the legislature.*
     d.  *\*Protein was impeached by the legislature.*

Similarly, the class of NPs that can occur in the *by*-phrase in passive sentences with a given verb is generally identical with the class of possible subjects that the verb can take in active sentences. For example, an NP can occur in the *by*-phrase of a passive sentence with main verb *be reapportioned* if and only if it can be the subject of *reapportion* in the corresponding active. Thus, corresponding to (5) and *\*(6) we have:

(9)  a.  *Parliament was reapportioned by George III.*
     b.  *The legislature was reapportioned by the governor.*
     c.  *Congress was reapportioned by the commission.*
     d.  *The state senate was reapportioned by the Twenty-fifth Amendment to the state constitution.*
(10) a.  *\*Congress was reapportioned by the wallpaper.*
     b.  *\*Congress was reapportioned by the artichoke.*
     c.  *\*Congress was reapportioned by the goldfish.*
     d.  *\*Congress was reapportioned by the explosion.*

So far we have illustrated two generalizations about selectional restrictions.

*Generalization 1*

The class of possible subjects that a verb can have in passive sentences is the same as the class of possible objects it can have in active sentences.

*Generalization 2*

The class of NPs that can occur in the *by*-phrase in passive sentences with a given verb is the same as the class of possible subjects that the verb can have in active sentences.

We will now show how generative grammarians have used these generalizations to argue for Hypothesis B.


## 3. AN ARGUMENT FOR DERIVING ACTIVES AND PASSIVES FROM THE SAME UNDERLYING STRUCTURE

### 3.1 The Statement of Selectional Restrictions Under Hypothesis B

Under Hypothesis B, active and passive sentence pairs are derived from the same source. We can account for the fact that the selectional restrictions on these sentences mirror each other by assuming that selectional restrictions are stated on underlying structures. If the underlying structure of sentences is active, then selectional restrictions are stated on active underlying forms.

*Selectional Restriction 1*

Subjects of *reapportion* must refer to humans, governing institutions, or laws promulgated by such institutions.

*Selectional Restriction 2*

Objects of *impeach* must refer to officials of government.

An optional transformation is posited to derive passives from actives. This transformation makes the old object NP into a new subject, places the old subject into a *by*-phrase and changes the verb form from active to passive.

Under this hypothesis, selectional restrictions for passives do not need to be stated separately; they follow automatically from the fact that passives are derived from actives. For example, the underlying structures

(11)   a.   *[*the legislature impeached the wallpaper*]
      b.   *[*the explosion reapportioned the legislature*]

violate selectional restrictions and hence are not well-formed. Therefore, both *(12) and *(13) are characterized as deviant.

(12)   a.   *The legislature impeached the wallpaper.*
      b.   *The explosion reapportioned the legislature.*
(13)   a.   *The wallpaper was impeached by the legislature.*
      b.   *The legislature was reapportioned by the explosion.*

If, on the other hand, the underlying structure of sentences is passive, then selectional restrictions are stated on passive underlying forms and an optional transformation is posited to derive actives from passives. Under this alternative, the selectional restrictions found in active sentences follow automatically from the fact that actives are derived from passives. Thus, whichever form is taken to be the underlying structure (active or passive), a grammar in which selectional restrictions are stated on underlying structures states the relevant selectional restrictions only once.

## 3.2 The Statement of Selectional Restrictions under Hypothesis A

Since active and passive sentence pairs have different underlying structures under Hypothesis A, there is no single structure on which to state selectional restrictions for both types of sentences. Thus, in addition to Selectional Restrictions 1 and 2 for active structures, Hypothesis A requires restrictions 3 and 4 for passive structures.

*Selectional Restriction 3*

NPs in the *by*-phrase with *be reapportioned* (passive sentences) must refer to humans, governing institutions, or laws promulgated by such institutions.

*Selectional Restriction 4*

Subjects of *be impeached* (passive sentences) must refer to government officials.

Since this duplication of selectional restrictions is repeated for all verbs in the language that have both active and passive forms, we must reject Hypothesis A in favor of Hypothesis B.

### 3.3 Capturing Generalizations and Missing Generalizations

There is another way to view the argument just given. Although both hypotheses can account for the data, Hypothesis B captures generalizations that Hypothesis A misses—Generalizations 1 and 2. The fact that Hypothesis B uses the same selectional restrictions to account for active and passive sentences means that it captures these generalizations. The fact that Hypothesis A is forced to use different selectional restrictions for actives and passives means that it misses them.

In the linguistic literature, there are many arguments based on capturing generalizations. Such arguments typically reduce to the claim that one hypothesis must state twice something that the other hypothesis need state only once. Such arguments constitute a special case of a more general form of argument: given a choice between two hypotheses that both account for the data, all other things being equal, we reject the one that forces us to posit otherwise superfluous statements, rules, or constraints.[2]

[2] For further discussion of the role of meaning in linguistic arguments like the one given above, see SFI-1 in Some Further Issues in the back of the book.

It should be pointed out that the argument in §3 (i.e., under heading 3) is not the only reason for adopting Hypothesis B. The answer to the problem in section 10 (Activization vs. Passivization) provides another argument for Hypothesis B. The matter is also taken up again in SFI-7 of Some Further Issues. This may be read after part 5. At that point we consider other proposals for capturing sameness of selectional restrictions and show that these proposals do not eliminate the need for a transformation relating actives and passives.

# 9

## *Grounds for Choice between Alternative Grammars*

### 1. ALTERNATIVE GRAMMARS THAT MAKE DIFFERENT EMPIRICAL PREDICTIONS

A grammar can be regarded as a *theory* of a language. When two grammars make different empirical predictions about the language, we obviously choose the grammar that makes the correct predictions. When we do this, we say that we are choosing between grammars on *empirical* or *theory-external* grounds. In such cases, the choice is made on the basis of empirical data, which is external to the theory (grammar) itself.

### 2. ALTERNATIVE GRAMMARS THAT MAKE THE SAME EMPIRICAL PREDICTIONS

There are cases in which two grammars make correct predictions even though they incorporate different devices to account for the same facts. If the grammars are comparable in all other respects, but Grammar A can account for the data only by positing some additional device(s) that Grammar B does not need, then Grammar B is adopted over Grammar A. Here the choice between the two grammars is made on grounds internal to the theories (grammars) themselves, or *theory-internal* grounds.

The extra devices that one grammar needs may be additional rules, extra restrictions on underlying structures, additional conditions governing rule interaction, or extra constraints of some other kind.[1] It should be emphasized, however, that it is possible to choose between alternative grammars on theory-internal grounds only if both grammars make correct empirical predictions. If one grammar makes correct predictions while the other does not, the choice between them must be made on theory-external grounds.

[1] Of course, there may be cases in which the devices posited by alternative grammars are not strictly comparable. In such cases we may have no clearcut sense that one grammar is simpler than the other, or that one grammar captures generalizations that the other does not. Hence, it may not always be possible to choose among grammars on theory-internal grounds. Nevertheless, in many cases the choices are clear and are recognized by working linguists. These are the cases that we will be concerned with in this book.

# 10

## *Activization vs. Passivization*

### *1. TWO CONFLICTING HYPOTHESES*

*Hypothesis A*

The underlying form of sentences is active. Passives are derived from actives by an optional rule of Passivization.

*Hypothesis B*

The underlying form of sentences is passive. Actives are derived from passives by an optional rule of Activization.

### *2. THE PHENOMENON: FIXED EXPRESSIONS*

English contains several syntactically complex phrases that function in certain ways like single verbs. One such phrase is the fixed expression *take advantage of.* The meaning of this expression is similar to that of the verb *exploit.* Thus,

(1)    *Everyone took advantage of their inexperience*

is similar in meaning to

(2)    *Everyone exploited their inexperience.*

The fixed expression *take advantage of* also has other interesting properties. First, corresponding to (1), there is not just one passive, but two.

(3)    *Advantage was taken of their inexperience by everyone.*
(4)    *Their inexperience was taken advantage of by everyone.*

Second, the noun *advantage* occurs without an article or other modifier in (1), (3), and (4). This is interesting because *advantage* can occur without an article or modifier only in a very limited range of environments.

(5)    a.    *She has a big advantage.*
       b.    *\*She has advantage.*
(6)    a.    *The other team has the advantage.*
       b.    *\*The other team has advantage.*
(7)    a.    *His advantage is significant.*
       b.    *\*Advantage is significant.*

Although *advantage* cannot occur without an article or other modifier in (\*5b–\*7b), it can occur alone in (1), (3), and (4).


## 3. THE PROBLEM

Use the above phenomenon to construct an argument to decide between Hypothesis A and Hypothesis B.

In working this problem, you should make the following three assumptions.

*Assumption 1*

If the underlying form of sentences is active, then the Passivization rule is capable of deriving both (3) and (4) from the structure underlying (1).

*Assumption 2*

If the underlying form of sentences is passive, there are two well-formed underlying structures:

(i)    [*advantage was taken of their inexperience by everyone*]
(ii)   [*their inexperience was taken advantage of by everyone*]

*Assumption 3*

The activization rule is capable of deriving (1) from either (i) or (ii).

Do not worry about how Activization and Passivization would have to be formulated in order to satisfy these assumptions. For purposes of this problem, simply assume that these assumptions are correct.

To solve this problem, compare how a grammar incorporating Hypothesis A would state the restrictions on the occurrence of *advantage* (without an article or other modifier) with the way that a grammar incorporating Hypothesis B would state these restrictions. Any solution must account for both the grammaticality of (1), (3), and (4) and the ungrammaticality of (*5b-*7b). Your solution should show how these facts can be accounted for without loss of generality under one of the two hypotheses but not the other.

Assume that restrictions on *advantage* state the conditions under which it can occur without an article or other modifier. It should be noted parenthetically that such restrictions are generally *not* referred to as selectional restrictions. Generative grammarians usually use the term *selectional restrictions* to refer to restrictions on *verbs* that limit such things as the type of subject and object a particular verb can have. Since *advantage* is not a verb, the restrictions on *advantage* that you formulate would generally not be called *selectional restrictions*.

## 4. POST MORTEM

After working the problem, determine whether or not your conclusion is affected if Assumption 2 is replaced by Assumption 2'.

*Assumption 2'*

If the underlying form of sentences is passive, there is only one well-formed underlying structure.

>    *Possibility A:* The underlying structure is (i).
>    *Possibility B:* The underlying structure is (ii).

# 11

## *Formulating the Passive Rule: A First Approximation*

The arguments in section 10 are based on the assumption that Passivization can derive both

 (1) *Advantage was taken of their inexperience by everyone*

and

 (2) *Their inexperience was taken advantage of by everyone*

from the structure underlying

 (3) *Everyone took advantage of their inexperience.*

This can be done if we say that *take advantage of* is a verb with internal structure, as in

 (4)

According to (4), *take* is a verb, *advantage* is a noun phrase, and *of* is a preposition, while the entire phrase *take advantage of* is a verb. If *take advantage of* has the structure (4), then the structure underlying (3), (1), and (2) is

(5)

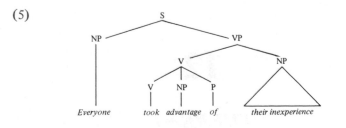

We now say that Passivization applies to structures of the form

(6)  NP – V – NP

Passivization will then be able to apply to (5) in two different ways.

(7)

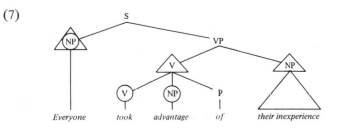

Application of Passivization to the circled constituents will produce sentence (1). Application of Passivization to the constituents in triangles will produce sentence (2).[1]

---

[1] Additional discussion of the formulation of Passive can be found in SFI-2.

# 12

## *THERE−1*

### *1. THE PHENOMENON*

Consider the word *there* which occurs in (1).

(1)    *There is a mouse in the bathtub.*

We must distinguish this word *there*, which is unstressed, from the stressed, demonstrative *there* which occurs in (2).

(2)    *The mouse is over there.*

### *2. THE PROBLEM*

What role does unstressed *there* play in sentences—is it a subject, direct object, indirect object, or what? The three arguments that follow show that *there* is a subject.[1]

---

[1] To say that *there* is a subject is not to say that it is a subject in underlying structure. The question of whether *there* is present in underlying structure or is inserted by a transformation will be taken up in THERE−2.

### 3. THREE ARGUMENTS

**3.1 Argument One**          *derived subjects*

(3)  a.  <u>They</u> were late.

   b.  Were they late?

(4)  a.  <u>The guy who bought the house</u> has found out what they were doing.

   b.  Has the guy who bought the house found out what they were doing?

(5)  a.  <u>That note</u> was written by Susan.

   b.  Was that note written by Susan?

(6)  a.  <u>There</u> was a mouse in the bathtub.

   b.  Was there a mouse in the bathtub?

The questions in (3–5) differ from the corresponding declaratives in that the subject[2] of the question (*they* in [3a], *the guy who bought the house* in [4a], and *that note* in [5a]) has been interchanged with a verbal element (in these examples, the "auxiliary verbs" *have* and *be*). The fact that *there* is inverted in (6b) is an argument that it is a subject.

**3.2 Argument Two**

(7) <u>Rodney was</u> eating an octopus, wasn't he?

(8) <u>It's</u> raining, isn't it?

(9) <u>Bill kissed</u> Harriet, didn't he?

(10) <u>Harriet was</u> kissed by Bill, wasn't she?

(11) *<u>Harriet was</u> kissed by Bill, wasn't he?

(12) *<u>Harriet was</u> kissed by Bill, didn't he?

(13) <u>You wrote</u> a letter to my uncle, didn't you?

(14) *<u>You wrote</u> a letter to my uncle, didn't it?

(15) *<u>You wrote</u> a letter to my uncle, didn't he?

(16) Last <u>Saturday was</u> a memorable day, wasn't it?

(17) *Last Saturday <u>the Red Sox won</u> the game, didn't it?

(18) Last Saturday <u>the Red Sox won</u> the game, didn't they?

(19) <u>There is</u> a lot of work to be done, isn't there?

[2] By *subject* we mean *derived subject*. Although in some cases the derived subject of a sentence may be the same as the underlying subject, in some cases, it is not. For example, the underlying subject of (5a) is *Susan*. However, its derived subject is *that note*. In (5b), it is this derived subject that is inverted with *be*.

In (7–9), the subject is repeated in pronominal form in what is called the *tag question* at the end of the sentence. The contrast between (10) and *(11–12) shows that it is the surface structure subject, not the underlying subject, that appears in tag questions. (13–18) show that an NP in the sentence other than the (surface structure) subject cannot appear in tag questions. The crucial sentence is (19). Since *there* appears in the tag question, we conclude that it is the (surface structure) subject of the sentence.

### 3.3 Argument Three

(20) *Susan said that the guy from Wyoming was happy, and so he was.*

(21) *Frank said that she had been elected, and so she had.*

(22) *Larry said that it was raining, and so it was.*

(23) *\*Harold said that Mary would win the match, and so he did.*

(24) *\*Mike said that Susan was waiting, and so the guy from Wyoming was.*

(25) *\*Mary said that Susan had beaten Harry, and so he had.*

(26) *Harriet said that last Saturday was a memorable day, and so it was.*

(27) *\*Harriet said that last Saturday the Red Sox won the game, and so it did.*

(28) *Harriet said that last Saturday the Red Sox won the game, and so they did.*

(29) *Joe said that there was a mouse in the bathtub, and so there was.*

In (20–22), (26) and (28), the (surface structure) subject of the embedded clause is repeated in pronominal form in the *and so* clause. Where this is not the case, as in *(23–25) and *(27), the sentence is ungrammatical. Thus, the fact that *there* appears in the *and so* clause in (29) is another argument that it is the (surface structure) subject.

## 4. THE NATURE OF THE ARGUMENTS

Each of the three arguments presented here has the same form.

(30) a.    *Only subjects appear in construction X.*

     b.    ***There** appears in construction X.*

     c.    *Therefore, **there** is a subject.*

Another way to put the point is to say that *there* behaves like a subject. To capture this generalization, we postulate that *there* is a subject.[3]

[3] In *Actives and Passives*, we indicated that arguments based on capturing a generalization constitute a special case of a more general form of argument: given the choice between two hypotheses that both account for the data, we reject the hypothesis that requires an additional statement, rule or constraint in favor of one that needs no such additional device. If we examine the arguments given above for the subjecthood of *there* we can see that they also are instances of this same general form of argument. In each case, two different grammars of English are being compared.

(i)    a.    *Grammar A:* **There** *is a subject.*
      b.    *Grammar B:* **There** *is not a subject.*

Each of the arguments shows that Grammar B is forced to include something that is unnecessary in Grammar A.

First consider Argument One. Let us assume for the moment that the derivation of the (b)-sentences in (3–6) involves the application of the following transformation.

*Subject-Auxiliary Inversion*

The subject of a question is inverted with the auxiliary (e.g., with the auxiliary verbs *have* and *be*).

If *there* is a subject, as it is in Grammar A, the same rule that derives (3b), (4b), and (5b) will automatically derive (6b) as well. In Grammar B, on the other hand, *there* is not a subject. Thus, in order to derive (6b), the rule that operates in (3b), (4b), and (5b) must be complicated. It now must state that either subjects or *there* are inverted with the auxiliary verb. Since the rule that is needed in Grammar B has to mention *there* in addition to subjects, it is more complicated than the rule of Subject Auxiliary Inversion that is posited by Grammar A. Thus, we prefer Grammar A to Grammar B.

Argument Two has exactly the same form. Let us assume that the tag questions in (7–10), (13), (16), and (18) are formed by a rule that reproduces both the subject (in pronominal form) and a verbal element at the end of the sentence. Under Grammar A, the same rule that forms these tag questions will automatically form the tag question in (19) as well. Under Grammar B, on the other hand, it is necessary to add something additional to the rule, saying that if the sentence contains *there,* it is *there* rather than the subject that must be copied in the tag question. The rule that forms tag questions under Grammar B is therefore more complicated than the rule that accounts for the same data under Grammar A. Because it accounts for the same data with less apparatus, we adopt Grammar A over Grammar B.

In exactly the same way, Argument Three reduces to an argument that Grammar B requires a more complicated rule or statement to account for the *and so* construction; we therefore reject Grammar B in favor of Grammar A.

# 13

## *THERE–2*

### *1. OVERVIEW*

In THERE-1 we argued that *there* is a subject in surface structure. Here we will do three things. First, we will show that although *there* is a surface subject, there are severe restrictions on the environments in which it may occur. Second, we will present traditional arguments used by transformational grammarians for postulating a rule of THERE-Insertion that derives sentences like (1b) and (2b) from the structures that also underlie (1a) and (2a).

(1)  a.  *A little girl is playing in the backyard.*
     b.  *There is a little girl playing in the backyard.*
(2)  a.  *Several candidates are running for president.*
     b.  *There are several candidates running for president.*

Third, we will discuss how the rule of THERE-Insertion might be formulated.

### *2. RESTRICTIONS ON THE DISTRIBUTION OF* THERE

*There* occurs in only a very limited range of environments. Note, for example, the ungrammaticality of

(3)  *\*There is nice.*
(4)  *\*There played hard yesterday.*

We will discuss three sets of restrictions on the distribution of *there*.

## 2.1 THERE and Verbs of Existence

The class of verbs with which *there* can occur is highly restricted.

(5)    *There was a mouse in the bathtub.*
(6)    *There exists a good argument for that.*
(7)    *There arose a controversy on that subject.*
(8)    *There ensued a wild melee.*
(9)    *There resulted a big discrepancy between their testimony and ours.*

The verbs that can take *there* seem to constitute a semantic class; they have something to do with existence or coming into existence. Other verbs cannot have *there* as subject.

(10) *\*There sang a popular singer a new song.*
(11) *\*There left early three guests.*

## 2.2 THERE and Selectional Restrictions

*There* occurs in structures of the form

(12)   *There, Verb of Existence, NP, . . .*

In general, a sentence of the form (12) is grammatical only if the corresponding sentence of the form (13) is also grammatical.

(13)   *NP, Verb of Existence, . . .*

The following examples illustrate this point.

(14)   a.    *A bird was chirping on the garage roof.*
        b.    *There was a bird chirping on the garage roof.*
(15)   a.    *Some dirt was under the rug.*
        b.    *There was some dirt under the rug.*
(16)   a.    *\*An injustice was in front of the fireplace.*
        b.    *\*There was an injustice in front of the fireplace.*
(17)   a.    *\*A theorem was sitting in the corner.*
        b.    *\*There was a theorem sitting in the corner.*

\*(16a) and \*(17a) violate selectional restrictions.[1] \*(16a) is deviant because an injustice is not the sort of thing that can be in front of a physical object. \*(17a)

---

[1] We are using the term *selectional restrictions* here in a broad sense. The term is sometimes used only for restrictions on the class of possible subjects or objects a particular verb can take. If the verb in both (15) and \*(16) is simply *was*, the notion *selectional restriction* must be broadened in order for it to characterize the contrast between normal sentences like (15) and deviant ones like \*(16).

is deviant because a theorem is not the kind of thing that can sit in a corner. The fact that *(16b) and *(17b) are deviant in the same way that *(16a) and *(17a) are shows that these restrictions carry over to sentences with *there.*

## 2.3 THERE and Indefinite NPs

In certain cases, sentences of the form (12) are not good even though the corresponding sentences of the form (13) are fully acceptable. For example, consider the contrast between (18a–b) on the one hand and (19a-*b) on the other.

(18)  a.    *A policeman was here today.*
      b.    *There was a policeman here today.*
(19)  a.    *The policeman was here today.*
      b.    **There was the policeman here today.*

Although there may be special contexts in which *(19b) could be given an interpretation, it is clearly different from (18b). Linguists have marked this difference by calling attention to the distinction between *indefinite* NPs like *a policeman* and *definite* NPs like *the policeman.* Linguists have usually assumed that *there* can only occur in structures in which the NP is indefinite.[2]

(20)  *There, Verb of Existence, Indefinite NP, . . .*


## 3. TRADITIONAL ARGUMENTS FOR THERE-INSERTION

### 3.1 Two Hypotheses

In this section we will consider traditional arguments that have been used to decide between the following two hypotheses.

[2] When *be* is the verb, *there* can be used with a definite NP, but only when giving a list. For example, if asked whether or not there were any witnesses to an accident, one might appropriately respond, "Well, there was the policeman; there was the shopkeeper; there was the old woman on the corner. . . . " With verbs of existence other than *be*, however, the list use is impossible and there cannot occur with a definite NP.

   (i)    **There arose the leader, there arose the general, . . .*
   (ii)   **There exists the even prime number, there exists the largest prime under 100, . . .*
   (iii)  **There ensued the riot, there ensued the melee, . . .*

An adequate grammar of English must characterize *(i–iii) as deviant. It must also characterize sentences like *(19b) as having a status different from that of sentences like (18b).

*Hypothesis A*

*There* is a subject in underlying structure. Constraints on its distribution are stated in underlying structure. Not only (14a) and (15a), but also (14b) and (15b) are underlying structures.

*Hypothesis B*

*There* is a derived subject that is introduced by a rule of THERE-Insertion. Constraints on its distribution are incorporated into the transformation that inserts it. (14b) and (15b) are derived from the structures underlying (14a) and (15a) by THERE-Insertion.

## 3.2  An Argument Based on Selectional Restrictions

In *Actives and Passives* we saw that the grammar of English must state selectional restrictions on the class of possible subjects that verbs can take. Such restrictions characterize (14a) and (15a) as grammatical, and *(16a) and *(17a) as deviant. Now consider the (b)-sentences, which contain *there* as subject. Whenever selectional restrictions characterize an (a)-sentence as deviant, the corresponding (b)-sentence is also deviant. Likewise, whenever an (a)-sentence satisfies selectional restrictions, the corresponding (b)-sentence does so as well.

This fact has been used to construct an argument in favor of Hypothesis B. The argument compares how the deviance of *(17b) would be accounted for under Hypothesis B with the way it would be accounted for under Hypothesis A. A parallel argument could be made for *(16b).

Under both Hypothesis A and Hypothesis B, the grammar must contain a selectional restriction that characterizes as deviant any sentence in which *theorem* is the subject of *sit*. Under Hypothesis B, *(17a) and *(17b) have the same underlying structure—one in which *a theorem* is the subject of *was sitting*. As a result, if selectional restrictions are stated on underlying structures (as was found to be necessary in the case of active and passive sentences), then the selectional restriction that characterizes *(17a) as deviant will automatically characterize *(17b) as deviant as well.

Under Hypothesis A, on the other hand, *(17a) and *(17b) have different underlying structures. In the structure underlying *(17a), *a theorem* is the subject of *was sitting*, and so the selectional restriction on the subject of *sit* will characterize *(17a) as deviant. In the structure underlying *(17b), however, the subject is *there*. The selectional restriction that prevents *a theorem* from being

With selection restrictions, HA fails to show a relationship between sentences with NP Subj and sent. w/'there'

2 sel. res. needed for every occurrence

the subject of *sit* will therefore fail to characterize *(17b) as deviant.[3] As a result, Hypothesis A requires some additional selectional restriction such as (21) that is not required by Hypothesis B.

(21)  **Sit** *cannot occur with* **a theorem** *in structures in which* **there** *is the subject.*

Since this duplication of selectional restrictions is needed for every verb that occurs with *there,* Hypothesis A must be rejected.

This argument can also be stated in terms of capturing a generalization. The generalization is that sentences with *there* as subject and the corresponding sentences without *there* have the same selectional restrictions. Since Hypothesis A requires stating the selectional restrictions separately for these sentences, it misses the generalization. Since Hypothesis B derives *there*-sentences from structures without *there,* it needs to state the selectional restrictions only once. Thus, Hypothesis B captures a generalization that Hypothesis A misses.

### 3.3  An Argument Based on Passive

(22)  *The policeman killed a demonstrator.*
(23)  **There killed the policeman a demonstrator.*
(24)  *A demonstrator was killed by the policeman.*
(25)  *There was a demonstrator killed by the policeman.*

In §2.1 it was pointed out that only a restricted class of verbs can have *there* as subject. Since *kill* is not such a verb, *(23) is ungrammatical. However, *be,* the auxiliary verb introduced by Passive, is one of the verbs that allows *there.*[4] As a result, (25) is grammatical.[5] Therefore, (24) has a corresponding grammatical

---

[3] A counterargument to this might run as follows.
The selectional restriction on *sit* must be stated roughly as follows:

(i)  *The subject of* **sit** *must designate a physical object.*

Since Hypothesis A postulates *there* as the underlying subject of *(17b), and since *there* does not designate a physical object, under Hypothesis A the same selectional restriction— namely (i)—will characterize both *(17a) and *(17b) as deviant even though they have different underlying structures.

This counterargument tacitly assumes that any sentence with *there* as subject of *sit* will be characterized as deviant. Thus, it incorrectly predicts that the sentence

(ii)  *There was a three-year-old child sitting in the corner*

will also be characterized as deviant. Since (ii) is a well-formed sentence, this counterargument does not go through.

[4] Normally *there* can only occur with verbs of existence, of which *be* is one. Examples like (25) show that *there* can also occur with the *be* that is introduced by Passive.

[5] Since *there* only occurs with indefinite NPs, application of Passive is also needed to interchange the definite *the policeman* with the indefinite *a demonstrator.*

*There can not be ruled out* THERE – 2 *based on underlying structures because Passive Tr. may allow for it. ⇒ There is derived.*

sentence with *there*, whereas (22) does not. Further, (22) and (24) are derived from the same underlying structure. Thus, it is impossible to characterize the structure underlying (22) and (24) as one that does or does not allow *there*.

Stated more generally, it is impossible to predict whether or not *there* will be grammatical on the basis of underlying structures alone, since subsequent application of Passive may make it possible for *there* to occur in a sentence in which it would not be able to occur otherwise. It follows then that the constraints on *there* cannot be stated on underlying structures, and that *there* must be introduced by a transformation. Consequently, Hypothesis A has been rejected in favor of Hypothesis B.

Under Hypothesis B, (25) can be derived without difficulty. First, Passive applies to the underlying structure

(26)  [*the policeman killed a demonstrator*]

producing

(27)  [*a demonstrator was killed by the policeman*]

Now that the environment for THERE-Insertion has been created, it can apply to derive (25).

## 4. *FORMULATING* THERE-*INSERTION*

### 4.1  Essentials

The rule of THERE-Insertion derives structures of the form

(28)  *There, Verb of Existence, Indefinite NP,* ____

from structures of the form

(29)  *Indefinite NP, Verb of Existence,* ____ .

Thus, THERE-Insertion derives the (b)-sentences from the structures underlying the (a)-sentences.

(30)  a.  *Someone is sleeping.*
     b.  *There is someone sleeping.*
(31)  a.  *A riot ensued.*
     b.  *There ensued a riot.*
(32)  a.  *A tape of the conversation exists.*
     b.  *There exists a tape of the conversation.*
(33)  a.  *A new leader arose.*
     b.  *There arose a new leader.*

## 4.2  Formulating THERE-Insertion:  A Preview

In the linguistic literature the rule of THERE-Insertion is often formulated as follows:

$$(34) \quad \begin{matrix} NP, \\ [-\text{Def}] \end{matrix} \quad \left\{ \begin{matrix} \text{be} \\ \text{exist} \\ \text{arise} \\ \cdot \\ \cdot \\ \cdot \end{matrix} \right\}, \quad X \Rightarrow \textit{There}, 2, 1, 3$$

$$\qquad\qquad\qquad 1 \qquad\qquad 2 \qquad\qquad 3$$

In essence, (34) is simply a shorthand for (28) and (29). The left side of (34) is the equivalent to (29). It specifies the class of structures to which THERE-Insertion can apply. The righthand side of (34) is short for (28). It tells what happens to a structure as a result of applying THERE-Insertion. *There* replaces the old subject (the indefinite NP), which moves to the immediate right of the verbal element. Everything else in the structure remains the same.

## 4.3  Optional vs. Obligatory Cases of THERE-Insertion

In all of the cases we have considered so far, THERE-Insertion is optional. However, there are also cases in which it appears to be obligatory.

(35)  a.   *Prime numbers between 90 and 100 are.*
      b.    *There are prime numbers between 90 and 100.*
(36)  a.   * Honest politicians are.*
      b.    *There are honest politicians.*
(37)  a.   * Ten-thousand species of beetles are.*
      b.    *There are ten-thousand species of beetles.*

In these sentences, *be* is used in the sense of *exist*. We will assume that (35b–37b) are derived from *(35a–37a), and hence that in these cases, THERE-Insertion is obligatory.

# 14

## *Notes on the Formalism of Transformational Grammar*

### *1. TREES*

(1)

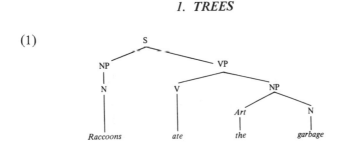

Trees such as this are produced by phrase structure rules. The bottom line consisting of lexical material is called the *terminal string*.

Trees provide several kinds of information.

### 1.1 Domination

A node A in a tree *dominates* a node B if and only if there is a uniformly downward path from A to B. For example, in (1) the *S*-node dominates everything else in the tree; the *NP*-node immediately beneath the *S*-node dominates both the *N*-node directly below it and *raccoons*; and so forth.

Note that domination is a transitive relation; if a node A dominates a node B, and if B dominates C, then A dominates C.

## 1.2 Immediate Domination

A node A *immediately dominates* an element B if and only if A is the first node above B. For example, the *S*-node immediately dominates the *NP*-node and the *VP*-node; the *VP*-node immediately dominates the *V*-node and the *NP*-node that is directly beneath it; and so forth.

## 1.3 Exhaustive Domination

A node A *exhaustively dominates* an element, or sequence of elements, Z of the terminal string if and only if A dominates Z and nothing else in the terminal string. For example, the *VP*-node in (1) exhaustively dominates the string *ate the garbage* although it does not exhaustively dominate any of these words individually.

The distinction between domination and exhaustive domination can be seen in any case in which a node branches. Thus, the distinction can be seen in the case of the *S*-node and the second *NP*-node in (1), but not in the case of the first *NP*-node. the *V*-node, the *Art*-node, or either *N*-node.

## 1.4 Constituent Types

We can use exhaustive domination to define the constituent types of expressions in a tree. Let T be a tree with terminal string s of lexical elements. For any substring x of s, x is a noun phrase in T if and only if x is exhaustively dominated by an *NP*-node in T. Analogous definitions could be given for the other constituent types—verb phrases, verbs, nouns, etc. Thus, (1) provides the following facts about constituent types:

(4)  a.  *Garbage is a noun.*
     b.  *The is an article.*
     c.  *Ate is a verb.*
     d.  *Raccoons is both a noun and a noun phrase.*
     e.  *The garbage is a noun phrase.*
     f.  *Ate the garbage is a verb phrase.*
     g.  *Raccoons ate the garbage is a sentence.*

## 1.5 Linear Order

In addition to providing information about domination, immediate domination, exhaustive domination, and constituent types, trees like (1) indicate the linear order in which elements appear. For example, in (1), *raccoons* precedes *ate the garbage, ate* precedes *the garbage,* and so on.

## 2. *FROM TREES TO TRANSFORMATIONS*

We have already seen that there are empirical arguments for distinguishing between underlying and surface structures. Consequently, there must be rules of grammar that convert underlying structures into surface structures.

What then is the nature of the underlying and surface structures, and what is the nature of the rules that derive one from the other? In this book we assume that both underlying and surface structures are *trees*. We will not, however, presuppose anything about the formal statement of the rules that derive surface structures from underlying structures. Since the question of how rules should be formally stated is an empirical one, the way to approach it is to first determine which rules are empirically motivated and then construct a formal theory for the statement of these rules.

The first theory of grammar to distinguish between underlying and surface structures and to attempt to state explicit rules to relate them was transformational grammar. In transformational grammar, the rules that derive surface structures from underlying structures are called *transformations*.

## 3. *TRANSFORMATIONS*

The key notion of transformational grammar is that of transformation. Each transformation has two parts.

(a) *A structure index or structural description that states the class of structures to which the transformation applies.*

(b) *A structural change that states the change produced by the application of the transformation.*

### 3.1 The Structural Description

#### 3.1.1 Analyzability

The structural description of a transformation is stated in terms of the notion of analyzability. A transformation with the structural description

(5)  A – B – C

will apply to any structure whose terminal string is *analyzable* as A – B – C, i.e., to any structure whose terminal string can be broken up into three successive substrings, the first of which is an A, the second of which is a B, and the third of which is a C. Thus, if a transformation has the structural description

(6)   NP – V – NP

it will apply to (1) because the terminal string *raccoons ate the garbage* can be broken up into three successive substrings first of which is a noun phrase (*raccoons*), the second of which is a verb (*ate*), and the third of which is a noun phrase (*the garbage*). The substrings specified by the structural description are called *terms of the structural description*. In practice, they are usually numbered. Thus, (6) would be written as

(7)   NP – V – NP

　　　 1　　 2　　 3

### 3.1.2 Variables in Structural Descriptions

Suppose there is a transformation that will apply to any structure in which a noun phrase is immediately followed by a verb; it does not matter what precedes the noun phrase or what follows the verb. In order to write such a transformation, one uses *variables over strings,* which are written by means of capital letters taken from the end of the alphabet: $X, Y, Z, W$, etc.

Using this notation, the structural description of the transformation in question can be written as follows:

(8)   X – NP – V – Y

　　　 1　　 2　　 3　　 4

The variables $X$ and $Y$ can stand for anything at all. Any structure in which a noun phrase is immediately followed by a verb satisfies (8): it does not matter how much material precedes the noun phrase or follows the verb. A structure in which a noun phrase in initial position is immediately followed by a verb also satisfies (8), as does a structure with a verb in final position which is immediately preceded by a noun phrase. In such cases, the variable in question is null. Thus, (1) satisfies (8), the initial variable being null.

Now suppose that there is a transformation that applies to any structure in which one noun phrase is followed by another, no matter what intervenes between the two. The structure index of such a transformation is given in (9).

(9)   X – NP – Y – NP – Z

　　　 1　　 2　　 3　　 4　　 5

The *Y* indicates that anything at all can intervene between the two noun phrases. *X* and *Z* indicate that it does not matter what precedes the first noun phrase or follows the second. Thus, (1) satisfies (9).

Variables over strings (*X, Y, Z,* etc.) can always be null. Only variables can be null.

### 3.1.3 The Cover-the-Tree Convention

In transformational grammar, the convention has been adopted that the structure index of a transformation must cover the entire structure to which it applies. We will refer to this as the *Cover-the-Tree Convention.*

Consider again a transformation that applies to any structure in which a verb immediately follows a noun phrase. Without the Cover-the-Tree Convention, the structural description of the rule would be stated as follows:

(10)  NP – V

The rule would apply to (1) since (1) contains a noun phrase immediately followed by a verb. With the Cover-the-Tree Convention, however, (10) will not apply to (1), because (1) does not consist of a noun phrase followed by a verb *and nothing more.* Adopting the Cover-the-Tree Convention means that if the rule in question is to apply to any structure in which a verb immediately follows a noun phrase, then its structural description must be stated as follows:

(8)   X – NP – V – Y

If the structural description of a transformation begins with the symbol *NP*, for example, instead of with a variable, the transformation will apply only to strings with a noun phrase in initial position. Similarly, a rule whose structure index ends in *V* will apply only to strings with a verb in a final position.

### 3.1.4 Multiple Analyses

A transformation can apply to a tree if and only if the tree is analyzable in accordance with the structural description of the transformation. It should be noted, however, that nothing we have said implies that for a given transformation R and tree T there must be just one way of analyzing T in accordance with the structural description of R. Consider, for example, the structural description (11) and the tree (12).

(11)  X – NP – V – NP – Y
       1    2    3    4    5

(12)

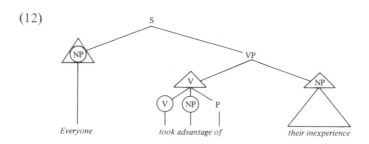

There are two ways of analyzing (12) in accordance with (11). Under one analysis, both $X$ and $Y$ are null and the sequence NP, V, NP is indicated by triangles. On the other analysis, $X$ is null, $Y$ is *of their inexperience,* and the sequence NP, V, NP is indicated by circles.

## 3.2 The Structural Change

The structural change of a transformation specifies what happens to each term of the factorization of the terminal string imposed by the structure index of the transformation. Three types of structural change will now be illustrated— deletion, insertion, and permutation.

### 3.2.1 Deletion

Suppose there is a transformation that deletes *that* if it immediately follows a verb

(13) $\ X - V - that - Y$

$\qquad 1 \quad 2 \quad\ \ 3 \quad\ \ 4 ====> 1, 2, \emptyset, 4$

Deletion is indicated by replacing the term of the structural description that is to be deleted by $\emptyset$ in the structural change of the transformation.

### 3.2.2 Insertions

Suppose there is a transformation that inserts an element $a$ between a verb and a noun phrase that immediately follows it. This transformation can be stated as

(14) $\ X - V - NP - Y$

$\qquad 1 \quad\ 2 \quad\ 3 \quad\ \ 4 =====> 1, 2, a, 3, 4$

### 3.2.3 Permutations

Suppose there is a transformation that moves a verb to the immediate right of a noun phrase that immediately follows it. This transformation can be stated as[1]

(15)  X – V – NP – Y

   1   2   3   4 ====> 1, 3, 2, 4

## 3.3  A Consequence of the Use of Variables in Transformations

Given the use of variables in the structural descriptions of transformations, we can write transformations that really make use of variables in the structural change that they produce. For example, with the devices that we have already introduced, it is possible to write a rule that moves a noun phrase to the beginning of the sentence.

(16)  X – NP – Y

   1   2   3 ====> 2, 1, $\emptyset$, 3

(16) moves a noun phrase over the variable to its left. Because of the Cover-the-Tree Convention, the variable $X$ necessarily encompasses all of the tree to the left of the noun phrase. Thus, moving the noun phrase to the left of the variable has the effect of moving it to the beginning of the sentence.

## 3.4  The Problem of Derived Constituent Structure in Transformational Grammar

Each transformation applies to the tree produced by the previous transformation. This means that the output of each transformation must be a tree. But the structural change of each transformation specifies merely what happens to each element in the *terminal string* to which the transformation applies. Hence, the structural change does *not* specify the resulting *tree structure*.

---

[1] For pedagogical reasons, our discussion of the structural changes produced by transformations differs from what is generally assumed in formal treatments of transformational grammar, in which certain basic transformational operations or *elementary transformations* are defined. More complex operations are treated as different combinations of these elementary transformations. In this approach, it is usually assumed that the operations of insertion and permutation are defined in terms of the elementary transformations of substitution and adjunction. The questions that this approach raises and its differences from the approach taken here are not relevant to the concerns of this book.

The problem of correctly specifying the resulting tree structure is known as the problem of *derived constituent structure*. Whenever we want to specify a certain derived constituent structure, we will simply state the rule in tree form, showing the kind of tree it takes as input and the kind of tree it yields as output.[2]

## 4. DIFFERENT VERSIONS OF TRANSFORMATIONAL GRAMMAR

At present there is no one theory of transformational grammar and no one formalism that all transformational grammarians accept. We have presented some of the essential elements of formalism common to many versions of transformational grammar, and although it is far from complete, it does provide some background necessary for reading the literature.

---

[2] In doing this we will be departing from the strict formalism of transformational grammar. Since rules written in this formalism do not provide full information about derived constituent structure, they must be supplemented by general principles that predict the derived constituent structure produced by each transformation on the basis of the kind of operation it performs. Although several different proposals have been made regarding such principles, they raise issues that go beyond the scope of this book.

# 15

## *Recursion*

### 1. SENTENTIAL SUBJECTS

Consider the sentence

(1)    *That the world is round is obvious.*

The subject of (1) is a sentence (*that the world is round*). Since subjects are NPs, *that the world is round* is dominated by *NP* in (1).[1]

(2)

To generate structures in which *NP* dominates *S*, the grammar must contain the phrase structure rule

(3)    NP – – ➤ S

which produces structures of the form

(4)        NP
           |
           S

---

[1] We ignore here the word *that*. It is discussed briefly in §4 below.

(3) can apply wherever *NP*-nodes are introduced into structures by other phrase structure rules.[2] After (3) has introduced an *S*-node under an *NP*-node, the phrase structure rule that expands *S* can reapply. Thus, entire sentence structures can be generated under the domination of *NP*-nodes.

## 2. SENTENTIAL OBJECTS

We have seen that object *NP*s undergo the Passive transformation. Now consider the following two sentences.

(5)    *Magellan proved that the world is round.*
(6)    *That the world is round was proved by Magellan.*

In the derivation of (6), *that the world is round* has undergone Passive. Consequently, it must be an NP. By introducing *S* under *NP*, (3) makes it possible to generate the structure that underlies (5–6).[3]

(7)

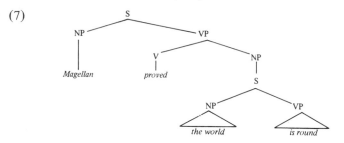

The fact that an *NP*-node is needed above *the world is round* in (7) constitutes additional evidence for the phrase structure rule 3.[4]

## 3. MECHANICS OF DERIVATIONS

Let's see how (7) is generated. The phrase structure rule that expands *S* as *NP* and *VP* and the rule that expands *VP* as *V* and *NP*, produce the structure

(8)

[2] Actually, there are some restrictions on *S*-nodes immediately dominated by *NP*-nodes, but we will not be concerned with them here.
[3] Here again we ignore *that*. See §4 below.
[4] The evidence for the *NP*-nodes above the complement *S*s in (7) and (2) is discussed further in section SFI-3 of *Some Further Issues*.

Now application of (3) produces

(9)

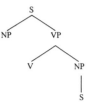

Subsequent application of phrase structure rules to the embedded *S*-node and insertion of lexical items results in (7).

In a similar way, application of (3) to the structure

(10)

produces

(11)

Expansion of *S* and *VP* produces the structure (2).

A sentence that is introduced into a structure by (3) is referred to as an *embedded sentence, a complement sentence,* or simply a *complement.* The word *that,* which serves to introduce the complement, is referred to as a *complementizer.* Material dominated by an *S* in a structure constitutes a *clause.* For example, in (7) *the world is round* is the *embedded clause,* while *Magellan proved that the world is round* is the *main* or *matrix clause.*

### 4. THE COMPLEMENTIZER

There are several ways in which the complementizer *that* could be introduced into structures. One possibility would be to adopt a new phrase structure rule.

(12)  S → *that* NP VP

Another possibility would be to introduce *that* by means of a transformation. We will not attempt to decide between these alternatives here. No matter which possibility is adopted, however, some mechanism is needed to restrict the distribution of the complementizer *that* to embedded sentences. Otherwise, ungrammatical examples like

(13) *\*That the world is round.*

would be generated in addition to grammatical sentences like

(14)   *The world is round.*


## 5. *RECURSION PRODUCES AN INFINITE SET OF SENTENCES*

The process by which the initial symbol $S$ is reintroduced into structures is called *recursion*. An $S$-node recursively introduced into a structure by a rule like (3) will itself contain *NP*-nodes to which (3) can reapply. In this way new $S$-nodes can be introduced into a structure without limit. For example, repeated application of (3) is involved in the production of

(15)   a.   *John believed that Magellan proved that the world is round.*
       b.   *Martin said that John believed that Magellan proved that the world is round.*
       c.   *Horace proved that Martin said that John believed that Magellan proved that the world is round.*
            .
            .
            .

Since processes such as this can be repeated indefinitely, the set of sentences generated by the grammar is infinite.

# 16

## *Extraposition*

### 1. EXTRAPOSITION

Consider the sentences

(1)  *That the world is round is obvious.*
(2)  *It is obvious that the world is round.*

(2) can be derived from the structure underlying (1) by means of a rule called *Extraposition*.

(3)

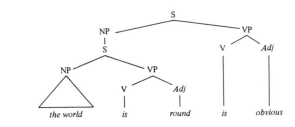

Extraposition applies to (3), substituting *it* for the sentential subject, which is moved to the end of the sentence. Extraposition also applies to derived sentential subjects produced by Passive. For example, application of Passive to the structure underlying.

(4)  *Magellan proved that the world is round.*

produces

(5)  *That the world is round was proved by Magellan.*

Application of Extraposition to this structure produces

(6)   *It was proved by Magellan that the world is round.*

## 2. THE DERIVED CONSTITUENT STRUCTURE PRODUCED BY EXTRAPOSITION

Which node in the tree is the extraposed S attached to? This question is one aspect of the problem of the *derived constituent structure*. Three possibilities are indicated by dotted lines in (7).[1]

(7)

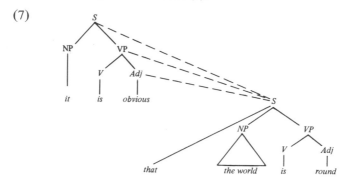

## 2.1 Possibility One:  Attaching the Extraposed S Under Adj

### 2.1.1 Empirical Claims

If the extraposed S is placed under the domination of *Adj*, the resulting tree will be[2]

---

[1] We assume here (without evidence) that there is no *NP*-node over the extraposed S in the derived constituent structure produced by Extraposition. Whether or not this is so must ultimately be decided on the basis of empirical evidence.

[2] Note that placing the extraposed *S* directly under the *Adj*-node entails that there is no *Adj*-node dominating *obvious* alone. To get such a structure, an additional *Adj*-node would have to be created, yielding

(i)

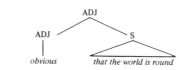

Such a structure is considered briefly in §2.1.3.

(8)

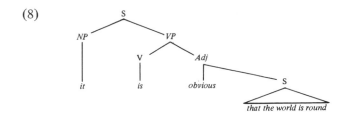

To say that (8) is the derived constituent structure produced by Extraposition is to make two claims.

*Claim 1*

*Obvious that the world is round* is an adjective (and hence a single constituent).

*Claim 2*

*Obvious* is not a constituent at all (and hence is not an adjective).

Claim 1 results from the fact that in (8), *obvious that the world is round* is exhaustively dominated by *Adj*. Claim 2 results from the fact that in (8) there is no node dominating *obvious* and nothing else.[3]

To test these claims we need to look for a transformation that applies to adjectives. If such a transformation can be shown to apply to *obvious* alone, and not to *obvious that the world is round*, then it will be shown that *obvious* is an adjective and that *obvious that the world is round* is not. If this is the case, then both Claim 1 and Claim 2 are false, and (8) is not the derived constituent structure produced by Extraposition.

### 2.1.2 An Argument Against Possibility One  *Tr. h test Adj.*

There is a transformation that can be used to test the empirical claims made by (8). This transformation preposes adjectives under certain conditions. For example, this rule is needed to derive the sentence

(9)   *True it is.*

from the structure that would otherwise be realized as

(10)   *It is true.*

---

[3] For a discussion of what it means for an element to be a constituent in a tree, review §§1.3–1.4 of section 14.

What happens when this rule applies to the output of Extraposition? If Claim 1 were correct, then *obvious that the world is round* would be an adjective and would undergo the rule, yielding

(11) *Obvious that the world is round it is.*

Since *(11) is ungrammatical, Claim 1 is false.
The correct output is

(12)  *Obvious it is that the world is round.*

In order for (12) to be derived, *obvious* must be an adjective in the derived structure produced by Extraposition. Since Claim 2 denies this, Claim 2 is also false. Thus, (8) is not the derived constituent structure of (2).

### 2.1.3  An Argument Against Another Possibility

The ungrammaticality of *(11) can be used to show that another possible derived structure is incorrect.

(13)

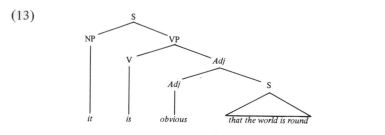

(13) is the structure that would be produced by creating a new *Adj*-node to dominate both the extraposed *S*-node and the *Adj*-node dominating *obvious*. (13) correctly indicates that *obvious* is an adjective. However, like (8), (13) incorrectly characterizes *obvious that the world is round* as an adjective. Consequently, the need to prevent the derivation of *(11) shows that (13) is also incorrect.

## 2.2  Possibilities Two and Three:  Attaching the Extraposed S under VP and S

(14)

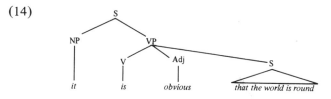

(15)

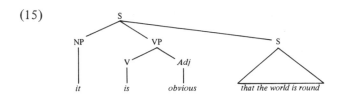

Since *obvious*, and not *obvious that the world is round*, is an adjective in (14) and (15), both of these structures account for *(11) and (12).

### 2.2.1 Empirical Differences

There are two major differences between (14) and (15). First, (14) claims that *is obvious that the world is round* is a verb phrase (and hence a constituent), whereas in (15) it is not a constituent at all. Second, (15) claims that *is obvious* is a verb phrase (and hence a constituent), whereas in (14) it is not a constituent at all.

The best way to decide between (14) and (15) would be to find a transformation that applies to VPs. If it applied to *is obvious that the world is round*, then (14) would be the correct derived constituent structure. If it applied to *is obvious* alone, then (15) would be correct. Unfortunately, we do not know of any transformations that provide the crucial test in this case.

### 2.2.2 A Further Argument

The behavior of structures under transformations provides the best means of determining derived constituent structure, but there is also another kind of evidence that has been used in cases where transformational tests are not available. This evidence involves features of a sentence such as intonation and the possibility of putting pauses and parenthetical expressions in various places. In the case of (2), it has been pointed out that (14) and (15) make different claims about the nature of the constituent break between *obvious* and *that the world is round*. It has been claimed that the break in (15) is a "major constituent break" while the break in (14) is not. It has also been claimed that pauses and parenthetical expressions are possible only at "major constituent breaks." Note, it is possible to put a pause between *obvious* and *that* when saying (2). Parenthetical expressions can also be inserted there.

(16) *It is obvious-don't you think?-that the world is round.*

It has therefore been concluded that (15) represents the correct derived constitutent structure of (2).

## 3. *FORMULATING EXTRAPOSITION*

We can state the rule of Extraposition in tree form as follows:

(17) *Extraposition*

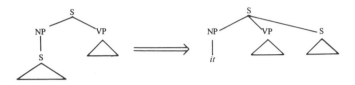

The same thing can be stated informally in words:

(18) **Extraposition**

> Substitute **it** for a sentential subject, move the sentential subject to the end of the sentence and attach it to the **S**-node of the matrix sentence.[4]

---

[4] The sentence in which a complement sentence is embedded is often referred to as the *matrix sentence.*

# 17

## The Derived Constituent Structure
## Produced by Passive

We have assumed that a sentence like

(1)  *Marge criticized Walter.*

has an underlying structure like

(2)

We will assume that the derived constituent structure produced by applying Passive to (2) is roughly

(3)
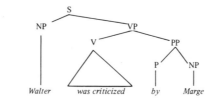

For convenience we will represent the derived verb form *was criticized* as being dominated by a single *V*-node; the correct representation of such verbal forms raises a number of questions that we do not want to go into here. Whenever we wish to avoid the question of the internal structure of constituents, we will indicate such constituents with a triangle, as we have in (3).

# 18

## *Two New Constructions*

### *1. TWO NEW CONSTRUCTIONS*

#### 1.1 NP-S Constructions

We will assume that the grammar of English contains the phrase structure rule

(1)   NP → NP S

(1) produces the structure

(2)

that underlies phrases like

        a.   *the idea that inflation is a necessary evil*
        b.   *the notion that summer is the time to take it easy*
        c.   *the fact that Ted arrived late*

#### 1.2 Infinitival Complements

We have discussed sentences like

(3)   *That the world is round is obvious.*

in which the embedded sentence is introduced by the complementizer *that*. There are also embedded sentences that are infinitival in form—e.g.,

(4)   *For Suzie to buy a polar bear might be unwise.*

Infinitival subject complements undergo Extraposition just as *that*-complements do. Thus,

(5)   *It might be unwise for Suzie to buy a polar bear.*

is derived by applying Extraposition to (4).

## 2. EXERCISE

For each sentence below, draw the underlying structure tree and work through the derivation, showing how transformations apply to produce the surface structure tree.[1]

(6)   *It was hypothesized by Professor Warhola that Venus is populated by Slovaks.*

(7)   *It amazes Carl that it annoys Mike that Sally likes celery juice.*

(8)   *It is absurd for Hilda to think that Snoopy is a CIA agent.*

(9)   *It is obvious that the notion that man is descended from the apes is not accepted by everyone.*

(10)   *It is doubted by no one that it surprised everyone that the fact that Marge likes Valentino bugs Pete.*

(11)   *It is outlandish for the fact that it is unnecessary for mountaineers to yodel to be ignored by experts.*

---

[1] If, in working through the derivations, you chance upon some sentences that strike you as ill-formed, and if you wish to pursue the matter further, read section SFI-4 of Some Further Issues in the back of the book.

*deep syntactic struct is to surface str. : phoneme is to phone*

*deep struct. is an unutterable "utterance"*

# 19

## *Part 1: Its Place in a Wider Context*

### 1. READINGS TO SUPPLEMENT PART 1

There are several papers that can be read without great difficulty at this point in the study of syntax. An excellent discussion of some of the topics treated in part 1 can be found in Postal (1964*b*); this paper should be read after sections 8 and 10, which deal with Passive. The classic study of reflexive and nonreflexive pronouns by Lees and Klima (1963) and Rosenbaum's (1967*b*) paper on phrase structure rules can also be read with profit once part 1 of this book has been completed. Two further papers dealing with the interest of studying linguistics are Chomsky (1966) and Postal (1968). For examples of some of the kinds of facts that an adequate linguistic theory must be able to account for, see Postal (1969, pp. 414–424).

### 2. ACKNOWLEDGMENTS FOR PART 1

Most of the material in part 1 forms part of the core of basic analyses in generative syntax that go back to the early days of the field (roughly 1955–1961). Key works from this period include Harris (1956, 1957), Chomsky, (1956, 1957, 1961, 1962), Lees (1960), Lees and Klima (1963), and Fillmore (1963). A number of important papers from this period are anthologized in Fodor and Katz (1964) and Reibel and Schane (1969). A useful work that includes results from this period as well as later is Stockwell, Schachter, and Partee (1973). Many of the arguments in part 1 are taken from the general stock of arguments dating from this period; where we give no specific acknowledgment, we are not aware of the ultimate source.

Our discussion of reflexive and nonreflexive pronouns is based in part on Lees and Klima (1963). Some aspects of it go back to Chomsky (1956). For further interesting discussion, see Postal (1963) and the discussion in the Proceedings following Postal's paper.

The argument about the interaction of Reflexivization and Imperative Deletion was apparently first given by Chomsky (1956). See also Postal (1964*b*).

The idea that two sentences must have the same selectional restrictions in order for them to be transformationally related is basic to the idea of "transformation" introduced by Harris (1956, 1957). The argument for Passive based on selectional restrictions, given by Chomsky (1957, pp. 42–43, and 1961, pp. 18–19), has its roots in Harris's work. The argument in section 10 developed out of some observations by Chomsky (1965, p. 190, and 1970, n. 29).

Our discussion of the formalism of transformational grammar is a highly simplified and incomplete version of some aspects of Chomsky (1961, 1963) and Chomsky and Miller (1963). An unusually clear introduction to the formalism can be found in Levelt (1974, vol. 2).

Our discussion of recursion has its antecedents in Chomsky (1965). See also Rosenbaum (1967*a*, 1967*b*).

We have taken the rule of Extraposition from Rosenbaum (1967*a*), but our treatment differs substantially from his. The material in section 18 has its antecedents in Rosenbaum (1967*b*).

### 3. SOME ADDITIONAL REFERENCES

Below we give some sources that should not be consulted by the student at this stage, but can profitably be reviewed after a broader background in syntax has been acquired. The list of readings here, as in the other sections of this book that cite relevant literature, is not intended to be exhaustive, but rather to provide a sample of work on different topics. We give no further references here on Passivization, which is treated at the end of part 5, or on reflexive and nonreflexive pronouns, which are discussed at the end of part 8.

On languages and linquistics as providing a means of studying human mental structure, see Chomsky (1965, chapter 1, and 1968).

On imperatives, see Katz and Postal (1964), Hasegawa (1965), Thorne (1966), Bolinger (1967), R. Lakoff (1968), Downing (1969), Stockwell, Schachter and Partee (1973), Green (1975), and Schmerling (1975, 1977).

Early work in transformational grammar took phrase structure grammar to be the appropriate formalization of most work in the framework of structural linguistics. In this connection, see Chomsky (1961) and Postal (1964*a*). For a rebuttal and another argument with the same conclusion, see Levelt (1974).

On phrase structure, see Nida (1943) and Harris (1946). These works can be viewed as antecedents of the $\bar{X}$ notation developed by Chomsky (1970) and Jackendoff (1977). Examples of grammar fragments incorporating both phrase structure rules and transformations (from the early days of transformational grammar) are to be found in Chomsky (1957, 1962).

On the formalism for transformations, in addition to Levelt (1974), see Chomsky (1956, 1961, 1963, 1965), Chomsky and Miller (1963), Gross (1972, chapter 8), Wall (1972), Kimball (1973*a*), and Gross and Lentin (1970). There has been a considerable discrepancy between the theory's formalism and the actual practice of linguists engaged in writing fragments of transformational grammars for particular languages. This led Peters and Ritchie (1973) to attempt to formalize the theory underlying many linguists' practice.

The rule of Extraposition was formulated in transformational terms by Rosenbaum (1967*a*), based in part on material in Jespersen (1965). This phenomenon has been treated in various different ways by Ross (1967), Emonds (1972, 1976), Higgins (1973), Hooper and Thompson (1973), and Koutsoudas (1973).

On existential *there*, see Jenkins (1975), Milsark (1977), and the references cited there.

# PART 2
## *Two-Story Rules*

With the introductory material of part 1 behind us, we now shift to a more problem-oriented format. The problems in part 2 will give you practice in constructing arguments to decide among alternative hypotheses about English sentence structure. The problem format is used to introduce rules whose domain of application includes both a matrix sentence and a complement. These two-story rules will provide the basis for the arguments about rule interaction in part 3.

# 20

## *Subject-to-Object Raising vs. S-Erasure*

### *1. ASSUMPTIONS*

*Assumption 1*

*Believe* takes direct objects in underlying structure.

(1)

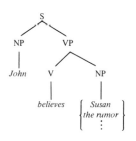

In some underlying structures, the direct object of *believe* is sentential. For example, the structure underlying

(2)    *Margaret believes that Harold is flawless.*

is roughly

(3)

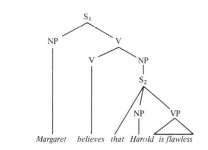

*Assumption 2*

Reflexive pronouns are possible only if the antecedent is in the same clause as the reflexive pronoun. Thus, the reflexive pronoun is grammatical in

(4)    a.    *Margaret convinced herself that Horatio betrayed her.*

        b.

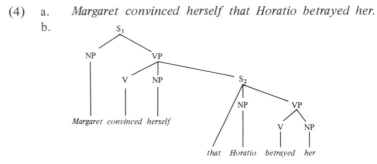

and ungrammatical in

(5)    a.    **Margaret convinced Harold that Horatio betrayed herself.*

        b.

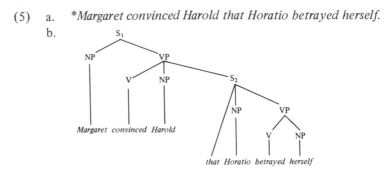

## 2. A NOTE ON PRONOMINALIZATION

In sections 2 and 3 of part 1 we assumed that noun phrases are marked for coreference in underlying structure. Thus, both

(6)

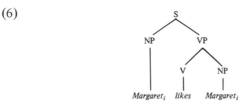

and

(7)

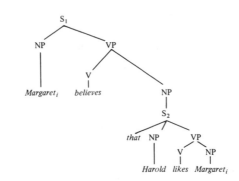

are possible underlying structures. In (6), the two coreferential noun phrases are in the same clause. Hence, Reflexivization applies to produce

(8)    *Margaret likes herself.*

In (7), the coreferential noun phrases are in different clauses and, consequently, Reflexivization cannot apply.

In considering cases like (7), transformational grammarians originally posited a rule of Pronominalization that replaced full noun phrases with non-reflexive pronouns. It was hypothesized that Pronominalization applied to (7) to produce

(9)    *Margaret$_i$ believes that Harold likes her$_i$.*

For purposes of exposition, we will temporarily adopt this hypothesis.[1]

## 3. THE PHENOMENON

In addition to sentences like

(2)    *Margaret believes that Harold is flawless.*

in which *believe* occurs with a *that* complementizer, there are also sentences like

---

[1] In part 8 we will make the hypothesis more explicit by specifying the conditions under which the rule of Pronominalization has been assumed to operate. This will allow us to test the hypothesis and compare it to various alternatives. For the present, it is only necessary to notice the complementary nature of Reflexivization and Pronominalization. Reflexivization applies to coreferential noun phrases in the same clause; Pronominalization applies to coreferential noun phrases in different clauses.

(10) *Margaret believes Harold to be flawless.*

in which the complement is infinitival. An interesting difference between infinitival complements of *believe* and those with the *that* complementizer involves examples in which the subject of the complement is coreferential with the subject of *believe.*

(11) a. *Margaret$_i$ believes that she$_i$ is flawless.*
    b. *\*Margaret$_i$ believes that herself$_i$ is flawless.*
(12) a. *\*Margaret$_i$ believes her$_i$ to be flawless.* [2]
    b. *Margaret$_i$ believes herself$_i$ to be flawless.*

If the subject of a *that*-complement is coreferential with the subject of *believe*, it cannot be reflexive. But if the subject of an infinitival complement is coreferential with the subject of *believe*, it must be reflexive. Why is this the case?

## 4. TWO ALTERNATIVE HYPOTHESES

### 4.1 The Subject-to-Object Raising Hypothesis

Sentences in which *believe* occurs with a *that*-complementizer and sentences in which the complement is infinitival are derived from the same underlying structure by an optional rule of Subject-to-Object Raising.[3] This rule raises the subject of the complement into the matrix (higher) sentence, making it the object of the matrix in derived structure. It also causes the *that* complementizer to be deleted and the "down-stairs" verb to be put in infinitival form. For example, application of Subject-to-Object Raising to the underlying structure

(13)

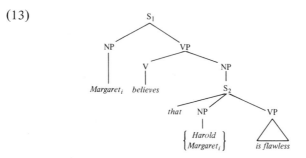

---

[2] Although (12a) is a grammatical sentence, it does not have a reading in which *Margaret* and *her* are coreferential. This is why it is starred.

[3] For further discussion of *that* and infinitival complements of *believe* see SFI-5 after working this problem.

produces

(14)

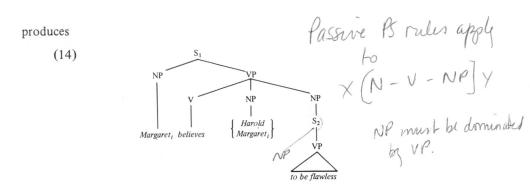

*Passive PS rules apply to*
$$X \left( N - V - NP \right) Y$$
*NP must be dominated by VP.*

Since the two occurrences of *Margaret* are in the same clause, Reflexivization can apply, and (12b) can be produced.

## 4.2 The S-Erasure Hypothesis

Sentences in which *believe* occurs with a *that*-complementizer and sentences in which the complement is infinitival are derived from the same underlying structure by an optional rule of *S*-Erasure. This rule erases the $S_2$-node, causing *that* to be deleted and the downstairs verb to be infinitivalized. Application of this rule to (13) results in

(15)

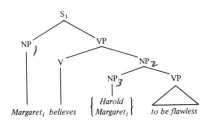

Since the two occurrences of *Margaret* are now in the same clause, Reflexivization applies, and (12b) is derived.

## 5. THE PROBLEM

Which of these two hypotheses should be adopted?

Construct two arguments to decide between them—one argument making use of Assumption 2 and one involving Passive. Feel free to draw on additional data.

*Reflexivization — Identical NP's not ~~presumit~~ necessarily*
*Subj + Obj. — tautoclausal NP's that are coref.*

# 21

## *The Triggering of Rules by Verbs*

### 1. VERBS THAT GOVERN SUBJECT-TO-OBJECT RAISING

Subject-to-Object Raising applies to structures of the form

(1)

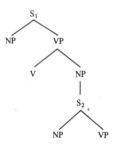

to produce structures of the form

(2)

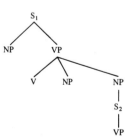

However, not all structures of the form (1) are possible inputs to Subject-to-Object Raising. Whether or not this rule applies depends on what verb occurs in the matrix (higher) clause. The grammaticality of

(3)   a.   *Dick* $\begin{Bmatrix} believed \\ proved \\ proclaimed \\ showed \\ imagined \end{Bmatrix}$ *that he was fearless.*

and

(3)   b.   *Dick* $\begin{Bmatrix} believed \\ proved \\ proclaimed \\ showed \\ imagined \end{Bmatrix}$ *himself to be fearless.*

indicates that Subject-to-Object Raising applies with the verbs in (3). Such verbs are said to *trigger* Subject-to-Object Raising. In the case of

(4)   a.   *Dick* $\begin{Bmatrix} insisted \\ forgot \\ learned \\ explained \\ hinted \end{Bmatrix}$ *that he was fearless.*

and

(4)   b.   *\*Dick* $\begin{Bmatrix} insisted \\ forgot \\ learned \\ explained \\ hinted \end{Bmatrix}$ *himself to be fearless.*

the ungrammaticality of *(4b) indicates that Subject-to-Object Raising does not apply with the verbs in (4). Although these verbs occur in structures of the form (1), they do not trigger Subject-to-Object Raising.[1]

---

[1] The inability of a verb to occur in a structure of the form

(i)   *NP$_i$ V Reflexive$_i$ Infinitive . . .*

provides evidence that the verb does not trigger Subject-to-Object Raising. However, this evidence is not always conclusive, i.e., there are verbs that trigger Subject-to-Object Raising but cannot have reflexive objects for independent reasons. For a detailed study of Subject-to-Object Raising, including a number of different tests for verbs that trigger it and discussion of the inability of certain verbs to have reflexive objects for independent reasons, see Postal (1974).

## 2. PREDICTABILITY, IDIOSYNCRASY, AND RULE GOVERNMENT

Many rules posited by transformational grammarians are triggered by individual lexical items. Another example of such a rule is THERE-Insertion. This rule applies to structures of the form

(5)   NP, V, X

where V is a verb of existence like *be, exist, ensue, arise,* and so on. Just as the verbs in (3) trigger Subject-to-Object Raising, so these verbs of existence trigger THERE-Insertion.

Once a rule has been shown to be triggered by individual lexical items, the next question is whether or not these items follow a predictable pattern. The verbs that allow THERE-Insertion to operate have something in common; they are verbs of existence. Whether or not a similar generalization can be found for Subject-to-Object Raising triggers is an open question.

Finally, one must be aware of idiosyncratic differences that exist among speakers of the same language. Although such speakers typically obey the same rules, the class of verbs triggering a particular rule may vary somewhat from speaker to speaker. For example, although

(6)   a.      *Mary$_i$ supposes that she$_i$ is more popular than anyone else.*

is generally acknowledged to be grammatical

(6)   b.      *?Mary supposes herself to be more popular than anyone else.*

is accepted by some speakers and rejected by others.[2] Thus, speakers differ with respect to whether or not *suppose* triggers Subject-to-Object Raising.

---

[2] We use a question mark to indicate that the sentence is not acceptable to all.

# 22

## *Missing Subjects*

### *1. ASSUMPTION*

*Want* takes direct objects in underlying structure.

(1)

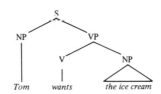

In some cases, the direct object of *want* is sentential. For example, the structure underlying

(2)   *Tom wants Sue to leave town.*

is

(3)

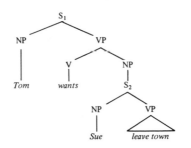

*Sue* is the subject of the complement, and *leave town* is the verb phrase.

## 2. THE PHENOMENON

Sentences with *want* differ from sentences with *believe* in an important respect. Although there are grammatical sentences like

(4)    *Tom wants to leave town.*

there is nothing comparable with *believe*:

(5)    a.    *\*Tom believes to leave town.*
       b.    *\*Tom believes to have left town.*
       c.    *\*Tom believes to be flawless.*

## 3. THREE CONFLICTING HYPOTHESES

*Hypothesis A*

The underlying structure of (4) is like (3), except that the subject of $S_2$ is coreferential with the subject of $S_1$. The subject of $S_2$ is deleted by a rule that deletes the complement subject if it is coreferential with the subject of the matrix sentence. We will refer to this rule as *Equi-NP Deletion,* or simple *Equi.*[1]

---

[1] The existence of an *NP*-node over the complement of *want* could be questioned on the basis of the ungrammaticality of passives like

(i)    *\*To leave town was wanted by Tom.*

However, this evidence is not clear-cut, since for many speakers some Passives with *want* are acceptable, e.g.,

(ii)    *?For Mark to leave was wanted by everyone.*

Other speakers do not accept such sentences. It is possible that the degree of acceptability of such Passives is due to factors other than the presence or absence of an *NP*-node over the complement of *want*. Evidence in support of this possibility comes from consideration of sentences like

(iii)    *Tom wants the ice cream*

and

(iv)    *?The ice cream is wanted by Tom.*

(iv) is as questionable as (ii). Since *the ice cream* is dominated by an *NP*-node in the structure underlying (iii), there must be factors other than the absence of an *NP*-node that make certain passives of *want* deviant.

*Hypothesis B*

The underlying structure of (4) is not like (3) but rather is

(6)

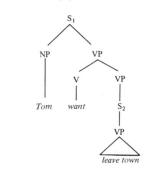

Thus, the complement of *want* has a subject in the structure underlying (2), but does not have a subject in the structure underlying (4). There is no rule of Equi-NP Deletion.

*Hypothesis C*

The underlying structure of (4) is not like (3) or (6), but rather is

(7)

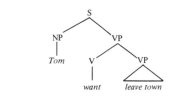

*Want* takes a sentential complement in the structure underlying (2), but not in the structure underlying (4). There is no rule of Equi.

## 4. AN ARGUMENT FOR HYPOTHESIS A

Consider what each of the three hypotheses must posit to account for the data discussed above. Hypothesis A posits a new transformation—Equi-NP

Deletion. Hypotheses B and C do not posit a new transformation; instead they require new phrase structure rules to generate (6) and (7).[2]

There is one thing that all three hypotheses have in common. They have to generate underlying structures like (3) to account for sentences like (2). Since such structures will be generated under all three hypotheses, there is nothing to prevent the generation of underlying structures in which the subject of the complement is coreferential with the subject of the matrix sentence.

(8)

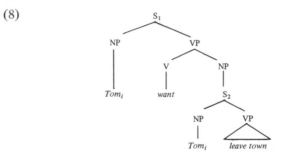

The existence of (8) poses no problem for Hypothesis A, since the rule of Equi-NP Deletion will convert it into the grammatical sentence (4). Under Hypotheses B and C, however, there is a problem. With no rule of Equi in the grammar, (8) will be realized as either (9) or (10).

(9) *$Tom_i$ wants $him_i$ to leave town.          Pronom T

(10) *$Tom_i$ wants $himself_i$ to leave town.[3]   Reflex T

[2] Hypothesis B requires the rule

(i)    $S \to VP$

and Hypothesis C requires the rule

(ii)    $VP \to V\ VP$

[3] Two comments about *(10) are in order. First, in this book we are dealing with sentences with normal intonation. In sentences with normal intonation, reflexive pronouns do not receive heavy stress. Thus, in the sentence

(i)    *Tom kicked himself*

the main stress is on *kicked*, and *himself* is unstressed. If *(10) is pronounced in the same way as (i), with main stress on *wants,* and with *himself* unstressed, it is ungrammatical. Since it is ungrammatical under normal intonation, we have starred it. However, if extra stress or emphasis is placed on *himself* as in

(ii)    *Tom wants **himself** to leave, not Marcia*

the sentence is acceptable. Needless to say, an adequate grammar of English must be able to account for such emphatic sentences. However, we will not be concerned with them here.

Since these sentences are ungrammatical, Hypotheses B and C need some additional device to prevent (8) from being generated. The fact that Hypothesis A needs no additional device is an argument in its favor.

## 5. THE PROBLEM

Find additional data that bears on the choice among these three hypotheses. Use the data to construct two arguments—one argument that is valid against both Hypotheses B and C, and one argument that is valid only against Hypothesis B. In each case, show that Hypothesis A automatically accounts for data that the alternative(s) cannot handle without additional complications.

*Footnote 3 continued*

Second, sentences like *(10) are much better for many speakers, even with normal intonation, if the complement is passive. Thus, sentences like

(iii)  *?Tom wants himself to be nominated*

and

(iv)  *?Georiga wants herself to be selected by the committee*

are marginal for some speakers and fully acceptable to others. For all speakers, it seems, they are much better than *(10). We have no explanation for this fact.

# 23

## *Coreference and Identity*

### *1. FORMULATING EQUI: COREFERENCE VS. IDENTITY*

Equi-NP Deletion applies to structures of the form

(1)

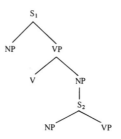

deleting the subject of $S_2$ under coreference with the subject of $S_1$. In formulating Equi it is important to distinguish between coreference and lexical identity. Roughly, expressions are coreferential if their intended reference is the same; they are lexically identical if they are made up of the same words. In

(2)    *She$_i$ is tall, and she$_j$ is short.*

and

(3)    **The man over there$_i$** *is happy, and* **the man over there$_j$** *is sad.*

the expressions in bold face are lexically identical but are not coreferential. In

(4)    *Tom hurt* **himself.**

92

and

(5)    ***Tom**$_i$ thinks that **he**$_i$ will be elected.*

the expressions in bold face are coreferential, but not lexically identical.
Sentences like

(6)    *The man over there wants to leave.*

show that Equi cannot be formulated solely in terms of lexical identity. If Equi
deleted the subject of the complement under *lexical identity* with the subject of
the matrix, then (6) would be derivable from both

(7)

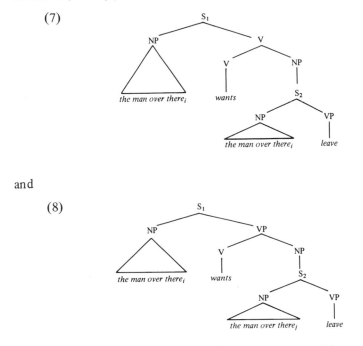

and

(8)

(7) asserts that a certain man desires his own departure. (8) asserts that one man
wants another man to leave. Since the meaning of (6) is represented by (7) and
not by (8), (6) must not be derived from (8). Consequently, Equi must be
formulated to delete under *coreference* rather than identity.

## 2. OPEN QUESTIONS

Several questions remain open regarding the formulation of Equi. One
possibility is that Equi deletes pronouns rather than full noun phrases. If this is

the case, the structure underlying (6) is not (7), but

(9)

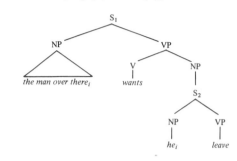

Under this alternative, the deleted subject is coreferential with, but not lexically identical to, the subject of the matrix clause. Another possibility is that Equi does delete full noun phrases. If this is the case, the structure underlying (6) is (7). Under this alternative, the deleted subject is both coreferential with and identical to the matrix subject. We will not try to decide between these possibilities here. The precise formulation of Equi and its interaction with coreference raise complicated issues that are beyond the scope of this book.[1]

---

[1] One unresolved issue involves the derivation of sentences like

(i)   *Each of the candidates wants to be elected.*

Since (i) does not mean the same thing as

(ii)   *Each of the candidates wants each of the candidates to be elected*

(i) cannot be derived from the structure underying (ii). Transformational grammarians have developed several different proposals to account for sentences like (i). However, the question of which of these proposals is correct is controversial and must be left open here.

# 24

## *LIKELY: Equi vs. Subject-to-Subject Raising*

### *1. DEFINITION*

We will use the term *verbals* to refer to both verbs and adjectives.

### *2. THE PHENOMENON*

The verbal *likely* occurs in underlying structures of the form

(1)

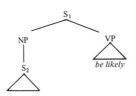

For example, the structure underlying

(2)    *That Martha is intelligent is likely.*

and

(3)    *It is likely that Martha is intelligent.*

is roughly

(4)

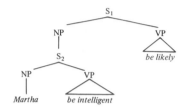

Now consider the sentence

(5)   *Martha is likely to be intelligent.*

In (5) *Martha* is the surface structure subject of *likely, is likely* is followed by an infinitival complement, and *Martha* is understood to be the semantic subject of *intelligent.*

## 3.  *TWO CONFLICTING HYPOTHESES*

### 3.1  The Subject-to-Subject Raising Hypothesis

The structure underlying (5) is roughly (4).[1] A rule that we will refer to as "Subject-to-Subject Raising" takes the subject of the complement ($S_2$) and makes it the subject of the matrix sentence ($S_1$). The rest of $S_2$ is moved to the right and placed under the *VP*-node in $S_1$. The derived constituent structure produced by Subject-to-Subject Raising is:

(6)

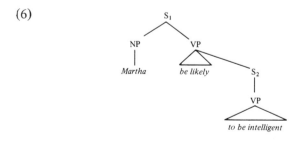

[1] We ignore here the status of the complementizer of $S_2$ in underlying structure. For purposes of this problem, it is irrelevant whether $S_2$ is infinitival in underlying structure or whether the infinitive in (5) results from the application of Subject-to-Subject Raising.

## 3.2 The Equi Hypothesis

The structure underlying (5) is roughly

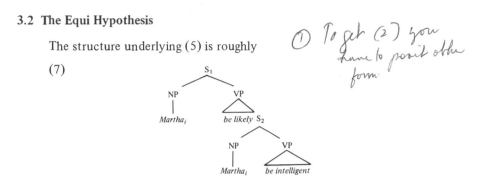

(7)

Equi deletes the subject of $S_2$ under coreferentiality with the subject of $S_1$. There is no rule of Subject-to-Subject Raising in English.

## 4. SELECTIONAL RESTRICTIONS IN $S_2$: A PHENOMENON BOTH HYPOTHESES ACCOUNT FOR

We have seen that there are selectional restrictions specifying the class of subjects individual verbals can take. When these restrictions are violated, the resulting sentence is deviant. For example,

(8) *The nineteenth letter of the alphabet is intelligent.*

is deviant because it violates selectional restrictions on *intelligent.*
 Now note that

(9) *The nineteenth letter of the alphabet is likely to be intelligent.*

is also deviant.
 Both hypotheses account for this fact. According to the Subject-to-Subject Raising Hypothesis, the structure underlying *(9) contains *(8) as a sentential subject.

(10)

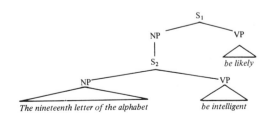

According to the Equi Hypothesis, *(8) is a sentential object.

(11)

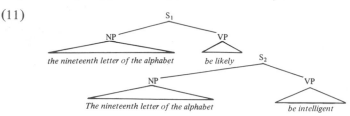

In each case, *(8) is a constituent of the underlying structure of *(9). Since *(8) violates selectional restrictions, neither (10) nor (11) is a well-formed underlying structure.[2] Consequently, both hypotheses correctly characterize *(9) as deviant.

## 5. A DIFFERENCE BETWEEN THE TWO HYPOTHESES

According to the Equi Hypothesis, the surface structure subject of *likely* in sentences of the form

(12)  *NP, is likely, infinitive . . .*

is also its subject in underlying structure. According to the Subject-to-Subject Raising Hypothesis, the underlying subject of *likely* is sentential. The subject of the complement sentence becomes the surface structure subject of *likely* through the application of Subject-to-Subject Raising.

The Subject-to-Subject Raising Hypothesis predicts that any noun phrase that gets to be the subject of the complement sentence through the application of a transformation may become the surface structure subject of *likely*. The Equi Hypothesis denies this. According to it, *likely*-sentences of the form (12)

---

[2] In some cases where *S violates selectional restrictions a larger sentence containing *S is fully grammatical. For example, although *(8) violates selectional restrictions,

(i)   *No one believes that the nineteenth letter of the alphabet is intelligent*

and

(ii)   *The clown said that the nineteenth letter of the alphabet is intelligent*

are nondeviant. This raises the question of how to account for both the deviance of *(9) and the nondeviance of (i) and (ii). This question is independent of the choice between the Equi Hypothesis and the Subject-to-Object Raising Hypothesis and will be left open here.

are derived by deleting the complement subject under coreference with the matrix subject. Thus, the Equi Hypothesis makes the following claims:

(13) a.    *The surface structure subject of the matrix sentence is also its underlying subject.*

b.    *The matrix subject is coreferential with the complement subject deleted by Equi.*

## 6. THE PROBLEM

Use the difference discussed in §5 to construct as many arguments as you can to decide between the Equi Hypothesis and the Subject-to-Subject Raising Hypothesis.

# 25

# *The Rationale for Multiple Arguments in Linguistics*

In section 24 you were asked to construct several arguments for Subject-to-Subject Raising. Like most linguists arguing for some conclusion, we are usually not content to present only one argument, but rather give several. One might wonder why this is so.[1]

The first and major reason for presenting more than one argument for the conclusion one wishes to establish is that doing so strengthens the case that one is trying to make. Each argument specifies a further class of data that any alternative analysis must account for.

The second reason for multiple arguments involves the fluidity of the field of generative grammar and the status of assumptions in syntactic argumentation. What an argument does is show that if certain assumptions are made, then certain conclusions follow. In generative grammar, arguments are based on assumptions about how a grammar is organized, what rules are or are not available, and so on. These assumptions may change or be called into question at any time. The grammarian who presents more than one argument increases the probability that his conclusion will be able to survive such changes. While one or two of his arguments may no longer be valid under changed assumptions some years later, his other arguments may still be sufficient to establish his result.

The third reason for multiple arguments is particular to this book. Our chief purpose is to teach syntactic argumentation. The more arguments one constructs, the more proficient one becomes.

---

[1] It should not be concluded that in those cases where we present only one argument no others could be given. In many cases additional arguments are not included because they are not directly relevant for our purposes, or because they involve additional complications that need not be introduced at this point.

Finally, it is important not to lose sight of the fact that doing linguistics can be interesting for its own sake. If you like linguistics, you'll like constructing arguments. Thus, the fourth reason for constructing more than one argument is that it is interesting to do so. After all, we could have given only one reason for multiple arguments in linguistics. Instead, we have given four.

# 26

# *EAGER: Equi vs. Subject-to-Subject Raising*

## *1. THE PHENOMENON*

*Eager* occurs in underlying structures of the form

(1)

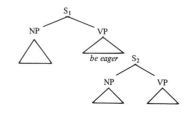

For example, the structure underlying

(2)    *Marie is eager for Marge to leave.*

is roughly:[1]

---

[1] The structure (3) omits a number of details which we will not be concerned with here. In particular, the grammaticality of sentences like

(i) *Marie is eager for a breakthrough*

suggests that *eager* occurs in underlying structures with prepositional phrases with the preposition *for*, such as:

(ii)

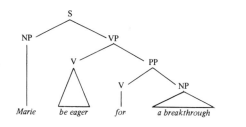

(3)

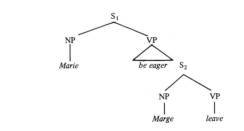

Now consider the sentence

(4)    *Tom is eager to go.*

In (4), *Tom* is the subject of *eager* in surface structure. *Is eager* is followed by an infinitival complement. *Tom* is understood to be the subject of *go*.

## 2. TWO CONFLICTING HYPOTHESES

### 2.1 The Subject-to-Subject Raising Hypothesis

The structure underlying (4) is not like (3), but rather is:

(5)

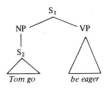

*Footnote 1 continued*
If this is correct, then the structure underlying (2) may be:

(iii)

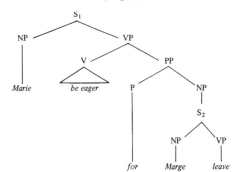

For our purposes, however, (3) will suffice.

Subject-to-Subject Raising obligatorily takes the subject of the complement (S₂) and makes it the subject of the matrix sentence (S₁).[2] The rest of S₂ is moved to the right, producing the derived structure:

(6)

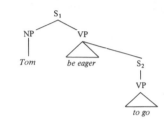

*Eager* occurs both in underlying structures like (3) and in underlying structures like (5). *Eager* does not trigger Equi.

## 2.2  The Equi Hypothesis

The structure underlying (4) is roughly:

(7)

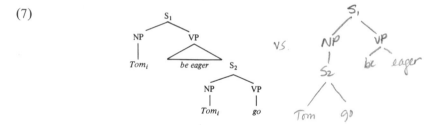

Equi obligatorily deletes the subject of S₂ under coreferentiality with the subject of S₁.[3] *Eager* does not occur in underlying structures like (5).

---

[2] Subject-to-Subject Raising must be made obligatory under this hypothesis in order to account for the ungrammaticality of

    (i)   *That Tom will go is eager*

and

    (ii)   *It is eager that Tom will go.*

[3] If the structure underlying sentences with *eager* is like (iii) in footnote 1, a rule will be needed to delete *for* when the complement subject has been deleted by Equi. This rule will be needed to derive (4) instead of

    (i)   *Tom is eager for to go.*

## 3. THE PROBLEM

Review the arguments in Section 24, LIKELY: Equi vs. Subject-to-Subject Raising. Construct analogous arguments to decide between the Subject-to-Subject Raising Hypothesis and the Equi Hypothesis in the case of *eager*. Where relevant, make explicit comparisons between sentences with *eager* and sentences with *likely*.

# 27

# *LIKELY, EAGER, and Sentence Idioms*

## *1. WHAT IS AN IDIOM?*

An idiom is an expression whose meaning cannot be predicted from the meaning of its parts. The portion of each of the following sentences in bold face is an idiom.

(1)  *My uncle finally **kicked the bucket.***
(2)  *That will **cook his goose.***
(3)  *The schedule conflict is **the fly in the ointment.***

(1) and (2) contain examples of VP-idioms, and (3) has an NP-idiom. Many sentences are ambiguous, having both a literal meaning and an idiomatic meaning. Someone who learns English must learn that *kick the bucket* has the idiomatic meaning "die" in addition to its literal meaning.

## *2. SENTENCE IDIOMS*

There are also sentence idioms in English.

(4)  *The cat is out of the bag.*
(5)  *The jig is up.*
(6)  *The shoe is on the other foot.*
(7)  *All hell broke loose.*

Here, too, the meaning of the whole cannot be predicted from the meaning of the parts. For example, in addition to its literal meaning, (4) also has an idiomatic meaning in which it means something like (8) or (9).

(8)   *The news is out.*

(9)   *The secret is out.*

The grammar of English must reflect this by listing these meanings of (4).


## 3. A DIFFERENCE BETWEEN IDIOMATIC AND LITERAL MEANINGS

An important difference between the literal and idiomatic meanings of (4) concerns the status of the NP *the cat.*

(10)   *With the literal meaning, the NP* **the cat** *in (4) refers to a small, furry animal; with the idiomatic meaning, it does not.*

In what follows, we will determine the consequences of (10) for the interaction of sentence idioms with *eager* and *likely.*


## 4. SENTENCE IDIOMS AND EAGER

On the basis of the problem in section 26, we postulate the following two things:

(11)   a.   *Sentences of the form* **NP is eager to VP** *are derived through deletion of the complement subject by Equi.*

b.   *Equi deletes the complement subject only if it is* **coreferential** *with the matrix subject.*

Taken together with (10), (11a-b) have important consequences for the structure:

(12)

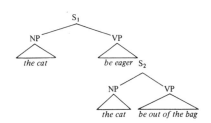

First consider the case in which the complement of (12) has its literal meaning and in which the complement subject is coreferential with the matrix subject. In this case, Equi will apply, producing

(13)  *The cat is eager to be out of the bag.*

Next consider the case in which the complement of (12) has its idiomatic meaning; the complement subject *the cat* is not coreferential with the matrix subject.[1] Thus, Equi cannot apply. This has two consequences. First, (13) does not have an idiomatic meaning. Second, the idiomatic meaning is realized in a sentence in which the subject of the complement is not deleted.

(14)  *The cat is eager for the cat to be out of the bag.*

This sentence reports the desire of a small, furry animal that deplores secrecy.[2]

## 5. STRUCTURES WITH LIKELY

On the basis of the problem in section 24, we hypothesize that sentences of the form

(15)  *NP is likely to VP.*

are derived by Subject-to-Subject Raising from structures in which *likely* has a sentential subject. Consider the structure

(16)

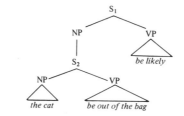

Regardless of whether the complement in (15) has the literal meaning or the idiomatic meaning, Subject-to-Subject Raising can apply, deriving the sentence

(17)  *The cat is likely to be out of the bag.*

Thus, (17) is ambiguous; it can have either the literal or the idiomatic meaning.

---

[1] It might be thought that with the idiomatic meaning the complement subject refers to the news or secret. However, since selectional restrictions on *eager* require its subject to be animate, the matrix subject cannot be coreferential with the subject of the idiomatic complement.

[2] Of course, (14) also has a nonidiomatic meaning.

## 7. EAGER AND LIKELY CONTRASTED

Sections 24 and 26 provide the basis for holding that *eager* and *likely* occur in different kinds of underlying structures, sentences with *eager* being derived by Equi and sentences with *likely* being derived by Subject-to-Subject Raising. In this section we have shown that this analysis makes correct predictions about sentences in which the complement is a sentence idiom. Since sentence idioms can occur in sentences derived by Subject-to-Subject Raising, but not in sentences derived by Equi, they can occur in sentences with *likely* but not in sentences with *eager*. Thus, (17) has the idiomatic meaning, while (13) does not. Similarly, the sentences

(18)  a.  *The jig is likely to be up.*
      b.  *The shoe is likely to be on the other foot.*
      c.  *All hell is likely to break loose.*

are grammatical, but the sentences

(19)  a.  *\*The jig is eager to be up.*
      b.  *\*The shoe is eager to be on the other foot.*
      c.  *\*All hell is eager to break loose.*

are not. The difference in grammaticality between (18) and \*(19) provides confirmation of the difference in structure that we have posited between *eager*-sentences and *likely*-sentences.

# 28

## *Some Differences Among Verbals*

### *1. WAYS VERBALS DIFFER*

#### 1.1 Two Ways Verbals Differ

In discussing *eager* and *likely* we have been concerned with two ways verbals may differ.

(1)  *They may occur in different structures.*
(2)  *They may trigger different rules.*

To some extent, (2) depends on (1). Only verbals that take sentential subjects can trigger Subject-to-Subject Raising. Thus, Subject-to-Subject Raising cannot apply with *eager*. Similarly, only verbals that take both a sentential complement and a nonsentential matrix NP can trigger Equi. Thus, Equi cannot apply with *likely*.

Often, however, (2) must be specified in addition to (1). For example, both *hope* and *believe* occur in structures of the form (3).

(3)

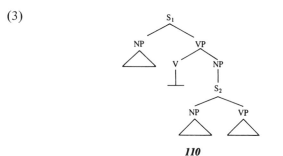

(4)   *Susan hopes that she will win the race.*

(5)   *Susan believes that she will win the race.*

Nevertheless, *hope* triggers Equi whereas *believe* does not.

(6)   *Susan hopes to win the race.*

(7)   *\*Susan believes to win the race.*

Similarly, both *likely* and *significant* take sentential subjects, and both trigger Extraposition.

(8)   a.   *That Harold has left is likely.*
      b.   *It is likely that Harold has left.*

(9)   a.   *That Harold has left is significant.*
      b.   *It is significant that Harold has left.*

But *likely* triggers Subject-to-Subject Raising, whereas *significant* does not.

(10)  *Harold is likely to have left.*

(11)  *\*Harold is significant to have left.*[1]

Thus, the structures that a verbal occurs in only partially determines which rule it triggers.

## 1.2  Another Way Verbals Differ

Verbals may also differ with respect to whether or not the rules they trigger are optional or obligatory. For example, both *be* and *exist* occur in

(12)

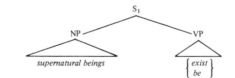

and both trigger THERE-Insertion.

---

[1] Further evidence that *significant* does not trigger Subject-to-Subject Raising is provided by the following.

(i)   a.   *That there is a mouse in the bathtub is significant.*
      b.   *\*There is significant to be a mouse in the bathtub.*

(ii)  a.   *That advantage was taken of their inexperience by everyone is significant.*
      b.   *\*Advantage is significant to have been taken of their experience by everyone.*

(iii) a.   *That it will rain is significant.*
      b.   *\*It is significant to rain.*

As has been noted earlier, the (b)-sentences above are all grammatical if the matrix verbal is *likely* instead of *significant*.

(13)  *There exist supernatural beings.*
(14)  *There are supernatural beings.*

However, when *be* occurs in a structure of the form (12), THERE-Insertion is obligatory:

(15) *\*Supernatural beings are.*

With *exist,* THERE-Insertion is optional:

(16)  *Supernatural beings exist.*

Equi and Subject-to-Subject Raising are also optional with certain verbals and obligatory with others. This fact will be important in working the problem below.

## 2.  A CHECKLIST OF VERBALS

### 2.1  Two Structures

(17)

(18)

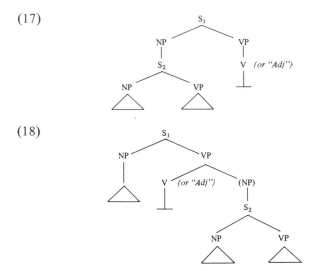

### 2.2  Two Rules

(19)  **Subject to Subject Raising**

> *This rule applies to the structures of the form (17), making the subject of $S_2$ the subject of the matrix and moving the remaining part of $S_2$ to the right of the matrix verbal.*

(20)  *Equi*

> *This rule applies to structures of the form (18), deleting the subject of $S_2$ under coreference with the subject of $S_1$.*

## 2.3  The Verbals

| reluctant | bound | seem |
|-----------|-------|------|
| anxious | apt | expect[3] |
| probable[2] | plan | certain |

## 2.4  The Problem

Use the arguments in sections 24–27 to construct tests that will enable you to answer Questions 1–3. Answer the questions using as many tests as you can.

*Question 1*

Which of the verbals in §2.3 occur in structure (17); which occur in (18); and which occur in both?

*Question 2*

Which of these verbals trigger Extraposition; which trigger Subject-to-Subject Raising; and which trigger Equi?

*Question 3*

Which verbals that trigger Subject-to-Subject Raising require this rule to apply? Which verbals require that either Subject-to-Subject Raising or Extraposition apply?[4]

The problems in part 3 (The Cycle) require you to be familiar with the arguments needed to answer these questions.

---

[2] Do not worry about the adverb "probably." In this problem, concern yourself with the adjective "probable."

[3] Do not worry about the passive forms "be expected" and "be planned."

[4] See SFI-6, A Note on Section 28, for a brief discussion of further issues raised by this question.

# 29

## Part 2: Its Place in a Wider Context

### 1. READINGS TO SUPPLEMENT PART 2

Two papers dealing with topics related to those covered in part 2 which can be read without great difficulty at this stage of the study of syntax are Rosenbaum (1967*b*) and Perlmutter (1970).

### 2. ACKNOWLEDGMENTS AND FURTHER REFERENCES

The theoretical framework proposed by Chomsky (1965) led to a great deal of research on complementation. The first major work on the subject is Rosenbaum (1967*a*). Other important studies of complementation include Lakoff (1966), Kajita (1968), Kiparsky and Kiparsky (1970), Bresnan (1970*b*, 1972), Chomsky (1973), Postal (1974), Brame (1976), and Emonds (1976). Useful discussion of work on complementation can also be found in Stockwell, Schachter, and Partee (1973). Work on complementation in the somewhat different theoretical framework of the earliest period of generative grammar is to be found in Chomsky (1962), Lees (1960), and Fillmore (1963).

Subject-to-Subject Raising has been posited in some form by most generative grammarians since Rosenbaum (1967*a*). Important studies bearing on it include Kajita (1968), Bresnan (1972), and Postal (1974). Postal (1974, pp. 33–39 and 369–374) summarizes a number of different arguments for Subject-to-Subject Raising in English. Ruwet (1972, chapter 2) gives some analogous arguments for French and presents a novel argument based on French data that has no counterpart in English. Novel arguments for Subject-to-Subject Raising are given for Italian by Rizzi (1976) and for Spanish by Aissen and Perlmutter (1976). A detailed study of Subject-to-Subject Raising in French is to be found in Ruwet (1976).

Subject-to-Object Raising has been the focus of considerable controversy. Called "IT-Replacement" by Rosenbaum (1967*a*), this rule has since been questioned by some and defended by others. Chomsky (1973) proposes an alternative analysis of certain aspects of English complementation without a rule of Subject-to-Object Raising. Postal (1974) is devoted to a defense of Subject-to-Object Raising. Other relevant literature includes Bresnan (1972, 1976*b*) and Postal (1977).

McCawley (1970*a*) argues that Subject-to-Subject Raising and Subject-to-Object Raising should be combined into a single rule, and that in order for this rule to be statable, the verb must be in clause-initial position in English underlying structures. Berman (1974) gives a critique of this proposal. Szamosi (1973) considers the question of whether there are two Raising rules or one. Chomsky (1970) proposes that Passive be broken down into two operations—postposing and preposing—and that the preposing operation be combined with Subject-to-Subject Raising.

The argument in SFI-5, THAT and Infinitives in Complements of BELIEVE, has not to our knowledge previously appeared in print. For an alternative analysis, see Bresnan (1970*b*).

The analysis of verbals into different classes according to which rules they trigger has been an important part of the study of complementation since Rosenbaum (1967*a*). Much research in this area has been concerned with questions of this kind. Relevant work includes Kajita (1968), Kiparsky and Kiparsky (1970), Bresnan (1972), and Postal (1974).

References for Equi include Rosenbaum (1967*a*, 1967*b*, 1970), Grinder and Postal (1971), and Brame (1976). Further references dealing with Equi and coreference are given in section 84.

# PART 3

# *The Cycle*

In part 3 we use the rules already introduced to motivate two general principles of rule interaction—the *cycle* and *strict cyclicity*. We will first show that these principles are needed to account for the data of English. We will then explore the hypothesis that the cycle and strict cyclicity are linguistic universals.

There are several ways of motivating the cycle for English, depending on whether or not one assumes that the rules of the grammar are *strictly ordered*. In sections 30–32, we explain what strict ordering is and show how the classical argument for the cycle depends on it. In sections 33–38, we free the argument for the cycle from assumptions about rule ordering by showing that the grammar of English must incorporate the cyclical principle even if rules are not ordered.

These results make it possible to use part 3 in different ways. Everyone should read sections 30–32. Those who do not assume strict ordering should do sections 33–38 as well; those who do postulate strict ordering may skip them.[1] The rest of part 3 should be read by everyone. There, we motivate strict cyclicity, summarize the arguments for the cycle, and illustrate the empirical predictions made by positing the cycle and strict cyclicity as linguistic universals.

---

[1] People who do not assume that rules are ordered fall into different cagetories, depending on what characterization of obligatory rules they adopt. This issue is discussed in section 33, which should be read by everyone who does not postulate rule ordering. Those who assume the *Immediate Characterization* of obligatory rules may skip sections 34–37; those who assume the *Frustrated Characterization* may skip section 38. However, since the issues in these sections have not been widely discussed elsewhere in the linguistic literature, we recommend these sections to everyone interested in freeing the argument for the cycle from assumptions about rule ordering.

# 30

# *Rule Ordering*

## *1. TWO THEORIES OF RULE APPLICATION*

In this section we examine two alternative theories of rule application.

*Strict Ordering Theory*

All the rules of a grammar are listed in a fixed order. In each derivation these rules are considered in turn until the end of the list is reached. If the structural description of a rule is met in its turn in the order, then it *may* apply if optional and *must* apply if obligatory. The derivation ends when the entire list has been considered.[1]

*Free Application Theory*

The rules of the grammar are not ordered and may apply whenever their structural descriptions are met. Each rule is available for application at all stages of derivation regardless of what rules have applied earlier or what rules will apply later.

## *2. AN EXAMPLE THAT BOTH THEORIES CAN HANDLE*

Many examples can be accounted for by both theories. One such example is

(1)   *There was a demonstrator arrested by the police.*

---

[1] The kind of ordering in the Strict Ordering Theory is also referred to as *linear ordering* and *extrinsic rule ordering.*

The structure underlying (1) is

(2)

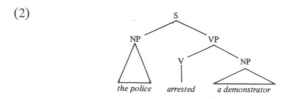

(1) is derived by applying Passive followed by THERE-Insertion.

Under the Free Application Theory, both Passive and THERE-Insertion are available for application at each stage of the derivation. (2) satisfies the structural description of Passive, but not THERE-Insertion. Thus, Passive can apply, producing

(3)

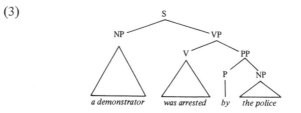

(3) satisfies the structural description of THERE-Insertion, but not Passive. Thus, THERE-Insertion may apply. In this way, (1) is derived by a theory in which rules apply freely whenever their structural descriptions are met.

(1) may also be derived by a theory in which rules are strictly ordered. Since (1) requires that THERE-Insertion be able to apply after Passive, the order must be

(4)                                    .
                                       .
                                       .
                                *Passive*
                                       .
                                       .
                                       .
                          *THERE-Insertion*
                                       .
                                       .
                                       .

rather than

(5)

             :
             :

*THERE-Insertion*

             :

*Passive*

             :
             :

Note that given the Strict Ordering Theory, (1) provides an argument for the ordering in (4). However, since (1) can be derived without rule ordering, it does not provide any reason for adopting the Strict Ordering Theory in the first place.

## 3. THE KIND OF ARGUMENT NEEDED TO JUSTIFY RULE ORDERING

The Strict Ordering Theory posits rule ordering constraints that the Free Application Theory does not. In order to adopt the Strict Ordering Theory, one must show that ordering is needed to account for linguistic data—i.e., one must show that allowing rules to apply freely either leads to the generation of ungrammatical sentences or makes it impossible to generate grammatical ones. Without such a demonstration, the Strict Ordering Theory cannot be adopted.

## 4. HYPOTHETICAL EVIDENCE

To illustrate the kind of evidence needed to justify rule ordering, we will construct a hypothetical example. Suppose the facts of English were such that sentential subjects extraposed, but sentential subjects produced by Passive did not. Then we would find data like the following.

(6)   a.   *That the world is round didn't surprise Magellan.*
        b.   *It didn't surprise Magellan that the world is round.*
(7)   a.   *Magellan proved that the world is round.*
        b.   *That the world is round was proved by Magellan.*
        c.   *\*It was proved by Magellan that the world is round.*

If the facts were as in (6-7), then the grammar would have to prevent Extraposition from applying to (7b) (the output of Passive). This could be accomplished by ordering Passive after Extraposition.

(8)                                            :
                                               :
                                               •

                              *Extraposition*
                                               :
                                               •
                                               :

                              *Passive*
                                               :
                                               •
                                               :

Thus, given (6–7), one could construct an argument for rejecting the Free
Application Theory in favor of the Strict Ordering Theory.[2]

  In reality, of course, Passive and Extraposition cannot be used to construct
such an argument. Since (7c) is grammatical, Extraposition must be able to
apply after Passive. Thus, the interaction of Passive and Extraposition is analogous to the interaction of Passive and THERE-Insertion discussed in §2. Both
pairs of rules *can* be ordered.

(9)                  :                                            :
                     :                                            :
                     •                                            •

        *Passive*                                    *Passive*
                     :                                            :
                     •                                            •
                     :                                            :

        *Extraposition*                              *THERE-Insertion*
                     :                                            :
                     •                                            •
                     :                                            :

However, neither pair of rules *must* be ordered.[3] In the absence of any evidence
that rule ordering is needed, we adopt the hypothesis that rules are free to apply
whenever their structural descriptions are met.[4]

---

  [2] If the facts were as in (6–7), then the Free Application Theory would be falsified.
The question would then arise as to whether we should adopt the Strict Ordering Theory or
a theory that orders some rules, but not all. Fortunately, we do not have to resolve this
question here. Since we have seen no cases that require rule ordering the question does not
arise.
  [3] Note, Extraposition and THERE-Insertion do not interact crucially. Thus, their interaction does not provide evidence for rule ordering and does not even determine how they
should be ordered in a theory in which all rules are ordered.
  [4] Note, the *it* of Extraposition does not undergo Passive.

    (i)   a.    *It surprised Pete that S.*
          b.    *\*Pete was surprised by it that S.*

However, the constraint preventing (ib) is not one ordering Passive after Extraposition. This
ordering is impossible, if, as we assume,

    (i)   c.    *It was proved by Pete that S*

is derived by applying Extraposition to the output of Passive. Although we cannot pursue
the point here, you may assume that the constraint blocking *(ib) is independent of rule
ordering.

## 5. *REFLEXIVE AND IMPERATIVE*

One example that might seem to require rule ordering is provided by the interaction of Reflexivization and Imperative Deletion. In Imperatives in part 1, we noted that the grammar of English must contain some mechanism to prevent Imperative Deletion from deleting the subject of

(10)

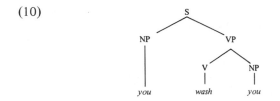

before Reflexivization has applied. If Reflexivization applies first,

(11) *Wash yourself*

is produced. If Imperative Deletion applies first, the environment for Reflexivization is destroyed and

(12) *\*Wash you*

is derived.

Examples like this led early transformational grammarians to adopt a Strict Ordering Theory in which Reflexivization is ordered before Imperative Deletion.[5]

(13)

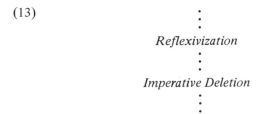

---

[5] Early transformational grammarians generally adopted the following assumption without argument.

   (i)   *If it can be shown that some rules must be ordered, then (all other things being equal) one should adopt the Strict Ordering Theory rather than a theory in which some rules are ordered and some are not.*

Thus, the argument for ordering Reflexivization and Imperative Deletion led these grammarians to adopt the Strict Ordering Theory.

In time, however, this theory began to be questioned. In part 4, we will show that there is another way of blocking *(12) that does not involve rule ordering. Consequently, one of the most important traditional arguments for the Strict Ordering Theory is not conclusive.

## 6. THE PRESENT STATUS OF RULE ORDERING IN TRANSFORMATIONAL GRAMMAR

At present many transformational grammarians no longer assume that the rules of a grammar must be ordered. However, the issue of rule ordering remains controversial. The field is very much in flux, various analyses of different grammatical phenomena have been proposed, and there is no widespread agreement on the status of particular analyses. Some of these analyses require rule ordering while others do not. If this were the *only* difference between them, then we would adopt the analyses without ordering to avoid positing extra grammatical devices (a classical form of argument). However, in most cases alternative analyses differ in many ways and often it is not obvious how to decide between them. Consequently, the issue of rule ordering does not stand out clearly, but is entwined with other controversial issues in the theory of grammar.

## 7. OUR STAND ON RULE ORDERING

It is not our purpose to try to resolve all disputes about rule ordering that have arisen among transformational grammarians. Our purpose is to teach syntactic argumentation. Since the rules we have presented in this book do not provide arguments for rule ordering,[6] we will not assume that rules are ordered. Instead we adopt the Free Application Theory.

---

[6] Examples like

(i)    *Myself was washed by me*

have sometimes beed cited as demonstrating that Reflexivization and Passive cannot be allowed to apply freely, but rather must be ordered.

(ii)            ⋮
             Passive
               ⋮
        Reflexivization
               ⋮

Note, however, that the result of applying Reflexivization after Passive is also deviant.

It should be noted that in certain cases traditional arguments for important principles of rule application have assumed the Strict Ordering Theory. In part 3 we free these arguments from controversial assumptions ⁻bout rule ordering by showing how the same principles can be motivated with or without ordered rules.

*Footnote 6 continued*
  (iii)  *I was washed by myself.*

*(iii) is possible only with extra constrastive stress on *myself*; without such stress, *(iii) is deviant. In this book we are concerned with the status of sentences only under normal intonation. Since *both* *(i) and *(iii) are deviant when given such intonation, the constraint needed to prevent them cannot be a rule ordering constraint.

It has also been objected that *(i) is worse than *(iii) and that therefore the grammar must contain a constraint preventing *(i) *in addition* to whatever constraint is responsible for the deviance of *(i) and *(iii). However, neither of the following can be assumed to be correct:

  (iv)  a.    *that *(i) violates two constraints in the grammar while *(iii) violates only one*
        b.    *that the additional constraint violated by *(i) is a rule ordering constraint.*

Unless both (*iva-b) can be shown to be correct, *(i) and *(iii) do not show that rule ordering is needed.

# 31

## *The Cyclical Theory in Early Transformational Grammar*

### *1. THE CYCLICAL THEORY*[1]

The basic idea of the Cyclical Theory is that rules apply from bottom to top. In a complex sentence structure like

(1)

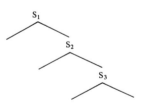

rules apply first to the most deeply embedded S, then to the next most deeply embedded S, and so on.

On the first cycle, all rules are given a chance to apply to $S_3$, but they can neither look at nor affect anything in $S_1$ or $S_2$. On the second cycle, rules apply to $S_2$ (which includes $S_3$) but they cannot look at or affect anything in $S_1$. On the final cycle rules apply to $S_1$. Only then can rule application affect the entire tree.

---

[1] The Cyclical Theory is referred to by a number of different names in the literature. They include the *Cyclical Theory*, the *Cyclical Principle of Rule Application*, and the *Cycle*.

## 2. THE ANYWHERE THEORY

Under the Cyclical Theory a complex structure like

(2)

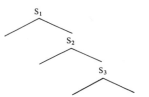

is broken up into three successive domains of rule application—$S_3$, $S_2$, and $S_1$. Under the Anywhere Theory, there is only one domain—the entire tree.

The Anywhere Theory allows rules to apply to any part of the tree that satisfies their structural descriptions. In some derivations rules may apply from bottom to top (as in the Cyclical Theory). In others, they may apply from top to bottom or in some mixed order. Unlike the Cyclical Theory, the Anywhere Theory does not *require* rule application on lower clauses to precede rule application on higher clauses.

## 3. A TRADITIONAL ARGUMENT FOR THE CYCLE

One of the most important traditional arguments for the cycle is based on sentences like

(3)  *The bomb was believed by the authorities to have been planted by the IRA.*

The structure underlying (3) is roughly[2]

(4)

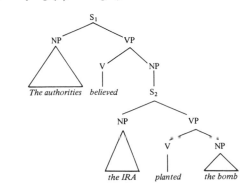

[2] For simplicity, we ignore the question of how tense is to be represented in tree diagrams. In (7), we represent as *be believed* what is realized in surface structure as *was believed*. In the same vein, we ignore the question of how the past tense of *planted* is to be represented. When it is infinitival, it appears in surface structure with *have*, as in *to have planted* or *to have been planted*. This *have* is systematically absent in the tree structures that we give here.

In the derivation of (3) from (4), Passive applies in $S_2$, producing the derived structure

(5)

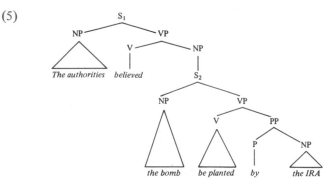

Subject-to-Object Raising then raises *the bomb*, making it the derived object of $S_1$. This produces the structure

(6)

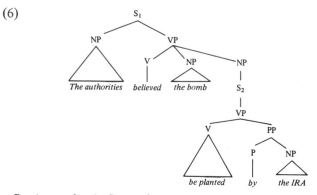

Finally, Passive applies in $S_1$ resulting in

(7)

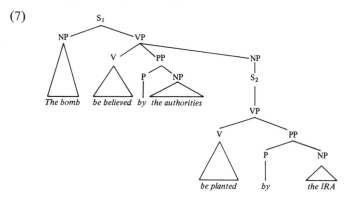

(7) is realized as (3).

   In Rule Ordering, we pointed out that early transformational grammarians assumed the Strict Ordering Theory. One consequence of this theory is that a rule can apply only when its turn comes up in the ordered list of rules. Since each rule occurs only once in the list, it gets only one chance to apply. However, in order to derive (3), rules must apply in the order

   (8)   *Passive*
         *Subject-to-Object Raising*
         *Passive*

Thus, it would seem that no matter how Passive and Subject-to-Object Raising are arranged in the list, (3) cannot be derived.

   Faced with this difficulty, early transformational grammarians had to choose between two alternatives.

   (9)   a.   *Abandon the Strict Ordering Theory.*
         b.   *Find some way of accounting for sentences like (3) without giving up the Strict Ordering Theory.*

Adopting the Cyclical Theory allowed them to select alternative (b).

   Under the Cyclical Theory the structure underlying (3) is divided into two domains of rule application (cycles). Since all rules get a chance to apply on each cycle, each rule is tested for application twice.

   (4)

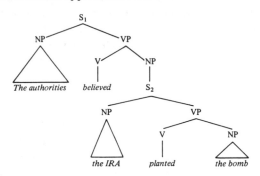

On the first cycle, Passive applies. On the second cycle, we run through the ordered list again applying Subject-to-Object Raising followed by Passive.[3] Since

---

[3] Note that under the Strict Ordering Theory, the ordering of Passive and Subject-to-Object Raising must be

   (i)          ⋮

         Subject-to-Object Raising
                 ⋮
         Passive
                 ⋮

the two applications of Passive are on different cycles, it is possible for Subject-to-Object Raising to apply between them.

Under the Anywhere Theory this is impossible since there is only one domain of rule application—the entire tree. *If all rules are ordered,* then each rule will get only one chance to apply. Hence, rules cannot be applied as in (8), and (3) cannot be derived. Thus, their adherence to the Strict Ordering Theory led early transformational grammarians to reject the Anywhere Theory and accept the Cyclical Theory.

## 4. UNORDERED RULES AND THE ANYWHERE THEORY

The argument just given is based on the assumption that the rules of a grammar are strictly ordered. Without this assumption, sentences like (3) provide no argument for the cycle.

Under the Cyclical Theory, (3) is derived from (4) by applying Passive on $S_2$ followed by Subject-to-Object Raising and Passive on $S_1$. If rules are unordered and are free to apply whenever their structural descriptions are met, then the same derivation is possible under the Anywhere Theory. Since (4) meets the structural description of Passive in $S_2$, Passive can apply, producing (5). Since (5) meets the structural description of Subject-to-Object Raising, this rule can apply, producing (6). Finally, Passive applies to (6), and (3) is derived. Thus, if rules are unordered, (3) can be generated in exactly the same way under the Anywhere Theory as it is under the Cyclical Theory.

## 5. EXERCISE

Consider the different possible applications of Passive, Subject-to-Object Raising, and Extraposition to the underlying structure (4). These rules can be used to derive ten different sentences from this structure. Show that if rules are unordered and are allowed to apply whenever their structural descriptions are met, then each of the ten sentences (and no ungrammatical sentences) can be derived by both the Anywhere Theory and the Cyclical Theory.

*Footnote 3 continued*

The reason for this is that when both rules apply *on the same cycle*, Passive follows Subject-to-Object Raising.

Also note that since both rules are optional, either one (or both) can be allowed not to apply. Thus, in the derivation of

(ii)  *That the bomb was planted by the IRA was believed by the authorities*

Passive, but not Subject-to-Object Raising, applies on $S_1$.

# 32

## *The Conceptual Independence of Rule Ordering and the Cycle*

In the previous two sections we have considered two pairs of theoretical alternatives involving rule application.

(1)   *The Strict Ordering Theory vs. the Free Application Theory*
(2)   *The Cyclical Theory vs. the Anywhere Theory*

These alternatives are logically independent. A priori there are four different possibilities to consider.

|          | Free Application | Strict Ordering |
|----------|:----------------:|:---------------:|
| Cyclical | Theory A         | Theory B        |
| Anywhere | Theory C         | Theory D        |

The argument in section 31 demonstrates that Theory D is incapable of deriving certain grammatical sentences and hence is empirically inadequate. Thus, if we have rule ordering, we must have the cycle as well. Much of the remainder of part 3 will be devoted to showing that Theory C is also empirically inadequate (either through generating ungrammatical sentences or failing to derive grammatical ones). Thus, the cycle must be adopted whether or not rules are ordered.[1]

---

[1] Note, our discussion in section 30 indicates that the rules in this book do not provide evidence for rule ordering. Consequently, we reject Theory B as well—not because it is empirically inadequate, but rather because it posits unnecessary grammatical devices. Thus, our discussion in part 3 is an attempt to show the superiority of Theory A over Theories B, C, and D.

# 33

# *Characterizing the Notion "Obligatory Rule"*

## *1. THE INTUITIVE NOTIONS OF "OBLIGATORY" AND "OPTIONAL"*

Intuitively, the difference between obligatory rules and optional rules seems clear. An obligatory rule *must* apply if its structural description is met. An optional rule *may* apply if its structural description is met, but it need not.

## *2. THE CHARACTERIZATION OF OBLIGATORY RULES IN A THEORY OF GRAMMAR WITH RULE ORDERING*

In a theory with rule ordering, rules are arranged in a list and come up for application in the order in which they are listed. Under this assumption, the characterization of the notion "obligatory rule" is straightforward:

(1)    *If a rule is obligatory, it must apply to a tree that satisfies its structural description **at the stage of the derivation at which it comes up in the list.***

## *3. CHARACTERIZING OBLIGATORY RULES IN A THEORY OF GRAMMAR WITHOUT RULE ORDERING*

### 3.1 The Problem

In a theory without ordering, rules may apply whenever their structural descriptions are satisfied. Since there is no single stage of derivation at which a particular rule comes up for application, (1) cannot be used to characterize obligatory rules. However, something must be said to characterize certain sentences as ungrammatical because an obligatory rule has failed to apply in their derivations. Thus, it is still necessary to distinguish obligatory from optional rules.

Although there are several different characterizations of obligatory rules that could be given, none seem obvious in the way that (1) does for a theory with ordered rules. Since generative grammarians have only recently begun to take seriously the possibility that rules are not ordered, much work remains to be done in exploring different characterizations of obligatory rules and determining their empirical consequences. Here we consider two possible characterizations.

### 3.2  The Immediate Characterization of the Notion "Obligatory Rule"

(2)   *The Immediate Characterization*

*If a rule is obligatory, it must apply to every tree in a derivation that satisfies its structural description.*

*(Intuitively: It must apply **immediately**, as soon in a derivation as its structural description is met.)*

In saying that an obligatory rule must apply right away, the Immediate Characterization imposes an order of application on rules: if a tree satisfies the structural description of both an obligatory and an optional rule, the obligatory rule must apply first.

In a theory of grammar that incorporates the cycle, the Immediate Characterization can be formulated as follows:

(3)   *The Immediate Characterization in the Cyclical Theory*

*If a rule is obligatory, on each cycle it must apply to every structure that satisfies its structural description.*

*(Intuitively: it must apply in each domain of rule application as soon as its structural description is satisfied.)*

### 3.3  The Frustrated Characterization of the Notion "Obligatory Rule"

(4)   *The Frustrated Characterization*

*If a rule is obligatory, no derivation can terminate leaving a surface structure that satisfies its structural description.*

*(Intuitively: a derivation cannot terminate if that would leave an obligatory rule **frustrated** because it has not applied, although its structural description remains satisfied.)*

An obligatory rule, like any other rule, may apply at any stage of the derivation at which it structural description is met. However, the Frustrated Characterization requires rule application to continue until a surface structure is generated that does not satisfy the structural description of any obligatory rule.

In a theory of grammar incorporating the cycle, the Frustrated Characterization can be formulated as follows:

(5)   ***The Frustrated Characterization in the Cyclical Theory***

*If a rule is obligatory, rule application on a particular cycle cannot terminate if the structural description of the rule is satisfied.*

*(Intuitively: rule application cannot cease on a particular cycle if that would leave an obligatory rule **frustrated** because it has not applied, although its structural description remains satisfied.)*

## 3.4  Some Empirical Differences Between the Two Characterizations

The question of which (if either) of the two characterizations of obligatory rules is correct is an empirical one. In order to decide between them one must find cases in which they make different predictions about linguistic data and determine which predictions are correct. In what follows, we illustrate some of the kinds of examples one could look for.

### 3.4.1  An Optional Rule that Destroys the Environment for Application of an Obligatory Rule

Suppose we had an example in which a tree satisfied the structural description of both an obligatory and an optional rule. Furthermore, application of the optional rule would destroy the environment for the obligatory rule, i.e., if the optional rule applied, the obligatory rule could no longer apply. A theory incorporating the Immediate Characterization predicts that in a case like this, the obligatory rule must apply right away. It therefore predicts that the derivation in which the optional rule applies first will result in an ungrammatical sentence.

The Frustrated Characterization allows either rule to apply to the structure in question. If the optional rule applies first, the resulting structure will not satisfy the structural description of the obligatory rule. Thus, the obligatory rule will not be "frustrated," and the derivation can terminate. The Frustrated Characterization thus predicts that the sentence resulting from this derivation will be grammatical.

With respect to cases like this, the Immediate Characterization and the Frustrated Characterization make different empirical predictions. If such cases can be found in natural languages, we can decide between them by determining whether the resulting sentences are grammatical or not.

### 3.4.2 An Obligatory Rule that Destroys the Environment for Application of an Optional Rule

Another class of cases for which the two characterizations make different empirical predictions are those in which application of an obligatory rule would destroy the environment for an optional rule. The Immediate Characterization states that the obligatory rule must apply first, thus predicting that sentences derived by applying the optional rule will be ungrammatical. The Frustrated Characterization, on the other hand, predicts that sentences in which the optional rule applies first will be grammatical, as long as application of the optional rule is followed by application of the obligatory rule. Here again the two characterizations make different empirical predictions. To decide between them one would have to find the appropriate examples in natural languages.

### 3.4.3 Structures that Satisfy the Structural Descriptions of More than One Obligatory Rule

The two characterizations also differ with respect to structures that satisfy the structural description of more than one obligatory rule. Under the Frustrated Characterization, the rules can apply in any order; it is necessary only that the derivation not terminate with the structural description of either of them satisfied. Under the Immediate Characterization, it is not clear what will happen in a case such as this, especially if the outputs of the two rules would be incompatible. One interpretation of the Immediate Characterization is that regardless of which rule applies first, there is still an obligatory rule that fails to apply immediately, and, therefore, both possible derivations will result in ungrammatical sentences. It might also be possible to interpret the Immediate Characterization differently for such cases. In any event, the Immediate Characterization stands in need of further refinement to handle such examples, if they are found in natural languages.[1]

---

[1] Cases like this are discussed in the discussion of section 38.

## 4. THE REASON FOR INCLUDING THE PROBLEM OF CHARACTERIZING OBLIGATORY RULES IN THIS BOOK

Our aim in part 3 is to motivate the cycle. We have already given a traditional argument for the cycle that depends on the assumption of rule ordering. The next task is to show that the cycle is needed even without this assumption. However, arguments for the cycle in a theory without rule ordering depend on which characterization of obligatory rules is adopted. Thus, we had to face the problem of how obligatory rules are to be characterized.

We have presented two characterizations, together with a brief indication of the kind of evidence that would decide between them. However, we will not be concerned with finding such evidence. Rather, we will show that, *regardless of which characterization of obligatory rules is adopted, we still need the cycle.* We will therefore construct arguments for the cycle, first assuming the Frustrated Characterization, and then asuming the Immediate Characterization. The final argument in section 39 is valid regardless of which of the two characterizations of obligatory rules is adopted.

# 34

## *Evidence for the Cycle in a Theory with the Frustrated Characterization of Obligatory Rules — 1*

### *1. ASSUMPTION*

The Frustrated Characterization of obligatory rules.

### *2. THE PROBLEM*

A.  Use the interaction of Subject-to-Object Raising and Reflexivization to construct an argument for rejecting the Anywhere Theory in favor of the Cyclical Theory.

B.  Use the interaction of Equi and Reflexivization to construct another argument for rejecting the Anywhere Theory in favor of the Cyclical Theory.

C.  Use the interaction of Subject-to-Subject Raising and Reflexivization to construct an argument similar to the ones in (A) and (B).

# 35

# Evidence for the Cycle in a Theory with the Frustrated Characterization of Obligatory Rules — 2

## 1. ASSUMPTIONS

*Assumption 1*

The Frustrated Characterization of obligatory rules

*Assumption 2*

The grammar of English contains a rule of Equi-*NP* Deletion that applies in the derivation of sentences like

(1)    *Tom wanted to go.*
(2)    *Tom expected to go.*
(3)    *Tom expected to be eager to go.*

Equi applies to structures of the form

(4)

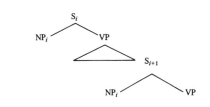

Equi deletes the subject of a complement sentence if it is coreferential with the subject of the sentence immediately above it—i.e., if it is coreferential with the subject of the matrix sentence in which it is embedded.

## 2. THE PROBLEM

Use the assumption that Equi deletes the subject of a complement only if it is coreferential with the subject of the sentence *immediately above it* to construct an argument for rejecting the Anywhere Theory in favor of the Cyclical Theory.

# 36

## *Evidence for the Cycle in a Theory with the Frustrated Characterization of Obligatory Rules — 3*

### *1. ASSUMPTIONS*

*Assumption 1*

THERE-Insertion is generally an optional rule. It converts the structure underlying.

(1)   *A mouse was in the bathtub.*

into

(2)   *There was a mouse in the bathtub.*

In some cases, however, THERE-Insertion is obligatory. For example, it obligatorily applies to

(3)   *\*A conspiracy was*

producing

(4)   *There was a conspiracy.*

*Assumption 2*

The Frustrated Characterization of obligatory rules

### *2. THE PROBLEM*

Use Assumptions 1 and 2 to construct an argument for rejecting the Anywhere Theory in favor of the Cyclical Theory. Base your argument on the interaction of THERE-Insertion and Subject-to-Subject Raising.

# 37

## *Summary of Evidence for the Cycle in a Theory with the Frustrated Characterization of Obligatory Rules*

In sections 34, 35, and 36, we have asked you to construct arguments for the cycle. Each of the arguments had the same form. Each involved the interaction of a two-story rule $R_1$ with an obligatory rule $R_2$ in a structure of the form

(1)

Under the Cyclical Theory, $R_2$ must apply on $S_2$ before $R_1$ applies on $S_1$. This order is possible under the Anywhere Theory as well. However, under the Anywhere Theory, it is also possible to destroy the environment for $R_2$ by applying $R_1$ before $R_2$ has applied. The Anywhere Theory (together with the Frustrated Characterization of obligatory rules) predicts that sentences derived in this way will be grammatical. The Cyclical Theory predicts them to be ungrammatical.

A priori, there is no way of determining which of these predictions is correct. However, when we look at the facts of English we find that the Cyclical Theory accounts for the data whereas the Anywhere Theory does not. Therefore, if the Frustrated Characterization of obligatory rules is adopted, then the Cyclical Theory must also be adopted.

# 38

# Evidence for the Cycle in a Theory with the Immediate Characterization of Obligatory Rules

## 1. BACKGROUND

We have shown that the cycle can be established using either of the following assumptions.

*Assumption 1*

All rules of a grammar are ordered.

*Assumption 2*

Rules are not ordered and the Frustrated Characterization of obligatory rules is adopted.

In this problem we will consider one final alternative.

*Assumption 3*

Rules are not ordered and the Immediate Characterization of obligatory rules is adopted.

## 2. THE NEED FOR NEW ARGUMENTS

Given the Frustrated Characterization, we saw that the cycle is needed to prevent two-story rules applying on $S_1$ from destroying the environment for obligatory one-story (or two-story) rules on $S_2$.

(1)

The Immediate Characterization of obligatory rules accomplishes this automatically. Since an obligatory rule must apply immediately whenever its structural description is met, the environment for such a rule can never be destroyed before it has had a chance to apply. Thus, if the Immediate Characterization is adopted, the data in sections 34, 35, and 36 can be handled by either the Anywhere Theory or the Cyclical Theory.

### 3. FORM OF ARGUMENT

In arguing for the cycle under the Immediate Characterization, we still need a two-story rule $R_1$ whose structural description is satisfied in $S_1$ and a one- (or two-) story rule $R_2$ whose structural description is satisfied in $S_2$. However, we have seen that no argument results if $R_2$ is obligatory, and $R_1$ is optional. Thus, the form of argument for the cycle is somewhat different under the Immediate Characterization than under the Frustrated Characterization.

### 4. THE PROBLEM

A.  Given the Immediate Characterization of obligatory rules, specify the form of argument needed for rejecting the Anywhere Theory in favor of the Cyclical Theory.

B.  Use the interaction of obligatory cases of Subject-to-Subject Raising with other rules to construct at least two such arguments.[1]

[1] See section 28, Some Differences Among Verbals, for verbals with which Subject-to-Subject Raising is obligatory.

# 39

# *Strict Cyclicity*

## *1. ASSUMPTIONS*

*Assumption 1*

The grammar of English incorporates the cyclical principle.

*Assumption 2*

Rules of a grammar are not ordered. Within each cycle, each rule is free to apply whenever its structural description is met.

*Assumption 3*

Subject-to-Object Raising is an optional rule that derives infinitival sentences like

(1)    *Tom believes Marie to be pregnant.*

from the structures that underlie sentences like

(2)    *Tom believes that Marie is pregnant.*

## *2. A PROPOSAL*

*Strict Cyclicity*

No cyclical rule can apply on a given cycle to any structure wholly within the domain of a lower cycle.

(3)

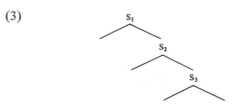

Suppose that in (3) all cyclical rules have already been given a chance to apply to $S_3$ and that we are now applying rules on the $S_2$ cycle. What the principle of Strict Cyclicity says is that we cannot now apply a rule to a structure wholly within $S_3$. Note, however, that neither the application of Equi on the $S_2$ cycle to delete the subject of $S_3$ nor the application of Subject-to-Object Raising on the $S_2$ cycle to move the subject of $S_3$ into $S_2$ would violate the principle of Strict Cyclicity. Since the matrix sentence ($S_2$) plays an essential role in satisfying the structural descriptions of these rules, it is included in their domain of application. On the other hand, application of Subject-to-Object Raising on the $S_1$ cycle to raise the subject of $S_3$ into $S_2$ would violate the principle, as would application of Passive on the $S_1$ cycle wholly within either $S_2$ or $S_3$.

## THE PROBLEM

Use Assumptions (1–3) and the interaction of Reflexivization with two-story rules to construct arguments for incorporating strict cyclicity into the grammar of English. Show that without this principle, Assumptions (1–3) lead to undesirable results.[1]

---

[1] This problem can be done with or without Assumption 2. For pedagogical reasons, however, we recommend that you first try to do the problem using Assumption 2. After checking your answer in §§1–3 of the discussion section, go on to §4 where you are asked to free the argument for strict cyclicity from dependence on Assumption 2.

# 40

## *Summary of Evidence for the Cycle*

You have now seen four different types of argument for the Cycle. The first type depends on the assumption that all rules in the grammar are strictly ordered. Under this assumption, the Cycle is needed to allow rules like Passive and Subject-to-Object Raising to apply in the order Passive-Raising-Passive in the derivation of sentences like

(1)   *The bomb was believed by the authorities to have been planted by the IRA.*

The Cyclical Theory makes this possible, since the two applications of Passive are on different cycles.

The second type of argument depends on the Frustrated Characterization of obligatory rules. Here the Cycle is needed to prevent two-story rules applying on $S_1$ from destroying the environment for obligatory rules on $S_2$. By preventing rules from applying in this way, the Cycle blocks the derivation of many ungrammatical sentences.

The third type of argument for the Cycle is based on the Immediate Characterization of obligatory rules. Under this characterization, the Cycle is needed to derive grammatical sentences that can be generated only by allowing rules in $S_2$ to apply before obligatory rules in $S_1$.

Finally, the arguments for Strict Cyclicity are also arguments for the Cycle. The reason for adopting this strengthened version of the Cycle is that it allows us to block ungrammatical sentences like

(2)   *Harold said that Bill expects Phyllis$_i$ to prove her$_i$ to be incompetent.
(3)   *Harold said that Betty$_i$ expects to prove her$_i$ to be electable.
(4)   *Harold said that Barbara$_i$ seems to expect her$_i$ to be flawless.

It should be emphasized that these arguments for the Cycle are independent of any assumptions about rule ordering and the characterization of obligatory rules.

Our purpose in considering several alternatives regarding rule ordering and obligatory rules has been to show that the Cycle can be motivated under a variety of different assumptions. We have not tried to decide between these assumptions or to suggest that they are the only ones that might be proposed. However, we have shown how different arguments for the Cycle can be constructed. On the basis of these arguments, we will adopt the Cyclical Theory for the remainder of this book.

In the case of rule ordering, we will assume that rules are unordered unless evidence to the contrary is presented. Since research has only just begun regarding the characterization of obligatory rules, we will not argue for any particular proposal. In what follows, explicit assumptions about the characterization of obligatory rules will be made only when relevant.

# 41

## *The Cyclical Theory vs. Multicyclical Theories*

### *1. THE ORDERED MULTICYCLICAL THEORY*

In the Ordered Multicyclical Theory, all the rules in a grammar are arranged in a list.[1] The order of the rules in this list is the order in which they are applied. The first rule on the list is tested for applicability to the most deeply embedded S in the tree, then to the next S up, and so on until the top of the tree is reached. The same is done with each rule until the list is completed. Although there are numerous cyclical applications of rules, each rule gets only one chance to apply cyclically.

### *2. THE UNORDERED MULTICYCLICAL THEORY*

The Unordered Multicyclical Theory is just like the Ordered Multicyclical Theory except that its rules are not ordered. As in the Ordered Multicyclical Theory, each rule is applied cyclically from the bottom of the tree to the top. Since the rules are unordered, however, any rule can be tested for applicability at any stage of the derivation. There is nothing to prevent a rule from applying cyclically several times; other rules may or may not apply cyclically between separate applications of the given rule.

---

[1] Each rule occurs in the list only once.

## *3. CHARACTERIZATIONS OF OBLIGATORY RULES IN THE MULTICYCLICAL THEORIES*

### 3.1 The Ordered Multicyclical Theory

If the structural description of an obligatory rule is met when it is being tested for application in a given domain, then the rule must apply.

### 3.2 The Unordered Multicyclical Theory

It is not easy to see how obligatory rules would be characterized in the Unordered Multicyclical Theory. We assume here that the characterization would meet the following three conditions.

(1) *If the structural description of an obligatory rule is met when the rule is being tested for application in a given domain, then the rule must apply.*

(2) *The fact that a rule is obligatory plays no role in determining at what stage or stages of the derivation the rule is tested for application.*

(3) *A derivation cannot be terminated if the structural description of an obligatory rule is satisfied anywhere in the tree.*

## *4. THE PROBLEM*

Contrast the Cyclical Theory with the Ordered and Unordered Multicyclical Theories. Assume the version of the Cyclical Theory in which rules are unordered and the Frustrated Characterization of obligatory rules is adopted.[2]

### *Part 1*

Construct five or six arguments in favor of the Cyclical Theory and against the Ordered Multicyclical Theory.

[2] For those who assumed rule ordering and skipped sections 33–38, contrast the Multicyclical Theories with the version of the Cyclical Theory in which rules are ordered. For those who assumed the Immediate Characterization and skipped sections 34–37, contrast the Multicyclical Theories with the version of the Cyclical Theory in which rules are unordered and the Immediate Characterization of obligatory rules is adopted.

*Part 2*

Construct six or seven arguments in favor of the Cyclical Theory against the Unordered Multicyclical Theory.

Arguments in favor of the Cyclical Theory and against the Multicyclical Theories are provided by

(i)   *grammatical sentence-types that are generated by the Cyclical Theory, but are not generated by one (or both) of the Multicyclical Theories, and*

(ii)  *ungrammatical sentence-types that are generated by one (or both) of the Multicyclical Theories, but are not generated by the Cyclical Theory.*

# 42

## *What Is Linguistic Theory?*

### 1. THE GOAL OF LINGUISTIC THEORY

It is the goal of linguistic theory to characterize what human language is. To achieve this goal, a linguistic theory must characterize the class of possible human languages. In so doing, it makes an empirical claim: every possible human language will be in the class it characterizes, and every language in that class will be a possible human language.

### 2. THE NOTION "POSSIBLE HUMAN LANGUAGE"

In order for a linguistic theory to be a theory of human language, it must characterize not only the class of languages that happen to be spoken in the world today, but the phenomenon of human language in general. Many languages that existed in the past are no longer spoken. Since languages are constantly changing, it is reasonable to expect that new languages will come into being. Dead languages and languages not yet born are part of the phenomenon of human language. To say that such languages are possible human languages is to say, among other things, that they could be learned by children in the same way that attested languages are learned. Any language that could not be learned by children as a native language is not a possible human language.

## 3. DEFINING THE CLASS OF POSSIBLE GRAMMARS

In order to define the class of possible human languages, a linguistic theory must do two things. First, it must define the class of grammatical devices that can be used in the grammars of natural languages. Whenever a particular grammatical device is found to be necessary in the grammar of some natural language, the device in question must be included in the class of grammatical devices defined by linguistic theory.

For example, we have provisionally adopted the following conclusions about the grammar of English.

(1)  *The grammar includes phrase structure rules that produce underlying structures.*

(2)  *There are grammatical transformations that derive surface structures from underlying structures.*

(3)  *The rules of English obey the cyclical principle and the principle of strict cyclicity.*

(4)  *The meaning of a sentence is represented in underlying structure.*

If we adopt these conclusions about the grammar of English, we are committed to the following conclusions about what linguistic theory makes available.

(5)  *Linguistic theory makes available phrase structure rules that produce underlying structures.*

(6)  *Linguistic theory makes available grammatical transformations that derive surface structures from underlying structures.*

(7)  *Linguistic theory makes available grammars whose rules obey the cyclical principle and the principle of strict cyclicity.*

(8)  *Linguistic theory makes available grammars in which the meaning of a sentence is represented in underlying structure.*

The second task of a linguistic theory is to formulate linguistic universals. To say that a principle is a linguistic universal is to say that it imposes a condition that is true of the grammar of every possible human language. Of course, we cannot establish that a given principle is a linguistic universal by studying a single language. However, certain conclusions that we have motivated for English have been posited by some transformational grammarians to hold for all human languages. Examples of such conclusions are:

(9)  *Every grammar includes phrase structure rules that produce underlying structures.*

(10)  *Every grammar includes transformations that derive surface structures from underlying structures.*

(11) *The rules of every grammar obey the cyclical principle and the principle of strict cyclicity.*

(12) *In every grammar, the meaning of a sentence is represented in underlying structure.*

To postulate these principles as linguistic universals is to make empirical claims about the common structure of all natural languages. To falsify these claims one would have to find a natural language whose grammar is not constructed in accordance with the above principles.

Note that to postulate (9) and (10) is not to postulate that all natural languages have the same phrase structure rules or the same transformations. The extent to which there are linguistic universals involving particular grammatical rules is a controversial issue that cannot be resolved without making detailed studies of many different languages.

A linguistic theory embodies a hypothesis about the ways in which languages differ and the ways in which all languages are the same. The devices made available by linguistic theory which are not posited as part of every grammar represent the ways languages differ. For each such device, there are possible languages whose grammars include it and possible languages whose grammars do not. The linguistic universals represent the ways in which languages are the same. Since linguistic universals impose conditions that are true of the grammars of all human languages, a linguistic theory predicts that any language whose grammar does not conform to some linguistic universal is not a possible human language.

# 43

## *The Cycle and Strict Cyclicity as Linguistic Universals: Evidence from Modern Greek*

### *1. INTRODUCTION*

In this book the cycle and strict cyclicity have been motivated solely on the basis of data from English. It is the purpose of this section to show that they make correct predictions about rule interaction of a novel type not found in English. To do this, we use an example from modern Greek.

### *2. SOME BACKGROUND ON GREEK*

#### 2.1 Verb Agreement and Adjective Agreement

In Greek, both verbs and adjectives agree with their subjects. A verb agrees with its subject in person and number, while an adjective agrees with its subject in gender and number. Consider the following examples.[1]

(1)  *Ego ime tixeros.*
     I    am   lucky
     'I am lucky.'

---

*This Section is based on an argument given in Joseph (1978) and Joseph and Perlmutter (to appear). Some of the material is taken from Joseph (1976). We gratefully acknowledge the help of Brian Joseph, without whom this section would not have been possible.

[1] Our transcription of Greek is roughly morphophonemic; it does not directly reflect either classical Greek orthography or contemporary pronunciation, though it is much closer to the latter. Our /d/ represents the voiced interdental fricative [ð], roughly the sound of *th* in English *this*. Our /g/ represents the voiced velar fricative [γ], which is not found in English. /θ/ represents the voiceless interdental fricative [θ], roughly the sound of *th* in English *thin*.

(2) *O filos   mu ine tixeros.*
the friend my is   lucky
'My friend is lucky.'
(3) *I   kopela ine tixeri.*
the girl   is   lucky
'The girl is lucky.'
(4) *Emis imaste tixeri.*
we   are   lucky
'We are lucky.'
(5) *I   kopeles ine tixeres.*
the girls   are lucky
'The girls are lucky.'

The verb *ime* is first person singular in (1), *imaste* is first person plural in (4), and *ine* in (2–3) and (5) is third person (singular and plural). The adjective, agreeing with the subject in gender and number, has the form *tixeros* (masculine singular) in (1) and (2), *tixeri* (feminine singular) in (3), *tixeri* (masculine plural) in (4), and *tixeres* (feminine plural) in (5).

## 2.2 Subject Pronoun Drop

Subject pronouns appear in surface structure in Greek only if they are being emphasized or contrasted. Otherwise, they are deleted. Thus, (1) and (4) have emphasis or contrast on *ego* and *emis*. Without such emphasis or contrast, the structures underlying (1) and (4) are actualized as

(6) *Ime   tixeros.*
'I am lucky.'
(7) *Imaste  tixeri.*
'We are lucky.'

## 2.3 Complements

Some complements in Greek are introduced by a complementizer such as *pos* or *oti*:[2]

(8) *Fenete    oti    i   dolofoni  skotosan ton idioktiti*
seem/3Sg COMP the murderers killed     the owner

---

[2] We use the following abbreviations:

| 1 | First person | NOM | Nominative | SUBJ | Subjunctive |
|------|--------------|------|------------|------|-------------|
| 3 | Third person | Pl | Plural | FUT | Future |
| ACC | Accusative | REFL | Reflexive | MASC | Masculine |
| COMP | Complementizer | Sg | Singular | | |

> *tu    magaziu.*
> of-the store
> 'It seems that the murderers killed the owner of the store.'

The complement in (8) is introduced by the complementizer *oti*; it contains the past tense verb form *skotosan*. Some complements have no overt complementizer. Some have the subjective marker *na*:

> (9)  *Afisa tis kopeles na    figun.*
>      I-let  the girls  SUBJ  leave
>      'I let the girls leave.'

The complement in (9) is a subjunctive complement, with the subjunctive marker *na*. The complement verb *figun* is finite, agreeing with its subject in person and number.[3] No complementizer appears in (9). Modern Greek has no infinitives. Subjunctive complements like the one in (9) are used in some of the environments where infinitives appear in English.

## 3. SUBJECT-TO-SUBJECT RAISING IN GREEK

There is a class of predicates in Greek that includes *piθano* 'likely,' *fenome* 'seem, appear,' and *arxizo* 'begin' that trigger Subject-to-Subject Raising. Consider *fenome* for example. We find sentences such as the following:

> (10) *Fenete    oti    i    kopeles    θa    fevgun.*
>      seem/3Sg  COMP  the girls/NOM  FUT  leave
>      'It seems that the girls will be leaving.'

Like *seem* in English, *fenome* in Greek triggers Extraposition. Note that unlike English, Greek has no dummy subject in surface structure in sentences in which Extraposition has applied.[4]

Alongside (10), there are also sentences derived by Subject-to-Subject Raising:

> (11) *I    kopeles    fenonde    na    fevgun.*
>      the girls/NOM seem/3PL  SUBJ  leave
>      'The girls seem to be leaving.'

---

[3] The nature of complement subjects will become clearer in §5.
[4] This fact could be accounted for in either of two ways:

 (i)  *Extraposition in Greek does not involve insertion of a dummy pronoun.*
 (ii) *The dummy pronoun, incapable of being emphasized or contrasted with anything else, is necessarily deleted by Subject Pronoun Drop.*

The question of which of these two alternatives is to be chosen is ignored here.

In (11) *i kopeles* is the derived subject of *fenonde*. The arguments for Subject-to-Subject Raising in Greek are analogous to those that have been given for English.

First, the word order in (11) is exactly what would result from Subject-to-Subject Raising, with *i kopeles* preceding the matrix verb, just as in the English translation of (11).

Second, the matrix verb *fenonde* is plural in agreement with the derived subject *i kopeles*. This can be seen by comparing it with the singular form *fenete* in (10).

Third, sentences like (13) in which Passive has applied in the complement are synonymous with those in which it has not:

(12) *Afti fenonde na     mas nikun.*
they seem     SUBJ us  defeat/3PL
'They seem to be defeating us.'

(13) *Emis fenomaste na     nikyomaste     apo aftus.*
we   seem          SUBJ be-defeated/1PL by  them
'We seem to be being defeated by them.'

Fourth, if a sentential idiom is embedded beneath *fenome*, its syntactic subject shows up as subject of *fenome*. One sentential idiom in Greek is:

(14) *O   kombos ftani   s  to  xteni.*
the knot     arrives at the comb
'Things are coming to a head.'

If (14) is embedded beneath *fenome*, *o kombos* can show up as surface subject of *fenome*, as in (16).

(15) *Fenete oti o kombos θa ftani s to xteni.*
'It is likely that things will come to a head.'

(16) *O kombos fenete na ftani s to xteni.*
'Things seem to be coming to a head.'
(Literally: 'The knot seems to be arriving at the comb.')

## 4. SUBJECT-TO-OBJECT RAISING IN GREEK

Greek has a small class of verbs that includes *afino* 'let,' *θeoro* 'consider,' *θelo* 'want,' and *perimeno* 'expect' that exhibit sentence pairs such as the following:

(17) a.  *Afisa na     kerdisi o  yanis       to pegnidi.*
I-let SUBJ win     the John/NOM the game

'I let John win the game.'
(Literally: 'I let that John win the game.')

b.  *Afisa ton yani       na     kerdisi to  pegnidi.*
    I-let  the John/ACC SUBJ win     the game
    'I let John win the game.'
    (Literally: 'I let John that he win the game.')

(17a) and (17b) are synonymous. (17a) consists of a matrix verb *afisa* and a complement clause *na kerdisi o yanis to pegnidi*. The complement verb *kerdisi* is third person singular in agreement with its subject *o yanis*. *O yanis*, being the subject, is in the nominative case.[5] In (17b), on the other hand, *ton yani* is in the accusative case, the case used for direct objects.

There is evidence that in (17b), *ton yani* is the direct object of the matrix clause.

First, there is the accusative case of *ton yani* in (17b), in contrast to the nominative case of *o yanis* in (17a). If *ton yani* in (17b) is the direct object of the matrix clause in (17b), its accusative case marking will be accounted for automatically by the rule that marks direct objects with the accusative case.

Second, the fact that *ton yani* immediately follows the matrix verb in (17b) would also follow automatically from its being direct object of the matrix clause, since a direct object usually immediately follows its verb.

Third, a direct object in Greek can appear as a *clitic pronoun* (unstressed pronominal form) preceding the verb of which it is direct object. The combination of clitic(s) plus verb is pronounced as a single word (although this fact is not reflected in Greek orthography). For example, in the sentence,

(18) *Ton       ida     xθes.*
     him/ACC saw/1Sg yesterday
     'I saw him yesterday.'

*ton* is the third person singular masculine clitic pronoun that is phonologically attached to the verb (*ida*) of which it is direct object. The evidence that *ton yani* is direct object of *afisa* in (17b) comes from the fact that if it is replaced by a pronoun, we find the clitic pronoun *ton* preceding the verb *afisa*:

(19) *Ton afisa na     kerdisi to  pegnidi.*
     him I-let SUBJ win     the game

_____

[5] In Greek, as in many other languages, a surface structure subject is in the nominative case, and a surface structure direct object is in the accusative case. In (17a), the complement subject is in postverbal position. Greek has considerable freedom of word order, and we will not be concerned here with the rules that determine the position of the complement verb in surface structure.

'I let him win the game.'
(Literally: 'I let him that he win the game.')

Fourth, in sentences in which the NP in question is coreferential with the matrix subject, it is realized as a reflexive pronoun:

(20) *O yanis     afise ton eafton tu     na     ksekurasθi.*
John/NOM let   REFL/3SgMASC SUBJ rest
'John let himself rest.'

As in English, a reflexive pronoun is possible in Greek only if the reflexive pronoun and its antecedent are in the same clause.

Fifth, with certain matrix verbs[6] the NP in question can undergo Passive in the matrix clause:

(21) a.   *Olos o kosmos θeori     ton yani   pos   ine eksipnos.*
everybody      considers John/ACC COMP is   smart
'Everybody considers John to be smart.'

b.   *O yanis     θeorite     pos   ine eksipnos apo*
John/NOM is-considered COMP is   smart     by
*olo ton kozmo.*
everybody
'John is considered to be smart by everybody.'

Thus, there are five independent pieces of evidence that the NP in question is direct object of the matrix clause. There is also evidence that this NP could not have been generated in the matrix sentence by the phrase structure rules of the base. One class of arguments for this consists of showing that sentences like (17b) behave differently in a variety of ways from superficially similar sentences (with verbs such as *piθo* 'persuade') in which the matrix direct object *is* generated in the matrix clause by the phrase structure rules of the base.[7] Another argument is based on sentential idioms such as *o kombos ftani s to xteni* 'things are coming to a head.' This idiom must be entered as such in the lexicon of Greek, and it must be inserted into underlying structures as a unit. The crucial fact is that if this sentential idiom is embedded beneath a Subject-to-Object Raising trigger, its subject *o kombos* can be raised. As a result, it appears in the matrix sentence in the accusative case:

[6] Some Subject-to-Object Raising triggers allow Passive in the matrix sentence, while others do not.

[7] The arguments for Greek can be found in Joseph (1978) and Joseph and Perlmutter (to appear). For arguments distinguishing the two types of verbals in English, see section 51 of this book.

(22) *O yanis      afise ton kombo na      ftani s to xteni.*
John/NOM let    the knot     SUBJ arrive at the comb
'John let things come to a head.'
(Literally: 'John let the knot that it arrive at the comb.')

With an appropriate verb in the matrix sentence, it can also passivize in the matrix clause:

(23) *O kombos θeorite oti ftani s to xteni.*
'Things are considered to be coming to a head.'
(Literally: 'The knot is considered to be arriving at the comb.')

The fact that the subject of the sentential idiom generated in the complement can appear in the accusative case in the matrix clause (and passivize in the matrix clause) shows that the direct object of this class of verbs cannot be the underlying object, but rather gets to be object of the matrix sentence as a result of Subject-to-Object Raising.

In sum, for sentences like (17b) there is evidence, first, that the complement subject is the direct object of the matrix clause, and second, that it could not have been generated in the matrix clause by the phrase structure rules of the base. It follows that the class of matrix verbs that allow this construction govern Subject-to-Object Raising, which makes the complement subject the direct object of the matrix sentence.

## 5. RAISING AS COPYING IN GREEK

Greek sentences with Subject-to-Subject Raising and Subject-to-Object Raising differ in an interesting way from their English counterparts: in Raising sentences, the complement verb is not an infinitive but a finite verb, agreeing with its subject. For example, consider the following sentences:

(24) a.    *Afisa ton yani     na      ksekurasθi.*
I-let  John/ACC Subj   rest/3Sg
'I let John rest.'
(Literally: 'I let John that he rest.')

   b.    *O yanis      me        afise na     ksekurasθo.*
John/NOM me/ACC let    SUBJ rest/1Sg
'John let me rest.'
(Literally: 'John let me that I rest.')

   c.    *O yanis      mas       afise na     ksekurasθume.*
John/NOM us/ACC let    SUBJ rest/1PL

'John let us rest.'
(Literally: 'John let us that we rest.')

In (24a), *ksekurasθi* is third person singular. *Ksekurasθo* in (24b) is first person singular. *Ksekurasθume* in (24c) is first person plural. It is the same for examples of Subject-to-Subject Raising:

(25) a. *Fenome    na    ime    fliaros    simera.*
seem/1Sg SUBJ be/1Sg talkative today
'I seem to be talkative today.'
(Literally: 'I seem that I am talkative today.')

b. *I    kopeles fenonde    na    ine    fliaros    simera.*
the girls      seem/3PL SUBJ be/3PL talkative today
'The girls seem to be talkative today.'
(Literally: 'The girls seem that they are talkative today.')

In (25a), both *fenome* and *ime* are first person singular. In (25b), both *fenonde* and *ine* are third person plural.

While superficially these Greek Raising sentences differ from their English counterparts only in having complements whose verbs are inflected to agree with their subjects, there is another, more fundamental difference, which is not immediately obvious. The Raising rules of Greek differ from those of English in an important way: the Greek Raising rules are *copying rules*. When the complement subject is raised into the matrix sentence by one of the two Raising rules, a *pronominal copy* of the raised NP (agreeing with it in person, gender, and number) is left behind in the complement. For example, the structure underlying (17a) and (17b) is:

(26)

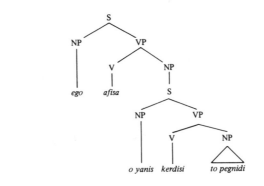

Application of Subject-to-Object Raising produces the structure[8]

---

[8] *O yanis* is represented here in the nominative case. The rule of Case Marking marks it as accusative, so that it appears as *ton yani* in (17b).

(27)

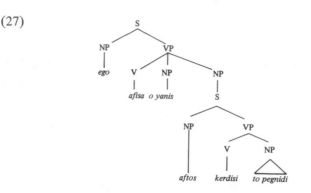

(27) underlies (17b). The NP *o yanis* is raised into the matrix sentence, and a pronominal copy of it (*aftos* 'he') is left behind in the complement.

The pronominal copy left behind by Raising rules in Greek does not appear in (17b), (24), or (25) because, like all pronouns that are not emphasized or contrasted, it is deleted by Subject Pronoun Drop. However, under the appropriate conditions, this pronoun actually does appear in the surface structure. It shows up most easily with a word like *mono* 'only' or with the emphatic *o idios*.

(28) *Afisa    ton yani    na      kerdisi aftos o idios to    pegnidi.*
let/1Sg John/ACC SUBJ win     he    himself the game
'I let John himself win the game.'
(Literally: 'I let John that he himself win the game.')

(29) *Olos o kozmos θeori       ti Maria    pos    mono*
everybody          considers Maria/ACC COMP only
*afti        ine eksipni.*
she/NOM is   smart
'Everyone considers only Maria to be smart.'
(Literally: 'Everyone considers Maria that only she is smart.')

(30) *I Maria       mas     afise na    ksekurasθume mono emis.*
Maria/NOM us/ACC let    SUBJ rest/1PL       only  we/NOM
'Maria let only us rest.'
(Literally: 'Maria let us that only we rest.')

(31) *O   filos   mu fenete      na     kerdizi     to  pegnidi*
the friend my seem/3Sg SUBJ be-winning  the game
*mono aftos.*
only  he/NOM
'Only my friend seems to be winning the game.'
(Literally: 'My friend seems that only he is winning the game.')

In (28), where *ton yani* has been raised, its pronominal copy *aftos* 'he' appears in the complement. *Afti* 'she' in (29) is the pronominal copy of the raised NP *ti*

*Maria*, while *emis* 'we' in (30) is the pronominal copy of *mas* 'us,' which has undergone Subject-to-Object Raising into the matrix sentence. In (31), *o filos mu* 'my friend' has undergone Subject-to-Subject Raising into the matrix sentence, leaving behind the pronominal copy *aftos* 'he.'

The fact that a pronominal copy of a raised NP can actually appear in the complement shows very clearly that both Subject-to-Subject Raising and Subject-to-Object Raising in Greek are copying rules.

Furthermore, it is possible to show that the appearance in the complement of a pronominal copy of the raised NP is a consequence of Raising; in the corresponding sentences without Raising, such a copy cannot appear. For example, consider the pair

> (32) a. *I    fili    mu afisan na    to krino    ego*
>        the friends my let     SUBJ it judge/1Sg I
>        'My friends let *me* judge that.'
>        (Literally: 'My friends let that I judge it.')
>
>    b. *I    fili    mu me afisan na    to krino.*
>        the friends my me let     SUBJ it judge/1Sg
>        'My friends let me judge that.'
>        (Literally: 'My friends let me that I judge it.')

(32a–b) are synonymous. (32a) is not derived by Raising, and the complement subject *ego* appears in the complement. (32b), on the other hand, is derived by Subject-to-Object Raising, and the raised NP appears as the accusative clitic pronoun *me* in the matrix sentence. The crucial point for the present discussion is that a pronominal copy of the raised NP is possible in (32b), but not in (32a):

> (33) a. *\*I    fili    mu afisan na    to    krino    ego mono ego.*
>        the friends my let     SUBJ that judge/1Sg I    only   I
>
>    b. *I    fili    mu me afisan na    to    krino    mono ego.*
>        the friends my me let     SUBJ that judge/1Sg only   I
>        'My friends let only *me* judge that.'
>        (Literally: 'My friends let me that only I judge that.')

The ungrammaticality of \*(33a) shows that the pronominal copy is not produced by a separate rule that is independent of Raising. The copy is possible only in sentences in which Raising has applied. Thus, the copy must be left by Raising itself.

## 6. THE INTERACTION OF PASSIVE AND RAISING

Examples have already been cited where the NP that undergoes Subject-to-Object Raising also undergoes Passive in the matrix sentence:

(34)  *I Maria     θeorite      pos   ine eksipni apo olo ton kozmo.*
      Maria NOM is-considered COMP is   smart   by   everybody
      'Maria is considered to be smart by everybody.'
      (Literally: 'Maria is considered that she is smart by everybody.')

As in English, there are also grammatical sentences where Passive applies first in the complement, so that the complement subject that is raised is the subject derived by Passive in the complement:

(35)  *Den  θa    afiso     ton idioktiti    tu magaziu na     skotoθi*
      NEG FUT let/1Sg the owner/ACC of-the-store SUBJ be-killed/3Sg
      *apo tus kleftes.*
      by   the thieves
      'I won't let the owner of the store be killed by the thieves.'

## 7. SNEAKY PASSIVES: THE PREDICTION OF STRICT CYCLICITY

The fact that both Raising rules in Greek are copying rules can be used to bring out an interesting empirical difference between two linguistic theories: Theory A, which does *not* incorporate the cycle and strict cyclicity as linguistic universals, and Theory B, which does.
    Consider the underlying structure

(36)

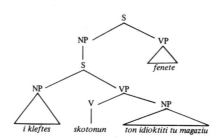

Extraposition applies to (36) to produce:

(37)  *Fenete oti i kleftes skotonun ton idioktiti tu magaziu.*
      'It seems that the thieves are killing the owner of the store.'

Application of Subject-to-Subject Raising to (36) produces the structure

(38)

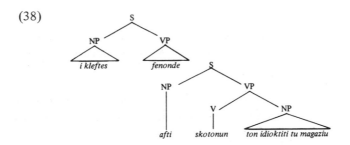

The complement subject *i kleftes* has been raised to subject of the matrix sentence, leaving behind a pronominal copy (*afti* 'they') in the complement. (38) is realized as the sentence

(39)   *I   kleftes fenonde na     skotonun ton idioktiti     tu magaziu.*
        the thieves seem     SUBJ kill/3PL   the owner/ACC of-the-store
        'The thieves seem to be killing the owner of the store.'
        (Literally: 'The thieves seem that they are killing the owner of the store.')

In a sentence with *mono* 'only' in the complement, the pronominal copy appears in surface structure:

(40)   *I   kleftes fenonde na     skotonun ton idioktiti     tu magaziu*
        the thieves seem     SUBJ kill/3PL   the owner/ACC of-the-store
        *mono afti.*
        only   they
        'Only the thieves seem to be killing the owner of the store.'
        (Literally: 'The thieves seem that only they are killing the owner of the store.')

Application of Passive in the complement of (38) followed by Subject-to-Subject Raising produces the structure

(41)

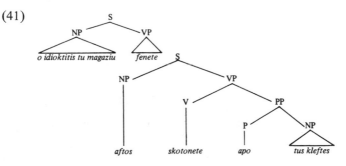

(41) is realized as the sentence

(42)  *O   idioktitis      tu magaziu fenete na     skotonete     apo tus*
the owner/NOM of-the-store seems SUBJ be-killed/3Sg by  the
*kleftes.*
thieves
'The owner of the store seems to be being killed by the thieves.'
(Literally: 'The owner of the store seems that he is being killed
by the thieves.')

With *mono* 'only' in the complement, the pronominal copy (*aftos* 'he') of the
raised *NP* appears in surface structure:

(43)  *O   idioktitis      tu magaziu fenete na     skotonete     apo tus*
The owner/NOM of-the-store seems SUBJ be-killed/3Sg by  the
*kleftes mono aftos.*
thieves only   he
'Only the owner of the store seems to be being killed by the thieves.'
(Literally: 'The owner of the store seems that only he is being killed
by the thieves.')

The difference between Theory A and Theory B appears when we consider
derivations with what we will call *sneaky passives*. The derivation proceeds as
follows: Subject-to-Subject Raising applies to (36), producing (38) with a pronominal copy (*afti* 'they') of the raised NP in the complement. Thus, the complement has a subject (the pronominal copy *afti*), verb, and direct object, so
Passive can now apply in the complement. The result will be the structure

(44)

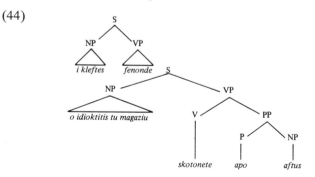

When Passive applies ("by stealth," so to speak) in the complement to the
pronominal copy created by Raising, we refer to the resulting passives as "sneaky
passives."

Theories A and B make different predictions about the status of (44) in
particular and of sneaky passives in general. Under Theory B, which incorporates

the cycle and strict cyclicity as linguistic universals, Subject-to-Subject Raising cannot apply until the second cycle. Since sneaky passives are produced by application of Passive within the complement *after* Subject-to-Subject Raising, their derivation violates strict cyclicity. Since Theory B posits strict cyclicity as a linguistic universal, it predicts that sneaky passives in Greek will be ungrammatical. Theory A, on the other hand, does not predict them to be ungrammatical.

The prediction of Theory B is correct, since sneaky passives in Greek are indeed ungrammatical. Thus, the sentence that results from (44) is ungrammatical:

(45) a.    *I*    *kleftes fenonde na*     *o*    *idioktitis tu magaziu*
         the thieves seem    SUBJ the owner     of-the-store
         *skotonete*     *apo aftus.*
         be-killed/3Sg by   them

     b.   **I kleftes fenonde na skotonete o idioktitis tu magaziu apo*
        *aftus.*

     c.   **I kleftes fenonde na skotonete apo aftus o idioktitis tu*
        *magaziu.*
        (Literally: 'The thieves seem that the owner of the store is being killed by them.')

Three variants of this sentence are given to show that it is ungrammatical regardless of word order. As predicted by Theory B, the resulting sentences are still ungrammatical if the complement contains a form of the emphatic *o idios* or a word like *mono* 'only':

(46) a.   **I kleftes fenonde na o idioktitis tu magaziu skotonete apo*
        *aftus tus idius.*

     b.   **I kleftes fenonde na skotonete o idioktitis tu magaziu apo*
        *aftus tus idius.*

     c.   **I kleftes fenonde na skotonete apo aftus tus idius o idioktitis*
        *tu magaziu.*
        (Literally: 'The thieves seem that the owner of the store is being killed by them themselves.')

Sneaky passives are ungrammatical in Greek, regardless of whether they arise through the interaction of Passive with Subject-to-Subject Raising, as in the examples above, or through the interaction of Passive with Subject-to-Object Raising. Subject-to-Object Raising raises the complement subject, regardless of whether or not Passive has applied in the complement.

(47)   *I melina*      *afise tus kleftes na*      *skotosun ton idioktiti*
      Melina/NOM let    the thieves SUBJ kill/3PL   the owner/ACC
      *tu magaziu.*
      of-the-store

'Melina let the thieves kill the owner of the store.'
(Literally: 'Melina let the thieves that they kill the owner of the store.')

(48) *I melina        afise ton idioktiti      tu magaziu na      skotoθi*
Melina/NOM let     the owner/ACC of-the-store SUBJ be-killed/3Sg
*apo tus kleftes.*
by   the thieves
'Melina let the owner of the store be killed by the thieves.'
(Literally: 'Melina let the owner of the store that he be killed by the thieves.')

However, if Subject-to-Object Raising applies when the complement is not passive, producing the structure

(49)

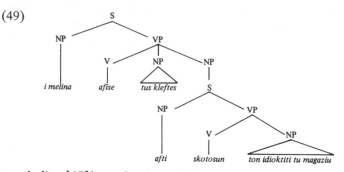

(which underlies [47]), application of Passive in the complement produces a sneaky passive, which is ungrammatical:

(50) a.  *\*I melina        afise tus kleftes na      o   idioktitis*
Melina/NOM let    the thieves SUBJ the owner/NOM
*tu magaziu skotoθi        apo aftus.*
of-the-store be-killed/3Sg by  them

b.  *\*I melina afise tus kleftes na skotoθi o idioktitis tu magaziu apo aftus.*

c.  *\*I melina afise tus kleftes na skotoθi apo aftus o idioktitis tu magaziu.*
(Literally: 'Melina let the thieves that the owner of the store be killed by them.')

Adding the emphatic *tus idius* 'themselves' or *mono* 'only' to accompany the pronominal copy *aftus* in \*(50) does not make the resulting sentences grammatical.[9]

---

[9] To account for the ungrammaticality of these examples under Theory A, one might propose an ad hoc constraint that rules out sentences in which an object of the preposition *apo* introduced by Passive is coreferential with an NP in the matrix clause. However, such a

Strict cyclicity was motivated on the basis of data in English that has nothing to do with sneaky passives in Greek. But Theory B, which incorporates strict cyclicity as a linguistic universal, automatically makes the correct prediction about the status of sentences with sneaky passives in Greek.

## 8. CONCLUSIONS

### 8.1 Strict Cyclicity as a Linguistic Universal

A linguistic theory that incorporates strict cyclicity as a linguistic universal makes predictions about the interaction of Passive with Subject-to-Subject Raising and Subject-to-Object Raising in languages in which one or both of these rules are copying rules. It has been shown here that the predictions of such a linguistic theory are confirmed for modern Greek. This provides additional evidence for strict cyclicity as a linguistic universal.

### 8.2 The Cycle as a Linguistic Universal

Strict cyclicity is not possible in a linguistic theory that does not incorporate the principle of the cycle. Thus, the evidence from Greek for the universality of strict cyclicity is also evidence for the universality of the cycle.

### 8.3 The Interaction between Linguistic Universals and Particular Languages

#### 8.3.1 How Linguistic Universals Provide an Explanation of Data in Particular Languages

Universal principles posited in linguistic theory make concrete empirical predictions about data in particular languages. When a linguistic theory makes correct predictions about novel data in particular languages, it provides an explanation of that data. The principle of strict cyclicity was proposed as a universal completely independently of sneaky passives in Greek. When it correctly

---

*Footnote 9 continued*

constraint cannot be maintained in the light of the grammaticality of sentences such as the following:

(i)  *Episa            ton yani$_i$      pos    i    Maria*
     persuaded/1Sg  the John/ACC  COMP  the  Mary/NOM

   *vlafθike          apo afton$_i$.*
   hurt+PASS/3Sg  by him

   'I persuaded John$_i$ that Mary was hurt by him$_i$.'

predicts sneaky passives such as *(45) and *(50) to be ungrammatical in Greek, it provides an explanation of their ungrammaticality.

### 8.3.2  How Linguistic Universals Affect the Grammars of Particular Languages

Imagine a linguist writing a grammar of Greek in terms of a theory of language that did not include a universal principle of strict cyclicity. A linguist in this position who noticed the ungrammaticality of sentences like *(45) and *(50) would most likely attempt to account for this by means of a constraint on rule application in the grammar of Greek. For example, he or she might propose that the following constraint be included in the grammar of Greek.

(51)  *A pronominal copy left by Subject-to-Subject Raising or Subject-to-Object Raising cannot undergo Passive.*

Both (51) and the principle of strict cyclicity account for the data in Greek; there is no evidence *internal to Greek* to decide between them. Thus, if we were concerned only with accounting for the data in Greek, we would have no grounds for choosing between (51) and strict cyclicity.

A linguist who posited (51) to account for sentences like *(45) and *(50) in Greek might even be tempted to propose that (51) is a linguistic universal. As such, it would make predictions about the interaction of Passive and Raising rules in additional languages in which they are copying rules.

The major difference between strict cyclicity and (51) (even if [51] is elevated to the status of a universal principle) lies in the domain of data about which each of these principles makes predictions. Strict cyclicity makes all the predictions that (51) makes, and more. For example, strict cyclicity accounts for the data in English discussed in section 39 concerning the interaction of Reflexivization and Subject-to-Object Raising with subject-removing rules such as Equi, Subject-to-Subject Raising, and Subject-to-Object Raising. (51) says nothing about this data. Thus, strict cyclicity is a more general principle than (51), accounting for everything that (51) accounts for and additional data as well. Once strict cyclicity is incorporated in linguistic theory as a universal, there is no need for (51), either in linguistic theory or in the grammar of Greek.

### 8.3.3  How Data in Particular Languages Affects Proposed Linguistic Universals

Since proposed linguistic universals make predictions about data in particular languages, it is necessary to examine the relevant data to see whether the predictions they make are confirmed or disconfirmed. If the predictions are confirmed, as was the case with the predictions of strict cyclicity for sneaky passives in Greek, the proposed universal receives additional supporting evidence. If, on the other hand, the predictions made by a proposed universal turn out to be incorrect, the principle in question is shown not to be universal, and it must either be modified or abandoned. In such a case it is necessary to review the evidence that had previously been marshalled in support of the putative universal and see whether the principle can be modified in some way so that it will still account for the data it previously accounted for, but will no longer be disconfirmed by the new data that has been brought to light. In other words, in such a case it is necessary to reduce or weaken the empirical content of the putative universal so that it will no longer make incorrect predictions about the new data that has been discovered. If this is possible, we have a new putative universal with different empirical content, whose empirical predictions must be tested in the same way. If reformulation of the disconfirmed universal in the light of new counterevidence is not possible without depriving the putative universal of all of its empirical content, then the proposed universal must be abandoned. A linguistic universal that makes no empirical predictions is of no interest.

Since it is only their predictions about data in particular languages that give substance to linguistic universals, the data in particular languages provide the standard against which linguistic universals must be tested. They affect proposed universals in the most direct way possible, playing the crucial role in determining which proposals are to be kept as tentative universals of language and which are to be abandoned.

One of the principal goals of linguistic theory is to make explicit the ways that human languages differ from each other and the ways that all human languages are alike. When data from some language confirms a proposed universal, it strengthens our belief that the principle in question is indeed universal. On the other hand, when data from some language disconfirms a proposed universal, it shows that something that had been thought to be the same in all human languages can vary from language to language. In either case, we would not have learned anything about the extent to which languages can differ if the universal had never been proposed. Both the confirmation and the disconfirmation of proposed universals by data from particular languages constitute advances in our knowledge and understanding of human language.

# 44

## Part 3: Its Place in a Wider Context

### 1. THE CYCLE

The basic discovery that led to the formulation of the cyclical principle was made by Fillmore (1963). Studying rule interaction, Fillmore concluded that there are many instances where transformations must apply in a complement prior to the application of transformations in the matrix sentence, but none where transformations must apply in the matrix prior to the application of transformations in the complement. Fillmore's generalization served as the basis for the first formulation of the cycle as a principle of grammar by Chomsky (1965, chapter 3).

The argument for the cycle in section 31, based on the assumption that syntactic rules are ordered, is due to Lakoff (1966). McCawley (1970a) gave a different argument for the cycle based on the same assumption. Another classic argument for the cycle was given by Ross (1969b). Postal (1971) points out problems with Ross's argument.

The arguments for the cycle in sections 34-38 of this book were developed in 1973-1974 and have not to our knowledge previously appeared in print. The arguments for strict cyclicity in section 39 date from the same period; they developed from a suggestion to us by Douglas O'Shaughnessy. Keyser and Postal (1976) present essentially the same argument. Pullum (1976) generalizes the argument along the lines it is generalized here in section 39. Jacobson and Neubauer (1976) give an argument for the cycle based on Super Equi-NP Deletion, which is discussed in part 5 of this book. Morgan and Green (1977) also contains a discussion of the cycle.

Arguments for the cycle based on languages other than English are given by Kayne (1975) for French, and Evers (1975) for Dutch and German.

## 2. ALTERNATIVES TO THE CYCLE

Few explicit alternatives to the cycle have been proposed. Kimball (1972*a*) contrasts cyclic grammars with what he calls "linear grammars." The latter, called "individual cyclic" by Postal (1974) and "epicyclic application" by Bach (1974), are grammars constructed in accordance with what we called the Ordered Multicyclical Theory in section 41. The student who has assimilated the arguments in the preceding sections will be able to construct arguments against the Ordered Multicyclical Theory.

Grinder (1972) argues for a version of the Ordered Multicyclical Theory, claiming that the cycle is unnecessary if Subject-to-Subject Raising and Subject-to-Object Raising leave a pronominal copy of the raised NP in subject position in the complement, to be deleted subsequently by Equi. Pullum (1976) argues that Equi cannot account for the failure of the pronominal copy to appear in surface structure, and that an ad hoc rule would be needed to delete it.

It is interesting that languages such as modern Greek, in which both Raising rules do leave a pronominal copy of the raised NP in the complement, provide a novel kind of argument for both strict cyclicity and the cycle, as shown in section 43. The Greek data would not provide an argument against Grinder's proposal, however, because he was assuming the Ordered Multicyclical Theory, which would avoid the problem by ordering Passive before the Raising rules.[1]

Neeld (1976) claims that the cycle is unnecessary. For a critique of Neeld's proposal, see Pullum (1976). Morin (1976) argues for a theory of grammar in which there is no rule ordering or cycle, and in which rules sometimes apply simultaneously and sometimes sequentially. He proposes a series of principles to determine when rules apply simultaneously and when one rule applies before another. Brame (1976) develops a different alternative to the cycle.

## 3. STRICT CYCLICITY

Chomsky (1973) proposes a principle of strict cyclicity which differs somewhat from the one used in this book. Bach and Horn (1976) propose another version of strict cyclicity.

---

[1] The version of the Ordered Multicyclical Theory given by Kimball and Grinder assumed a derivation of certain sentences involving both Raising and Passive that is different from the one assumed here. For an argument against the derivation assumed by Kimball and Grinder, see section 54. That section thus provides an additional argument against Kimball and Grinder's alternative to the cycle.

As mentioned above, the arguments given here for strict cyclicity developed from a suggestion made to us by Douglas O'Shaughnessy. Keyser and Postal (1976) use the same line of argument to argue for the cycle. The argument for strict cyclicity based on modern Greek is due to Joseph (1978) and Joseph and Perlmutter (to appear).

It has sometimes been claimed that the cyclical principle makes no sense without strict cyclicity. However, as sections 39 and 43 make clear, this is not so. A linguistic theory that incorporates both the cycle and strict cyclicity as linguistic universals makes different empirical predictions than a theory that incorporates the cycle as a universal, but does not make strict cyclicity available to particular grammars. Although both theories are conceptually coherent, the data from English and modern Greek in sections 39 and 43 supports the former theory, but not the latter.

## 4. RULE ORDERING

From the inception of transformational grammar, transformational grammarians assumed that the rules of a grammar are ordered. For a long while, serious alternatives to the rule ordering hypothesis were neither proposed nor tested empirically. Movement away from the assumption of rule ordering was slow, and took place in a series of steps. For example, the Ordering Strain Principle in Perlmutter (1971) in effect called for a minimization of the use of rule ordering in grammars. G. Lakoff (1971) and Postal (1972a) espoused the view that rule ordering statements, like other grammatical devices, are not to be merely assumed as part of every grammar, but must be justified.

In a related line of work, Koutsoudas (1972) showed that many of the supposed arguments for rule ordering actually presupposed it, initially assuming what they claimed to show. Lehmann (1972) and Ringen (1972) also argued against earlier arguments in favor of rule ordering. This line of work led to the claim, stated in Koutsoudas, Sanders, and Noll (1974), that grammars do not contain language-particular rule ordering statements. This led to attempts to discover universal principles that would correctly predict rule interaction. In addition to Koutsoudas, Sanders and Noll (1974), the relevant literature includes Ringen (1972, 1974), Sanders (1974a, 1976), Eckman (1974), Koutsoudas (1976b), Hastings (1976), and Pullum (1976).

The work of Chomsky also shows a progression from the assumption that all grammatical rules are ordered to a framework without rule ordering. Syntactic rules are assumed to be ordered in Chomsky (1962) (a paper given at a conference in 1958). Chomsky (1965, p. 133) operates on the assumption that "singular transformations are linearly ordered (perhaps only partially ordered)." Chomsky (1973) relies crucially on certain rules being ordered with respect to other rules. Chomsky and Lasnik (1977) assumes that syntactic rules are not ordered.

## 5. CHARACTERIZING THE NOTION "OBLIGATORY RULE"

Soames (1974) discusses the relationship between assumptions about rule ordering and alternative characterizations of obligatory rules. A characterization is given for a theory with ordered rules, and suggestions for further investigations are made regarding the characterization of obligatory rules in theories without ordering. Unfortunately, relatively little empirical work has been done in this area. The Immediate Characterization and Frustrated Characterization used in this book are only two of the possible characterizations that could be given. We briefly review here some of the other characterizations that have been given.

G. Lakoff (1971) attempts to formalize the notions "rule ordering constraint," "obligatory rule," and "optional rule." For a discussion of Lakoff, see Soames (1974). Ringen (1972) assumes that "an obligatory rule is a rule which must apply to a phrase marker if that phrase marker meets the structural description of the rule." She says that what she calls the "Obligatory-Optional Principle" follows from this. The principle states that if a phrase marker meets the structural description of both an optional and an obligatory rule, then the obligatory rule must apply first. This is very close (perhaps identical) to the Immediate Characterization of obligatory rules.[2] Further discussion of the Obligatory-Optional Principle can be found in Ringen (1974) and Hastings (1976).

Koutsoudas, Sanders, and Noll (1974) are also very close to the Immediate Characterization in proposing that an obligatory rule must apply whenever its structural description is met, unless its application is precluded by some universal principle. They claim that it follows from this requirement that rules will apply simultaneously if possible; otherwise they will apply sequentially. Essentially the same characterization is given in Koutsoudas (1976b).

Sanders (1974b) is an attempt to remove the distinction between obligatory and optional from linguistic theory. See also Fiengo (1977) and Chomsky and Lasnik (1977).

---

[2] Ringen's (1972) characterization of obligatory rules appears to be identical with the Immediate Characterization. However, there may be other ways to interpret what she has in mind. For example, in Ringen (1974) she accepts a (universal) principle that would allow certain optional rules to apply to phrase markers satisfying an obligatory rule before the obligatory rule has a chance to apply.

# PART 4

# *Cycle-Type of Rules*

In addition to cyclical rules, syntacticians have posited a class of post-cyclical rules that apply after all cyclical rules have applied. Unlike cyclical rules, which apply first to the most deeply embedded S, then the next S up, and so on up the tree, postcyclical rules can apply to the whole tree, or to any part of it that satisfies their structural description. (We assume that postcyclical rules are not subject to the principle of strict cyclicity.)

It is not important here to go into the various reasons that have been given for postulating a class of postcyclical rules. What is important is to understand the task that such a postulation imposes on a linguist constructing a grammar. Since each rule must be classified as either cyclical or postcyclical, arguments must be found for making the correct classification in each case. Arguments for the cyclicity of a given rule are designed to show that it cannot be postcyclical. Arguments for the postcyclicity of a rule are designed to show that it cannot be cyclical.

Part 4 is devoted to finding arguments of this type. Here we ask you to establish the cycle-type (cyclical or postcyclical) of the rules introduced earlier. Constructing these arguments provides a deeper understanding of the way these rules interact, and of the cyclical principle in general.

# 45

## Cycle-Types

### 1. ASSUMPTIONS

*Assumption 1*

There are two kinds of rules:

A.   Cyclical rules, which apply first to the most deeply embedded S, then to the next S up, and so on.

B.   Postcyclical rules, which apply only after all cyclical rules have applied. A postcyclical rule can apply anywhere in a tree where its structural description is satisfied.

*Assumption 2*

A given rule is either cyclical or postcyclical; no rule can apply both cyclically and postcyclically.

### 2. DEFINITION

If two rules are either both cyclical or both postcyclical, we say that they are of the same *cycle-type*. If one rule is cyclical and the other is post-cyclical, then they are of different cycle-types.

## 3. THE PROBLEM

Determine whether Reflexivization, Subject-to-Object Raising, Passive, and Subject-to-Subject Raising are cyclical or postcyclical. Show that the cycle-type of these rules is the same under both the Immediate and the Frustrated Characterization of obligatory rules.

In working this problem, proceed in three steps.

*Step 1*

Show that all four rules must be of the same cycle-type—i.e., either all are cyclical or all are postcyclical. This can be shown independently of any assumptions about the characterization of obligatory rules.

*Step 2*[1]

Assuming the Frustrated Characterization of obligatory rules, determine the cycle-type of Reflexivization and Subject-to-Object Raising. The results of Step 1 will then give you the cycle-type of all four rules under the Frustrated Characterization.

*Step 3*

Assuming the Immediate Characterization of obligatory rules, determine the cycle-type of Passive and Subject-to-Subject Raising. Then use the results of Step 1 to determine what the cycle-type of all four rules must be.

---

[1] Those who assumed in part 3 that the rules of a grammar are strictly ordered may use this assumption together with the results of Step 1 to determine the cycle-type of all four rules.

# 46

## Equi and THERE-Insertion

### 1. ASSUMPTIONS

*Assumption 1*

There are two kinds of rules: cylical and postcyclical.

*Assumption 2*

A given rule is either cyclical or postcyclical; no rule can apply both cyclically and postcyclically.

### 2. THE PROBLEMS

*Problem 1*

Use the results of section 45 to determine the cycle-type of Equi.

*Problem 2*

Do the same for THERE-Insertion.

# 47

# *Reflexivization and Imperative Deletion*

## 1. THE INTERACTION OF REFLEXIVIZATION AND IMPERATIVE DELETION

In sections 4 and 30 we saw that Imperative Deletion must be prevented from applying before Reflexivization in order to block the derivation of examples like

(1) *Wash you.*

We also saw that early transformational grammarians used examples like *(1) to motivate a theory of strict linear ordering in which Reflexivization is ordered before Imperative Deletion. It is now possible to show why the interaction of these two rules does not provide a conclusive argument for rule ordering.

## 2. REFLEXIVIZATION, IMPERATIVE DELETION, AND THE IMMEDIATE CHARACTERIZATION OF OBLIGATORY RULES

Under the Immediate Characterization, an obligatory rule must apply immediately to any structure in a derivation that satisfies its structural description. Since Reflexivization is obligatory and Imperative Deletion is optional, Reflexivization must apply to

(2)

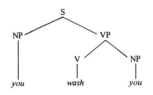

before Imperative Deletion. As a result, Imperative Deletion can never destroy the environment for Reflexivization, and *(1) cannot be generated. Thus, if the Immediate Characterization of obligatory rules is adopted, then examples like *(1) provide no evidence for rule ordering.[1]

## 3. REFLEXIVIZATION, IMPERATIVE DELETION, AND THE FRUSTRATED CHARACTERIZATION OF OBLIGATORY RULES

Under the Frustrated Characterization, it is possible for an optional rule to destroy the environment of an obligatory rule. Thus, obligatory Reflexivization does not prevent Imperative Deletion from applying to (2) to produce *(1). Some other mechanism is needed.

The distinction between cyclical and postcyclical rules is just such a mechanism. We have seen that a grammar must mark each rule as either cyclical or postcyclical. Reflexivization is cyclical. If Imperative Deletion is postcyclical, then it can never apply before Reflexivization, and *(1) will not be generated.

This shows that if the Frustrated Characterization is adopted, then Imperative Deletion is postcyclical. The argument for this conclusion can be reconstructed as follows.

(4)  a.   *Each rule must be either cyclical or postcyclical.*
     b.   *If Imperative Deletion is postcyclical, then examples like *(1) are accounted for automatically.*
     c.   *If Imperative Deletion is cyclical, then some additional device is needed to block the derivation of examples like *(1).*[2]

---

[1] Note, this argument holds for any characterization of obligatory rules that has the consequence that the environment of an obligatory rule cannot be destroyed by the application of other rules.

[2] This is where the assumption of the Frustrated Characterization comes in. If the Immediate Characterization were adopted, then obligatory Reflexivization would block *(1). Thus, a grammar in which Imperative Deletion is cyclical would not require any additional device. However, if the Frustrated Characterization is adopted, then a grammar in which Imperative Deletion is cyclical would require an additional mechanism to block *(1).

d.    *Since a grammar in which Imperative Deletion is cyclical requires an extra device that is not needed by a grammar in which Imperative Deletion is postcyclical, we adopt the hypothesis that Imperative Deletion is postcyclical.*

Consequently, Reflexivization and Imperative Deletion need not be ordered.

## 4. CONCLUSION

No matter which characterization of obligatory rules is adopted, the interaction of Reflexivization and Imperative Deletion does not provide evidence for rule ordering.

# 48

## *What Cycle-Type is Extraposition?*[1]

### *1. ASSUMPTIONS*

*Assumption 1*

There are two kinds of rules: cyclical and postcyclical.

*Assumption 2*

A given rule is either cyclical or postcyclical; no rule can apply both cyclically and postcyclically.

*Assumption 3*

Subject-to-Subject Raising is a cyclical rule.

### *2. THE PROBLEM*

Use Assumptions 1–3 to determine the cycle-type of Extraposition.

---

[1] This problem is somewhat more complex than most problems in part 4. Although we recommend it to everyone, those who want to go through the book as quickly as possible may omit it. This problem is a prerequisite for the problem in section 49.

# 49

## *Cycle Arguments and Cycle-Types*[1]

In Section 45 it was shown that the rules in

(1)   *Reflexivization*
      *Subject-to-Object Raising*
      *Passive*
      *Subject-to-Subject Raising*

are cyclical. In sections 46 and 48 you were asked to determine the cycle-type of the rules in

(2)   *THERE-Insertion*
      *Equi*
      *Extraposition*

In each case, this could be done by showing that the relevant rule in (2) must be able to apply before one of the rules in (1).

The arguments for the cyclicity of the rules in (1) were based on the cycle arguments of part 3. Sections 46 and 48 showed that if the rules in (1) are cyclical, then the rules in (2) are also cyclical. Thus, the arguments in part 3 provide the basis for establishing the cyclicity of each of the rules in (1) and (2).

Having shown that these rules are cyclical, we will put aside this conclusion for the moment in order to establish a more abstract result. In Step 1 of section 45 we showed that *no matter what arguments one might use to motivate the cycle,* the rules in (1) must all be of the same cycle-type. We can now extend this result to cover the rules in (2) as well. To do this we must show that *no*

---

[1] Section 48 is a prerequisite for this problem.

*matter how the cycle is motivated, the rules in (2) must be of the same cycle-type as the rules in (1).* For this purpose, it is sufficient to establish (3) and (4).

(3)     *For each rule in (2), there are grammatical sentences that can be derived only by applying the rule **before** some rule in (1). (If the rules in [1] are cyclical, then so are the rules in [2].)*

(4)     *For each rule in (2), there are grammatical sentences that can be derived only by applying the rule **after** some rule in (1). (If the rules in [2] are cyclical, then so are the rules in [1].)*[2]

In doing sections 46 and 48, you have already established (3). The only thing that remains to be established is (4). Once you have done this you will have shown that no matter what assumptions are made about obligatory rules, and no matter how the cycle is motivated, the rules in (1) and (2) must be of the same cycle-type. Thus, if a grammar posits all seven rules, then any argument for the cyclicity of one of them can be used to demonstrate the cyclicity of all of them.

## EXERCISE

Construct examples that show that (4) is true.

---

[2] If the Cycle were motivated using the rules in (2), then (4) would allow us to use such cycle arguments to establish the cyclicity of the rules in (1). In section 57 of part 5 we will present just such an argument; we will show that the interaction of Extraposition and Super Equi-NP Deletion provides us with a new argument for the Cycle.

# 50

## *Part 4: Its Place in a Wider Context*

### *1. ARGUMENTS FOR POSTCYCLICAL RULES*

One type of argument for the postcyclicity of a rule consists of showing that if Rule A applies in the complement before a two-story rule, Rule B, applies in the matrix sentence, ungrammatical sentences will be generated. But if Rule A is postcyclical, then ungrammatical sentences will not be produced. It is concluded that Rule A is postcyclical.

Another type of argument for postcyclicity is based on strict cyclicity.[1]

(1) *Strict Cyclicity*

> *No cyclical rule can apply on a given cycle to any structure wholly within the domain of a lower cycle.*

In this type of argument, it is shown first, that Rule A must apply in a complement; second, that it cannot apply in the complement on the initial cycle for that complement; and third, that if it applies in the complement on a subsequent cycle, it will violate strict cyclicity. It is concluded that Rule A is postcyclical. With Rule A postcyclical, its application in the complement after the first cycle on that complement will not violate strict cyclicity.

Among the earliest papers arguing that not all rules can be cyclical are Lakoff (1966) and Matthews (1970). Arguments for the postcyclicity of par-

---

[1] The formulation of strict cyclicity in Chomsky (1973) is not restricted to cyclical rules. Arguments for postcyclicity of the type mentioned here would thus provide counterexamples to Chomsky's formulation of the principle. For further discussion of how strict cyclicity should be formulated, see Bach and Horn (1976).

ticular rules are given in Hankamer (1974), Moyne and Carden (1974), Breckenridge (1975), Kayne (1975), Pullum (1976), and Quicoli (1976). This list is by
no means complete. Emonds (1976) gives a typology of rules that is related to
the distinction between cyclical and postcyclical rules. Noll (1976) argues
against postcyclical rules. Extensive discussion of the topic can be found in
Pullum (1976).

## 2. ARGUMENTS FOR THE CYCLICITY OF RULES

A number of different arguments have been given in the literature for the
cyclicity of particular rules. The nature of these arguments has been different,
depending on the general assumptions about rule interaction made by the
author. For example, many arguments for the cyclicity of particular rules are
based on the assumption that all syntactic rules are strictly ordered. Under this
assumption, one shows that Rule A is cyclical by showing examples in which it
must apply before Rule B and examples in which it must apply after Rule B.

The arguments for the cyclicity of six of the seven rules of English shown
to be cyclical in part 4 are based largely on data that has figured in earlier arguments for the cycle. We present our own argument for the cyclicity of Extraposition.

Our presentation in part 4 emphasizes that all seven rules must be of the
same cycle-type. Thus, any argument for the cyclicity of one of them can be
used to demonstrate the cyclicity of all of them. The arguments for the cyclicity
of these rules are thus freed from assumptions about rule ordering and obligatory rules; regardless of how the cycle is motivated, the rules in question must all
be cyclical.

## 3. LAST-CYCLICAL RULES

The linguistic literature contains some reference to "last-cyclical rules." The
idea of last-cyclical rules was originally suggested by Noam Chomsky, at a time
when transformational grammarians generally assumed that syntactic rules were
ordered. The basic idea can be simply stated. Instead of a class of postcyclical
rules, there is a class of last-cyclical rules that apply *only during the last cycle,*
that is, during the cycle on the topmost S. Since last-cyclical rules could not
apply on earlier cycles, the category of last-cyclical rules had some of the same
properties as what are now considered to be postcyclical rules. The crucial
difference between them lies in the fact that last-cyclical rules could apply
*before* cyclical rules, but *only on the last cycle.* Since at that time rules were
generally assumed to be ordered, the idea of last-cyclical rules permitted the

linguist to order these rules *before* certain cyclical rules, and still prevent them from applying on earlier cycles. In the mid-1960s, George Lakoff and John Ross gave an argument that this notion of last-cyclical rules is needed, based on some pronominalization facts in English. The Lakoff-Ross argument depended on certain assumptions about pronominalization which subsequent work on pronominalization has led most linguists to abandon. Their argument also depended on the assumption that syntactic rules are ordered.

At present, there seems to be no evidence that the notion of last-cyclical rules is needed in linguistic theory. For discussion of the question, see Pullum (1976). To show that last-cyclical rules are needed, it would be necessary to show that there are rules that must be prevented from applying on any but the last cycle, and that these rules must be able to apply *before* some cyclical rule on the last cycle. The former is needed to show that the rules in question are not cyclical, and the latter, to show that they are not postcyclical. In the absence of such evidence, we assume that there are no last-cyclical rules in syntax.

## 4. PRECYCLICAL RULES

Several times in the development of transformational grammar it has been proposed that there exists a class of "precyclical rules" which apply to the entire tree before any cyclical rules apply. Lakoff (1966) gave an argument for one such rule in English, but it was based on assumptions about pronominalization that many linguists no longer accept. More recently, arguments for precyclical rules have been given by Aissen (1974a) and Newmeyer (1976). The kind of evidence that would be needed to establish that a rule is precyclical would be of the following kind: Consider an S, $S_i$, which is embedded in another S, $S_j$. To show that a rule is precyclical, it is necessary to show that it must apply to $S_j$ *before* the application of cyclical rules to $S_i$. Aissen (1974a) and Newmeyer (1971, 1975, 1976) give arguments of this type; for a critique, see Pullum (1976). The assumptions on which the arguments for precyclical rules are based are controversial; as a result, the existence of such rules is controversial as well.

## 5. SUMMARY

While the cycle and strict cyclicity make many correct predictions about rule interaction in syntax, work in transformational grammar has brought to light facts about rule interaction that cannot be accounted for by these two principles alone. It has therefore been necessary to posit the existence of non-cyclical rules. The best supported of these are postcyclical rules. For this reason, we have assumed the existence of both cyclical and postcyclical rules, and shown how certain rules can be shown to be cyclical, on the assumption that both cyclical and postcyclical rules exist. The existence of last-cyclical rules and pre-cyclical rules is much more problematic. We have therefore not assumed their existence here.

Since noncyclical rules have been posited in transformational grammar, it has become necessary to argue for the cyclicity of particular rules. It has been the purpose of part 4 to show how arguments of this kind can be constructed. Two extensive syntactic studies that contain arguments for the cyclicity or postcyclicity of particular rules are Postal (1974) and Kayne (1975).

# PART 5

# *Further Issues in Complementation*

In part 5 we present several remaining issues involving complementation. Section 51, Force and Expect, introduces a new underlying structure and object-controlled Equi. Sections 52 and 53 are review problems that extend familiar forms of argument to new cases. The next two sections are concerned with new rule interactions—section 54 with the interaction of Passive and the two Raisings, and section 55 with the interaction of THERE-Insertion and Verb Agreement. The last two sections in part 5 introduce the notion of *primacy relations* (*precede* and *command*) and illustrate their utility in the formulation of a rule called *Super Equi*. The problem on Super Equi develops arguments for the cycle-type of various rules as well as new arguments for the cycle and strict cyclicity.

# 51

# *FORCE and EXPECT*

## *1. THE PHENOMENON*

The two sentences

(1)    *I expected Tom to go.*

and

(2)    *I forced Tom to go.*

appear to have surface structures of exactly the same form. In this problem we will consider evidence that their underlying structures differ in important respects.

## *2. TWO COMPLEMENTARY HYPOTHESES*

*Hypothesis A*

*Expect* occurs in underlying structures of the form[1]

---

[1] More generally, *expect* occurs in underlying structures of the form

(i)

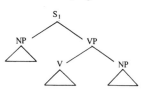

of which (3) is a special case.

(3)

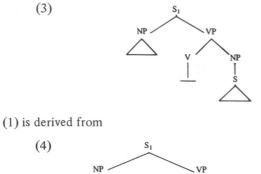

(1) is derived from

(4)

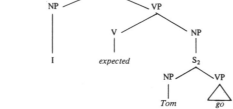

by the application of Subject-to-Object Raising.

*Hypothesis B*

*Force* occurs in underlying structures of the form[2]

(5)

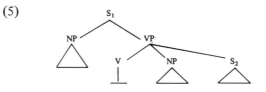

[2] To generate underlying structures of the form (5), we will need the phrase structure rule

    (i)   VP → V NP S

Since we already have the phrase structure rule

    (ii)   VP → V (NP)

(i) and (ii) can be combined as the single rule

    (iii)   VP → V (NP [S]).

(iii) says that *VP* can be expanded as any of the following:

    (iv)  a.   V
          b.   V NP
          c.   V NP S

(2) is derived from

(6)

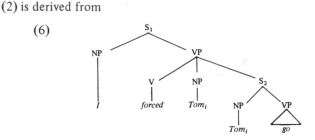

by the application of Equi. Note, in the derivation of (2) Equi deletes the subject of $S_2$ under coreferentiality with the *object* (rather than the subject) of $S_1$[3],[4]

Under Hypothesis A, *expect* does not occur in underlying structures of the form (5). Under Hypothesis B, *force* does not occur in underlying structures of the form (3).

---

[3] This requires either that we reformulate Equi to allow objects to trigger deletion as well as subjects, or that we posit a new rule of Object-Controlled Equi. We leave it open which of these alternatives is correct.

[4] Once *force* is allowed to occur in underlying structures of the form (5), there is nothing to prevent underlying structures like (i) from being generated.

(i)

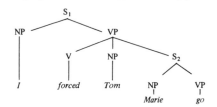

(i) has no grammatical output

(ii)  a.    *I forced Tom for Marie to go*
      b.    *I forced Tom Marie to go.*

Some constraint is needed to characterize sentences like *(ii) as ungrammatical.

At first it might seem that all that is needed is to make Equi obligatory with *force*. However, this will not solve the problem,. Since the complement subject in (i) is not coreferential with the matrix object, the structural description of Equi is not satisfied. Regardless of which characterization of obligatory rules is adopted, the fact that (i) does not satisfy the structural description of Equi means that making Equi obligatory with *force* will not characterize *(ii) as ungrammatical.

One possible solution to this problem is to require Equi to actually apply in derivations with *force*. Failure of Equi to apply in the derivations of *(iia-b) will therefore characterize these sentences as ungrammatical.

## 3. THE CLAIMS MADE BY THE TWO HYPOTHESES

*Hypothesis A*

Claim 1. The surface object of *expect* is not its underlying object, but rather becomes the object of *expect* during the course of derivation.

Claim 2. Subject-to-Object Raising applies in the derivation of sentences with *expect*. Object-Controlled Equi does not.[5]

*Hypothesis B*

Claim 1. The surface object of *force* is also its underlying object.

Claim 2. Object-Controlled Equi applies in the derivation of sentences with *force*. Subject-to-Object Raising does not.

## 4. THE PROBLEM

Contrast *expect*-sentences with *force*-sentences. Use the contrasts between these sentences to construct as many arguments as you can for Hypotheses A and B.

---

[5] Recall that with *expect*, Equi optionally deletes the complement subject under coreference with the matrix subject. For example, if Equi applies to

(i)

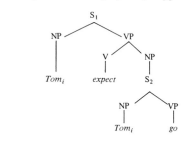

then

　　(ii) *Tom expects to go*

is derived. If Subject-to-Object Raising applies, then

　　(iii) *Tom expects himself to go*

is produced.

An argument for Hypothesis A is an argument that sentences like (1) are not derived from structures of the form (5) by Equi, but rather are derived structures of the form (3) by Subject-to-Object Raising.

An argument for Hypothesis B is an argument that sentences like (2) are not derived from structures of the form (3) by Subject-to-Object Raising, but rather are derived from structures of the form (5) by Equi.

# 52

## A Checklist of Verbs

### 1. TWO UNDERLYING STRUCTURES

(1)

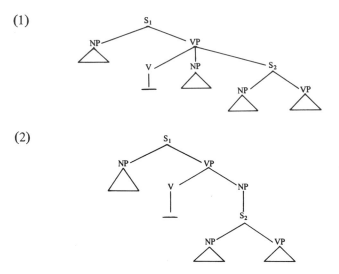

(2)

### 2. THREE RULES

(3) **Subject-to-Object Raising**

*This rule applies to structures of the form (2), moving the subject of $S_2$ out of the complement and making it the derived object of $S_1$.*

(4) **Subject-Controlled Equi**

*This rule applies to structures of the form (2), deleting the subject of $S_2$ under coreference with the subject of $S_1$.*

(5)   *Object-Controlled Equi*[1]

> *This rule applies to structures of the form (1), deleting the subject of $S_2$ under coreference with the object of $S_1$.*

## 3. THE TRIGGERING OF RULES BY VERBS

Only verbs that occur in structure (1) can trigger Object-Controlled Equi, for example, *force*. Only verbs that occur in structure (2) can trigger Subject-to-Object Raising, for example, *expect*. Some verbs occurring in (2) trigger Subject-Controlled Equi—e.g., *want* and *expect*. So far, it is an open question whether or not there are any verbs occurring in structure (1) that trigger Subject-Controlled Equi.

## 4. A CHECKLIST OF VERBS

| | | |
|---|---|---|
| persuade | tell | advise |
| intend | consent | assure |
| encourage | promise | ask |
| affirm | imagine | |

## 5. THE EXERCISE

Review the discussions of Subject-to-Object Raising, Subject-Controlled Equi and Object-Controlled Equi. Use the material in those discussions to construct tests that will enable you to answer Questions 1 and 2. Answer the questions using as many tests as you can.

*Question 1*

Which of the verbs in §4 occur in structures of the form (1), and which occur in structures of the form (2)?

*Question 2*

Which of the verbs in §4 trigger Subject-to-Object Raising, which trigger Subject- or Object-Controlled Equi, and which do not trigger any of these rules?

---

[1] We leave open the question of whether Subject-Controlled Equi and Object-Controlled Equi are the same rule or two separate rules.

# 53

## Two Analyses of the Passive

### 1. TWO HYPOTHESES

*Hypothesis A*

The Sentence

(1)   *Morris was bitten by a mosquito.*

is derived from the underlying structure

(2)

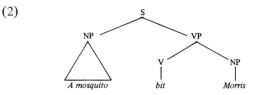

The Passive transformation then makes the object into the subject, post-poses the old subject, making it the object of the preposition *by,* inserts the auxiliary verb *be,* and puts the verb in its past participle form. The result is (1).

*Hypothesis B*

(1)   *is derived not from (2), but rather from the structure*

(3)

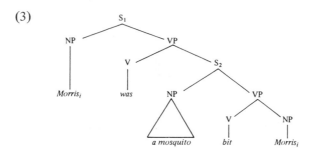

in which the surface subject of (1) is also its underlying subject. The Passive transformation, applying on the $S_2$-cycle, makes the object into the subject, postposes the old subject, making it the object of the preposition *by,* and puts the verb in its past participle form. Since *be* is present in $S_1$ in the underlying structure, the Passive Transformation does not insert *be.* On the $S_1$-cycle, Equi-NP Deletion applies, deleting the derived subject of the embedded sentence to produce the surface structure (1).

## 2. THE PROBLEM

Construct as many arguments as you can to decide between these two hypotheses. Hint: several arguments can be constructed which parallel those presented in section 51.

# 54

## *Raising/Passive Sentences*

### *1. THE PROBLEM*

Sentences like

(1)  *The bomb was believed by the authorities to have been planted by the IRA*

were discussed in section 31 where it was shown that they provide an argument for the cycle in theories of grammar that assume role ordering. According to this argument, (1) is derived from the underlying structure

(2)

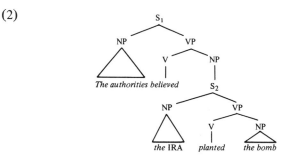

by applying Passive on $S_2$ and Subject-to-Object Raising on $S_1$ to produce the derived structure

(3)

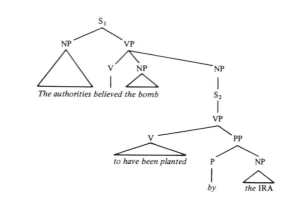

Application of Passive on the $S_1$-cycle generates (1). Since this derivation makes crucial use of Subject-to-Object Raising, we will call it the Subject-to-Object (S-O) derivation.

However, there is another way that (1) might be generated from (2). Suppose that Passive applies on the $S_2$-cycle, but Subject-to-Object Raising does not apply on $S_1$. Rather, Passive applies on the $S_1$-cycle, producing the derived structure

(4)

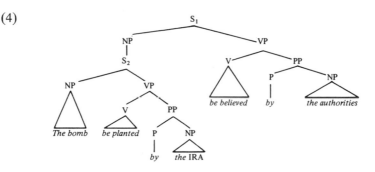

If passive forms like *be believed* are Subject-to-Subject Raising triggers, then Subject-to-Subject Raising will apply to (4), producing (1). Since this derivation makes crucial use of Subject-to-Subject Raising, we will refer to it as the Subject-to-Subject (S-S) derivation.

It is conceivable then that sentences like (1) could be derived from (2) in either of two ways—one involving Subject-to-Object Raising and the other involving Subject-to-Subject Raising. The question arises as to whether or not such *Raising/Passive sentences* are in fact derived in both of these ways. In §2 we will argue that they are not, but rather have only S-O derivations.

## 2. *ARGUMENT BASED ON A MYSTERIOUS CONSTRAINT WITH* SEEM

### 2.1 Strategy

Consider the contrast between the following two sentences:

(5)   *It is likely to seem that Hanrahan is guilty.*
(6)   *\*It is believed to seem that Hanrahan is guilty.*

We will show that if Raising/Passive sentences are derived by Subject-to-Object Raising rather than by Subject-to-Subject Raising, the ungrammaticality of \*(6) will follow automatically from a constraint that is needed in the grammar independently.

### 2.2 S-S Derivations Do Not Block \*(6)

First consider sentences with *likely*. Application of Extraposition on the $S_2$-cycle to the underlying structure

(7)

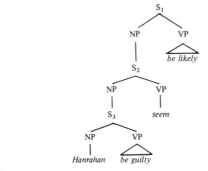

produces the structure

(8)

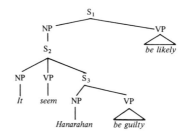

Application of Subject-to-Subject Raising to (8) generates

(9)   *It is likely to seem that Hanrahan is guilty.*

This shows that grammatical sentences result from application of Subject-to-

Subject Raising to structures in which *it seems that Hanrahan is guilty* is embedded beneath a Subject-to-Subject Raising trigger.

If passive forms like *be believed* were Subject-to-Subject Raising triggers, analogous derivations could be constructed for examples like \*(6) and \*(10).

(10) \**It is believed by everyone to seem that Hanrahan is guilty.*

The structure underlying \*(10) would be

(11)

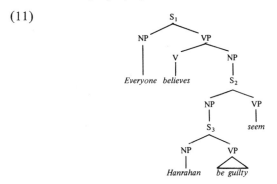

Application of Extraposition on the $S_2$-cycle and Passive on the $S_1$-cycle would produce the structure

(12)

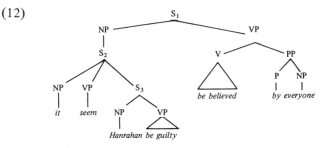

Application of Subject-to-Subject Raising to (12) would generate the ungrammatical \*(10). Thus, if *be believed* were a Subject-to-Subject Raising trigger, there would be nothing to prevent the rule from applying to (12) to produce ungrammatical sentences like \*(6) and \*(10).[1]

---

[1] \*(10) differs from \*(6) only in that it contains the *by*-phrase *by everyone*. Generative grammarians have postulated that the absence of a *by*-phrase in sentences like \*(6) is due to two factors:

   (i) *The presence of an element* **pro** *which is the subject of* **believe** *in the underlying structure of* \*(6).

   (ii) *A rule of* **Agent Deletion** *which deletes by-phrases containing* **pro**.

## 2.3 S-O Derivations Block *(6) and *(10)

We will now show that ungrammatical Raising/Passive sentences like *(6) and *(10) cannot be derived via S-O derivations. Consider again the underlying structure (11). Applying Extraposition on the $S_2$-cycle produces

(13)

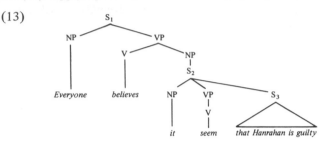

If no further transformations apply, this results in the grammatical sentence

(14) *Everyone believes that it seems that Hanrahan is guilty.*

However, if Subject-to-Object Raising were to apply to (13), the result would be

(15)

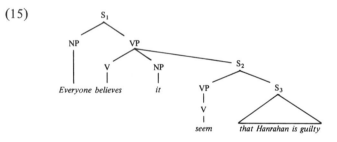

which yields the ungrammatical sentence

(16) *Everyone believes it to seem that Hanrahan is guilty.*

Although we have no explanation of why *(16) is ungrammatical, the fact that it is shows that the grammar must include a constraint preventing *(15) from being generated:

(17) *Mystery Constraint*

*Subject-to-Object Raising cannot apply to structures like (13) to produce structures like (15).*[2]

---

[2] The formulation of this constraint is vague since it is not specified what structures are *like* (13) and *(15). However, this does not affect the argument. For more on this point, see footnote 3 below.

In addition to blocking *(16), this constraint has the consequence that *(6) and *(10) cannot be derived by S-O derivations. To derive *(10) in this way, Extraposition would have to apply first, producing (13); Subject-to-Object Raising would have to apply next, producing (15); and Passive would have to apply last, producing *(10). Since the Mystery Constraint does not allow Subject-to-Object Raising to produce (15), this derivation is blocked. Hence, *(10) does not have an S-O derivation. The same conclusion holds for *(6).[3]

## 2.4 Conclusion

So far we have seen three things:

(18) a.    *If Raising/Passive sentences could be derived via S-S derivations, then passive verbs like* **be believed** *would have to be Subject-to-Subject Raising triggers.*

     b.    *If these verbs were Subject-to-Subject Raising triggers, then there would be nothing to prevent ungrammatical sentences like *(6) and *(10) from being derived.*

     c.    *If, on the other hand, Raising/Passive sentences can be derived only via S-O derivations, then these ungrammatical sentences will be blocked by a constraint that is needed in the grammar independently.*

We conclude that Raising/Passive sentences have S-O derivations, not S-S derivations.

## 3. THE FORMULATION OF THE MYSTERY CONSTRAINT

In referring to the constraint that prevents the derivation of structures like *(15) as the "Mystery Constraint," we are indicating that its nature and proper

---

[3] Note also that *(16) contrasts with the grammatical sentence

(i)    *Everyone believes it to be likely that Hanrahan is guilty.*

The Mystery Constraint must be stated so as to apply only to structures in which the verbal in $S_2$ is in the *seem* class, but not to structures in which the $S_2$ verbal is in the *likely* class. This fact, in conjunction with the hypothesis that Raising/Passive sentences are derived by S–O derivations, makes a further prediction: that the Raising/Passive sentence that is like *(10) except that the $S_2$ verbal is *likely* will be grammatical. And it is:

(ii)    *It is believed (by everyone) to be likely that Hanrahan is guilty.*

(ii) is grammatical because it is derived from the structure that also underlies (i) by application of Passive in $S_1$. The ungrammaticality of *(10) is due to the ill-formedness of *(15).

formulation are not yet understood. Fortunately, this does not affect our argument. The important point is that no matter how the constraint is ultimately formulated, a grammar that derives Raising/Passive sentences only via S-O derivations will be able to account for such sentences with devices that are needed independently in the grammar. Thus, even though the constraint blocking *(15) remains a mystery, it can be used to construct an argument about how Raising/Passive sentences are derived.[4]

[4] Recall the Ordered Multicylical Theory of rule interaction discussed in section 41 of part 3. Under this theory, Raising/Passive sentences could be derived *only* by the S–S derivation. The argument presented here showing that such sentences are derived by the S–O derivation, and not by the S–S derivation, is thus also an argument against the Ordered Multicyclical Theory.

# 55

# THERE-Insertion and Verb Agreement

## 1. THE PHENOMENON

In English, the verb agrees in number with its subject.

(1)  a.  *A mouse is in the bathtub.*
     b.  *\*A mouse are in the bathtub.*

(2)  a.  *\*Some mice is in the bathtub.*
     b.  *Some mice are in the bathtub.*

In derivations in which THERE-Insertion applies, *there* becomes the derived subject, replacing the former subject. The agreement patterns in sentences in which THERE-Insertion has applied are the same as those in the corresponding sentences without *there*.

(3)  a.  *There is a mouse in the bathtub.*
     b.  *\*There are a mouse in the bathtub.*

(4)  a.  *\*There is some mice in the bathtub.*
     b.  *There are some mice in the bathtub.*

## 2.  TWO CONFLICTING HYPOTHESES

### 2.1  Hypothesis A

The way to account for the agreement facts in (3-4) is to impose a rule ordering constraint preventing THERE-Insertion from applying until after Verb Agreement has already applied. THERE-Insertion will then operate on forms like (1a) and (2b) to which Verb Agreement has already applied. Thus, (3a) and (4b) will be generated and *(3b) and *(4a) will be blocked.

### 2.2  Hypothesis B

The way to account for the agreement facts in (3-4) is to add a mechanism to the grammar ensuring that if the subject is *there,* then the verb agrees with the NP that *there* replaced when it was inserted, regardless of where that NP may be located in the tree.[1]

Under this hypothesis, there is no need to impose a constraint preventing THERE-Insertion from applying before Verb Agreement. For example, even if THERE-Insertion applies before Verb Agreement in the derivation of (4b), the new mechanism will ensure that the verb agrees with the plural NP *some mice.* Thus, (4b) will be generated, and *(4a) will not.

### 2.3  Comparison of the Two Hypotheses

Hypothesis A and Hypothesis B account for the agreement facts in (3-4) in different ways. Each posits something that the other does not. Hypothesis A posits a rule ordering constraint, but leaves verb agreement intact. Hypothesis B adds a new mechanism involving verb agreement, but requires no rule ordering constraint.

## 3.  AN EMPIRICAL DIFFERENCE BETWEEN THE TWO HYPOTHESES

Hypotheses A and B make the same predictions about simple sentences without embedding. To find an empirical difference between them, one has to find sentences whose derivations involve the application of THERE-Insertion, Verb Agreement, and other cyclical rules on different cycles. It is particularly

---

[1] There are several different formal mechanisms that could be used to ensure that agreement operates in this way. Since we haven't discussed these mechanisms, you may ignore the question of how agreement is formalized in working this problem.

important to find cases in which the noun phrase with which the verb agrees was not the subject of the verb at any stage of derivation. If it is possible to construct an agrument for Hypothesis B, the crucial evidence will come from sentences of this kind.

## 4. THE PROBLEM

Construct two arguments for rejecting Hypothesis A in favor of Hypothesis B. Each argument should be based on the interaction of THERE-Insertion and Verb Agreement with a cyclical rule or combination of cyclical rules.

# 56

## *Primacy Relations*[1]

### *1. COMMAND*

#### 1.1  A Definition

A constituent A *commands* a constituent B if and only if every *S*-node that dominates A also dominates B.

#### 1.2  Unilateral Command

A constituent A *unilaterally commands* a constituent B if and only if A commands B, but B does not command A.

#### 1.3  Examples in which A Unilaterally Commands B

(1)

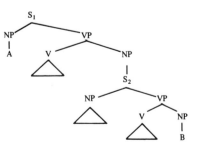

---

[1] The notions discussed in this section are drawn from Langacker (1969).

(2)

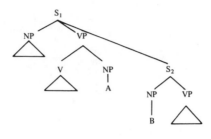

(3)

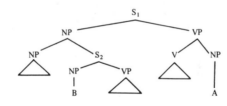

(4)

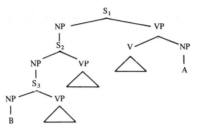

(5)

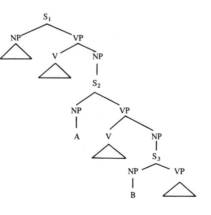

(6)

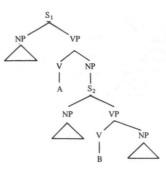

## 1.4 Examples in which A and B Command Each Other

(7)

(8)

(9)

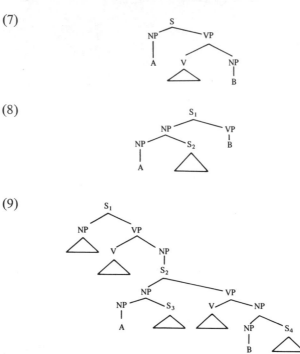

## 1.5 Examples in which Neither A nor B Commands the Other

(10)

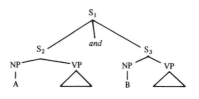

(11)

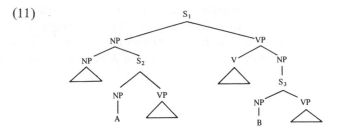

## 1.6 An Equivalent Definition of Command

In §1.1 we gave a definition of *command.*

A constituent A commands a constituent B if and only if every *S*-node that dominates A also dominates B.

There is a different, but equivalent, definition that is sometimes given.

A constituent A commands a constituent B if and only if the first *S*-node above A that dominates A also dominates B.

Check back through examples (1–11) to see that whenever A commands B according to one definition, A also commands B according to the other definition.

## 1.7 Command, Clause Mates, and Simplex Sentences

In formulating the rule of Reflexivization, we saw that an NP can reflexivize an NP to its right only if the two NPs are clause mates—that is, only if the two NPs are members of the same simplex sentence. We can now use the notion of *command* to define what it is for two constituents to be clause mates.

*Clause Mates: A Definition*

A and B are clause mates if and only if A and B command each other.

## 2. PRIMACY RELATIONS

### 2.1 A Definition

A constituent A bears a *primacy relation* to a constituent B if and only if either (i) A commands B, or (ii) A precedes B in left-to-right order in the string.

There are two primacy relations—the command relation and the precedence relation. If A both commands B and precedes B in left-to-right order, then A bears both primacy relations to B. If, on the other hand, A only commands B, or if A only precedes B in left-to-right order, then A bears only one primacy relation to B.

# 57

## *Super Equi-NP Deletion*[1]

### *1. THE PHENOMENON*

A.    We will call *Super Equi-NP Deletion* the rule that derives each (b) sentence below from the structure corresponding to the (a) sentence.

(1)  a.    *Roger$_i$ thinks that it will be easy for him$_i$ to protect himself.*
     b.    *Roger thinks that it will be easy to protect himself.*
(2)  a.    *Phyllis$_i$ is sure that it will be possible for her$_i$ to find her way in the dark.*
     b.    *Phyllis is sure that it will be possible to find her way in the dark.*
(3)  a.    *Sandra$_i$ insists that it was difficult for her$_i$ to hold her breath for more than six minutes.*
     b.    *Sandra insists that it was difficult to hold her breath for more than six minutes.*

B.    There is no limit to the number of embedded Ss over which Super Equi may operate.

(4)  a.    *Michael$_i$ felt that it was clear that it would turn out to be impossible for him$_i$ to get himself ready on time.*
     b.    *Michael felt that it was clear that it would turn out to be impossible to get himself ready on time.*

---

[1] This problem is based on work by John Grinder.

## 2. DEFINITIONS

A.   The NP that triggers deletion is the *trigger*.

B.   The NP that gets deleted is the *victim*.

C.   A *potential trigger* is an NP that satisfies all the conditions for being a trigger except that it is not coreferential with the victim. Assume, however, that the *it* of Extraposition and *the fact* in structures of the form

D.

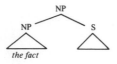

never count as potential triggers.

## 3. AN ILLUSTRATION

We will assume that the structure underlying (1a) is[2]

(1)   c.

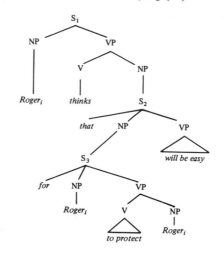

[2] To make the structures in this problem easier to read, we will sometimes represent them as including the complementizers *for* and *that*. Similarly, when structures contain pronouns we will represent them in the case (nominative or accusative) in which they occur in the surface structure.

(1a) is derived from (1c) by applying Reflexivization in $S_3$, Extraposition in $S_2$, and Pronominalization in $S_1$. Thus, the derived structure of (1a) is

(1)

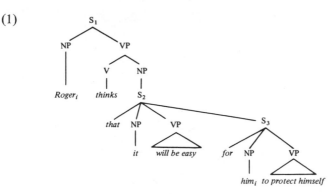

The subject of $S_1$ is the trigger. The subject of $S_3$ is the victim. There is no potential trigger. Super Equi applies to (1d) to produce (1b).[3]

## 4. THE PROBLEM

What conditions must be satisfied in order for an NP to trigger Super Equi? In particular, what happens when, in addition to the actual trigger, there is also a potential trigger?[4]

Once you have a solution to this problem, use it to answer Subsidiary Questions 1 and 2.

### Subsidiary Question 1

What is the derived constituent structure produced by applying Subject-to-Subject Raising to a structure of the form

---

[3] For purposes of this problem it does not matter whether Pronominalization applies before Super Equi or not.

[4] In working this problem, one could make either of two different assumptions:

*Assumption A*

All deletions in the problem are produced by Super Equi.

*Assumption B*

Deletions in which the victim is embedded in the sentence immediately beneath the trigger are produced by ordinary Equi. Other deletions are produced by Super Equi.

It is not part of this problem to decide between Assumptions A and B. Further, adopting one or the other should not affect your solution.

E.

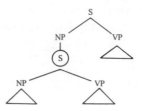

Is the resulting structure

F.

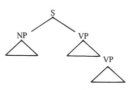

or is it

G.

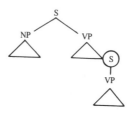

## Subsidiary Question 2

What cycle-type are Super Equi and Extraposition?

In answering Subsidiary Question 2, assume that Subject-to-Subject Raising is cyclical. (In the case of Extraposition, there are two arguments determining its cycle-type. One depends on Subject-to-Subject Raising and one does not. Try to find both.)

## 5. AN INITIAL HYPOTHESIS

Any number of different solutions to the problem could be given that would be consistent with the data in sentences (1–4). However, we suggest the following as an initial hypothesis.

*Hypothesis 1*

Super Equi may delete the subject of an embedded sentence (the victim) under coreferentiality with another NP (the trigger) if and only if:

(i)   *the trigger precedes the victim*

and

(ii)   *the trigger unilaterally commands the victim.*

## 6. THE BASIC STRATEGY FOR SOLVING THIS PROBLEM

Begin with Hypothesis 1 above. Apply it to further data. If modifications are necessary, make them explicit. This will result in a new hypothesis that must be tested against still further data. Continue in this way until all relevant data is accounted for. Your solution will thus consist of a series of hypotheses that account for larger and larger sets of sentences. The final result should be a hypothesis that accounts for all the data.

## 7. THE DATA

There is considerable variation among speakers with respect to judgments of grammaticality of some of these sentences. For the purpose of this problem, assume that the distribution of asterisks is as given here.

(5)   a.   *Eric said that Roxanne$_i$ knew that it would be difficult for her$_i$ to criticize herself.*

   b.   *Eric said that Roxanne knew that it would be difficult to criticize herself.*

(6)   a.   *Eric$_i$ said that Roxanne knew that it would be difficult for him$_i$ to criticize himself.*

   b.   *\*Eric said that Roxanne knew that it would be difficult to criticize himself.*

(7)   a.   *The girl$_i$ that Tom loved said that it would be difficult for her$_i$ to get herself ready on time.*

   b.   *The girl that Tom loved said that it would be difficult to get herself ready on time.*

(8)   a.   *The girl that Tom$_i$ loved said that it would be difficult for him$_i$ to get himself ready on time.*

   b.   *\*The girl that Tom loved said that it would be difficult to get himself ready on time.*

(9)   *That washing herself in public was enjoyable surprised Louise.*[5]

(10)   *That washing herself with mud disturbed Louise surprised Pete.*

[5] In most cases Super Equi is optional. However, in cases like (9) it may seem to be obligatory. Do not worry about this. It is not part of the problem to determine whether Super Equi is optional or obligatory in particular cases.

(11) *\*That washing himself with mud disturbed Louise surprised Pete.*

(12) *That it disturbed Louise to wash herself with mud surprised Pete.*

(13) *\*That it disturbed Louise to wash himself with mud surprised Pete.*

(14) *It surprised Pete that washing herself with mud disturbed Louise.*

(15) *It surprised Pete that washing himself with mud disturbed Louise.*

(16) a.     *John said that making a fool of herself in public disturbed Sue.*

      b.     *John said that making a fool of himself in public disturbed Sue.*

(17) a.     *John said that it disturbed Sue to make a fool of herself in public.*

      b.     *\*John said that it disturbed Sue to make a fool of himself in public.*

(18) a.     *Max$_i$ told Maxine that it would be easy for him$_i$ to protect himself.*[6]

      b.     *Max told Maxine that it would be easy to protect himself.*

(19) a.     *Max told Maxine$_i$ that it would be easy for her$_i$ to protect herself.*

      b.     *Max told Maxine that it would be easy to protect herself.*

(20) a.     *It irritated Eileen that washing herself in public was likely to disturb Pete.*

      b.     *That washing herself in public was likely to disturb Pete irritated Eileen.*

(21) *The fact that protecting himself will be easy is likely to please Pete.*

(22) *John said that to wash himself in public would disturb Sue.*

(23) *\*John said that it would disturb Sue to wash himself in public.*

---

[6] For purposes of this problem, assume that the sentences in (18) are derived from an underlying structure of the form

(i)

# 58

## *Part 5: Its Place in a Wider Context*

The material on *force* and *expect* has its origins in the discussion of *persuade* and *expect* in Chomsky (1965, pp. 22-24), but much additional material has been added.

The argument in section 54 has not to our knowledge appeared elsewhere. The ungrammaticality of sentences like *Everyone believes it to seem to Tom that he is mistreated,* on which the argument is based, was pointed out to us by Geoffrey Pullum. Postal (1977, n. 5) shows how various restrictions on Subject-to-Subject Raising discussed in Postal (1974, chapter 9) can be used to construct arguments for the same conclusion.

The problem in section 53 was suggested by the proposal for passives made by Hasegawa (1968). One of the arguments against this proposal was first made by Chomsky (1970, n. 29). Chomsky (1970) proposes breaking Passive up into two rules—a postposing rule and a preposing rule. R. Lakoff (1971) studies a number of different aspects of passivization. Alternative proposals for passivization are made by Fillmore (1968), Langacker and Munro (1975), Freidin (1975), Brame (1976), Perlmutter and Postal (1977), Wasow (1977), Bresnan (1978), and Dik (1978).

The facts on which section 55 is based have been discussed by generative grammarians since the late 1960s.

The notion of *command* and the idea that "precede" and "command" are primacy relations are contributions of Langacker (1969). Somewhat different notions have been proposed by Klima (1964a), Reinhart (1976), and Lasnik (1976).

Super Equi-NP Deletion was discovered by Grinder (1970). The problem on Super Equi in this book was originally based on that article, but we have added additional data and arguments that are not in Grinder's original paper. Grinder's paper has given rise to a whole literature on Super Equi, some of which gives arguments that are in our discussion of the problem, and some of which takes different positions. See Kimball (1971), Grinder (1971), Neubauer (1972), Clements (1975), Kuno (1975a), Jacobson and Neubauer (1976), Hayes (1976), Kuno and Kaburaki (1977), and Rouveret (1977). Jacobson and Neubauer (1976) give the argument for the cyclicity of Extraposition based on the Intervention Constraint affecting Super Equi, and they use this to argue for the cycle against some other theories of rule application.

# PART 6
## *Movement Rules*

In part 6 we motivate four movement rules—Topicalization, Nonsubject Raising, Question Movement, and Relativization. Nonsubject Raising represents an addition to the two Raisings postulated thus far. The other three rules move an NP to the left over an indefinite distance and hence must be formulated as moving the NP over a variable. These rules have received a great deal of attention from generative grammarians, and a large literature has developed around them. Part 6 provides necessary background for understanding work in this area, as well as for part 7 on Ross's constraints.

# 59

# *Topicalization*

There are English sentences with an "extra NP" in initial position:[1]

(1)  *Harriet I spotted yesterday at the movies.*
(2)  *Those people I've had just about enough of.*
(3)  *The Bahamas you said were warm in January.*
(4)  *Prices going down I'm not ready to count on.*

Two facts about these sentences stand out.

*Fact 1*

Each contains a "gap," i.e., there is a constituent missing from somewhere in each sentence. This can be seen from the fact that each sentence minus the "extra NP" in initial position is ungrammatical.

(1')  *I spotted _____ yesterday at the movies.*
(2')  *I've had just about enough of _____ .*
(3')  *You said _____ were warm in January.*
(4')  *I'm not ready to count on _____ .*

*Fact 2*

In each case the "extra NP" that is in initial position bears a semantic relation to a constituent elsewhere in the sentence. in (1), *Harriet* is understood as the object of *spotted*; in (2), *those people* is the object of the preposition *of*; in (3), *the Bahamas* is semantically the subject of *(were)*

---

[1] These sentences are often pronounced with extra emphasis on the initial NP–e.g., HARRIET I spotted yesterday at the movies.

*warm*; and in (4), *prices going down* is the object of *count on.* In all of these cases the "extra NP" bears the semantic relations it would have if it were in the gap.

We will now consider three alternative hypotheses for accounting for these sentences.

## 2.  THE PHRASE STRUCTURE HYPOTHESIS

Under this hypothesis, phrase structure rules generate sentences (1–4) in underlying structure. Thus, it is necessary to add to the grammar the phrase structure rule

(5)   $S \rightarrow NP\ S$

which produces structures of the form

(6)

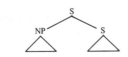

The NPs *Harriet, those people, the Bahamas,* and *prices going down* in (1–4) occupy the initial NP position in underlying structures of the form (6).
There are three important difficulties with this hypothesis.

**Difficulty One**

Consider the position occupied by the triangle dominated by the lower *S* in (6). Under the Phrase Structure Hypothesis, sentences *(1′–4′) must be able to occupy this position even though they are ungrammatical in isolation. Thus, the grammar will have to say that the rules for expanding the lower *S* in (6) are different from the phrase structure rules that expand *S* in isolation. This is a problem in itself. The problem becomes even worse when we consider that the gap in the lower S in structures of the form (6) may be indefinitely far away from the initial NP.

(7)   *Those people Sally said she had forgotten to tell Joe to remind Sue to invite_____.*

(8)   *Those people Sally said she had forgotten to tell Joe to remind _____ to invite Louise.*

It is not clear how any modification of the phrase structure rules could handle this fact.

## Difficulty Two

Even if it were possible to generate sentences like (1–4) in underlying structure, the grammar would need some device to capture the fact that the "extra NP" in initial position bears the semantic relations it would have if it were in the "gap."

## Difficulty Three

The Phrase Structure Hypothesis can be shown to be inadequate in yet another respect: there must be an NP in the "gap" at some stage of the derivation in order for certain transformations to apply. Consider, for example, the sentences

(9) *Roger she says she was taken in by* _____ .
(10) *Roger she says* _____ *was taken in by Pete.*

Since the Passive transformation requires two NPs in order to operate, there must have been two NPs in the complement sentences of (9) and (10) at some stage of derivation. The Phrase Structure Hypothesis cannot account for this fact.

Finally, note the contrast between

(11) *The boys she said* _____ *were coming.*

and

(12) *\*The boys she said* _____ *was coming.*

This contrast should follow automatically from the difference between (13a) and (13b).

(13) a. *She said the boys were coming.*
b. *\*She said the boys was coming.*

Under the Phrase Structure Hypothesis, it does not.

For all of these reasons, the phrase structure hypothesis must be rejected.

## 3. TWO ADDITIONAL HYPOTHESES

The difficulties with the Phrase Structure Hypothesis arose from postulating that the gap in sentences of the form (6) is present in underlying structure. These difficulties can be avoided if the S in underlying structure is an ordinary S, and the gap is created during the course of derivation. There are two ways that the gap could be created—by a deletion rule or by a movement rule.

*The Deletion Hypothesis*

Sentences with a topicalized NP in initial position are derived from underlying structures of the form (6). However, there is no gap in the underlying structure. The gap is produced during the course of the derivation by a rule that deletes an NP in the S under identity with the NP in initial position.

*The Movement Hypothesis*

Sentences (1-4) are not derived from structures of the form (6), but rather are derived from the structures that also underlie

(14)  *I spotted Harriet yesterday at the movies.*
(15)  *I've had just about enough of those people.*
(16)  *You said the Bahamas were warm in January.*
(17)  *I'm not ready to count on prices going down.*

In the derivation of (1-4), a movement rule applies, moving an NP to S-initial position. We will refer to this rule as *Topicalization*.


## 4. THE SUPERIORITY OF THE DELETION AND MOVEMENT HYPOTHESES TO THE PHRASE STRUCTURE HYPOTHESIS

It is easy to see how the Deletion and Movement Hypotheses avoid the difficulties encountered by the Phrase Structure Hypothesis.

### 4.1 Phrase Structure Rules

Since underlying structures do not contain gaps, the same phrase structure rules that expand *S* in isolation can be used for topicalized sentences. [Although the Deletion Hypothesis must include (5) among the phrase structure rules, it does not need phrase structure rules that leave a gap in the lower S in sentences of the form (6).]

### 4.2 Semantic Relations

Under the Movement Hypothesis, the NP that ends up in the initial position in (1-4) starts out in the same position it occupies in the structures underlying (14-17). Since semantic relations are stated in underlying structure, it follows that the semantic relations in (1-4) will be the same as those in (14-17).

Under the Deletion Hypothesis, the initial NP is not itself in the position it would occupy in the structures underlying (14–17). However, an NP identical to it is. It is this NP that bears the relevant semantic relations in underlying structure.

## 4.3 Undergoing Transformations

Under the Movement Hypothesis, the NP that ends up in initial position can undergo transformations before it is moved to initial position. Under the Deletion Hypothesis, the NP that is identical to the S-initial NP can undergo transformations before it is deleted. Thus, both of these hypotheses can account for sentences like (9–13).

# 5. THE DELETION HYPOTHESIS VS.
# THE MOVEMENT HYPOTHESIS: FOUR ARGUMENTS

## 5.1 Two Theory-Internal Arguments[2]

### 5.1.1 Argument One: Phrase Structure Rule

The Deletion Hypothesis requires that phrase structure rule (5) be added to grammar, while the Movement Hypothesis does not. All other things being equal, the fact that the Deletion Hypothesis requires this extra device constitutes an argument against it.

### 5.1.2 Argument Two: Overgeneration

Under the Deletion Hypothesis, phrase structure rule (5) produces underlying structures like (6). Thus, both (18) and (19) will be generated as underlying structures.

[2] Under the Deletion Hypothesis, the question arises as to whether the deletion rule in question requires the deleted NP to be *coreferential* with the NP in initial position, or lexically *identical* to it. If coreferentiality is required, it is difficult to see how the Deletion Hypothesis can account for sentences like (4), where the NP that would have to be deleted is a clause rather than a referring expression. If, on the other hand, only lexical identity is required for deletion, the Deletion Hypothesis could derive sentences like (1) from an underlying structure in which the two occurrences of *Harriet* are not coreferential, but only lexically identical—an undesirable result.

(18)

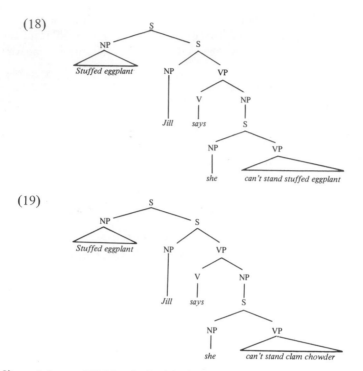

(19)

(18) contains an NP identical with the initial NP in the structure. Therefore, the structural description of the deletion rule is met. Since this rule is obligatory, it will apply to (18) producing

(20)  *Stuffed eggplant Jill says she can't stand.* ·

Structure (19) does not satisfy the structural description of the deletion rule. As a result, deletion will not take place, and the ungrammatical sentence

(21) *\*Stuffed eggplant Jill says she can't stand clam chowder.*

will be generated.

There are at least two ways that the Deletion Hypothesis could state a restriction to prevent sentences like *(21) from being generated. First, the grammar could require that the sentence-initial NP be followed in underlying structure by an NP identical to it somewhere in the sentence. Alternatively, the grammar could say that in structures of the form (6), the deletion rule must actually apply. Either way, the Deletion Hypothesis must postulate an additional restriction that is not needed under the Movement Hypothesis.[3]

---

[3] We are not arguing against this *type* of constraint (we saw it in the case of *force*). However, if we have two hypotheses, one that requires the constraint and one that does not, then, all other things being equal, we choose the one that does not require it.

## 5.2 Two Empirically-Based Arguments

The Deletion Hypothesis and the Movement Hypothesis give different accounts of the derivational history of the sentence-initial NP. Under the Movement Hypothesis, it starts out elsewhere in the sentence and gets moved to sentence-initial position. Under the Deletion Hypothesis, it starts out in sentence-initial position and remains there throughout the derivation. Evidence to decide between the two hypotheses might therefore come from examples in which the sentence-initial NP shows evidence of having been present elsewhere in the sentence. Two such arguments are given below.

### 5.2.1 Argument Three: Reflexivization

There are grammatical sentences in which the topicalized *NP* is a reflexive pronoun:

(22) *Myself I can't stand.*

Under the Movement Hypothesis, (22) is derived from

(23)

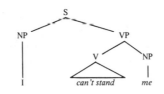

by first applying Reflexivization and then applying Topicalization. Under the Deletion Hypothesis, (22) is a problem. Applying Reflexivization to the underlying structure

(24)

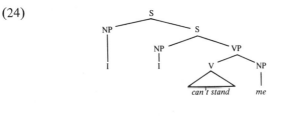

results in

(25)

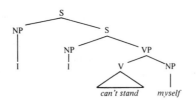

However, there is no way to make the initial NP reflexive. Thus, (22) can't be derived, and the Deletion Hypothesis must be rejected.[4]

### 5.2.2 Argument Four:  Deleted Subjects

There are grammatical sentences in which the topicalized *NP* is a sentence whose subject has been deleted:

(26)  *Criticizing herself I think Sue finds difficult.*

Under the Movement Hypothesis, (26) is derived from[5]

(27)

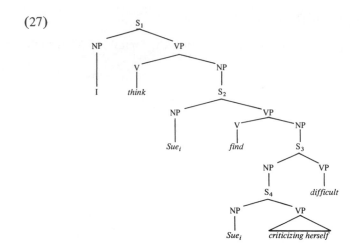

by first deleting the subject of $S_4$ and then moving *critizing herself* (which is now exhaustively dominated by the *NP*-node above $S_4$ to sentence-initial position. Thus, the same rule that deletes the subject of *criticizing* in

(28)  *I think Sue finds criticizing herself difficult.*

automatically accounts for the absence of the subject of *criticizing* in (26).

---

[4] Another way of looking at this argument is as follows: Under the Movement Hypothesis, the same rule of Reflexivization that accounts for the reflexive pronoun in

(i)   *I can't stand myself*

automatically accounts for the reflexive pronoun in (22). Under the Deletion Hypothesis, the only way to account for the reflexive pronoun in (22) would be to posit an additional and otherwise unmotivated rule that reflexivizes a sentence-initial NP in structures of the form (6) just in case the deleted NP has undergone ordinary Reflexivization. The need for such a rule is an argument against the Deletion Hypothesis.

[5] (25) is the structure that results after Reflexivization has applied on $S_4$.

Under the Deletion Hypothesis, on the other hand, (26) is derived from[6]

(29)

In order for (26) to be derived from (29), three things must happen: the subject of $S_6$ must be deleted under coreference with the subject of $S_4$; the subject of $S_2$ must be deleted under coreference with the subject of $S_4$; and the subject of $S_5$ must be deleted under identity with the initial NP. For our purposes, the important deletion is the second one. For this operation, the Deletion Hypothesis would have to posit an additional rule deleting an NP higher in the tree under coreference with an NP in a lower S. Unless this rule can be shown to be needed independently, the fact that it is required by the Deletion Hypothesis constitutes a further argument for movement over deletion.

## 6. THE FORMULATION OF TOPICALIZATION

Since Topicalization is capable of moving an NP to sentence-initial position over an indefinite distance, it must be formulated with a variable, roughly as follows:[7]

*Topicalization*

X NP Y $\Rightarrow$ 2, 1, 3
1  2  3

This formulation expresses the fact that there is no upper limit on the distance that the topicalized NP can travel on its way to initial position.

[6] (29) is the structure that results after Reflexivization has applied on $S_2$ and $S_6$.

[7] Additional factors (such as the definiteness or indefiniteness of the topicalized NP) are relevant to Topicalization. We have ignored these factors here.

# 60

## *Types of Arguments for Movement Rules*

Whenever there is a movement rule like Topicalization, the following must hold:

(1)  *There is a gap somewhere in the sentence and an "extra constituent" somewhere else.*

(2)  *The "extra constituent" bears the semantic relations it would have had if it had started out in the gap.*[1]

Sometimes there is also an argument of the following kind:

(3)  *There must have been a constituent in the gap at some stage of the derivation in order for some transformation to apply.*

Our arguments for rejecting the Phrase Structure Hypothesis in the case of Topicalization were based on facts of types (1-3). Although such facts provide evidence against phrase structure hypotheses, they do not furnish arguments against deletion hypotheses.

There are two types of arguments favoring movement over deletion—theory-internal arguments like those in §5.1 of section 59 and empirically-based arguments of the following kind:

---

[1] By "semantic relations" we mean relations like those in sentences (1–4) discussed under Fact (2) at the beginning of the discussion of *Topicalization*. The conclusion that there can be no movement rule if (2) does not hold is based on the assumption that these semantic relations are stated in underlying structure.

(4) *The "extra constituent" itself shows evidence of having been else-
    where in the sentence.*

Facts like (4) are explained by a rule that moves the "extra constituent" during
the course of the derivation. Because arguments of this type provide evidence
not only against phrase structure hypotheses, but also against deletion hypotheses, they constitute the strongest kind of argument in support of movement
rules.

# 61

## *Nonsubject Deletion vs. Nonsubject Raising*

### *1. THE PHENOMENON*

English has a class of sentences like

(1)   *Those books are impossible for children to read.*
(2)   *That proposal is impossible for me to make sense out of.*
(3)   *Those children are difficult to read stories to.*
(4)   *Marie is difficult to talk to about politics.*
(5)   *Politics is difficult to talk to Marie about.*

In place of *impossible* and *difficult,* we can also have predicates like *easy, hard, tough, a breeze, a cinch, a snap,* and others. Three facts about these sentences should be noted.

*Fact 1*

Each of these sentences contains a gap—i.e., there is a constituent missing from somewhere in the complement sentence.

    (1)   *These books are impossible for children to read _____ .*
    (2)   *That proposal is impossible for me to make sense out of*
        _____ .
    (3)   *Those children are difficult to read stories to _____ .*
    (4)   *Marie is difficult to talk to _____ about politics.*
    (5)   *Politics is difficult to talk to Marie about _____ .*

*Fact 2*

In each case, the surface subject of the matrix sentence bears semantic relations to elements of the complement clause. These semantic relations are the ones that the matrix subject would have if it were in the gap. For example, in (1), *those books* is understood as the object of *read.*

*Fact 3*

The gap may be located indefinitely far from the surface subject of the matrix.

(6) *Politics is hard for me to imagine anyone talking to Marie about* _____ .

(7) *Marie is hard for me to imagine anyone talking to* _____ *about politics.*

In addition, sentences like (1–7) are also subject to several constraints.

*Constraint 1*

The gap in the complement sentence cannot be located in subject position.

(8) a. *Those books are hard for children to read* _____ .
   b. *\*Children are hard (for)* _____ *to read those books.*

(9) a. *The manuscript will be easy for me to arrange for you to see* _____ .
   b. *\*You will be easy for me to arrange (for)* _____ *to see the manuscript.*

*Constraint 2*

For some speakers the gap cannot be located in a that-clause.

(10) a. *Those books are hard to imagine anyone enjoying* _____ .

   b. *\*?Those books are hard to imagine that anyone would enjoy* _____ .

    (Speakers vary with respect to their judgments about sentences like \*?(10b).)

*Constraint 3*

Transformations cannot always apply in the complement containing the gap. For example, Passive cannot apply in the complement.

(11) a. *Those books are hard for children to read* _____ .
   b. *\*Children are hard for those books to be read by* _____ .

(12) a. *The manuscript will be easy for me to arrange for you to read* _____ .
   b. *\*You will be easy for me to arrange for the manuscript to be read by* _____ .

In §2 we will outline three different hypotheses for deriving sentences like (1–5). Constraints 1–3 are common to each of the hypotheses and will not be used to decide among them.

## 2.  *THREE CONFLICTING HYPOTHESES*

### 2.1  **The Phrase Structure Hypothesis**

The structure underlying (1) is:

(13)
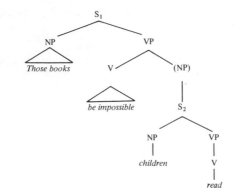

(The fact that the *NP* above $S_2$ is in parentheses means that it is not relevant for this problem whether or not there is an *NP*-node above $S_2$ in [13].)

### 2.2  **The Deletion Hypothesis**

The structure underlying (1) is:

(14)
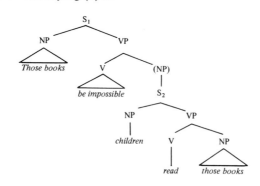

A rule we will refer to as *Nonsubject Deletion* deletes an NP to the right of the verb in $S_2$ if it is identical[1] to the subject of the matrix sentence.

## 2.3 The Movement Hypothesis

The structure underlying (1) is:

(15)

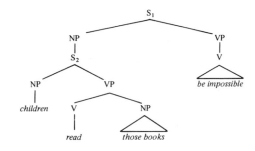

A rule we refer to as *Nonsubject Raising* takes an NP to the right of the verb in $S_2$ and makes it the subject of $S_1$, moving the rest of $S_2$ to the right.

## 3. ARGUMENTS AGAINST THE PHRASE STRUCTURE HYPOTHESIS

### 3.1 The Gap in the Complement

As was the case with Topicalization, sentences (1–5) contain a gap. Under the Phrase structure Hypothesis, new phrase structure rules would be needed to produce complements that contain gaps in underlying structure. This problem is compounded by the fact that the gap can be indefinitely far from the matrix subject. Moreover, the complement can contain only one gap. Thus, while both

(16) *Mary is difficult to talk to* _____ *about Joe*

and

(17) *Joe is difficult to talk to Marie about* _____ .

are grammatical, a sentence with two gaps in the complement is ungrammatical.

(18) *\*Marie is difficult to talk to* _____ *about* _____ .

---

[1] As in the case of the Deletion Hypothesis considered in Topicalization, the question arises as to whether the deletion rule requires the deleted NP to be coreferential with the initial NP or lexically identical with it (or both). See footnote 2 of Topicalization for a discussion of this issue.

It is not clear how the phrase structure rules could be modified to account for such facts.

Finally, under the Phrase Structure Hypothesis, some device would be needed to prevent the usual phrase structure rules—which do *not* produce sentences with gaps—from applying in the complement of *impossible, difficult,* and so on. Without such a device, the phrase structure rules that we already have would produce underlying structures like

(19)

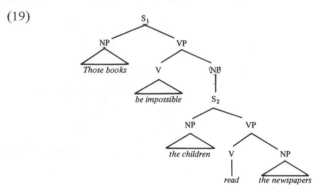

and

(20)

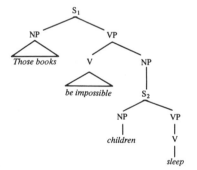

## 3.2  Semantic Relations

The second argument against the Phrase Structure Hypothesis is that surface structure subjects of sentences like (1–5) bear the semantic relations that they would have if they were in the gap. For example, *those books* in (1) is understood as being the object of *read*. The Phrase Structure Hypothesis does not account for this fact.

As we have seen elsewhere, such semantic relations are reflected in selectional restrictions. Thus,

(21) *\*Those bricks are easy for us to interview.*

is deviant in exactly the same way as

(22) *\*We interviewed those bricks.*

The Phrase Structure Hypothesis does not make the deviance of *(21) follow automatically from the deviance of *(22).

## 4. THE DELETION HYPOTHESIS VS. THE MOVEMENT HYPOTHESIS

### 4.1 Exercise

Show why the arguments that were given above against the Phrase Structure Hypothesis are not arguments against the Deletion or Movement Hypotheses.

### 4.2 The Problem[2]

Crucial evidence to decide between the Deletion Hypothesis and the Movement Hypothesis is provided by the sentence

(23) *Getting herself arrested on purpose is hard for me to imagine Betsy being willing to consider.*

Which hypothesis should be adopted and why?

[2] This problem is based on work by Postal and Ross. If, after working the problem and consulting the discussion section you wish to explore the issues it raises further, see SFI-8, TOO-Deletion.

# 62

## *What Cycle-Type Is Nonsubject Raising?*

### *1. ASSUMPTIONS*

*Assumption 1*

English has a rule of Nonsubject Raising.

*Assumption 2*

Every rule is either cyclical or postcyclical. No rule can apply both cyclically and postcyclically.

### *2. THE PROBLEM*

Is Nonsubject Raising cyclical or postcyclical? Construct arguments based on its interaction with other rules whose cycle-types have already been established.

# 63

# *Nonsubject Raising and FOR-Phrases*[1]

## *1. ASSUMPTIONS*

*Assumption 1*

   (1)   a.   *To talk to Mark about politics is unpleasant.*
          b.   *It is unpleasant to talk to Mark about politics.*
          c.   *Mark is unpleasant to talk to about politics.*
          d.   *Politics is unpleasant to talk to Mark about.*
   (2)   a.   *To talk to Mark about politics is exciting.*
          b.   *It is exciting to talk to Mark about politics.*
          c.   *Mark is exciting to talk to about politics.*
          d.   *Politics is exciting to talk to Mark about.*

The (c) and (d) sentences are derived from the structure underlying the corresponding (a)-sentences by Nonsubject Raising.[2] The (b)-sentences are derived from the structure underlying the (a)-sentences by Extraposition.

*Assumption 2*

   (3)   a.   *For his father to talk about the old country is exciting for Frank.*

---

[1] This problem is based on Berman (1974) and Berman and Szamosi (1972).

[2] Nonsubject Raising makes an NP in the verb phrase of an embedded sentence the subject of an upstairs verbal like *unpleasant, exciting*, etc., moving the rest of the downstairs sentence to the right of the main clause verbal.

        b.     *It is exciting for Frank for his father to talk about the old country.*

(4)  a.     *For Martha to borrow money from him is unpleasant for Harold.*

        b.     *It is unpleasant for Harold for Martha to borrow money from him.*

The structure underlying (3) is

(5)

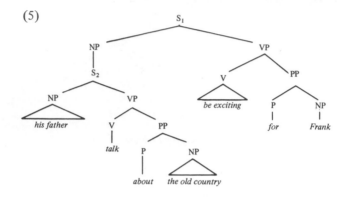

Thus, in (3) the phrase *for Frank* originates in the matrix S and the phrase *for his father* originates in the embedded S.[3] Similarly, in (4) *for Harold* originates in the matrix and *for Martha* originates in the embedded S.

## 2. A QUESTION

(6)  a.     *For Louise to discuss politics would be unpleasant.*

        b.     *To discuss politics would be unpleasant for Louise.*

        c.     *It would be unpleasant for Louise to discuss politics.*

        d.     *Politics would be unpleasant for Louise to discuss.*

(7)  a.     *For Louise to discuss politics would be exciting.*

        b.     *To discuss politics would be exciting for Louise.*

        c.     *It would be exciting for Louise to discuss politics.*

        d.     *Politics would be exciting for Louise to discuss.*

The existence of structures like (5) shows that there can be *for*-phrases both in the matrix sentence and in the complement. This raises a question: *Do*

---

[3] The *for* in *for his father* is a complementizer. In this problem we will follow our practice of not representing complementizers in tree diagrams.

*the **for**-phrases in (6c–d) and (7c–d) originate in the matrix or the embedded sentence?* The following three sets of data should help you answer this question.

*First Set of Data*

(8)  *\*The old country is exciting for Frank for his children to talk about.*

(9)  *\*Money is unpleasant for Frank for Martha to borrow from him.*

*Second Set of Data*

(10)  a.  *For it to be hot and stuffy in the classroom is unpleasant.*
      b.  *It's unpleasant for it to be hot and stuffy in the classroom.*
      c.  *\*The classroom is unpleasant for it to be hot and stuffy in.*

(11)  a.  *For there to be Koala bears in the backyard would be exciting.*
      b.  *It would be exciting for there to be Koala bears in the backyard.*
      c.  *\*Koala bears would be exciting for there to be in the backyard.*
      d.  *\*The backyard would be exciting for there to be Koala bears in.*

*Third Set of Data*

(12)  a.  *For the children to find themselves in that position would be unpleasant.*
      b.  *To find themselves in that position would be unpleasant for the children.*
      c.  *It would be unpleasant for the children to find themselves in that position.*
      d.  *That position would be unpleasant for the children to find themselves in.*

(13)  a.  *For the children to find themselves in that position would be exciting.*
      b.  *To find themselves in that position would be exciting for the children.*
      c.  *It would be exciting for the children to find themselves in that position.*
      d.  *That position would be exciting for the children to find themselves in.*

## 3. THE PROBLEM

A.  Formulate a constraint that accounts for the sentences in the three sets of data. Be sure to indicate how this constraint blocks the deviation of ungrammatical sentences like \*(8), \*(9), \*(10c), and \*(11c–d). In addition, show what consequences the constraint has for the derivation of grammatical sentences like (12d) and (13d).

Note: In formulating the constraint, you may have to modify an assumption made in §2.3 of section 61 regarding the kind of structures to which Nonsubject Raising applies.

B.     Test your constraint to make sure that it accounts for the semantic facts illustrated by the sentences in (14).

(14)   a.     *For Martians to land in Las Vegas would be unpleasant.*
       b.     *To land in Las Vegas would be unpleasant for Martians.*
       c.     *It would be unpleasant for Martians to land in Las Vegas.*
       d.     *Las Vegas would be unpleasant for Martians to land in.*

(14a) and (14b) differ in meaning. In (14b) it is the Martians who would experience unpleasantness. In (14a) it is not specified who would experience unpleasantness. Both of these meanings are present in (14c), which is subtly ambiguous between the two. The crucial sentence is (14d). It is unambiguous, having only the meaning of (14b), in which the Martians are the ones who would experience unpleasantness. The constraint formulated in your answer to part A of this problem should account for these facts. It should also allow you to determine the position of the *for*-phrases in (6d), (7d), (12d), (13d), and (14d).

# 64

## Questions

### 1. MOVEMENT IN QUESTIONS

(1)  *What will Jojo bring _____ for Sue?*
(2)  *Who did Sidney expect Mary Lou to invite _____ ?*
(3)  *Where did Curtis see Nate _____ yesterday?*
(4)  *When will the doctor arrive _____ ?*
(5)  *Which team do you think _____ is likely to win?*

These questions contain a question word or pharse in initial position and a gap elsewhere in the sentence. In this respect they are like sentences that have undergone Topicalization. The arguments that were used to show that topicalized sentences are not generated directly by phrase structure rules, with an NP in initial position and a gap elsewhere, can also be used to show that questions are not generated directly by phrase structure rules. Thus, a transformation is needed. Generative grammarians have assumed that the rule in question is one which moves question phrases to sentence initial position, thereby creating a gap.

(6)

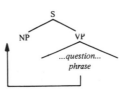

This rule is referred to as *Question Movement.*[1]

---

[1] See SFI-9, Movement in Questions, for an argument in support of Question Movement.

In addition to examples like (1–5), in which the question phrase is moved to sentence-initial position, there are also cases in which it is moved to the front of an embedded sentence.

(7)  *I wonder **what** Jojo will bring* _____ *for Sue.*
(8)  *I wonder **who** Sidney expects Mary Lou to invite* _____ .
(9)  *I wonder **where** Curtis saw Nate* _____ *yesterday.*
(10)  *I asked Red **when** the doctor would arrive* _____ .
(11)  *I am going to ask Tommy **which team** he thinks* _____ *is likely to win.*

Although we will not attempt to give a formal statement of Question Movement in this section, it is clear that the rule must be able to distinguish full-fledged questions like (1–5) (in which the question phrase is moved to the front of the entire sentence) from embedded questions like (7–11) (in which it is moved to the front of the embedded clause).[2]

## 2. INVERSION

When a question phrase is preposed to sentence-initial position, the subject inverts with the auxiliary verb.

(12)  a.    *He was working downtown.*
       b.    *Where was he working?*
       c.    *\*Where he was working?*
(13)  a.    *Your cousin from Chicago has offended someone influential.*
       b.    *Who has your cousin from Chicago offended?*
       c.    *\*Who your cousin from Chicago has offended?*
(14)  a.    *The Red Sox can beat that team.*
       b.    *Who can the Red Sox beat?*
       c.    *\*Who the Red Sox can beat?*

In some cases, inversion causes a form of *do* to appear.

(15)  a.    *Mary likes rodeos.*
       b.    *What does Mary like?*
       c.    *\*What Mary likes?*

If the question phrase is the subject of the matrix, then inversion does not take place.

(16)  a.    *The candidates will leave early.*

---

[2] The formulation of Question Movement is discussed in the discussion of section 65.

      b.    *Which candidates will leave early?*

      c.    *\*Will which candidates leave early?*

(17) a.    *Sam can do the job.*

      b.    *Who can do the job?*

      c.    *\*Can who do the job?*

The rules accounting for inversion and the appearance of *do* need not concern us here. It should be pointed out, however, that the mechanism causing inversion is not part of Question Movement, but rather is an independent rule.

This can be seen in two ways. First, there are instances of Question Movement that do not result in inversion—e.g., embedded questions.

(18) a.    *Judy is certain to wonder who he has been seeing _____ .*

      b.    *\*Judy is certain to wonder who has he been seeing _____ .*

(19) a.    *Harry wondered what Mary liked _____ .*

      b.    *\*Harry wondered what did Mary like _____ .*

(20) a.    *Dick wondered who the Red Sox could beat _____ .*

      b.    *\*Dick wondered who could the Red Sox beat _____ .*

Second, there are instances of inversion without Question Movement.

(21) *Seldom have I heard such stirring words.*

(22) *Nowhere will you find a braver man.*

(23) *Never had I seen anything like it.*

Roughly speaking, inversion is governed by the following generalization:

(24) *Inversion of the matrix subject with an auxiliary element (**be, have, can,** etc.) occurs when either a question-word (phrase) or a "negative" adverb (**seldom, nowhere, never, scarcely, rarely,** etc.) is in S-initial position preceding the matrix subject.*

Since Question Movement and Inversion are capable of occurring independently, they must be separate rules.

## 3. YES-NO QUESTIONS AND WHETHER

So far we have discussed *wh-questions*, which contain question-words. *Yes-no questions* do not contain question-words.

(25) *Are the officials honest?*

(26) *Will Charlie find happiness at MacDonald's?*

(27) *Can Winifred defeat her opponents?*

(28) *Has Marty given up?*

(29) *Did the match end in a tie?*

Just as there are embedded *wh*-questions, there are also embedded *yes-no* questions.

    (30)  *Red asked whether the officials were honest.*

    (31)  *I wonder whether Charlie will find happiness at MacDonald's?*

    (32)  *Ripley is anxious to find out whether Winifred can defeat her opponents.*

    (33)  *I wonder whether Marty has given up.*

    (34)  *John asked whether the match ended in a tie.*

Although embedded *yes-no* questions are introduced by the question-word *whether,* they do not contain gaps and are not the result of question movement. As before, inversion does not occur in embedded clauses.

One way to account for the distribution of *whether* is to generate it freely in front of all *yes-no* questions, both in the matrix sentence and in complements, and to posit a rule deleting it in matrix clauses. In addition to accounting for the occurrence of *whether* in embedded *yes-no* questions, this hypothesis accounts for inversion in sentences like (25–29). According to generalization (24), inversion occurs when the matrix subject is preceded by a question-word or a negative adverb. If (25–29) are derived from

    (35)  [*whether the officials are honest*]

    (36)  [*whether Charlie will find happiness at MacDonald's*]

    (37)  [*whether Winifred can defeat her opponents*]

    (38)  [*whether Marty has given up*]

    (39)  [*whether the match ended in a tie*]

then the inversion of subject and auxiliary in (25–29) will follow automatically from (24).[3] In this way we can maintain generalization (24) and eliminate the need for a special exception governing inversion in *yes-no* questions.[4]

## 4. OBLIGATORY QUESTION MOVEMENT

Generative grammarians have traditionally assumed that Question Movement is obligatory. Thus the underlying structure

---

[3] This hypothesis requires that the grammar contain some mechanism preventing *whether* from being deleted before inversion occurs. We leave open the question of how this is to be accomplished.

[4] This argument comes from Ross (1970).

(35)  [*you are going to do what*]

is obligatorily transformed into

(36)  *What are you going to do?*

and

(37) \**You are going to do what?*

is ungrammatical. Note that \*(37) is not to be confused with the echo or incredulity question.

(38)  *You are going to do what?*

Incredulity questions are pronounced with special emphasis and intonation, convey a sense of disbelief on the part of the speaker and have far fewer restrictions on them than ordinary questions do—e.g.,

(39)  a.  *Sam is in your backyard.*
       b.  *Sam is in your backwhat?*
       c.  \**What is Sam in your back?*

Differences like these have led generative grammarians to regard ordinary questions and incredulity questions as separate phenomena with different underlying structures. Question Movement applies only to the structures underlying ordinary questions.

## 5.  THE SOURCE OF QUESTION WORDS

We will now consider two hypotheses about how question words like *who* and *what* are represented in underlying structure.

### 5.1  Multiple Sources:  An Inadequate Proposal

Under this hypothesis, any inanimate noun phrase can be changed to *what* and any human noun phrase can be changed to *who* in questions. For example,

(40)  *Who took my notebook?*

could be derived from both

(41)  *Your cousin took my notebook.*

and

(42)  *The man living next door who likes to play the trombone until 3 a.m. took my notebook.*

Under the assumption that the meaning of a sentence is represented in underlying structure, this hypothesis incorrectly predicts that questions like (20) are
ambiguous. Since there are an infinite number of noun phrases from which *who*
and *what* could be derived, the hypothesis actually predicts that sentences containing these words are infinitely ambiguous, which they are not. Thus, we need
a hypothesis in which each of them is derived from a single underlying source.

## 5.2  Question Words and Indefinite Pro-Forms

### 5.2.1  Indefinite Pro-Forms and the Distribution of ELSE

In English the word *else* has a very restricted distribution. It can occur
with question words like *who* and *what*.

(43)  *Who else left early?*
(44)  *What else fell over?*

However, it cannot occur with most noun phrases.

(45) *\*Your cousin else took my notebook.*
(46) *\*A visitor else is leaving tomorrow.*
(47) *\*The guy next door else was complaining.*
(48) *\*Three people else were complaining.*

There is only a small class of elements with which *else* can occur; they are the
indefinite pro-forms.

(49)  *Someone else left early.*
(50)  *No one else left early.*
(51)  *Everyone else left early.*
(52)  *Did anyone else leave early?*

Notice also that the indefinite pro-forms that can occur with *else* form
paradigms:

(53)  | *who*   | *someone*   | *anyone*   | *no one*   | *everyone*   |
      |---------|-------------|------------|------------|--------------|
      | *what*  | *something* | *anything* | *nothing*  | *everything* |
      | *where* | *someplace* | *anyplace* | *noplace*  | *everyplace* |

In addition to being able to occur with *else,* the forms in these paradigms exhibit
a regular morphological pattern to which only the question words *who, what,*
and *where* are exceptions.

### 5.2.2 The Source of Pro-Forms and Question Words: A Hypothesis

The regularities in (53) can be captured if we assume that those forms have the following underlying representations:

(54) *wh one*   *some one*    *any one*   *no one*   *every one*
     *wh thing*  *some thing*  *any thing*  *no thing*  *every thing*
     *wh place*  *some place*  *any place*  *no place*  *every place*

Two rules are needed to generate the surface forms in (53) from the underlying representations in (54). One rule combines *some* and *one, any* and *thing,* and the rest into single words—*some+one, any+thing,* and so on. The other rule specifies that *wh+one, wh+thing,* and *wh+place* are realized as *who, what,* and *where* respectively.

Under this analysis, the indefinite pro-forms in (53) are made up out of morphemes which (with the sole exception of *wh*) also occur independently in the language. This simplifies the lexicon since it will now need to list only the morphemes out of which the elements in (54) are made up.[5] It also simplifies the restriction on *else,* which can now be stated as follows:

(55) ***Else** occurs with:* _____ *+one*
                         _____ *+thing*
                         _____ *+place*

Without the analysis in (54), it would be necessary to list all fifteen forms in (53) as being able to occur with *else.*

### 5.2.3 A Wider Class of Facts

(53) does not exhaust the indefinite pro-forms of English. First, there are some additional regular forms. Corresponding to who, there are pro-forms *somebody, anybody, nobody,* and *everybody.* Corresponding to *where,* we find the pro-forms *somewhere, anywhere, nowhere* and *everywhere.* These forms exhibit a morphological regularity and can occur with *else.* Second, there are some additional question words that do not have the full range of corresponding indefinite pro-forms.[6]

---

[5] The lexicon is that part of the grammar which lists the morphemes occurring in the language—morphemes being, roughly, the minimal syntactically and semantically significant elements in the language.

[6] Although *no time* and *every time* occur as separate words, they do not occur as single-word pro-forms. Although there is a word *anyhow,* it is not a pro-form corresponding to the question word *how*—e.g., it cannot occur in sentences such as \**Do it anyhow you can.*

(56)  *when*        *sometime*      *anytime*    *\*notime*    *\*everytime*
      *how*         *somehow*       *\*anyhow*   *\*nohow*     *\*everyhow*
      *why*         *\*somewhy*     *\*anywhy*   *\*nowhy*     *\*everywhy*

These question words can occur with *else* under certain conditions,[7] but *sometime, anytime,* and *somehow* cannot. Although irregularities like these must be accounted for in one way or another, we will not be concerned with them here.

[7] For example,

  (i)   *When else might he have been there?*
  (ii)  *How else could you do it?*
  (iii) *Why else would he have withheld evidence?*

# 65

## *Two Hypotheses about Question Movement*[1]

### *1. ASSUMPTIONS*

*Assumption 1*

Question Movement is an obligatory rule.

*Assumption 2*

Question Movement can move a question phrase over an unbounded distance.

(1)  *Who did Joe say Sally thought Mona wanted to try to convince Sandy to invite _____ ?*

### *2. TWO CONFLICTING HYPOTHESES*

*The Single Movement Hypothesis*

Question Movement preposes question phrases to *S*-initial position in a single movement.

(2)

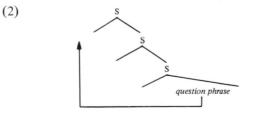

[1] This problem is based on work by Paul Postal.

*The Successive Cyclic Hypothesis*

Question Movement operates cyclically, preposing the question phrase to
the front of each successive S until it reaches initial position.

(3)

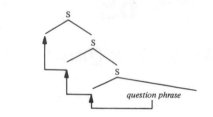

## 3. THE PROBLEM

Below you are given two sets of data about Question Movement. First
figure out what each set of data shows. Then use each set of data to construct an
argument to decide between the two hypotheses above.

*First Set of Data*[2]

(4)   a.   *Whom did you say you spoke with?*
      b.   *With whom did you say you spoke?*

*Second Set of Data*

(5)   *Which charges did you think it was easy for Louise to deny?*
(6)   *Which charges did you think were easy for Louise to deny?*[3]

---

[2] The distinction between *who* and *whom* plays no role in this problem.

[3] A constraint irrelevant to this problem has the consequence that if the complementizer *that* were present after *think* in (6), the result would be ungrammatical.

(i)   *Which charges do you think that were easy for Louise to deny?*

Examples like *(i) may be ignored in working this problem.

# 66

## *Relativization*

### 1. SYNTACTIC PROPERTIES OF RELATIVE CLAUSES

English contains a class of constructions like the following:

(1)  a.  *the candidate who(m) I supported _____ in the last election*
     b.  *a table that we piled books on _____*
     c.  *that man who Susan thinks _____ is trying to catch her*
     d.  *the hypothesis which Anne thinks she has refuted _____*

Each of these examples consists of an initial NP followed by a clause which is introduced by a relative pronoun—*who, which,* or *that.* The initial NP is called *the head*; the clause that follows it is called a *relative clause.* For example, in (1d) the relative clause is *which Anne thinks she has refuted* and the head of the relative clause is *the hypothesis.*

These *NP*-plus-relative-clause constructions have several important properties.

*Property 1*

They are NPs. This is shown by the fact that they undergo transformations that apply to NPs.

(2)  a.  *To beat the candidate who(m) I supported in the last election would be easy for almost any politician.*
     b.  *The candidate who(m) I supported in the last election would be easy for almost any politician to beat.*
          *(Nonsubject Raising)*

(3)  a.    *A table that we piled books on is in the bedroom.*
    b.    *There is a table that we piled books on in the bedroom.*
                      *(THERE-Insertion)*

(4)  a.    *The man who Susan thinks is trying to catch her shot a policeman.*
    b.    *A policeman was shot by the man who Susan thinks is trying to catch her.*
                      *(Passive)*

(5)  a.    *That the hypothesis which Anne thinks she has refuted is correct is unlikely.*
    b.    *The hypothesis which Anne thinks she has refuted is unlikely to be correct.*
                      *(Subject-to-Subject Raising)*

*Property 2*

The relative clauses in (1) each contain a gap. The gap in a relative clause can be embedded indefinitely deeply.[1]

(6)  *(The books that Nora expects Mark to tell Winifred to remind*
     NP
    *Harold to bring* _____ *to class) are very rare.*
                NP

*Property 3*

The surface structure of constructions like those in (1) is roughly

(7)

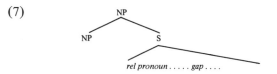

## 2. DERIVING THE CONSTRUCTIONS

One proposal for accounting for examples like those in (1) is given by (A–C) below.

---

[1] Some relative clauses appear to have no gaps, e.g.,

  (i)    *The woman **who** left early*
  (ii)   *The bomb **that** exploded*
  (iii)  *The weeds **which** have grown in the garden*

This is the case when the relativized NP is the subject of the relative clause.

A.    Structures of the form

(8)

are generated in underlying structure by the phrase structure rule

(9)    $NP \rightarrow NP\ S$

B.    The S in (8) does not contain a gap. Rather, the grammar requires that this S contain an NP identical to and coreferential with the head of the relative clause.

(10)

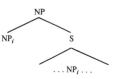

This NP can be embedded indefinitely deeply in the clause.

C.    The rule of *Relativization* moves the coreferential NP to clause initial position and replaces it with a relative pronoun.[2,3]

(11)

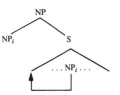

For example, the underlying structure of

(12)   *The man who(m) I met in the hospital*

---

[2] It is an open question whether the Relativization transformation replaces the relativized NP with a relative pronoun or whether this is accomplished by another rule that operates in conjunction with Relativization.

[3] When the relativized NP is the subject of the relative clause, Relativization does not change the linear order of elements since the relativized NP is already in clause-initial position. In such cases, the only difference is that the relativized NP is replaced by a relative pronoun.

is

(13)

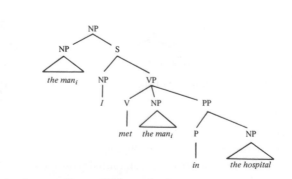

Relativization applies to (13), producing

(14)

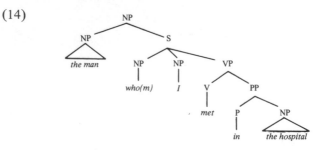

## 3. PIED PIPING

Normally, Relativization moves only the NP that is coreferential with the head. However, in certain cases the rule can optionally move larger constituents in which the relativized NP is embedded. This phenomenon is known as *Pied Piping*.[4] For example, the relative clauses in

(15)  a.  *reports **which** the government regulates the height of the lettering on the covers of* _____
      b.  *reports **the covers of which** the government regulates the height of the lettering on* _____
      c.  *reports **the lettering on the covers of which** the government regulates the height of* _____
      d.  *reports **the height of the lettering on the covers of which** the government regulates* _____

are all derived from the underlying form

[4] This phenomenon was discovered and named by Ross (1967). We have used some of Ross's examples here.

(16)

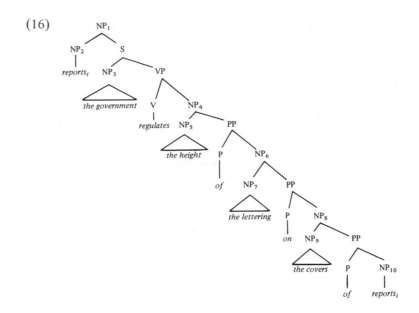

If only the relativized NP, NP$_{10}$, is preposed, (15a) is produced. (15b), (15c), and (15d) are derived by moving NP$_8$, NP$_6$, and NP$_4$, respectively.

This kind of pied piping does not occur in questions:

(17) a.　*What does the government regulate the height of the lettering on the covers of* _____ *?*

b.　*\*The covers of what does the government regulate the height of the lettering on* _____ *?*

c.　*\*The lettering on the covers of what does the government regulate the height of* _____ *?*

d.　*\*The height of the lettering on the covers of what does the government regulate* _____ *?*

However, a phenomenon similar to pied piping does occur in both questions and relative clauses.

(18) a.　*the man **who(m)** I spoke with* _____

b.　*the man **with whom** I spoke*

(19) a.　***Who(m)** did I speak with* _____ *?*

b.　***With whom** did I speak* _____ *?*

In (18b) and (19b) the preposition has been optionally transported to the front along with the moved NP.

## 4.  TWO HYPOTHESES CONCERNING RELATIVIZATION

### 4.1  Assumptions

*Assumption 1*

Relativization is an obligatory rule.

*Assumption 2*

Relativization can move a relativized constituent over an unbounded distance.

### 4.2  Two Conflicting Hypotheses

*The Single Movement Hypothesis*

Relativization moves relativized constituents to clause-initial position in a single movement.

(20)

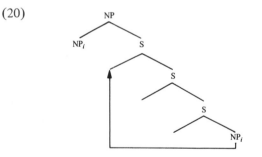

*The Successive Cyclic Hypothesis*

Relativization operates cyclically, preposing the relativized constituent to the front of each successive S until clause-initial position is reached.

(21)

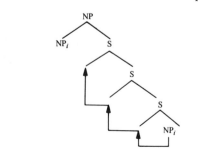

## 4.3 Exercise

Show that arguments analogous to those constructed in section 65 can be used to demonstrate the superiority of the Single Movement Hypothesis for Relativization. First construct two sets of relative clauses corresponding to the two sets of questions in section 65. Then construct two arguments based on the two sets of data. Finally, show that for Relativization, the argument based on preposition stranding can be generalized to pied piping of the kind found in (15).

## 5. THE DISTINCTION BETWEEN RESTRICTIVE AND APPOSITIVE RELATIVE CLAUSES

### 5.1 Appositive Relatives

There are two kinds of relative clauses in English—*restrictive relatives* and *appositive relatives*. All of the relative clauses so far discussed have been restrictives. They must be distinguished from appositive relative clauses like

(22) a.  *The President, who we all know will run for re-election, won't take a stand on that issue.*
   b.  *My parents, who live in Oregon, called me last night.*
   c.  *Susan read the book on the table, which is a bestseller.*

Appositive relatives are pronounced with comma intonation—i.e., with pauses after the head and the relative clause. Restrictive relatives do not have this comma intonation.

### 5.2 Semantic Differences

A restrictive relative clause in a sentence of the form

(23)  [*NP relative clause*]$_{NP}$ *Predicate*

restricts the predication to the class of individuals specified in the relative clause. An appositive relative clause does not.[5] When the clause in (23) is appositive, the predication is made of all those individuals specified by the head NP; it is further asserted that this set of individuals is the same as the set of individuals specified by the relative clause.

[5] The semantic difference between restrictive and appositive relatives shows up in sentences with many different forms. We have chosen sentences of the form (23) to illustrate this difference.

This difference is illustrated by (24).

(24)  a.    *Philosophers who have read the works of Bertrand Russell*
            *appreciate the value of formal logic.*
            *(Restrictive)*

      b.    *Philosophers, who have read the works of Bertrand Russell,*
            *appreciate the value of formal logic.*
            *(Appositive)*

In (24a), the predication is restricted to those philosophers who have read Russell. (24a) asserts that these philosophers appreciate the value of formal logic.[6] (24b), on the other hand, asserts that

(i)    *philosophers in general appreciate the value of formal logic*

and

(ii)   *philosophers in general have read the works of Bertrand Russell.*

A situation in which (a) would be true but (b) false is one in which only a few philosophers have read Russell, but all who have read him appreciate formal logic.

Further examples that illustrate the basic semantic difference between restrictive and appositive relative clauses are:

(25)  a.    *Athletes who keep in shape live longer than the average person*
            *(Restrictive)*

      b.    *Athletes, who keep in shape, live longer than the average*
            *person*
            *(Appositive)*

and

(26)  a.    *Squash which is harvested in the summer is sweet.*
            *(Restrictive)*

      b.    *Squash, which is harvested in the summer, is sweet.*
            *(Appositive)*

## 5.3  Related Differences

Proper names are used to refer to specific individuals. As a result, when the head NP of a relative clause is a proper name, it picks out the subject of predication, leaving no role for a restrictive clause to play. Consequently, proper

---

[6] (24a) says nothing about philosophers who have not read Russell. It leaves open the question of whether some or all of them also appreciate the value of formal logic.

names cannot be heads of a restrictive clauses; however, they can be heads of appositives.

(27) a.  *John, who had already seen the play, told us about it. (A)*
 b.  *\*John who had already seen the play told us about it. (R)*

By contrast, certain indefinite NPs can be heads of restrictive relative clauses, but cannot be heads of appositives.

(28) a.  *Any law which is about taxes is bound to be complicated. (R)*
 b.  *\*Any law, which is about taxes, is bound to be complicated. (A)*
(29) a.  *I've got to find someone who can advise me on this. (R)*
 b.  *\*I've got to find someone, who can advise me on this. (A)*

In this book the only relative clauses that we will be concerned with are restrictive relatives; the proposals in §§ 1-4 apply only to them. The question of how appositive relatives are derived is left open.


## 6. ADJECTIVES

The devices that have been proposed to generate relative clauses will also generate relative clauses whose predicates are adjectives—e.g.

(30) *Yesterday I met a person who is unusual.*

Adjectives in English also occur preceding the head noun that they modify:

(31) *Yesterday I met an unusual person.*

It has been proposed that structures like (31), with a prenominal adjective, are derived from structures like (30), with an adjective in a relative clause. Two rules have been posited to accomplish this:

(32) a.  *WH IS Deletion (pronounced "Whiz Deletion"), which deletes the relative pronoun and a form of the copula be*
 b.  *Adjective Flip, which preposes the adjective to prenominal position*

Schematically, the derivation of an NP such as **an unusual person** would look like this:

(33) a.  *[a person who is unusual]*
 b.  *[a person unusual]*
 c.  *an unusual person*

It might appear at first that the proposed analysis adds two otherwise unnecessary rules to the grammar of English. For example, it might be thought that Adjective Flip can be dispensed with by using phrase structure rules to generate adjectives directly in prenominal position instead of deriving them from relative clauses. However, this is not the case.

To show this, we will contrast a grammar of English (Grammar A) that generates all adjectives in prenominal position with a grammar (Grammar B) in which adjectives are derived from relative clauses by means of WH IS Deletion and Adjective Flip. The point of this argument is to show that Adjective Flip is independently motivated by showing that both grammars need a rule to move adjectives. Consequently, Grammar A does not save a rule by generating adjectives in prenominal position in underlying structure.

The crucial evidence comes from examples where the head is an indefinite pronoun (*someone, something,* etc.). In such cases, the adjective does not precede the head, but follows it.

(34)  a.  *Yesterday I met unusual someone.*
      b.  *Yesterday I met someone unusual.*

Such examples show that whether the adjective precedes or follows its head depends on the nature of the head. Grammar A would need a rule of Adjective Postposing to account for examples like (34b), while Grammar B needs Adjective Flip to account for the prenominal position of adjectives in other cases. Since both grammars need a rule to move adjectives, nothing would be saved by generating adjectives only in prenominal position by phrase structure rules. Thus, the rule of Adjective Flip that is needed by the analysis that derives adjectives from relative clauses does not make the grammar more complex than it would be otherwise.

The question now arises as to whether WH IS Deletion represents the addition of an otherwise unmotivated rule, or whether some rule of this kind would be needed in any event. Here the answer is not so clear. Any grammar of English will need a rule to delete the relative pronoun to account for examples such as

(35)  a.  *the man I met*
      b.  *the people I talked to*
      c.  *the group I worked with*

If the rule that is needed for these examples can be formulated so it will also delete the copula in copula-adjective constructions, then WH IS Deletion will also result from a rule that the grammar needs independently.

Further support for the analysis in (32) comes from examples of prenominal adjectives that are ambiguous, where one reading corresponds to a restrictive relative clause and the other corresponds to an appositive relative.

(36)  *The affluent Germans travel all over Europe.*

(36) has two meanings:

(37)  *The Germans who are affluent travel all over Europe.*
(38)  *The Germans, who are affluent, travel all over Europe.*

The ambiguity of (36) would be accounted for by a grammar that derives it from the structures underlying both (37) and (38) by WH IS Deletion and Adjective Flip.

It is important to note, however, that not all adjectives can be derived from relative clauses. This can be seen by comparing the sentences in (39) with those in *(40), which cannot be their source.

(39)  a.   *He is a mere child.*
     b.   *He is a potential candidate.*
(40)  a.   *\*He is a child who is mere.*
     b.   *\*He is a candidate who is potential.*

The sentences in (39) seem rather to be related to certain adverbial constructions:

(41)  a.   *He is merely a child.*
     b.   *He is potentially a candidate.*

However, there are other examples of prenominal adjectives that neither have a relative clause source nor are related to adverbial constructions.

(42)  a.   *He is a complete idiot.*
     b.   *He is a presidential candidate.*

# 67

## *Part 6: Its Place in a Wider Context*

The movement rules that are the focus of part 6 have been studied extensively in the framework of transformational grammar—perhaps more than any other aspect of grammar. Since the literature dealing with them is vast, we will limit ourselves to mentioning the sources of the arguments we have used here, plus a small number of additional references.

The Nonsubject Raising construction has been formulated in many ways and has gone under several names—e.g., *Tough Movement* in Postal (1971) and *IT-Replacement* in Chomsky (1973). It is also discussed in Chomsky (1962), Berman (1973), Bresnan (1971), and Berman and Szamosi (1972). The problem in section 61 is based on Postal and Ross (1971). A reply is to be found in Akmajian (1972). An alternative analysis is proposed in Lasnik and Fiengo (1974), and replied to in Jackendoff (1975).

The problem on Nonsubject Raising and FOR-Phrases in section 63 is based on Berman (1973). Additional discussion can be found in Jackendoff (1972) and Chomsky (1973).

Relative clauses have been an object of interest in transformational grammar since its inception. Most of the analyses presented in section 66 draw on the earliest transformational works on the subject, particularly Smith (1961, 1964). See also Klima (1964*a*, 1964*b*), Kuroda (1968), Peranteau, Levi, and Phares (1972), and the references cited there. An analysis of relative clauses under which the head is "created" by a rule that moves it out of the relative clause itself has been proposed by Schachter (1973) and Vergnaud (1974).

Questions have also spawned a huge literature. Some of the key earlier works on the subject are Chomsky (1957, 1962, 1964), Klima (1964*a*, 1964*b*), Katz and Postal (1964), Baker (1970), Bresnan (1970*b*), Bach (1971), and Langacker (1974). The discussion of *Whether*-Deletion in section 64 draws on Ross (1970). The problem *Two Hypotheses Concerning Question Movement* in section 65 is based on Postal (1972*b*). An alternative analysis is proposed by Chomsky (1973, 1977).

# PART 7

# *Ross's Constraints*

In part 7, we present a few of the central ideas from John Ross's unpublished but highly influential doctoral thesis, *Constraints on Variables in Syntax,* completed in 1967. Ross proposed a set of constraints, many of them universal, on the operation of a class of syntactic rules of which movement rules are the most prominent. These constraints were proposed to account for some phenomena that had previously been discussed in the literature and a range of new phenomena that Ross himself discovered. Since 1967, Ross's analyses have given rise to a number of reanalyses and new proposals, which limitations of space prevent us from dealing with here. This has been one of the most fertile areas for transformational research, and most specific proposals in this area remain controversial. Nonetheless, Ross's work serves as a benchmark against which subsequent work in this area has been, and will continue to be, judged. We have selected a few key topics to serve as an introduction to Ross's work as a whole.

# PART 7

## Ross's Constraint

# 68

## *Island Constraints*

### *1. ISLANDS*

#### 1.1 Complex Noun Phrases

(1)

Ross refers to the structure in (1) as a *complex noun phrase*. The following are examples of complex NPs in English:

(2)  a.    *the claim that Tom is innocent*
       b.    *the fact that no one told him that she arrived late*
(3)  a.    *the man who bought a car*
       b.    *the woman who Tom says Sally met in Chicago*

In some languages, complex noun phrases have the form

(4)

#### 1.2 Sentential Subjects

Ross refers to an embedded sentence that is the subject of a clause as a *sentential subject.*

(5)

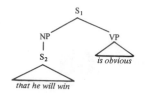

In (5), *that he will win* is a sentential subject.

Complex NPs and sentential subjects are two types of syntactic *islands*.

## 2. ISLAND CONSTRAINTS

### 2.1 The Complex Noun Phrase Constraint

(6)  a.   *Marcia believes that Tom will say something.*
     b.   *What does Marcia believe that Tom will say?*
(7)  a.   *Marcia believes the claim that Tom will say something.*
     b.   *\*What does Marcia believe the claim that Tom will say?*

The structure underlying *(7b) is roughly

(8)

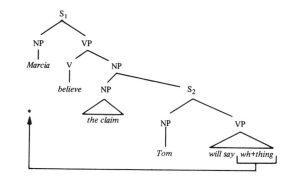

In (8), *wh+thing* is inside a complex noun phrase. The ungrammaticality of
*(7b) illustrates the fact that Question Movement cannot move anything out of
a complex NP.

Since relative clauses are also complex NPs, Question Movement cannot
move anything out of a relative clause either.

(9)  a.   *Marie knows the man who said something.*
     b.   *\*What does Marie know the man who said?*

(10)

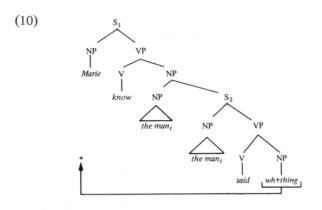

The ungrammaticality of *(7b) and *(9b) shows that Question Movement *obeys the Complex Noun Phrase Constraint.* In general, to say that a movement rule obeys the Complex Noun Phrase Constraint is to say that it cannot move anything out of *the S in the configuration (11).*[1]

(11)

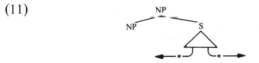

## 2.2 The Sentential Subject Constraint

To say that a movement rule obeys the Sentential Subject Constraint is to say that it cannot move anything out of a sentential subject. Question Movement obeys the Sentential Subject Constraint.

(12)

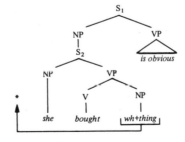

[1] Ross's formulation of the Complex NP Constraint is slightly different. The points at issue are discussed in section 71.

(13)  a.     *That she bought something is obvious.*
      b.     *\*What is that she bought obvious?*

If the complement sentence is extraposed, however, it is no longer a subject.

(14)

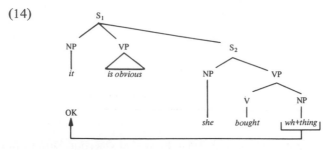

As a result, Question Movement can apply.

(15)  a.     *It is obvious that she bought something.*
      b.     *What is it obvious that she bought?*

## 3. EXERCISE

We have shown that Question Movement cannot move NPs out of two kinds of structural configurations—complex NPs and sentential subjects. In each case, the structural configuration is one in which an S is immediately dominated by an *NP*-node. It might, therefore, be thought that the Complex NP Constraint and the Sentential Subject Constraint are just particular cases of a broader generalization—namely that a rule such as Question Movement cannot move anything out of an S immediately dominated by *NP*.

Show that this is not the case by finding grammatical sentences in which Question Movement moves a constituent out of the complement of *prove*. (For arguments that the complement of *prove* is dominated by an *NP*-node, see Some Further Issues-3). After doing this, find other verbs which could be used to make the same point.

# 69

# *Which Rules Obey Island Constraints?*

## 1. HOW TO SHOW THAT A RULE OBEYS ISLAND CONSTRAINTS

To show that a rule obeys island constraints, one must not only cite ungrammatical sentences where the constraint is violated, but also show that the ungrammaticality is due to the violation (rather than to something in the formulation of the rule itself). In the case of Question Movement we showed that movement of a *wh*-constituent out of an island results in ungrammaticality. To demonstrate that this ungrammaticality is due to island constraints rather than to something in the formulation of the rule itself, one must show that the structural description of Question Movement does not specify the kinds of structures out of which it can move constituents.

This can be done by considering some of the structures across which Question Movement can move an NP.

(1) *What did you say _____?*

(2) *What does Marcia think you said _____?*

(3) *What did Marcia tell Tom to tell Louise to say _____?*

(4) *What does Jeff think Marcia wanted Louise to tell Tom to remind Pete to deny _____?*

(5) *What do you think Tom expects Louise to tell Pete to have Matilda make sure Sally reminds Wenceslas to remember _____?*

Since there is no limit to the amount of material over which movement can occur, it would be impossible to list in the structural description of the rule all of the structures over which a constituent can be moved. Consequently, a variable is needed to express the fact that movement can occur over an unlimited distance.

(6)    *Question Movement*[1]

$$X - wh+NP - Y \Rightarrow 2, 1, 3$$
$$1 \quad 2 \quad \quad 3$$

If Question movement is formulated in this way, then nothing in its structural description prevents it from moving an element out of an island. For example, just as (6) would allow us to generate

(7)    *What do you believe that Sally said?*

it would also allow us to generate

(8)    **What do you believe the claim that Sally said?*

*(8) shows that some independent constraint is needed to prevent movement in certain cases. (7) shows that the constraint does not prevent movement out of complements of *believe* in general. Taken together, these sentences provide evidence that it is movement out of a complex NP that results in ungrammaticality. (7) and *(8) are said to be a *minimal pair* showing that Question Movement obeys the Complex NP Constraint.

Another way to show that Question Movement obeys the Complex NP Constraint, is to test it on structures containing relative clauses

(9)    a.    *Sally knows the man who won which trophy?*
       b.    **Which trophy does Sally know the man who won?*[2]

Examples like *(9b) show that a *wh*-constituent cannot be moved out of a complex NP that consists of a head plus a relative clause.[3]

---

[1] We ignore here the issue of how Question Movement is to be formulated so that it moves a *wh*-NP to initial position in the complement of verbs that embed indirect questions, as in:

(i)    a.    *I wonder **what** she said _____ .*
       b.    *I don't know **what** Tom thinks she said_____ .*
       c.    *I'm not sure **what** Tom thinks Mary told George to make sure to remind to tell Geraldine to say_____ to Lester.*

In each of these examples, the *wh*-word has moved to initial position in the embedded question clause rather than in the entire sentence. This issue may be ignored here since our only concern is to show that Question Movement moves constituents across a variable.

[2] (9a) is an echo question in which no movement occurs. *(9b) would mean roughly

(i)    *Which trophy is such that Sally knew the man who won it*

if it were grammatical. However, the Complex *NP* Constraint prevents *(9b) from being derived.

[3] Ross (1967) subsumed both NP-plus-relative clause structures and complex NPs like *the claim that S* and *the fact that S* under a single constraint. However, subsequent research

Finally, if Question Movement is formulated as in (6), then minimal pairs like

(10) *\*What is that Sally said ———— likely?*
(11) *What is it likely that Sally said ———— ?*

show that it obeys the Sentential Subject Constraint. Since nothing in the structural description of the rule itself discriminates sentential subjects from other embedded sentences, the Sentential Subject Constraint is needed to block \*(10).[4]


## 2. TESTING SOME RULES OF ENGLISH


### 2.1 Topicalization

Topicalization preposes an NP to initial position.

(12)  a.   *Timothy I don't like ————.*
     b.   *Matilda I think Sally said Harold doesn't like ————.*
     c.   *Sam I would never tell Marcia to try to get Phyllis to tell Morris to invite ————.*

Since there is no upper limit to the distance across which Topicalization can move an NP, it must be formulated with a variable along the following lines.[5]

*Footnote 3 continued*
has indicated that some speakers allow violations of the Complex NP Constraint in examples of the latter kind, but not in relative clauses. Further, most speakers find violations in relative clauses much worse than violations with complex NPs like *the claim that S.*

(i)   *\*\*What does Mary know the man who said?*
(ii)   *\*What does Mary believe the claim that the man said?*

Facts like these make it worthwhile to test both types of complex NPs separately to see whether a given rule can move elements out of it.
    [4] The result of applying Question Movement is also grammatical if Subject-to-Subject Raising has destroyed the sentential subject.

(i)   *What is Sally likely to have said ————?*

    [5] Some additional factors (such as, for example, the definiteness or indefiniteness of the *NP* being topicalized) enter into the applicability of Topicalization. We have ignored such factors in this formulation of the rule.

(13)  *Topicalization*

X – NP – Y
1     2     3 ⇒ 2, 1, 3

The contrast between

(14)  *Phyllis I don't believe that Harold likes* _____ .

and

(15) *\*Phyllis I don't believe the claim that Harold likes* _____ .

shows that Topicalization cannot move a constituent out of complex NPs of the form *the claim that S*. Since NP-plus-relative clause structures are of the form

(16)

the Complex NP Constraint should also prevent Topicalization from moving an NP out of a relative clause.

(17)

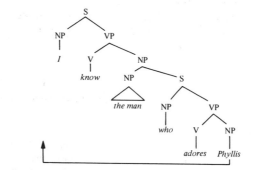

The ungrammaticality of

(18) *\*Phyllis I know the man who adores* _____ .

shows that it does.[6]

---

[6] Since Topicalization is formulated as in (13), nothing in its formulation prevents it from applying to (17). Thus, examples like \*(18) led Ross to conclude that the Complex *NP* Constraint prevents Topicalization from moving constituents out of relative clauses.

The structure

(19)

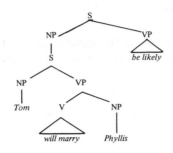

allows us to test whether Topicalization obeys the Sentential Subject Constraint. Topicalizing *Phyllis* results in the ungrammatical sentence

(20) **\*Phyllis** *that Tom will marry* _____ *is likely.*

However, if Extraposition applies to (19), producing

(21)  *It is likely that Tom will marry Phyllis.*

then Topicalization can apply, yielding the grammatical output

(22)  **Phyllis** *it is likely that Tom will marry* _____ .

The contrast between \*(20) and (22) shows that Topicalization obeys the Sentential Subject Constraint.


## 2.2  Relativization

Relativization moves a relative pronoun to initial position inside the relative clause.[7]

(23)  a.   *the man* **who** *Sally met* _____ .
      b.   *the man* **who** *Sally says Marcia met* _____ .
      c.   *the man* **who** *Sally told me Marcia said Harold thinks Janey has been trying to meet* _____ .

---

[7] Some analyses of relative clauses claim that there are two separate rules involved—a rule of Relativization that converts the relativized NP into a relative pronoun and a rule of Relative Movement or WH-Movement that moves the relative pronoun to the front of the relative clause. Other analyses claim that both are accomplished by a single rule, which is generally called *Relativization*. For our purposes, it does not matter which of these two types of analysis is correct. We therefore speak loosely of "Relativization" moving the relative pronoun, although a more detailed analysis might make it necessary to posit distinct rules.

d.   *the man **who** George said Marcia wants Sally to remind _____ to sign up for photography*

Since there is no upper limit on the distance across which Relativization can move a relative pronoun, it must be formulated as moving a constituent over a variable. The contrast between

(24)  *the man **who** I believe that Sally met _____ .*

and

(25) *\*the man **who** I believe the claim that Sally met _____ .*

shows that Relativization cannot move a relative pronoun out of complex NPs of the form *the claim that S.* To show that Relativization cannot move a relative pronoun out of complex NPs of the form *NP+relative clause,* we need a sentence like

(26)  *The Globe has reviewed the book which denounced the man.*

The structure of (26) is roughly

(27)

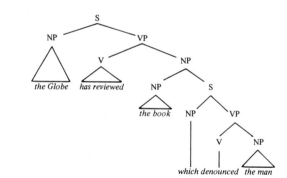

Now suppose that we try to embed (27) as a relative clause on *the man* in the sentence

(28)  *Sally met the man.*

The resulting structure is

(29)

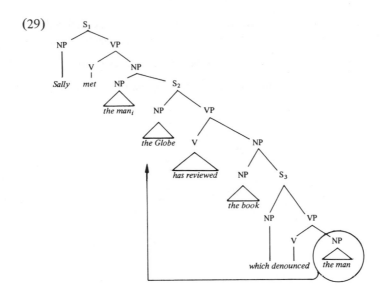

$S_2$ is a relative clause modifying *the man* in $S_1$. The NP in this relative clause that is coreferential with the head is itself inside another relative clause ($S_3$) modifying *the book*. Application of Relativization to this NP (*the man*) should convert it into a relative pronoun (*who*) and move it to the front of $S_2$. But this produces an ungrammatical sentence:

(30) *\*Sally met the man **who** the Globe has reviewed the book which denounced* _____ .

The Complex NP Constraint accounts for the ungrammaticality of this sentence by preventing Relativization from moving *who* out of the complex NP, *the book which denounced the man*.

Structures like

(31)

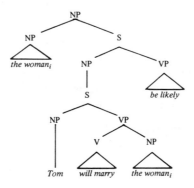

can be used to show that Relativization also obeys the Sentential Subject Constraint. Relativization of *the woman* in (31) produces the ungrammatical

(32) *\*the woman **who** that Tom will marry* _____ *is likely.*

However, if Extraposition applies inside the relative clause, producing

(33)

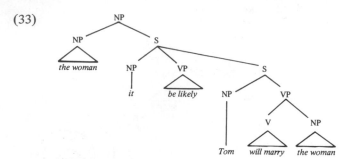

then Relativization is possible.

(34)  *the woman **who** it is likely that Tom will marry* _____ .

The contrast between *\*(32) and (34) shows that Relativization obeys the Sentential Subject Constraint.


### 2.3  Adjective Preposing

In

(35)  ***Pretty** as Maggie is* _____ , *I still think that Alice is prettier.*

and

(36)  ***Pretty** though Maggie is* _____ , *I still think that Alice is prettier.*

we find the adjective *pretty* in initial position instead of in its usual position after the copula *be*. Thus, English must have a rule of Adjective Preposing that applies in the derivation of these sentences.

Many things about this rule are not clear—for example, the nature of the structures to which it applies and the precise formulation of the rule itself. One thing that is clear, however, is that it operates across a variable.

(37)  ***Pretty** as Tom reported that Marcia thinks that Maggie is* _____ ,
       *most people would still say that Alice is prettier.*

Since Adjective Preposing can move a constituent over an unbounded distance, it must be formulated as involving movement over a variable. Having established this, we can now ask whether it obeys Island Constraints.

To demonstrate that it obeys the Complex NP Constraint, we show that although it can prepose an adjective out of the complement of *believe,* it cannot move one out of a complex NP.

(38) *Pretty as I believe that Maggie is* _____ , *I still believe that Alice is prettier.*

(39) *\*Pretty as I believe the claim that Maggie is* _____ , *I still believe that Alice is prettier.*

*\*(41) shows that Adjective Preposing cannot move an adjective out of a relative clause.

(40) *I know the man who said that Maggie is pretty.*

(41) *\*Pretty as I know the man who said that Maggie is*_____ , *I still think that Alice is prettier.*

It is more difficult to show that Adjective Preposing obeys the Sentential Subject Constraint, since judgments on the relevant sentences are not clear. For example, while

(42) *?Though that Maggie is pretty is clear, I still think Alice is prettier*

is quite awkward, it is probably grammatical. Certainly, it is much better than the sentence that results from the application of Adjective Preposing.

(43) *\*Pretty though that Maggie is* _____ *is clear, I still think Alice is prettier.*

This seems to show that Adjective Preposing obeys the Sentential Subject Constraint. Still, we cannot consider this conclusion established until we are sure that the ill-formedness of *\*(43) is not due to other factors. Although

(44) *Though it is clear that Maggie is pretty, I still think Alice is prettier.*

is well-formed, the result of applying Adjective Preposing to it sounds somewhat strange, even though no sentential subject is involved.[8]

(45) *?Pretty though it is clear that Maggie is* _____ , *I still think Alice is prettier.*

Whatever makes ?(42) and ?(45) sound strange may also play a role in the ill-formedness of *\*(43). Of course, *\*(43) is much worse than either of these

[8] (45) results from applying Extraposition to (44). After Extraposition has applied, the complement is no longer a sentential subject and movement out of it should be possible.

examples, and the Sentential Subject Constraint would account for this. Never-theless, our ignorance of the factors involved in ?(42) and ?(45) renders tentative our conclusion that Adjective Preposing obeys the constraint.

Despite these uncertainties about preposing out of sentential subjects, we did establish that Adjective Preposing obeys the Complex NP Constraint. This is interesting not only for its own sake, but also because it illustrates how a rule can be shown to obey an island constraint even when one is not sure how the rule is formulated or exactly what structures it applies to.

## 3. EXERCISE

### 3.1 Instructions

Assume that the (b)-sentences below are derived from the structures underlying the corresponding (a)-sentences by rules that prepose constituents from the underlined positions to sentence-initial position. For each rule, first determine whether it operates across a variable. (Do this without formulating the rule itself.) Then determine whether it obeys the Sentential Subject and Com-plex NP constraints. Assume that the Complex NP Constraint prevents move-ment of a constituent out of the S in the configuration

(46)

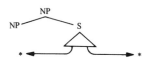

In testing whether a rule obeys this constraint, use both examples like *the claim that S* and relative clauses.

### 3.2 The Rules

*VP Preposing*

    (47)  a.    *They said that Mike would pay up.*

           b.    *They said that Mike would pay up, and **pay up** he will* _____ .

*Exclamation Preposing*

    (48)  a.    *[Our soldiers are how brave!]* *(This is assumed as the structure underlying [48b].)*

           b.    ***How brave** our soldiers are* _____ *!*

*Left Dislocation*

> (49) a. *Everyone thinks your father is a great guy.*
> b. ***Your father,** everyone thinks **he** is a great guy.*

Note that Left Dislocation differs from the other rules in that it leaves a *pronominal copy* in the position previously occupied by the dislocated NP. The pronominal copy agrees in gender and number with the dislocated NP.

> (50) a. *Everyone thinks your mother is wonderful.*
> b. ***Your mother,** everyone thinks **she** is wonderful.*
> (51) a. *No one told me those kids were sick.*
> b. ***Those kids,** no one told me **they** were sick.*

Do this exercise before proceeding.

## 4. *WHICH RULES OBEY THE CONSTRAINTS? A GENERALIZATION*

By now you have considered each of the following rules:

> (52) a. *Question Movement*
> b. *Topicalization*
> c. *Relativization*
> d. *Adjective Preposing*
> e. *VP Preposing*
> f. *Exclamation Preposing*
> g. *Left Dislocation*

All of these rules have the following two properties:

> (53) a. *They move a constituent to the left.*
> b. *They move a constituent across a variable.*

Left Dislocation differs from the other rules in that it leaves a pronominal copy of the moved constituent in the position it previously occupied. Ross (1967) called rules that do this *copying rules*. Rules like those in (52a–f), which do *not* leave a pronominal copy, he called *chopping rules*. The distinction between these two types of rules is crucial with respect to island constraints. Chopping rules obey the constraints; copying rules do not. Thus, Left Dislocation, alone of the rules in (52) can violate the constraints.

> (54) **Complex NP Constraint with THE CLAIM THAT S**
> ***Your father,*** *I will never believe the claim that **he** is guilty.*
> (55) **Complex NP Constraint with a Relative Clause**
> ***Your father,*** *I know the man who accused **him.***

(56)  **Sentential Subject Constraint**
      *Your father, that no one understands **him** is obvious.*

On the basis of data such as that considered here, Ross reached conclusion (57).

(57)  *Chopping rules that move a constituent across a variable obey island constraints. Copying rules do not.*[9]

Ross's research was not limited to English. Having considered data from a wide variety of languages, he concluded that (57) was not limited to English, but rather is a *linguistic universal.*


## 5. ISLAND CONSTRAINTS AND THE DISTINCTION BETWEEN OPTIONAL AND OBLIGATORY RULES

No constituent can be moved outside an island by a chopping rule. If the rule is optional, a grammatical sentence results from the derivation in which it has not applied. This is the case for Topicalization with respect to (17):

(58)  a.   *I know the man who adores Phyllis.*
      b.   *\*Phyllis I know the man who adores _____ .*

Although the Complex NP Constraint blocks *(58b), (58a) is still grammatical.

If the rule is obligatory, the situation is different. Because it is obligatory, a derivation in which the rule does *not* apply will yield an ungrammatical sentence. But because application of the rule would violate an island constraint, a derivation in which it *does* apply will also result in ungrammaticality. This is the case for Relativization with respect to the structure (29). If Relativization does not apply, no grammatical sentence can result. If it does apply, it violates the Complex NP Constraint, producing the ungrammatical sentence

(30) *\*Sally met the man **who** the Globe has reviewed the book **which** denounced _____ .*

Thus, examples in which an obligatory rule cannot apply without violating an island constraint constitute a class of cases where no grammatical surface structure corresponds to an otherwise well-formed underlying structure.

---

[9] This characterization must be considered tentative for several different reasons. First, we have not established that rules that do not operate across variables are not subject to island constraints. Second, we have not shown that the direction of movement (leftward vs. rightward) is irrelevant, since we have not yet considered rightward movement rules. Third, there are additional (nonmovement) rules discussed by Ross that we have not yet considered. Some of these matters will be discussed further in sections 71 and 72.

# 70

## Picture Nouns and Krispy Klauses

### 1. PICTURE NOUN CONSTRUCTIONS

There is a large class of nouns in English called *picture nouns*. The class includes items such as *picture, photograph, sketch, portrait, story, anecdote, joke, poem, novel, book, movie, play, rumor, lie,* and others.[1] Reflexivization can operate into picture noun constructions if the picture noun has the indefinite article.

    (1)    a.    *Tom showed me a picture of himself.*

Reflexivization is worse with the definite article or a demonstrative (*this,that*).

    (1)    b.    *?Tom showed me the picture of himself.*[2]
            c.    *??Tom showed me that picture of himself.*

It is still worse with a possessive.

    (1)    d.    *\*Tom showed me Mary's picture of himself.*

---

[1] Harris (1976), who called attention to the properties of picture nouns, gives a much longer list. Although her paper was published for the first time in 1976, it was actually written in 1964–1965, and circulated in mimeographed form for a number of years.

[2] Examples of this kind are better with a relative clause, e.g.,

    (i)    *Tom showed me the picture of himself that he had hung in the den.*

We are concerned here only with such constructions that are *not* modified by a relative clause.

Judgments of grammaticality thus form a continuum in (1a–d); in each successive sentence, one would be more likely to use the nonreflexive *him*.

Ross (1967) noted that the ability of chopping rules to move an element out of picture noun constructions is correlated with the ability of Reflexivization to operate into them. Where Reflexivization is possible, chopping is, too, and where Reflexivization is questionable or impossible, so is chopping. Thus, corresponding to (1a–d) we have

(2)    a.    *Who did Tom show you a picture of* _____ *?*
       b.    *?Who did Tom show you the picture of* _____ *?*
       c.    *??Who did Tom show you that picture of* _____ *?*
       d.    *\*Who did Tom show you Mary's picture of* _____ *?*

These examples show that certain picture noun constructions are islands. The correlation between Reflexivization and chopping rules with respect to islands like these forms the basis for Ross's ultimate characterization of islands, which we discuss in section 72.


## 2. KRISPY KLAUSES

There is a class of manner-of-speaking verbs in English whose complements are islands.[3] This class includes *snort, chortle, guffaw, mumble, grumble, moan, shriek, titter,* and other verbs whose meaning specifies not only saying something, but also the way it is said.[4] Since this class of verbs includes, *snap, crackle,* and *pipe up,* we will refer to complements of verbs of this class as *Krispy Klauses.* The islandhood of these clauses is illustrated by contrasting them with the complement of *say*:

(3)    a.    *She said that she met someone in Oswego.*
       b.    *Who did she say that she met* _____ *in Oswego?*
(4)    a.    *She snapped that she met someone in Oswego?*
       b.    *\*Who did she snap that she met* _____ *in Oswego?*
(5)    a.    *She cackled that she met someone in Oswego.*
       b.    *\*Who did she cackle that she met* _____ *in Oswego?*
(6)    a.    *She piped up that she met someone in Oswego.*
       b.    *\*Who did she pipe up* _____ *that she met in Oswego?*

---

[3] The islandhood of complements of verbs of this class was apparently first noted by Fodor (1967).

[4] For a discussion of other interesting properties of manner-of-speaking verbs, see Zwicky (1971).

### 3. EXERCISE

Show that none of the chopping rules discussed in section 69 can move constituents out of picture noun islands or Krispy Klauses. Show that Left Dislocation *can* move constituents out of these constructions, leaving a pronominal copy in the island.

# 71

# *Rightward Movement Rules and the Right Roof Constraint*

## *1. RIGHTWARD MOVEMENT RULES*

Each of the rules listed below derives the (b)-structure from the corresponding (a)-structure. We assume here that the constituent moved to the right is attached to the *S*-node in each case.

*Extraposition of Relative Clauses*

(1)   a.

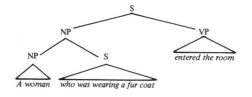

*A woman who was wearing a fur coat entered the room.*

b.

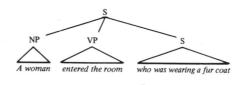

*A woman entered the room who was wearing a fur coat.*

*Extraposition from NP*

(2)  a.

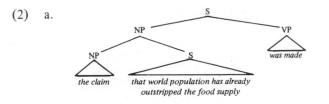

The claim that world population has already outstripped the food supply was made.

b.

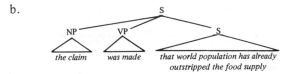

The claim was made that world population has already outstripped the food supply.

We leave it as an open question whether Extraposition of Relative Clauses and Extraposition from NP are the same rule or two distinct rules.

*Extraposition of PP*

(3)  a.

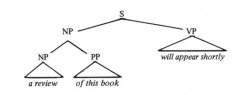

A review of this book will appear shortly.

b.

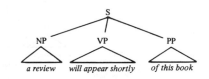

A review will appear shortly of this book.

*Extraposition of Comparative Clauses*

(4)   a.

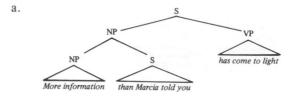

*More information than Marcia told you has come to light.*

b.

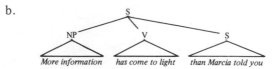

*More information has come to light than Marcia told you.*

*Heavy NP Shift*

(5)   a.

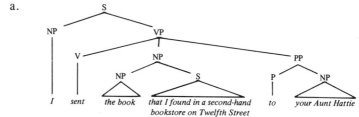

*I sent the book that I found in a second-hand bookstore on Twelfth Street to your Aunt Hattie.*

b.

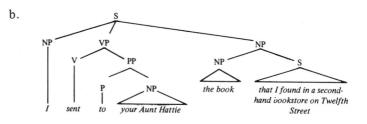

*I sent to your Aunt Hattie the book that I found in a second-hand bookstore on Twelfth Street.*

Heavy NP Shift applies only to direct objects that are "heavy." This is indicated by the contrast between (5) and (6).

(6)   a.   *I sent the book to your Aunt Hattie.*
   b.   *\*I sent to your Aunt Hattie the book.*

Note that Extraposition of Relative Clauses and Extraposition from NP break up complex NPs of the form

(7)

This is the reason why we said that it is the S in configurations of the form (7) that is an island. If $NP_1$ were the island, Extraposition from NP and Extraposition of Relative Clauses would violate the Complex NP Constraint.[1]

## 2. A GENERALIZATION CONCERNING RIGHTWARD MOVEMENT RULES

### Generalization

(8)   *A rightward movement rule can move a constituent to the end of its clause (that is, to the end of the first S above it)—and no farther.*

Consider the structure

(9)

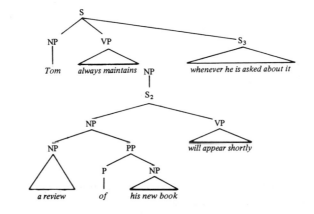

---

[1] The issue of what in (7) is the island is far from resolved. $NP_2$ cannot be moved by chopping rules. If $NP_1$ were the island, this fact would be accounted for. However, Extraposition from NP and Extraposition of Relative Clauses would then be counterexamples to the Complex NP Constraint. The ultimate formulation of the Complex NP Constraint remains an open question.

(9) underlies the sentence

(10)  *Tom always maintains a review of his new book will appear shortly whenever he is asked about it.*

If Extraposition of PP applies to *of his new book*, the result is

(11)

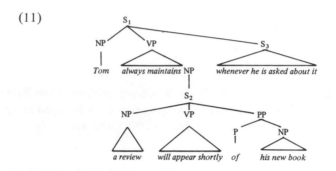

*Tom always maintains a review will appear shortly of his new book whenever he is asked about it.*

In (11), *of his new book* has moved only to the end of $S_2$. If it had moved to the end of $S_1$, the result would be the ungrammatical

(12)

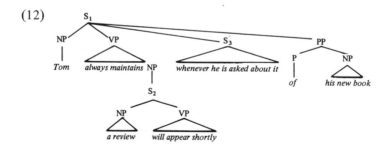

*\*Tom always maintains a review will appear shortly whenever he is asked about it of his new book.*

Extraposition of Comparative Clauses and Extraposition of Relative Clauses behave in exactly the same way. Consider the structure

(13)

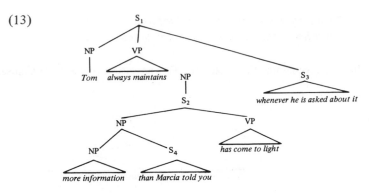

which underlies the sentence

(14) *Tom always maintains more information than Marcia told you has come to light whenever he is asked about it.*

Application of Extraposition of Comparative Clauses to (13) produces

(15)

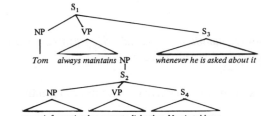

*Tom always maintains more information has come to light than Marcia told you whenever he is asked about it.*

and not

(16)

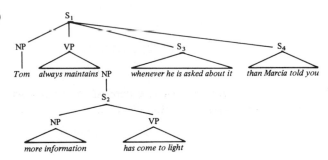

*Tom always maintains more information has come to light when-
ever he is asked about it than Marcia told you.*

The same generalization holds for Extraposition of Relative Clauses. The
structure

(17)

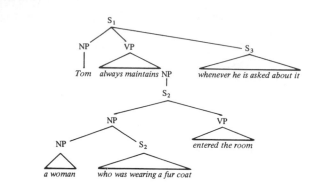

underlies the sentence

(18)  *Tom always maintains a woman who was wearing a fur coat entered
the room whenever he is asked about it.*

Application of Extraposition of Relative Clauses to (17) produces

(19)

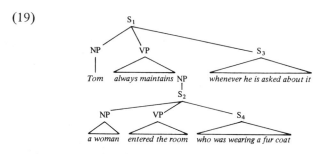

*Tom always maintains a woman entered the room who was wearing
a fur coat whenever he is asked about it.*

and not

(20)

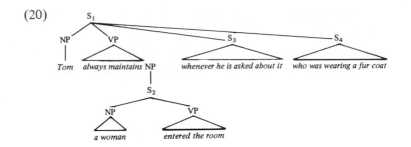

*\*Tom always maintains a woman entered the room whenever he is asked about it who was wearing a fur coat.*

These examples illustrate the fact that a rightward movement rule can move a constituent only to the end of its clause—and no farther. This generalization distinguishes rightward movement rules from leftward movement rules, which can move constituents out of their clauses in structures like those under consideration here. For example, an NP in the position of *that review* in (21) can be moved out of its clause by leftward movement rules.

(21)

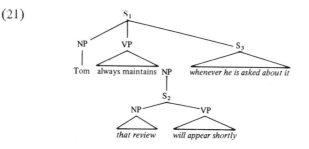

*Tom always maintains that review will appear shortly whenever he is asked about it.*

Topicalization of *that review* in (21) produces

(22)

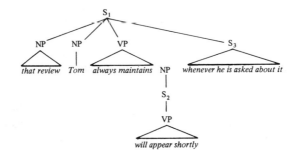

> **That review** *Tom always maintains* _____ *will appear shortly when-ever he is asked about it.*

Similarly, an NP in the position of *that review* in (21) can be moved out of its clause by Question Movement and Relativization, producing sentences like

(23)

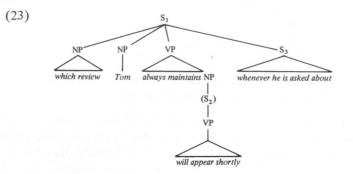

> **Which review** *does Tom always maintain* _____ *will appear shortly whenever he is asked about it?*

and

(24)

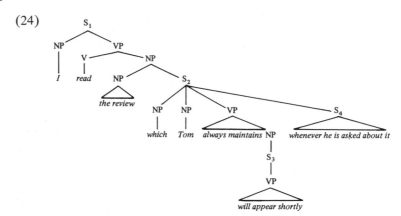

> *I read the review* **which** *Tom always maintains* _____ *will appear shortly whenever he is asked about it.*

These examples also show that $S_2$ in structures like (9–20) is not an island. Thus, the fact that rightward movement rules cannot move constituents out of $S_2$ cannot be due to an island constraint.

## 3. THE ARGUMENT FOR A VARIABLE IN RIGHTWARD MOVEMENT RULES

### 3.1 The Argument

The rightward movement rules we have been discussing have been formulated in transformational grammar as rules that move a constituent across a variable. For example, Extraposition of PP has been formulated as follows:

(25) *Extraposition of PP*

$$X - [NP - PP]_{NP} - Y$$
$$1 \quad 2 \quad 3 \qquad 4 \Rightarrow 1, 2, 4, 3$$

"$[NP\ PP]_{NP}$" means "a string consisting of an NP immediately followed by a PP such that that string is also an NP," i.e., anything of the form

(26)

Given generalization (8), we obviously cannot show that rightward movement rules can move constituents an indefinite distance. What then is the evidence that these rules are to be formulated as moving constituents across a variable?

First, rightward movement rules can move elements across *any kind of constituent*. If they were not formulated with a variable, it would be necessary to list the types of constituents over which movement is possible (this list would include all possible constituent types that can occur to the right of the element to be moved). By abbreviating the full range of possible constituent types with a variable, we achieve the desired result.

Second, rightward movement rules can move an element over any *combination* of constitutents (consistent with generalization [8]). For example, consider the structure[2]

___

[2] (27) raises certain questions we would like to leave open. First, it is not clear whether or not *yesterday* and *at 5 P.M.* constitute two separate constituents or a single constituent. Second, it is not clear whether the *Adv* and *PP*-nodes dominating *yesterday, at 5 P.M.*, and *near Zelda's* are immediately dominated by the *S*-node or the *VP*-node. Third, the adverb node dominating *yesterday* is arbitrary; it is not clear how such constituents are to be represented. However, these questions are not relevant to the issue at hand. What is important here is the fact that Extraposition of Relative Clauses moves relative clauses across a combination of different constituents.

(27)

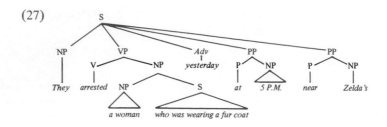

which is realized as the sentence

(28)   *They arrested a woman who was wearing a fur coat yesterday at
       5 P.M. near Zelda's.*

Application of Extraposition of Relative Clauses to (27) produces the structure

(29)

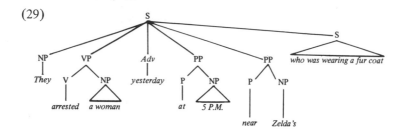

which is realized as

(30)   *They arrested a woman yesterday at 5 P.M. near Zelda's who was
       wearing a fur coat.*

If Extraposition of Relative Clauses were not formulated with a variable, it
would be necessary to complicate the structural description of the rule by listing all the different combinations of constituents over which it can move a
relative clause. If it is formulated with a variable, no such complication results.

   Below we consider the rightward movement rules one by one, and show
the range of constituents over which they can move elements. In each case,
the (b)-sentence is derived from the (a)-sentence by application of the rule in
question. The bold constituent has been moved across the constituent or constituents in italics.

## 3.2 Extraposition of Relative Clauses

   (1) shows Extraposition of Relative Clauses moving a relative clause across
a VP. It can also move a relative clause across a PP, as in (31), an adverb, as in
(32), an NP, as in (33), or across an adjective, as in (34).

(31) a.   I met a woman **who was wearing a fur coat** *at Brando's.*
     b.   I met a woman *at Brando's* **who was wearing a fur coat.**
(32) a.   I met a woman **who was wearing a fur coat** *yesterday.*
     b.   I met a woman *yesterday* **who was wearing a fur coat.**
(33) a.   They consider anyone **who so much as speaks to a member of the occupying army** *a traitor.*
     b.   They consider anyone *a traitor* **who so much as speaks to a member of the occupying army.**
(34) a.   They consider anyone **who dresses ostentatiously** *neurotic.*
     b.   They consider anyone *neurotic* **who dresses ostentatiously.**

(27) and (29) show Extraposition of Relative Clauses moving a relative clause across a combination of nodes.

The arguments that other rightward movement rules must be formulated with a variable have exactly the same form. Rather than repeating the argument in each case, we simply give relevant data to supplement that in (1–5). Readers can reconstruct the arguments for themselves.

## 3.3  Extraposition from NP

(35) a.   The ambassador made the claim **that world population has already outstripped the food supply** *yesterday.*
     b.   The ambassador made the claim *yesterday* **that world population has already outstripped the food supply.**
(36) a.   The ambassador made the claim **that world population has already outstripped the food supply** *at this conference.*
     b.   The ambassador made the claim *at this conference* **that world population has already outstripped the food supply.**
(37) a.   They consider the claim **that world population has already outstripped the food supply** *preposterous.*
     b.   They consider the claim *preposterous* **that world population has already outstripped the food supply.**
(38) a.   They consider the claim **that world population has already outstripped the food supply** *a proven fact.*
     b.   They consider the claim *a proven fact* **that world population has already outstripped the food supply.**
(39) a.   The ambassador made the claim **that world population has already outstripped the food supply** *yesterday at 5 P.M. at this conference before all the assembled delegates.*
     b.   The ambassador made the claim *yesterday at 5 P.M. at this conference before all the assembled delegates* **that world population has already outstripped the food supply.**

(2) shows Extraposition from NP operating across a VP.

## 3.4 Extraposition of PP

(40) a.  Sally told me that the paper will publish a review **of her new book** *soon*.

b.  Sally told me that the paper will publish a review *soon* **of her new book**.

(41) a.  Sally told me that the paper will publish a review **of her new book** *this week*.

b.  Sally told me that the paper will publish a review *this week* **of her new book**.

(42) a.  Sally told me that the paper will publish a review **of her new book** *in its Sunday edition*.

b.  Sally told me that the paper will publish a review *in its Sunday edition* **of her new book**.

(43) a.  Sally told me that the paper will publish a review **of her new book** *this week in its Sunday edition*.

b.  Sally told me that the paper will publish a review *this week in its Sunday edition* **of her new book**.

(3) shows Extraposition of PP moving a PP across a VP.

## 3.5 Extraposition of Comparative Clauses

(44) a.  The detectives discovered more clues **than had previously come to light** *last week*.

b.  The detectives discovered more clues *last week* **than had previously come to light**.

(45) a.  The detectives discovered more clues **than had previously come to light** *in their most recent investigations*.

b.  The detectives discovered more clues *in their most recent investigations* **than had previously come to light**.

(46) a.  They consider more evidence **than has been unearthed to date** *necessary to establish his guilt*.

b.  They consider more evidence *necessary to establish his guilt* **than has been unearthed to date**.

(47) a.  They found more evidence **than had previously come to light** *last week in their most recent investigations*.

b.  They found more evidence *last week in their most recent investigations* **than had previously come to light**.

(4) shows Extraposition of Comparative Clauses moving a comparative clause across a VP.

## 3.6 Heavy NP Shift

(48)  a.    They consider **anyone who so much as speaks to a member of the occupying army** *a traitor*.

b.    They consider *a traitor* **anyone who so much as speaks to a member of the occupying army**.

(49)  a.    They consider **anyone who dresses ostentatiously** *neurotic*.

b.    They consider *neurotic* **anyone who dresses ostentatiously**.

(50)  a.    I sent **the book that discusses the prehistoric migrations across the Bering Strait** *to your Aunt Hattie last Thursday by special delivery*.

b.    I sent *to your Aunt Hattie last Thursday by special delivery* **the book that discusses the prehistoric migrations across the Bering Strait**.

To see the difference between sentences derived by Heavy NP Shift and those derived by Extraposition of Relative Clauses, compare (48–49) with (33–34).


## 4. THE RIGHT ROOF CONSTRAINT

Now that it has been shown that the rightward movement rules under discussion must be formulated so as to move a constituent to the right *across a variable*, the question arises as to how generalization (8) is to be incorporated in the grammar. What will ensure that rightward movement rules do not move constituents outside their clauses?

It would be unsatisfactory to attempt to incorporate generalization (8) into the statement of the rightward movement rules themselves. To do that would be to repeat the same thing in the statement of each rule, missing the generalization that all rightward movement rules are clause-bounded. Further, one cannot account for the clause boundedness of rightward movement rules by making them cyclical. To be sure, if a rightward movement rule applies on the first cycle on which it is applicable, then moved constituent will be placed correctly in the sentence. Because the rightward movement rules under discussion are optional, however, it is possible for them not to apply on the first cycle on which they are applicable. Thus, on a later cycle, there is nothing to prevent them from moving a constituent too far to the right. For example, consider the structure

(51)

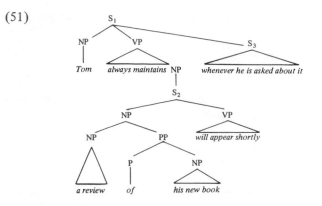

If Extraposition of PP does not apply to the structure

(52)

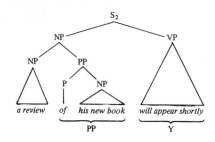

on the $S_2$-cycle, then there is nothing to prevent it from applying to the structure

(53)

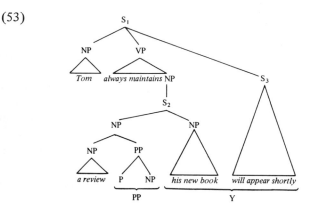

on the $S_1$-cycle. Thus, given the formulation of Extraposition of PP in (25), the ungrammatical sentence

(54) *\*Tom always maintains that a review will appear shortly whenever he is asked about it of his new book*

will be produced.

Note also that strict cylicity will not prevent *(54) from being generated. Strict cyclicity only prevents a rule from applying to a structure entirely contained in a lower S. Since the structure indicated in (53) is available only on the last cycle, strict cyclicity will not prevent Extraposition of PP from applying to it.

Consequently, it is necessary to incorporate generalization (8) in the grammar of English as an independent constraint. Having discovered the generalization, Ross (1967) stated the constraint in terms of the notion "command."[3]

### (55) **The Right Roof Constraint**

*In all rules whose structural description is of the form ... – A – Y, and whose structural change specifies that A is moved to the right across the variable Y, A can be moved across only those constituents that it commands in the structure that serves as input to the rule.*

Verify for yourself that the formulation in (55) has the desired effect.

---

[3] Our formulation of the Right Roof Constraint differs slightly from Ross's in ways that are not directly relevant here.

# 72

## *Islands, Command, and Maximal Strips*

### *1. ISLANDS*

One of the basic ideas in Ross (1967) is that there is a correlation between the behavior of three kinds of rules with respect to syntactic islands:

(1)   a.   *chopping rules*
       b.   *feature-changing rules*
       c.   *a subclass of deletion rules*

We will use Reflexivization to illustrate the feature-changing rules, and TOO-Deletion to illustrate the relevant subclass of deletion rules.[1]

The basic correlation can be seen in picture noun constructions, which do not act as islands with an indefinite article, but get progressively worse with the definite article, with a demonstrative, and with a possessive.[2] This is illustrated for Question Movement by the following sentences:

(2)   a.   ***Who*** *did you show Bob a picture of* _____ *?*
       b.   *?****Who*** *did you show Bob the picture of* _____ *?*
       c.   *??****Who*** *did you show Bob that picture of* _____ *?*
       d.   *\****Who*** *did you show Bob Sue's picture of* _____ *?*

---

[1] For a characterization of the relevant class of deletion rules and a better indication of what is meant by "feature-changing rules," see Ross (1967). For a discussion of TOO-Deletion, see SFI-8.

[2] See the discussion of this in section 70.

The same continuum of judgments is found with Reflexivization:

(3)   a.   *I showed Bob a picture of himself.*
       b.   *?I showed Bob the picture of himself.*
       c.   *??I showed Bob that picture of himself.*
       d.   *\*I showed Bob Sue's picture of himself.*

Now consider TOO-Deletion, the rule that derives (4b) from the structure that also underlies (4a).

(4)   a.   *This rock is too heavy for me to pick it up.*
       b.   *This rock is too heavy for me to pick _____ up.*

The same continuum of grammaticality judgements that is found with Question Movement and Reflexivization is also found with TOO-Deletion:

(5)   a.   *Sally is pretty enough to show Bob a picture of her.*
       b.   *Sally is pretty enough to show Bob a picture of _____ .*
(6)   a.   *Sally is pretty enough to show Bob the picture of her.*
       b.   *?Sally is pretty enough to show Bob the picture of _____ .*
(7)   a.   *Sally is pretty enough to show Bob that picture of her.*
       b.   *??Sally is pretty enough to show Bob that picture of _____ .*
(8)   a.   *Sally is pretty enough to show Bob Sue's picture of her.*
       b.   *\*Sally is pretty enough to show Bob Sue's picture of _____ .*

The (b)-sentences get progressively worse just as the sentences in (2) and (3) do. Ross's claim was that syntactic islands block the application of the three classes of rules in (1) in the same way.

## 2. A PRINCIPLE GOVERNING MOVEMENT RULES

Ross proposed a principle governing movement rules that has the following effect:

(9)   *A constituent that is moved across a variable can only be moved to a position in the output structure that commands its position in the input structure.*

This principle has two important consequences.

First, it assigns derived constituent structure in certain cases. For example, consider the structure[3]

---

[3] We are assuming here the existence of "Adv" nodes above *tonight* and *yesterday*, but the point that we wish to make does not depend on this assumption. The existence of such

(10)

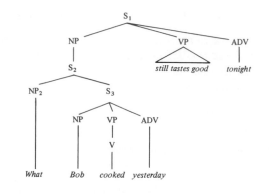

which underlies the sentence

(11)  *What Bob cooked yesterday still tastes good tonight.*

English has a rule of Adverb Preposing that preposes an adverb to initial position over a variable. The result of applying this rule to *tonight* in (10) is

(12)  *Tonight, what Bob cooked yesterday still tastes good.*

Now consider the derived constituent structure produced by Adverb Preposing in a case such as this. Is the preposed adverb immediately dominated by $S_1$, $NP_1$, $S_2$, or $NP_2$?

(13)

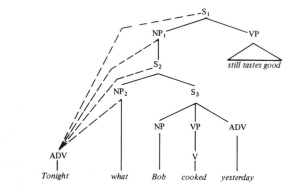

*Footnote 3 continued*

"Adv" nodes is controversial, since many adverbs are NPs or PPs and behave as such with respect to certain transformations. Elsewhere in this book, we have trees in which adverbs are dominated by *NP*- or *PP*-nodes.

In accordance with (9), (12) is assigned the derived constituent structure in (14).[4]

(14)

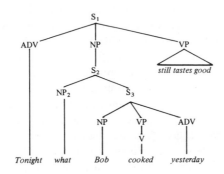

This makes the intuitively correct prediction that *tonight* is a constituent by itself, and that neither *tonight what* or *tonight what Bob cooked yesterday* is a constituent, as would be predicted by the other possible derived constituent structures in (13).

The second consequence of (9) is that it defines *maximal strips* for the operation of movement rules. We turn to this in §3.

### 3. MAXIMAL STRIPS

Consider the structure

(15)

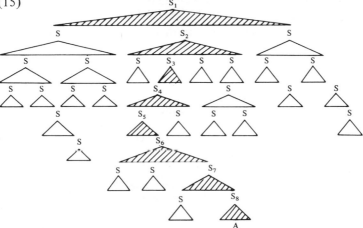

---

[4] (14) is not the only possible derived constituent structure for (12) that is consistent with (9); if *tonight* were immediately dominated by $NP_1$ in the output structure, (9) would

According to (9), a movement rule that moves constituent A across a variable can only move it to a position in the shaded portion of (15), since only these positions command the position occupied by A in the input to the rule. Thus, (9) defines a *maximal strip* for A in the tree; A cannot be moved off its maximal strip by a rule that moves it across a variable.[5]

Where A can move is restricted even further by the Right Roof Constraint. A rule that moves a constituent to the right across a variable will attach it to the first $S$-node above its position in the input tree. Thus, if A is moved to the right across a variable in (15), it will end up immediately dominated by $S_8$.

The notion of maximal strips also plays a role in defining the domain of operation of what Ross called "feature-changing" rules. These rules effect a change in one element under the influence of a "trigger" element. The relevant principle is that the triggering element must command the element undergoing change. Thus, if A in (15) undergoes a change as the result of a feature-changing rule, the trigger must be somewhere in the shaded strip. Maximal strips thus define the maximal domains of application not only for movement rules, but for feature-changing rules as well. An element A cannot be moved off its maximal strip, nor can any element that is not on this strip trigger a feature-changing rule that affects A.


## 4. MAXIMAL STRIPS AND ISLANDS

How do islands affect the maximal strip of rule application for an element A in a tree? If the maximal strip of A contains a structure that defines an island, then the maximal strip of A is *cut* into a smaller strip at that node. The resulting substrips define the maximum domain of application for rules of the relevant types.

*Footnote 4 continued*

not be violated either. Ross gives a principle whose intended effect is to rule out this possibility, leaving (14) as the only possible derived constituent structure in this case.

[5] Ross apparently assumed that no rule—whether it operates across a variable or not—can move a constituent off its maximal strip. While this may be correct, it does not follow from (9), which covers only rules that move a constituent across a variable. An obvious way to capture Ross's intention would be to reformulate (9) as follows:

    (i)    *A transformation can only move a constituent to a position in the output tree that commands its position in the input tree.*

(i) is not restricted to movement across a variable.

# 73

## *Part 7: Its Place in a Wider Context*

The point of departure for Ross's (1967) work·was the A-over-A Principle first proposed by Chomsky (1964). According to this principle, if the structural description of a transformation mentions an element A, and if a particular tree in which one A dominates another A satisfies the structural description in two different ways, then the transformation can apply only to the dominating A, not to the dominated one. Several versions of this principle have been proposed at one time or another. Part of Ross (1967) is devoted to arguments that linguistic theory should incorporate island constraints instead of the A-over-A Principle.

Ross's arguments are based on cases where island constraints and the A-over-A Principle make different empirical predictions. These include cases where a constituent of type A is inside a syntactic island dominated by a node B (where A≠B). Some such cases involve a VP or Adj inside a complex NP. Others involve an NP inside a coordinate VP, which is subject to the Coordinate Structure Constraint (cf. below). The clearest cases of these kinds involve chopping rules. Island constraints predict that the constituents in question cannot be chopped, while the A-over-A Principle predicts that they can, because these are not instances of A-over-A. Ross shows examples of this kind, where chopping is impossible, thus confirming the predictions of the island constraints in question. Ross also gives another type of argument against the A-over-A Principle, citing cases of what he calls *Pied Piping,* where there is a nested structure of one NP dominating another NP. He shows that either the dominated NP or the dominating one can be moved to the left under Relativization.

In addition to arguments against the A-over-A Principle and the topics included in this book, Ross (1967) deals with a host of other issues. We briefly mention some of them here.

## 1. THE COORDINATE STRUCTURE CONSTRAINT

This is another one of Ross's island constraints, proposed as a linguistic universal. The basic idea is that *coordinate structures,* such as those coordinated by means of the conjunctions *and, but,* and *or* in English, are islands. Thus, a chopping rule cannot move an entire conjunct or a constituent of a conjunct.

## 2. THE UNIVERSALITY OF THE CONSTRAINTS

Ross proposes that the basic island constraints—the Complex NP Constraint, the Sentential Subject Constraint, and the Coordinate Structure Constraint—are universal. However, he points out certain cases that cast doubt on the universality of the Sentential Subject Constraint. He also proposes some language-particular constraints. One of the areas of research stimulated by Ross's work has been the investigation of which of these constraints are universal and which are language-particular.

## 3. THE CLASS OF RULES THAT OBEY ISLAND CONSTRAINTS

Ross discusses in great detail the question of whether it is predictable which rules obey island constraints. Among movement rules, he distinguishes between chopping rules and copying rules, showing that the former obey island constraints and the latter do not. He discusses deletion rules in detail, showing that some obey island constraints and some do not, pointing out that those deletion rules that obey island constraints also obey constraints on Pronominalization, and concluding that unidirectional deletion rules obeying constraints on Pronominalization also obey island constraints. Ross also discusses so called "feature-changing rules," showing that they obey island constraints, but also pointing out examples of such rules that do not obey the Complex NP Constraint.

## 4. THE LEFT BRANCH CONDITION

The structure underlying *Whose book did you borrow?* cannot be realized as *\*Whose did you borrow book?* Ross calls the constraint operative here the "Left Branch Condition," which prevents movement of the possessive NP *whose* because it is on the left branch in the input structure to Question Movement. In later work, Ross abandoned the Left Branch Condition in favor of a condition preventing chopping of possessives, regardless of whether they are on a left branch or a right branch.

## 5. PRUNING

Ross proposed a condition for what he calls "tree-pruning," i.e., erasure of an *S*-node in a tree as the result of the operation of transformations. A somewhat different version of the pruning condition is proposed in Ross (1969a).

## 6. FURTHER READING

A short excerpt from Ross's thesis can be found in Harman (1974). For a summary of some of the main results of the thesis and further development of several points, see Ross (1974).

Work on constraints on movement since Ross's thesis has gone in a number of different directions. First, there has been work on the various particular constraints proposed by Ross. On the Complex NP Constraint, see Bolinger (1972) and Koutsoudas (1973). The Sentential Subject Constraint and alternative approaches to it are discussed by Kuno (1973), Grosu (1974b, 1974c, 1975) and Grosu and Thompson (1977). The Right Roof Constraint is discussed by Grosu (1973b). Kaufman (1974) and Kohrt (1975) argue that it cannot be universal. Akmajian (1975) extends the idea of bounding rightward movement to *NP*-nodes. Grosu (1973a) argues that Ross's Coordinate Structure Constraint cannot be a single phenomenon, showing cases where conjuncts behave differently from constituents of conjuncts. Grosu (1974a) discusses the Left Branch Condition, showing that possessives are "frozen" regardless of whether they are on a left branch or a right branch.

Second, a number of different proposals have been made to account for some or all of the data handled by Ross's constraints. These range from modifications or reformulations of Ross's constraints to totally different constraints based on different analyses of the relevant syntactic phenomena. They include Schwartz (1972), Perlmutter (1972), Chomsky (1973), Horn (1974), Bresnan (1975, 1977), Cattell (1976), Culicover and Wexler (1977), and Cole, Harbert, Sridhar, Hashimoto, Nelson, and Smietana (1977).

Third, various proposals have been made to account for some of Ross's data by nonsyntactic means. Grosu (1972) attempts to account for the data in terms of perceptual strategies. The discussion in Kimball (1973b) is also relevant. Erteschik (1973) develops the idea that the constraints are not syntactic but semantic, constructing a theory of "bridges" that make movement possible. Kuno (1975b, 1976) argues that the constraints on relativization follow from the requirement that a relative clause must be "about" the head.

# PART 8
## *Pronominalization*

In part 8 we investigate the phenomenon of pronominal anaphora. Sections 74-82 are concerned with the rise and fall of the first and one of the most important theories of anaphora developed by generative grammarians—the Pronominalization Hypothesis. The final section surveys the major alternatives to this hypothesis and discusses their significance for alternative programs of research and for the thesis that all aspects of meaning are represented in underlying structure.

# 74

# *Pronominalization*

## *1. PRONOUNS AND COREFERENCE*

### 1.1 The Basic Contrast

Theories of pronominal coreference in generative grammar have been motivated by the contrast between sentences like

(1)   a.   *Tom said that he was hungry.*
       b.   *Tom went out after he ate dinner.*
       c.   *Tom sold the car that Helen gave him.*

and

(2)   a.   *He said that Tom was hungry.*
       b.   *He went out after Tom ate dinner.*
       c.   *He sold the car that Helen gave Tom.*

The pronouns in (1) can be understood in two ways—one in which they are assumed to be coreferential with *Tom* and one in which they are not. The pronouns in (2) can only be understood as noncoreferential with *Tom*. When a pronoun is understood as coreferential with another NP in the sentence, it is called an *anaphoric* pronoun. When a pronoun cannot be understood in this way, it is called *nonanaphoric*.

### 1.2 Three Assumptions

In the section on Reflexivization in part 1, we posited

(3)   [$he_i$ washed $him_i$]

as the structure underlying

    (4)   *He washed himself.*

and

    (5)   [*he$_i$ washed him$_j$*]

as the structure underlying

    (6)   *He washed him.*

Under this analysis, pronouns are present in underlying structure, where they are marked for coreference or noncoreference.

    Given this analysis, one might propose to account for the contrast between (1) and (2) by deriving the sentences in (2) from the underlying structures

    (7)   a.    [*he$_i$ said that Tom$_j$ was hungry*]
            b.    [*he$_i$ went out after Tom$_j$ ate dinner*]
            c.    [*he$_i$ sold the car that Helen gave Tom$_j$*] [1]

and deriving sentences in (1) from both the underlying structures

    (8)   a.    [*Tom$_i$ said that he$_i$ was hungry*]
            b.    [*Tom$_i$ went out after he$_i$ ate dinner*]
            c.    [*Tom$_i$ sold the car that Helen gave him$_i$*]

and the underlying structures

    (9)   a.    [*Tom$_i$ said that he$_j$ was hungry*]
            b.    [*Tom$_i$ went out after he$_j$ ate dinner*]
            c.    [*Tom$_i$ sold the car that Helen gave him$_j$*]

More generally, one might propose a theory of pronominal coreference based on the following three assumptions:

*Assumption 1*

The meaning of a sentence, including coreference information, is represented in underlying structure.

*Assumption 2*

Pronouns occurring in surface structure are present in underlying structure. [2]

---

[1] For ease of exposition, underlying structures containing relative clauses will be represented in this discussion as having already undergone Relativization.

[2] Assumption 2 should be understood to allow for certain exceptions—e.g., the *it* inserted by Extraposition.

*Assumption 3*

The only mechanism accounting for pronominal coreference is one that marks pronouns for coreference or noncoreference in underlying structure.

## 1.3 An Incorrect Claim

It follows from Assumptions 1–3 that transformations neither introduce pronouns into structures nor affect the interpretation of pronouns that are already there. Thus, these assumptions give rise to the claim

(10) *A pronoun and another NP in a sentence are coreferential if and only if they are marked for coreference in underlying structure. The operation of transformations does not affect coreference relations.* [3]

The falsity of this claim can be seen by considering sentences involving Extraposition and Passive.

(11) a. *That Tom won the election surprised him.*
    b. *It surprised him that Tom won the election.*
(12) a. *The fact that Tom won the election surprised him.*
    b. *He was surprised by the fact that Tom won the election.*
(13) a. *He jilted the girl who Tom was supposed to marry.*
    b. *The girl who Tom was supposed to marry was jilted by him.*

In each case, the interpretation of a pronoun is affected by the operation of a transformation. In (11a) and (12a), *Tom* and *him* can be either coreferential or noncoreferential; in (11b) and (12b), they can only be noncoreferential. The situation is reversed in (13). *Tom* and *he* can only be noncoreferential in (13a), whereas both interpretations are possible in (13b). Since transformations can both create and destroy the environment for coreferential interpretations, (10) is false, and Assumptions 1–3 cannot be jointly maintained.

## 2. SYNTACTIC PRONOMINALIZATION

### 2.1 The Traditional Strategy for Handling Pronominal Anaphora

We have seen that one or more of Assumptions 1–3 must be rejected. We have also seen in parts 1 through 7 that there is evidence that meaning is

*Footnote 2 continued*
    We are also concerned here only with nonreflexive pronouns. In the rest of this discussion we will use the term *pronouns* to refer only to nonreflexives.
    [3] In formulating (10), we are implicitly restricting ourselves to cases in which both the pronoun and the NP appear in surface structure as well as underlying structure. For present purposes there is no reason to consider derivations in which deletion occurs.

represented in underlying structure. Because of such evidence and because Assumption 1 was a basic postulate guiding research in the early years of transformational grammar, generative grammarians tried to construct an account of pronominal anaphora compatible with it. Thus, they retained Assumption 1 and rejected Assumptions 2 and 3.

## 2.2  The Pronominalization Hypothesis

Rejecting Assumption 2 means that some pronouns appearing in surface structure are not present in underlying structure, but rather are produced by a transformation. Generative grammarians called this transformation *Pronominalization*. They adopted three assumptions about this rule.

*Assumption 4*

Pronominalization applies to structures containing two coreferential, identical, nonpronominal noun phrases. Applying it results in the substitution of a pronoun for one of the two noun phrases.

*Assumption 5*

Every pronoun that is coreferential with a full (nonpronominal) noun phrase in the same sentence is produced by Pronominalization.

*Assumption 6*

Pronouns that are not coreferential with a full noun phrase in the same sentence are present in underlying structure.

These assumptions, together with Assumption 1, are the core of the Pronominalization Hypothesis. Under this hypothesis (1a) can be derived from both the underlying structure

(14)

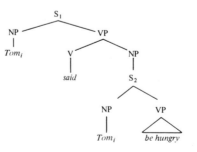

and the underlying structure

(15)

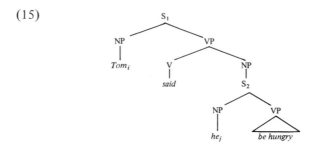

Pronominalization applies to (14), replacing *Tom* in S₂ (the *victim*) with *he* on the basis of coreference with *Tom* in S₁ (the *trigger*).

## 2.3 Precede and Command[4]

In each of the sentences in (1), the trigger precedes the victim. Cases like this are sometimes referred to as instances of *forward pronominalization*. When a sentence contains two identical, coreferential NPs (in different clauses), the first can pronominalize the second.[5] Thus, the pronouns in (16) can each be derived from full, coreferential NPs by Pronominalization.

(16) a. **Herbert** *is drunk and **he** will feel sick in the morning.*
    b. **Marcia** *and the man **she** is dating just met.*
    c. **Hartley** *is not as dumb as **he** looks.*
    d. *The woman who hired **Morton** will see **him** tomorrow.*
    e. *That **Karen** is unpopular is bound to bother **her**.*
    f. *I will give the money that **Horace** told me about to the woman who will hide it for **him**.*

(16) g. *The woman who told Martha to remind Sarah to expect **Bart** to be late hates **him**.*
    h. **Morris** *tried to remain calm after Kathy reminded Loretta that Shirley had told the police to arrest **him**.*

Not all cases of Pronominalization are instances of forward pronominalization. For example, the pronoun and NP can be coreferential in each of these sentences.

(17) a. *That **he** was unpopular didn't bother **Tom**.*
    b. *The woman who hired **him** will see **Morton** tomorrow.*
    c. *The fact that **she** went to Saint Mary's impressed **Susan's** boss.*

---

[4] The material in this section is based on Langacker (1969) and Ross (1969b).
[5] When two coreferential NPs are in the same clause, Reflexivization occurs.

d.   *The girl who loves **him** thinks that the woman who divorced*
     ***Larry** is a fool.*

e.   *The book that **she** is writing was commissioned by a publisher*
     *who thinks that **Charlotte** will be a big success.*

Examples like these are sometimes referred to as instances of *backward pro-nominalization*. Here again Pronominalization derives pronouns from full NPs.

Cases in which backward pronominalization is possible must be distinguished from cases like (18) in which it is not.[6]

(18) a.   ***He**ᵢ said that **Tom**ᵢ was hungry.*
     b.   ***He**ᵢ went out after **Tom**ᵢ ate dinner.*
     c.   ***He**ᵢ sold the car that Helen gave **Tom**ᵢ.*
     d.   **I will give **it**ᵢ to the girl who lost the **dog**ᵢ.*
     e.   ***Susan told **him**ᵢ that **Bill**ᵢ couldn't come to dinner.*

The fact that these pronouns and NPs cannot be coreferential shows that Pronominalization cannot be used to derive the sentences in (18) from the structures in (19).[7]

(19)  a.

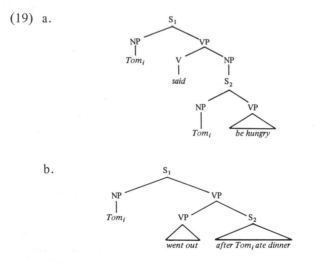

[6] The asterisks in (18) indicate that the underlined pronoun and NP cannot be coreferential.

[7] Backward Pronominalization does not occur in (19); rather Pronominalization applies forward producing

(i)  a.   *Tom said that **he** was hungry*
     b.   *Tom went out after **he** ate dinner*
     c.   *Tom sold the car that Helen gave to **him***
     d.   *I will give the **dog** to the girl who lost **it***
     e.   *Susan told **Bill** that **he** couldn't come to dinner.*

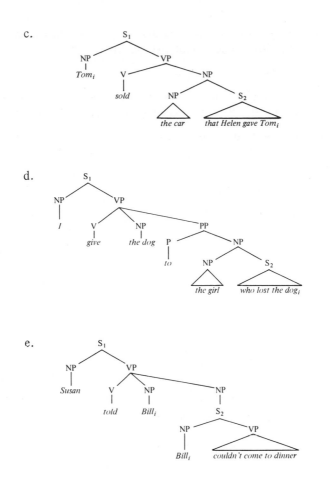

The difference between examples like (17), in which backward pronominalization is possible, and examples like (18), in which it is not, can be neatly described using Langacker's notion of *command*, introduced in *Primacy Relations* in part 5.

### Definition

A constituent A commands a constituent B if and only if every S-node that dominates A also dominates B.

In (18) the victim commands the trigger. In (17) it does not; either the trigger unilaterally commands the victim, as in (17a–c), or neither commands the other as in (17d–e). Thus, backward pronominalization is possible whenever the victim does not command the trigger.

Since forward pronominalization is always possible, this means that the rule of Pronominalization can be formulated roughly as follows:

*Pronominalization*

A nonpronominal NP[b] can be pronominalized under coreference with an identical NP[a] unless NP[b] both precedes and commands NP[a].[8]

This rule allows the trigger to pronominalize the victim in structures like

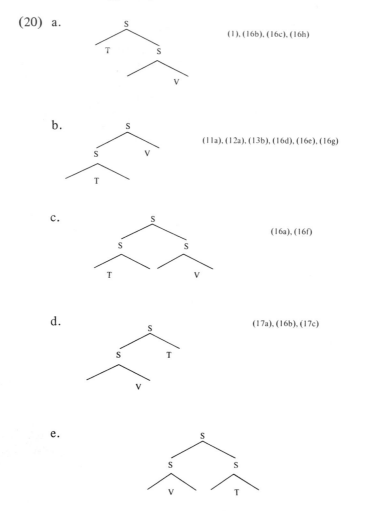

(20)  a.                                        (1), (16b), (16c), (16h)

     b.                                        (11a), (12a), (13b), (16d), (16e), (16g)

     c.                                        (16a), (16f)

     d.                                        (17a), (16b), (17c)

     e.

---

[8] To distinguish Pronominalization from Reflexivization, we assume that NP[a] and NP[b] are in different clauses.

f.

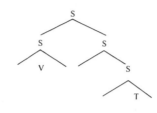

Pronominalization is not possible in:[9]

---

[9] The Pronominalization Rule stated in this section is somewhat too liberal. It would allow the derivation of

(i)   *$He_i$ is drunk and $Herbert_i$ will feel sick in the morning*

from the same structure that underlies (16a)—i.e.,

(ii)

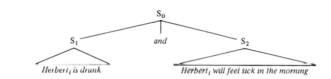

Forward pronominalization produces (16a) and is unproblematic. However, since *Herbert* in $S_1$ does not command *Herbert* in $S_2$, our Pronominalization rule should also allow backward pronominalization. The ungrammaticality of *(ii) shows that this must be prevented.

Examples like (17d) indicate that one cannot require the trigger to command the victim in order for backward pronominalization to work. Thus, it appears that conjoined structures like (ii) require us to complicate the Pronominalization Rule presented in the text. Langacker (1969) notes this and, at one place, formulates Pronominalization as follows:

(iii) *Pronominalization*

A nonpronominal $NP^b$ can be pronominalized under coreference with an identical $NP^a$ unless

(i)   *$NP^b$ precedes $NP^a$; and*
(ii)  *either (a) $NP^b$ commands $NP^a$, or*
      *(b) $NP^b$ and $NP^a$ are elements of separate conjoined structures.*

Langacker goes on to argue that since an element in one conjoined sentence can never command an element in another, the notion of command is irrelevant to the relationship between such elements. In these cases, the only relevant primacy relation (section 56) is precedence. This leads him to restate Pronominalization a final time as follows:

(iv) *Pronominalization*

A nonpronominal $NP^b$ can be pronominalized under coreference with an identical $NP^a$ unless $NP^b$ bears all relevant primacy relations to $NP^a$.

(21)

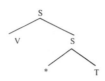

## 2.4 Obligatory Pronominalization

Most generative grammarians assumed that Pronominalization was obligatory. Under this analysis, Pronominalization must apply to

(22)

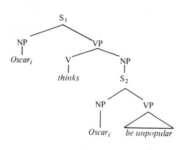

producing

(23)  ***Oscar thinks that he is unpopular.***

This means that (24) cannot be derived.

(24) **Oscar<sub>i</sub> thinks that Oscar<sub>i</sub> is unpopular.**

and that

(25)  ***Oscar thinks that Oscar is unpopular.***

can be derived only from

---

*Footnote 9 continued*

In order to simplify our discussion in part 8, we will continue to use the precede and command conditions incorporated into the Pronominalization Rule given in the text. When considering conjoined sentences, the student is asked to bear in mind that these conditions are somewhat oversimplified and can be modified along the lines suggested here.

(26)

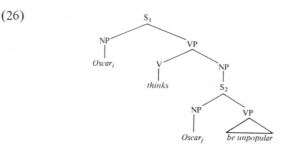

Thus, the analysis predicts that the two occurrences of *Oscar* in (25) can only be understood to be noncoreferential. If the coreferential interpretation is desired, one must use (23).

Although Pronominalization was assumed to be obligatory, it was recognized that some structures provide an option as to how it can apply. For example, Pronominalization can apply either forward or backward to (27).[10]

(27)

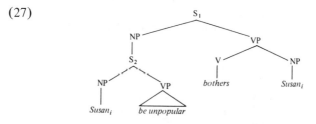

(28)  a.    *That **Susan** is unpopular bothers **her**.*
      b.    *That **she** is unpopular bothers **Susan**.*

Since Pronominalization must apply to (27), this analysis predicts that

(29) *\*That Susan$_i$ is unpopular bothers Susan$_i$.*

cannot be derived.

---

[10] Although Pronominalization can apply either forward or backward to (27), it cannot apply both ways simultaneously, producing

  (i)    *That **she** is unpopular bothers **her**.*

Since the pronouns in (i) are not coreferential with a full NP in the same sentence, Assumption 6 of the Pronominalization Hypothesis dictates that both pronouns are present in underlying structure. Thus, (i) can be derived from both

  (ii)    [*that she$_i$ is unpopular bothers her$_i$*]

and

  (iii)    [*that she$_i$ is unpopular bothers her$_j$*]

## 3. PRONOMINALIZATION, PASSIVE AND EXTRAPOSITION

In §1 we cited three pairs of sentences that undermined the theory of pronominal anaphora based on Assumptions 1-3.

(11)  a.    *That Tom won the election surprised him.*
      b.    *It surprised him that Tom won the election.*

(12)  a.    *The fact that Tom won the election surprised him.*
      b.    *He was surprised by the fact that Tom won the election.*

(13)  a.    *He jilted the girl who Tom was supposed to marry.*
      b.    *The girl who Tom was supposed to marry was jilted by him.*

We will now show how the Pronominalization Hypothesis accounts for this data. The noncoreferential interpretation of these sentences is unproblematic. What must be explained is why *Tom* and *he/him* can be coreferential in (11a), (12a), and (13b), but not in (11b), (12b), and (13a).

First consider (11) and (12). The structures underlying (11a) and (12a) are

(30)

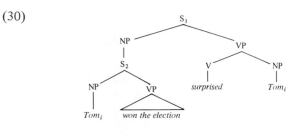

and

(31)

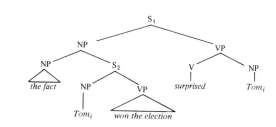

Since the trigger precedes the victim, Pronominalization can apply to these structures, producing (11a) and (12a). Suppose, however, that Extraposition applies to (30), and Passive applies to (31).

(32)

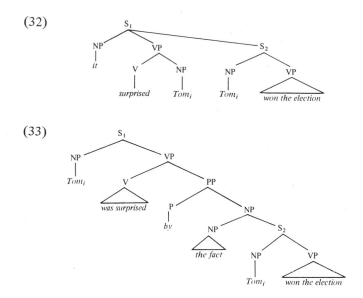

(33)

Since *Tom* in $S_1$ both precedes and commands *Tom* in $S_2$, Pronominalization cannot apply backward, and

(34) *\*It surprised him$_i$ that Tom$_i$ won the election.*

and

(35) *\*He$_i$ was surprised by the fact that Tom$_i$ won the election.*

cannot be derived.[11] Thus, *Tom* and *he/him* in (11b) and (12b) can only be understood to be noncoreferential.

Next consider (13). The structure underlying (13b), on the coreferential interpretation, is

(36)

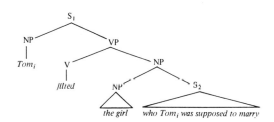

---

[11] Pronominalization can only apply forward to (32) and (33), producing

(i) *It surprised **Tom** that **he** won the election*

and

(ii) ***Tom** was surprised by the fact that **he** won the election.*

Since the occurrence of *Tom* in $S_1$ both precedes and commands the occurrence of *Tom* in $S_2$, backward Pronominalization cannot take place. Thus, (13a) cannot be derived from (36) and *he* and *Tom* cannot be coreferential. However, if Passive applies, producing

(37)

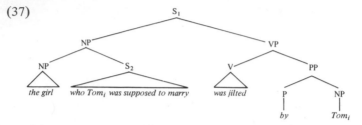

then *Tom* in $S_2$ can pronominalize *Tom* in $S_1$, and (13b) can be derived.

It should be noted that this explanation of (11–13) presupposes that Pronominalization is able to apply after Passive and Extraposition, and, crucially, that the grammar contains some mechanism preventing these rules from applying in the opposite order. Without such a mechanism (11b–12b) could be derived from (11a–12a). We will not be concerned here with the various mechanisms posited by generative grammarians to prevent this from happening.

# 75

# *A Pronominalization Problem*[1]

## *1. ASSUMPTIONS*

*Assumption 1*

Pronouns that are anaphoric with full NPs in the same sentence are produced by Pronominalization. This rule is capable of pronominalizing an $NP^b$ under coreference with a nonpronominal $NP^a$ unless $NP^b$ both precedes and commands $NP^a$.

*Assumption 2*

Pronominalization is obligatory.

*Assumption 3*

Equi deletes the subjects of a variety of embedded clauses.

> (1)   *Joe wants to play the piano.*
> (2)   *Joe likes hunting wombats.*
> (3)   *Hunting wombats amuses Joe.*

## *2. THE PROBLEM*

There are apparent counterexamples to Assumption 1—e.g.,

(4)   *\*Realizing that Tom$_i$ was unpopular didn't brother him$_i$.*

[1] This problem is based on Ross (1969b).

Our formulation of Pronominalization has the consequence that forward pronominalization is always possible. Nevertheless, *Tom* and *him* cannot be coreferential in *(4). Note, however, that *he* and *Tom* can be coreferential in

(5)    *Realizing that he$_i$ was unpopular didn't bother Tom$_i$.*

Is there a non-ad hoc way of accounting for *(4) and (5) without modifying
Assumptions 1–3?

# 76

# *Dative Movement and Pronominalization*

## *1. THE PHENOMENON*

English contains pairs of sentences like

(1)  a.    *Marie gave the watch to Tom.*
     b.    *Marie gave Tom the watch.*

If the direct object is a pronoun, the (b) sentence is ungrammatical.

(2)  a.    *Marie gave it to Tom.*
     b.    *\*Marie gave Tom it.*

## *2. ASSUMPTIONS*

*Assumption 1*

(1b) is derived from the structure underlying (1a) by a rule called *Dative Movement.*

*Assumption 2*

The ungrammaticality of sentences like \*(2b) is accounted for by a constraint preventing Dative Movement from applying if the direct object is a pronoun.

*Assumption 3*

Dative Movement is cyclical.

*Assumption 4*

Pronouns that are coreferential with a full NP in the same sentence are
produced by the rule of Pronominalization discussed in section 74.

*Assumption 5*

Pronouns that do not have an antecedent in the same sentence are present
in underlying structures. (This is the case in [2].)

*Assumption 6*

Every rule is either cyclical or postcyclical.


# 3. EXERCISE

Give an argument in support of Assumption 3. (Take Assumption 1 as
given.)


# 4. THE PROBLEM

Construct an argument showing that Assumptions 1-6 cannot all be
correct.

# 77

# *Particle Movement and Pronominalization*

## *1. THE PHENOMENON*

English has pairs of sentences like

(1)   a.    *Mark called up his cousin.*
       b.    *Mark called his cousin up.*

If the object is a pronoun, the (a) sentence is ungrammatical.

(2)   a.    *\*Mark called up her.*
       b.    *Mark called her up.*

## *2. ASSUMPTIONS*

*Assumption 1*

(1b) is derived from the structure underlying (1a) by an optional rule of Particle Movement.

*Assumption 2*

The ungrammaticality of sentences like (1a) is accounted for by making Particle Movement obligatory when the direct object is a pronoun.

*Assumption 3*

Particle Movement is cyclical.

*Assumption 4*

Pronouns that are coreferential with a full NP in the same sentence are produced by the rule of Pronominalization discussed in section 74.

*Assumption 5*

Pronouns that are not coreferential with a full NP in the same sentence are present in underlying structures. (This is the case in [2].)

*Assumption 6*

Every rule is either cyclical or postcyclical.

*Assumption 7*

All cyclical rules obey the principle of Strict Cyclicity.


### 3. THE PROBLEM

Construct an argument showing that Assumptions 1–7 cannot all be correct.

# 78

## *Particle Movement, Dative Movement, and Pronouns*

### *1. OVERVIEW*

The previous two sections were designed to show that combining the Pronominalization Hypothesis with seemingly plausible assumptions about Dative Movement and Particle Movement produces unacceptable results. Given these results, one has two choices: to reject the Pronominalization Hypothesis or to reject some of the assumptions about Particle Movement and Dative Movement. In this section we show that certain crucial assumptions about these rules must be rejected on independent grounds. As a result, the Pronominalization Hypothesis need not be given up on the basis of the material in sections 76 and 77.

### *2. ASSUMPTIONS AND DATA*

*Assumption 1*

English has an optional rule of Particle Movement which derives sentences like

    (1)   *Susan called Bill up.*

and

    (2)   *Harriet handed the paper in.*

from the structures underlying

    (3)   *Susan called up Bill.*

and

    (4)   *Harriet handed in the paper.*

Particle Movement moves postverbal particles like *up* and *in* around an immediately following an NP—e.g., the direct objects *Bill* and *the paper* in (1) and (2).

*Assumption 2*

English has an optional rule of Dative Movement which derives sentences like

    (5)   *Martin gave Harriet the watch.*

and

    (6)   *Larry sent the congressman a letter.*

from the structures underlying

    (7)   *Martin gave the watch to Harriet.*

and

    (8)   *Larry sent a letter to the congressman.*

In deriving (5) and (6), Dative Movement deletes *to* and interchanges the direct and indirect objects.

*Data*

    (9)  a.    *The boss gave it to John.*
          b.   **The boss gave John it.*
   (10)  a.   **They called up her.*
          b.   *They called her up.*

*Assumption 3*

The correct way to account for (9) and (10) is to adopt the following two constraints:

   (11) *Dative Movement cannot apply if the direct object is a pronoun. (Assumption 2 of section 76)*
   (12) *Particle Movement is obligatory if the direct object is a pronoun. (Assumption 2 of section 77)*

## 3. EXERCISE

Show that Assumption 3 cannot account for the grammaticality of

(13)  *John was given it by the boss.*

Do this before proceeding further.

## 4. THE SIGNIFICANCE OF SENTENCE (13)

Sentence (13) is derived from the underlying structure

(14)  [*the boss gave it to John*]

by applying Dative Movement followed by Passive. Since Dative Movement applies to (14) even though the direct object is pronominal, constraint (11) cannot be correct.

The grammaticality of (13) shows that examples like *(9b) cannot be accounted for by preventing Dative Movement from applying when the direct object is pronominal. This suggests that Dative Movement is free to apply to (14) and that the grammar contains an output constraint marking structures like *(9b) as ill-formed.

## 5. THE CONSTRAINT

*(9b) and *(10a) have something in common. In both cases a pronominal object is separated from the verb by some other constituent—an NP in *(9b), and a particle in *(10a). In (13), on the other hand, the pronominal object immediately follows the verb, and the sentence is grammatical.

In many languages, pronouns have what is known as a *strong form*, which is used under contrast or emphasis, and a *weak* or *clitic form*, which is used otherwise. The clitic form is attached to the verb and forms a single phonological unit with it. In such languages, clitic pronouns cannot be separated from the verb, and typically must appear in a fixed order when there is more than one. The data in (9), (10), and (13) suggests that English is one of these languages.

Positing that pronominal objects in English are clitics on the verb accounts for three kinds of data. First, it accounts for the fact that pronominal objects, when not under emphasis or contrast, are pronounced together with a verb as a single phonological unit. For example, in (10b), *called her* is pronounced [kaldɹ̩], with *her* realized only as a syllabic /r/. Second, the clitic hypothesis accounts for the ungrammaticality of *(9b) and *(10a) and the grammaticality of (13). Third, the clitic hypothesis accounts for the fact that when pronominal objects bear extra stress under contrast, they can be separated from their verbs.

(15)  *They called up her, not him.*
(16)  *The commissioner gave our team him, not them.*

When bearing extra stress, pronominal objects are not clitics and do not fall under the constraint requiring clitics to be attached to the verb. Thus, the pronominal objects in (9) and (10) are clitics whereas those in (15) and (16) are not.

Unlike (11) and (12), which were conditions on transformations, the constraint requiring clitic pronouns to be phonologically attached to the verb allows rules to apply freely. Those surface structures that violate the constraint are characterized as ungrammatical. Comparing this constraint with Assumption 3, we see that it both accounts for (13) and succeeds in bringing (9) and (10) under a single generalization. We therefore opt for it instead of (11) and (12).[1]

## 6. *NONINTERVENTION AND PRONOMINALIZATION*

### 6.1  Particle Movement and Pronominalization Revisited

Under the Pronominalization Hypothesis,

(17)  *Susan$_i$ hopes that Harry will call her$_i$ up.*

is derived from

(18)

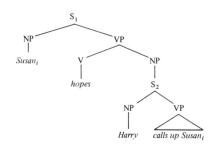

by applying Particle Movement and Pronominalization. In section 77 we assumed that Particle Movement is cyclical and that the ungrammaticality of sentences like *(10a) is accounted for by constraint (12), which makes Particle

---

[1] The idea of accounting for examples like *(9b) and *(10a) by a surface structure constraint is due to Ross (1967). For more specific proposals regarding clitics and surface structure constraints, see Perlmutter (1971).

Movement obligatory when the direct object is a pronoun. Given these assumptions, one has no way of blocking

(19) *\*Susan$_i$ hopes that Harry will call up her$_i$.*

which would be derived by optionally allowing Particle Movement not to apply to (18) on $S_2$ and then doing forward pronominalization on $S_1$. (Strict Cyclicity keeps Particle Movement from applying after *Susan* has been replaced by a pronoun.)

Examples like this show that the assumptions in section 77 cannot all be correct. However, if constraint (12) is replaced by the clitic hypothesis, then the remaining assumptions involving Pronominalization and Particle Movement can be retained. Particle Movement can be allowed not to apply, and Pronominalization can replace *Susan* in $S_2$ with a pronoun. Since the resulting surface structure violates the constraint requiring clitics to be phonologically attached to the verb, *(19) will be correctly characterized as ungrammatical. Thus, examples like this can be handled without abandoning any of the assumptions that make up the Pronominalization Hypothesis.

## 6.2 Dative Movement and Pronominalization Revisited

An argument analogous to the one just given can be constructed regarding the interaction of Pronominalization and Dative Movement. Given the assumptions listed in section 76, one has no way of preventing

(20) *Susan prepared **the report**$_i$, and the boss gave John **it**$_i$.*

from being derived from

(21)

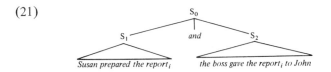

However, if constraint (11) is replaced by the requirement on clitics, then *(20) can be accounted for without giving up the remaining assumptions about Dative Movement and Pronominalization.

# 79

## *Pronominalization and THERE-Insertion*[1]

### *1. THE PHENOMENON*

Some pronouns are anaphoric with nonpronominal, indefinite NPs in the same sentence. For example, in

(1)    *A woman in the back of the room* is passing out leaflets that *she* made up for this meeting

*she* is anaphoric with the indefinite NP; this is not the case in

(2)    *She* is passing out leaflets that *a woman in the back of the room* made up for this meeting.

### *2. ASSUMPTIONS*

*Assumption 1*

THERE-Insertion applies only with indefinite NPs. It does not apply with pronouns or other definite NPs.

(3)    a.    *A woman in the back of the room is handing out leaflets.*

b.    *There is a woman in the back of the room handing out leaflets.*

---

[1] This problem is based on work by Joan Bresnan.

(4) a. *The woman in the back of the room is handing out leaflets.*

 b. *\*There is the woman in the back of the room handing out leaflets.*

(5) a. *She is handing out leaflets.*

 b. *\*There is she handing out leaflets.*

*Assumption 2*

Nonpronominal, indefinite NPs that are anaphoric with other *NP*s in the same sentence can undergo THERE-Insertion.

(6) *There is **a woman in the back of the room** handing out leaflets that **she** made up for this meeting.*

*Assumption 3*

THERE-Insertion is cyclical.

*Assumption 4*

Pronominalization is cyclical.

## 3. TWO CONFLICTING HYPOTHESES

*Hypothesis A*

Pronouns that are anaphoric with indefinite NPs in the same sentence are produced by Pronominalization. This rule derives (1) from the underlying structure

(7) [*a woman in the back of the room$_i$ is passing out leaflets that a woman in the back of the room$_i$ made up for this meeting*]

*Hypothesis B*

Pronouns that are anaphoric with indefinite NPs are present in underlying structure. Thus, the pronoun that appears on the surface in (1) also occurs in underlying structure. The question of how such pronouns get marked anaphoric with indefinite NPs is left open.

## 4. THE PROBLEM

Use the phenomenon together with Assumptions 1–4 to construct an argument in favor of Hypothesis B over Hypothesis A.

# 80

## Question Movement and Pronominalization[1]

### 1. THE PHENOMENON

Question Movement can move entire NPs along with question words to sentence-initial position.

(1)   *Which of the men that you described did Walter criticize?*

### 2. PROBLEM 1

*Assumption 1*

Pronouns that are anaphoric with a full NP in the same sentence are produced by Pronominalization. This rule can pronominalize a non-pronominal $NP^b$ under coreference with another nonpronominal $NP^a$ unless $NP^b$ both precedes and commands $NP^a$.

*Assumption 2*

Pronominalization is cyclical.

*Assumption 3*

Question Movement is postcyclical.

Use the above phenomenon to show that Assumptions 1–3 cannot all be correct.

---

[1] This problem is based on a discussion in Postal (1971).

### 3. PROBLEM 2

It might be thought that the conflict between Question Movement and Pronominalization could be resolved simply by rejecting Assumption 3 and postulating that Question Movement is cyclical. Show that this is not so by demonstrating that Assumptions 1, 2, 4, and 5 cannot all be correct.

*Assumption 4*

Pronominalization is obligatory.

*Assumption 5*

Question Movement preposes question phrases to sentence-initial position in a single movement.

# 81

## *Problems with Pronominalization*

### *1. BACKGROUND*

In section 74 we explained the Pronominalization Hypothesis and showed that it was motivated essentially by an assumption and an observation.

*The Assumption*

Meaning, including coreference information, is represented in underlying structure.

*The Observation*

Coreference possibilities between pronouns and full NPs are determined in derived rather than underlying structure.

By positing a pronominalization transformation incorporating the precede and command conditions discussed in section 74, generative grammarians tried to construct a theory that was compatible both with their basic assumptions about meaning and with their empriical observations about pronouns in English. In this section we will examine several difficulties with this theory. In section 83 we will sketch a number of alternatives to it.

### *2. QUESTION MOVEMENT, THERE-INSERTION AND PRONOMINALIZATION*

The results of sections 79 and 80 pose problems for the Pronominalization Hypothesis. In section 75 you saw that in order to account for sentences like

(1)  *\*Realizing that Tom$_i$ was unpopular didn't bother him$_i$.*

and

(2)  *\*The fact that he$_i$ isn't bothered by the possibility that that Tom$_i$ will lose surprises him$_i$.*

Pronominalization must be both cyclical and obligatory. However, sections 79 and 80 contradict this conclusion. If, as we have argued, Question Movement operates in a single movement, then making Pronominalization both cyclical and obligatory prevents us from deriving the grammatical

(3)  *Which of the men that Mary$_i$ saw did you say she$_i$ criticized?*

In addition, if

(4)  **A woman in the back of the room$_i$ made up leaflets, and she$_i$ is passing them out.**

is derived from

(5)  **A woman in the back of the room$_i$ made up leaflets, and a woman in the back of the room$_i$ is passing them out.**

then cyclical Pronominalization allows the derivation of the ungrammatical[1]

(6)  **\*A woman in the back of the room$_i$ made up leaflets, and there is she$_i$ passing them out.**

Thus, the Pronominalization Hypothesis leads to a paradox. On one hand it seems that Pronominalization must be both cyclical and obligatory. On the other, it seems that it cannot be both.

## 3. MARKING COREFERENCE IN UNDERLYING STRUCTURE: A DIFFICULTY

In addition to problems involving the interaction of Pronominalization with other rules, there are also other difficulties with the Pronominalization Hypothesis. One such difficulty involves the mechanism for marking coreference.

Under the Pronominalization Hypothesis, full noun phrases are marked for coreference or noncoreference in underlying structure. Sentences like

(6)  *He thinks that he will win.*

---

[1] The argument involving THERE-Insertion is compatible with but not dependent upon the assumption that Pronominalization is cyclical.

show that it must also be possible to mark pronouns coreferential or noncoreferential with other pronouns. Since the pronouns in (6) can be understood to be either coreferential or noncoreferential, the Pronominalization Hypothesis must derive (6) from both

(7)   *[he$_i$ thinks that he$_i$ will win]*

and

(8)   *[he$_i$ thinks that he$_j$ will win]* .

Thus, the Pronominalization Hypothesis must posit a mechanism that

(a)   *marks full NPs coreferential or noncoreferential in underlying structure;*

and

(b)   *marks pronouns coreferential or noncoreferential in underlying structure.*

It is important to notice that any mechanism capable of accomplishing (a–b) will also be able to

(c)   *mark pronouns coreferential or noncoreferential with full NPs in underlying structure*

unless some additional constraint is imposed to prevent this. Without such a constraint, the Pronominalization transformation would be superfluous because:

(i)   *Every sentence derivable by Pronominalization would also be derivable from an underlying structure in which a pronoun is marked coreferential with a full NP.*[2]

(ii)  *The sentences that the precede and command conditions on Pronominalization are designed to block would be derivable from underlying structures in which pronouns are marked coreferential with full NPs.*

Point (ii) can be illustrated by considering structures (11–13).

(11)

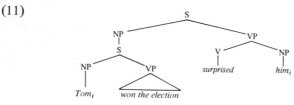

---

[2] Lasnik (1976) calls attention to this point.

(12)

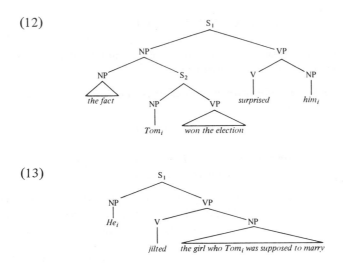

(13)

If there is no constraint preventing pronouns from being marked coreferential with full NPs in underlying structure, then (11–13) will be generated as underlying structures. But then all the problems that the precede and command conditions on Pronominalization were designed to avoid will be back with us. For example, applying Extraposition to (11) will produce

(14) *It surprised him*$_i$ *that Tom*$_i$ *won the election;*

applying Passive to (12) will produce

(15) *He*$_i$ *was surprised by the fact that Tom*$_i$ *won the election;*

and failing to apply Passive to (13) will produce

(16) *He*$_i$ *jilted the girl who Tom*$_i$ *was supposed to marry.*

To avoid these undesirable consequences, the Pronominalization Hypothesis must not allow (11–13) to be generated as underlying structures with *Tom* and *he/him* marked coreferential. Thus, a special constraint is required preventing pronouns from being marked coreferential with full NPs in underlying structure. Since the Pronominalization Hypothesis allows (a and b), the required constraint is an ad hoc device for which there is no independent motivation. The need for such a device detracts significantly from the explanatory value of the Pronominalization Hypothesis.[3]

---

[3] For other problems with the Pronominalization Hypothesis, see the Appendix to this section.

## 4. INTRACTABLE DATA

Finally, there is a class of data that simply cannot be handled by the Pronominalization Hypothesis in it present form.

(17) a.  *Each of the women thinks that she is the most qualified candidate.*

b.  *Most people feel sure that they are more intelligent than the average person.*

c.  *All of the children bathed before they ate dinner.*

d.  *Only the man in front is justified in thinking that he will win.*

Each of these sentences has a reading in which the pronoun is anaphoric with the preceding full noun phrase.[4] Nevertheless, these pronouns cannot be derived from NPs identical with their antecedents in accordance with the Pronominalization Hypothesis.

(18) a.  *Each of the women thinks that each of the women is the most qualified candidate.*

b.  *Most people feel sure that most people are more intelligent that the average person.*

c.  *All of the children bathed before all of the children ate dinner.*

d.  *Only the man in front is justified in thinking that the man in front will win.*

Since the sentences in (17) differ in meaning from those in (18), the former cannot be derived from the structures underlying the latter without giving up the assumption that meaning, including coreference, is represented in underlying structure. Thus, we must abandon either our central assumption about meaning, or our assumption that all pronouns that are anaphoric with full NPs are derived from full NPs by the Pronominalization transformation. Each alternative seriously weakens the Pronominalization Hypothesis.

---

[4] Each of these sentences is ambiguous between anaphoric and nonanaphoric interpretations. For example, if the pronoun in (17a) is understood nonanaphorically, then what is asserted is that some one woman (whose identity must be inferred from the context) is believed by each of the women to be the most qualified candidate. However, if the pronoun is understood anaphorically, what is asserted is that each woman regards herself as the most qualified.

The situation with (17d) is analogous to that of (17a), though it is a bit trickier. The anaphoric interpretation that is problematic for the Pronominalization Hypothesis is one in which what is asserted is (roughly) that the only person who has reason to be confident of winning is the man in front.

## 5. SUMMARY

In this section we have discussed three difficulties with the Pronominalization Hypothesis. First, we showed that the interaction of Pronominalization with other rules leads to an apparent paradox: on one hand, it appears that Pronominalization must be both cyclical and obligatory; on the other, it appears that it cannot be both. Second, we saw that in order to account for the very cases that motivated it, the Pronominalization Hypothesis must posit an ad hoc device that is not independently justified. Last, we indicated that there is an important class of data that the Pronominalization Hypothesis cannot handle.

Difficulties such as these have led many generative grammarians to look for alternative accounts of pronominal anaphora. Several of these accounts will be outlined in section 83. However, before turning to these accounts, we will discuss a phenomenon (in section 82) which, more than any other, led generative grammarians to look for alternatives to the Pronominalization Hypothesis.

# Appendix to Problems with Pronominalization

## 1. IDENTITY: ANOTHER THEORY-INTERNAL PROBLEM

In §3 of Section 81 we saw that the Pronominalization Hypothesis is forced to posit an ad hoc constraint preventing pronouns from being marked coreferential with full NPs in underlying structure. Another problem with this hypothesis is illustrated by the underlying structures

(1)   [*the tall man$_i$ ate a sandwich before the tall man$_i$ went to bed*]

(2)   [*Tom$_i$ ate a sandwich before Tom$_i$ went to bed*]

(3)   [*Tom$_i$ ate a sandwich before the tall man$_i$ went to bed*]

In each case, the subject of *ate* is marked coreferential with the subject of *went*. (Since the Pronominalization Hypothesis allows full NPs to be marked coreferential, there is nothing to prevent (1-3) from being generated as underlying structures.) Application of the Pronominalization transformation to (1) and (2) produces

(4)   *The tall man ate a sandwich before he went to bed*

and

(5)   *Tom ate a sandwich before he went to bed.*

However, if Pronominalization applies to (3), then (5) will also be derived from a structure that does not represent its meaning. Since (3), but not (5), contains the information that the man who went to bed is tall, the Pronominalization Hypothesis must not allow Pronominalization to derive (5) from (3).

For this reason, it has often been suggested that there is an *identity condition* on Pronominalization requiring the victim to be not only coreferential with the trigger, but also word-for-word identical to it. Since *the tall man* is not identical to *Tom,* this condition ensures that Pronominalization cannot apply to (3).

However, this is not enough. Although the identity condition prevents (5) from being derived from (3), it does not prevent

(6)    *Tom ate a sandwich before the tall man went to bed.*

from being derived from (3). Since (6) does not have a reading in which *Tom* and *the tall man* are coreferential, deriving (6) from (3) violates the assumption that coreference information is represented in underlying structure.

## 2. AN INADEQUATE PROPOSAL

It might be thought that this problem can be handled by imposing an identity constraint on underlying structures rather than the Pronominalization transformation.

### The Underlying Identity Constraint

Only noun phrases that are word-for-word identical can be marked coreferential in underlying structure.

Under this constraint, (3) would not be a possible underlying structure. Thus, the problem of preventing (5) and (6) from being derived from (3) would not arise. In addition, this constraint could be used to handle the problem discussed in §3 of Section 81. Since pronouns are not identical with full NPs, they could not be marked coreferential with such NPs in underlying structure.

Although the Underlying Identity Constraint seems to be an attractive means of handling some of the problems with the Pronominalization Hypothesis, there are counterexamples to it.

(7)    *When Sam entered the room, everyone scowled at the bastard.*

Since *Sam* and *the bastard* can be understood to be coreferential, the assumption that coreference information is represented in underlying structure requires that they be marked coreferential in underlying structure. This falsifies the Underlying Identity Constraint.

## 3. A NOTE ON EPITHETS

(8)   a.    That **Sam**$_i$ *humiliated the little girl didn't bother* **the bastard**$_i$.
      b.    *\*It didn't bother* **the bastard**$_i$ *that* **Sam**$_i$ *humiliated the little girl.*
(9)   a.    That **Sam**$_i$ *humiliated the little girl didn't bothe* **him**$_i$.
      b.    *\*It didn't bother* **him**$_i$ *that* **Sam**$_i$ *humiliated the little girl.*

Examples like these show that transformations that alter precede and command relations affect the possible coreference relationships between full NPs and epithets (like *the bastard*) in much the same way that they affect coreference relationships between full NPs and pronouns. Since the contrast between (8a) and *\*(8b) cannot be accounted for by the Pronominalization transformation, the Pronominalization Hypothesis cannot provide a unitary explanation of (8) and (9).[1]

## 4. THE SIGNIFICANCE OF THESE DIFFICULTIES

The Pronominalization Hypothesis was designed to account for the contrast between cases in which a pronoun can be coreferential with a full NP and cases in which it cannot. To account for this contrast, a mechanism was posited for marking coreference and noncoreference relations in underlying structure. However, such a mechanism gives rise to as many problems as it handles:

(i)    *The problem of preventing pronouns from being marked coreferential with full NPs in underlying structure*
(ii)   *The identity problem*
(iii)  *The problem of giving a unified account of sentences like (8) and (9).*

These problems, together with the other difficulties discussed in *Problems with Pronominalization*, cast serious doubt on the validity of the Pronominalization Hypothesis.

---

[1] Jackendoff (1972) makes this point. G. Lakoff (1968) also contains a discussion of epithets.

# 82

## *Paradox Lost*

### 1. BACKGROUND

One commonly speaks of a paradox when assumptions whose truth seems to be beyond question are shown to lead to an unacceptable or contradictory result. The assumptions that make up the Pronominalization Hypothesis had this status for most generative grammarians in the 1960s. In the late 1960s, an argument was produced which purported to show that these assumptions led to an unacceptable result and hence that the Pronominalization Hypothesis had to be given up. It is a testimony to the widespread acceptance of the hypothesis at the time that this argument was standardly referred to as a "paradox."

The discovery of the "paradox" had an electrifying effect on the study of pronominal anaphora. It was almost universally taken as showing that there is no Pronominalization transformation that replaces full NPs with pronouns. Given this negative result, theorists started looking for alternative accounts (which we will discuss in section 83). Later, a few linguists pointed out that the negative lesson drawn from the pronominalization "paradox" was far from conclusive. However, by this time the damage had been done; the Pronominalization Hypothesis had fallen into nearly universal disrepute.

Whether genuine or not, the pronominalization "paradox" changed the study of pronominal anaphora in a way unmatched by any other single argument. In this section we will present the "paradox," show why it is inconclusive, and discuss some subsequent research involving the data on which it was based.

### 2. THE "PARADOX"

#### 2.1 An Informal Statement of the Argument[1]

Under the Pronominalization Hypothesis, the Pronominalization transfor-

---

[1] The argument below is an informal statement of the Bach-Peters Paradox given in Bach (1970).

mation replaces a full NP with a pronoun under coreference and (word-for-word) identity with the trigger. Thus, a sentence like

(1)    *The man that I met yesterday$_i$ said that he$_i$ was tired*

is derived by Pronominalization from the underlying structure

(2)    [*the man that I met yesterday$_i$ said that the man that I met yester-day$_i$ was tired*]

The crucial point is that since the pronoun *he* in (1) is coreferential with the entire NP-plus-relative-clause structure (*the man that I met yesterday*), it must be derived from an identical NP-plus-relative-clause structure.

Now consider sentences (3) and (4).

(3)    *The pilot who shot it$_j$ down$_i$ misidentified the plane that he$_i$ fired on$_j$.*
(4)    *I gave the man who wanted it$_{ij}$ to the book that he$_j$ asked for$_i$.*

Each of these sentences contains two pronouns that are coreferential with full NPs. In (3), *it* is coreferential with *the plane that he fired on,* and *he* is coreferential with *the pilot who shot it down.* In (4), *it* is coreferential with *the book that he asked for* and *he* is coreferential with *the man who wanted it.*

Under the Pronominalization Hypothesis neither of these sentences can be derived. (Since the argument is the same in both cases, we will concentrate only on [3].) The hypothesis requires *it* in (3) to be derived from

(5)    *The plane that he fired on*

and *he* to be derived from

(6)    *The pilot who shot it down.*

Thus, the structure immediately underlying (3) must be

(7)

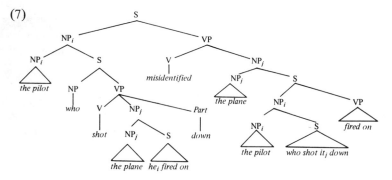

[*the pilot who shot the plane that* he*ᵢ fired on down*ᵢ misidentified *the plane that the pilot who shot* it*ⱼ down fired on*ⱼ]

(this structure is the result of replacing *it* and *he* in [3] with [5] and [6] respectively.)

But this structure still contains two pronouns that are coreferential with full NPs. The Pronominalization Hypothesis requires *he* in (7) to be derived from

(8)    *The pilot who shot the plane that he fired on down*

and *it* to be derived from

(9)    *The plane that the pilot who shot it down fired on.*

Thus, the structure immediately underlying (7) must be

(10)

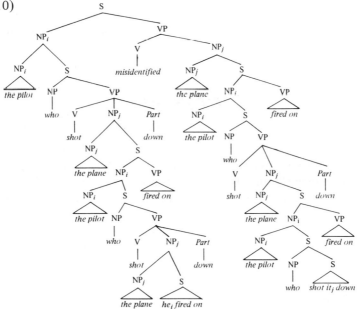

[*the pilot who shot the plane that the pilot who shot the plane that* he*ᵢ fired on down fired on down*ᵢ *misidentified the plane that the pilot who shot the plane that the pilot who shot* it*ⱼ down fired on down fired on*ⱼ]

(This structure is the result of replacing *he* and *it* in [7] with [8] and [9] respectively)

Here again we have a structure that contains two pronouns coreferential with full NPs. What's more, these pronouns cannot be eliminated. Under the Pronominalization Hypothesis, (10) must be derived from a still larger underlying structure containing the same two pronouns—and so on to infinity. Thus, the Pronominalization Hypothesis leads to the conclusion that (3) does not have any finite underlying structure. However, this conclusion cannot be correct. Since all underlying structures must be finite, the Pronominalization Hypothesis is incapable of deriving (3) and hence must be rejected.

### 2.2 The Argument Made Explicit

The assumption that leads to the erroneous conclusion that (3) does not have a finite underlying structure is

*Assumption A*

Whenever a pronoun is coreferential with an NP-plus-relative-clause structure, it is derived (only) from an identical NP-plus-relative-clause structure.

Examples like (3) and (4) show that this assumption is false.

## 3. PARADOX LOST

### 3.1 A Question

The informal presentation of the "paradox" in §2.1 was supposed to show that the Pronominalization Hypothesis is incorrect. However, when the argument was made explicit in §2.2, we pointed out that what the "paradox" demonstrates is that Assumption A is false. But Assumption A does not say anything about the Pronominalization Hypothesis. So why should the fact that it is false lead one to conclude that the Pronominalization Hypothesis is incorrect?

### 3.2 Pronominalization and Identity

### 3.2.1 The Motivation of Assumption A

In §2.1 we motivated Assumption A by claiming that since the Pronominalization transformation requires (word-for-word) identity in order to operate, the pronoun *he* in

(1)    **The man that I met yesterday$_i$ said that he$_i$ was tired**

is derived from the NP-plus-relative-clause structure

(11)  *The man that I met yesterday*

Taking this as a paradigmatic case, one might suppose that Assumption A is a consequence of Assumptions B and C.

*Assumption B*

All anaphoric pronouns are produced by the Pronominalization transformation.

*Assumption C*

The Pronominalization transformation requires (word-for-word) identity in order to operate.

If Assumption A really were a consequence of these assumptions, then the falsity of A would show that B and C could not both be correct, and hence that the Pronominalization Hypothesis must be rejected.

However, A is not a consequence of B and C. In what follows we will show why it isn't. Our explanation will show why one who rejects Assumption A need not also reject the Pronominalization Hypothesis.

### 3.2.2 Underlying Structures for (3)

First consider the underlying structure[2]

(12)

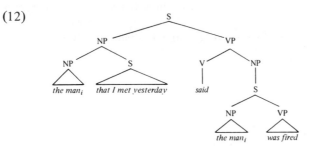

The head of the relative clause must be marked for coreference in order to allow Relativization to operate.[3] Since NPs are generated with referential indices, there is nothing to prevent the subject of the complement from being marked coreferential with the head of the relative clause. Thus, under the Pronominalization Hypothesis, (12) is a well-formed underlying structure.

---

[2] This is the structure after Relativization has applied.
[3] See section 66.

Note that (1) can be derived from (12) in accordance with Assumptions B and C by letting the head of the relative clause pronominalize the subject of the complement. Since the head of the relative clause has the same referent as the entire NP-plus-relative-clause structure, it follows that the resulting pronoun will have the same referent as the entire NP-plus-relative-clause structure. Consequently, the derivation of (1) from (12) violates Assumption A. The fact that it violates A, but not B and C, shows that Assumption A is not a consequence of B and C.

Similar derivations can be provided for sentence (3). Consider the following underlying structure.[4]

(13)

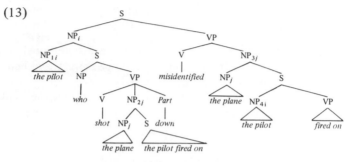

In this structure $NP_3$ is identical with $NP_2$, and $NP_1$ is identical with $NP_4$. As a result, $NP_3$ can pronominalize $NP_2$, and $NP_1$ can pronominalize $NP_4$, producing (3). Consequently, Assumptions B and C allow (3) to be derived from a finite underlying structure.

Other underlying structures from which (3) can be derived are:

(14)

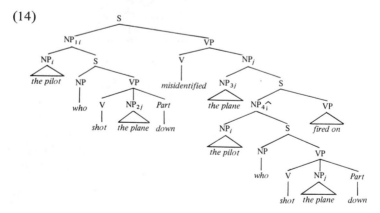

[4] This is the structure after Relativization and Particle Movement have applied. For simplicity, the underlying structures in this section will all be represented in this way. The

(15)

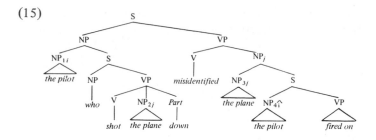

In both of these cases, $NP_1$ pronominalizes $NP_4$, and $NP_3$ pronominalizes $NP_2$.[5]

### 3.2.3 Pronouns Within Relative Clauses

#### 3.2.3.1 An Independent Argument that Assumption A Does Not Follow from Assumptions B and C

In our presentation of the "paradox" in §2, we implicitly used Assumption A to conclude that since the pronoun in

(8)    *The pilot who shot the plane that* he$_i$ *fired on down*$_i$

has the same referent as the entire NP-plus-relative-clause structure which contains it, (8) must be derived from

(16)    *The pilot who shot the plane that the pilot who shot the plane that* he$_i$ *fired on down fired on down*$_i$

Since this process can be repeated indefinitely, we concluded that (3) cannot have any finite underlying source.

Now consider a simpler example.

(17)    *The man who thinks that* he$_i$ *will be elected*$_i$ *is conceited.*[6]

Here the pronoun *he* has the same referent as the entire NP-plus-relative-clause structure that contains it. Thus, it is a consequence of Assumption A that (17) has no finite underlying structure.

---

*Footnote 4 continued*

*i*'s and *j*'s in trees like (13) are referential indices. The numbers 1, 2, 3, . . . are heuristic devices that allow us to refer to various NPs.

[5] The argument in this subsection is based in part on Karttunen (1971).

[6] Jacobson (1977) calls attention to sentences like these.

Assumptions B and C do not have this consequence. Under the Pronominalization Hypothesis, the structure underlying (17) is

(18)

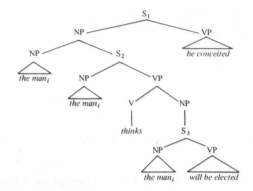

(17) is derived from (18) by pronominalizing the subject of $S_3$ and relativizing the subject of $S_2$.[7] The fact that Assumptions B and C allow (17) to be derived from (18), whereas Assumption A does not, constitutes an independent argument that A does not follow from B and C.


### 3.2.3.2 The Significance of Examples like (17)

Examples like (17) clearly illustrate the confusion inherent in our informal presentation of the "paradox" in §2.1. The assumption that is needed to make the argument go through is Assumption A. If this is not clearly realized, however, the argument based on examples like (3) and (4) is likely to be interpreted not as an argument against Assumption A, but rather as an argument against Assumptions B and C, which are central to the Pronominalization Hypothesis. Once it is realized that A is the crucial assumption, it is easy to see that it can be falsified by means of simple examples like (17), and that it is unnecessary to resort to complicated sentences like (3) and (4). Since (17) can be derived by Pronominalization, the falsity of Assumption A does not tell us anything about the Pronominalization Hypothesis.


[7] For purposes, it is irrelevant whether the subject of $S_2$ or the head of the relative clause triggers Pronominalization.

### 3.2.4 Another Underlying Structure for (3)

So far the only derivations we have provided for (3) are ones in which the *head*, rather than the entire head plus relative clause, triggers Pronominalization outside the clause ([13], [14], and [15]). We will now show that even if such Pronominalization were prohibited,[8] it would still be possible to derive (3).

Consider the underlying structure:

(19)

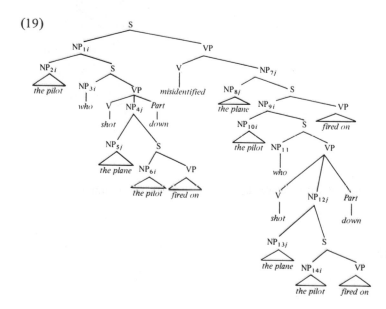

First, $NP_6$ and $NP_{14}$ are pronominalized. These instances of pronominalization are exactly analogous to the instance of pronominalization discussed in (17) and (18). For our purposes, it does not matter whether $NP_6$ and $NP_{14}$ are pronominalized by the heads of their respective relative clauses (i.e., by $NP_2 \, NP_{10}$) or whether they are pronominalized by $NP_3$ and $NP_{11}$ before these NPs are turned into relative pronouns.[9] Either way, the resulting structure is:

---

[8] Some proponents of the paradox did assume (rightly or wrongly) that such pronominalization was impossible.

[9] Prior to being turned into relative pronouns, these NPs are both occurrences of *the pilot*. The pronominalization of $NP_6$ and $NP_{14}$ in (19) parallels the pronominalization of the subject of $S_3$ in (18) discussed in footnote 7.

(20)

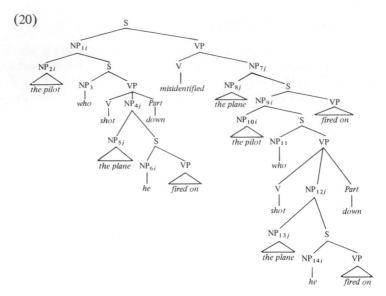

Next, the full NP-plus-relative clause-structure NP$_1$ pronominalizes NP$_9$, producing

(21)

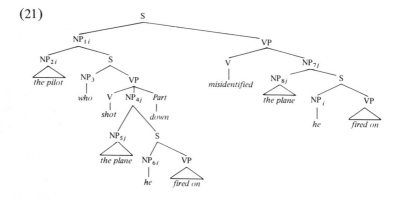

Finally, NP$_7$ pronominalizes NP$_4$, producing (3).

(3)    *The pilot who shot it down misidentified the plane he fired on.*

Since (3) can be derived in accordance with the Pronominalization Hypothesis, the "paradox" dissolves.

### 3.2.5 Summary

(i)    *Assumption A leads to the conclusion that sentences like (3) and (4) do not have finite underlying structures.*

(ii)   *Since this conclusion is incorrect, Assumption A is false.*

(iii)  *Assumption A is not a consequence of the Pronominalization Hypothesis (in particular it is not a consequence of Assumptions B and C). Thus, the falsity of A does not show that the Pronominalization Hypothesis is false.*

(iv)  *The Pronominalization Hypothesis allows sentences like (3) to be derived from a variety of finite underlying structures.*

(v)   *Once the asumptions that constitute the Pronominalization Hypothesis are distinguished from Assumption A, the "paradox" dissolves.*

## 4. A FINAL IRONY: TOO MANY UNDERLYING STRUCTURES?

Sentences like (3) were originally used to argue that the Pronominalization Hypothesis must be rejected because it does not provide such sentences with finite underlying structures. Having realized that this argument does not go through, some linguists have turned the tables by arguing that the Pronominalization Hypothesis must be rejected because it provides *too many* (finite) underlying structures for (3).

We have already seen that the Pronominalization Hypothesis allows (3) to be derived from (13), (14), (15), and (19). These are not the only underlying structures that it can be derived from. For example, a derivation exactly analogous to the one from (19) can be constructed from[10]

---

[10] In the derivation of (3) from (22)

(i)    $NP_9$ and $NP_{15}$ *are pronominalized (either by $NP_5$ and $NP_{11}$ or by the NPs that become relative pronouns as a result of Relativization on $NP_4$ and $NP_{10}$. Although these latter NPs are not graphically represented in (22), they would be present in a complete representation).*

(ii)   $NP_{10}$ *pronominalizes* $NP_4$.

(iii)  $NP_1$, *which by this time is **the pilot who shot it down**, pronominalizes $NP_{12}$ (remember that $NP_{15}$ has already become it).*

(22)

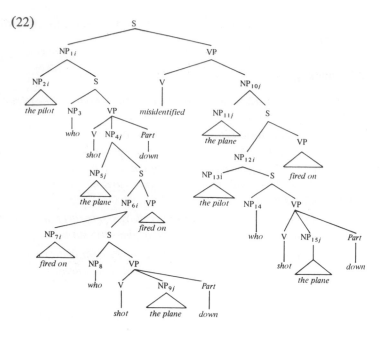

Now note the relationship between (13) and (19) and between (14) and (22). (19) can be constructed from (13) by substituting a copy of the entire subject expression for NP$_4$ in (13). (22) can be constructed from (14) by substituting a copy of the entire object expression for NP$_2$ in (14). Several linguists[11] have pointed out that this process can be repeated indefinitely so as to yield infinitely many underlying structures from which (3) can be derived.[12]

This result has been used to argue that if the following principle about meaning and underlying structure is adopted, then the Pronominalization Hypothesis will incorrectly predict that (3) is infinitely ambiguous:[13]

*Principle 1*

Each different underlying structure represents a different meaning.

However, it is important to distinguish Principle 1 from Principle 2.

[11] Fauconnier (1971), Wasow (1972), Jacobson (1977).
[12] For example, by substituting a copy of the entire object in (19) for NP$_4$ we get the structure

*Principle 2*

Each different meaning is represented by a different underlying structure.

Principle 2 is just another way of stating the assumption that meaning is represented in underlying structure. Thus, it is part of the Pronominalization Hypothesis. Principle 1 is not.[14] Since a proponent of Pronominalization need not accept Principle 1, the fact the Pronominalization Hypothesis allows (3) to be derived from an infinite number of underlying structures does not show that it incorrectly predicts (3) to be infinitely ambiguous.[15]

This does not mean that no problems remain. The issue of what (3) means and whether its meanings are correctly represented by the structures provided by the Pronominalization Hypothesis has not been resolved. As a result, the full import of sentences like (3) and (4) has yet to be determined.

*Footnote 12 continued*

(i)

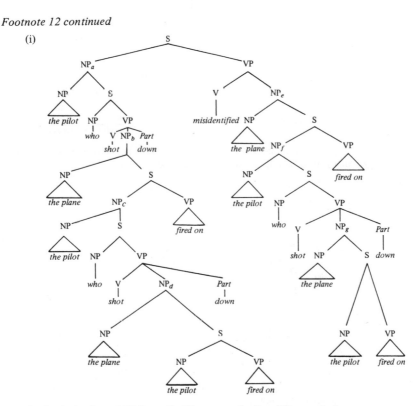

In the derivation of (3) from (i), $NP_f$ pronominalizes $NP_c$, producing

*Footnotes continued*

(ii)

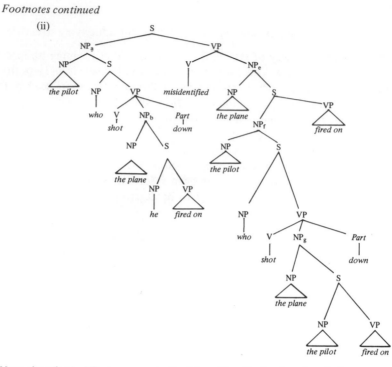

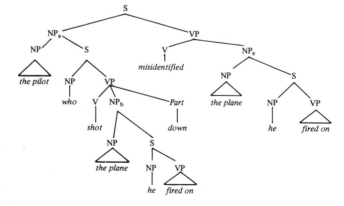

Next *the pilot* in NP$_g$ is pronominalized by either the head or the relative pronoun of NP$_f$. Since NP$_f$ is now identical to NP$_a$, it can be pronominalized, producing

(iii)

Finally, NP$_e$ pronominalizes NP$_b$, and (3) is derived.

   Exactly the same thing can be done by substituting a copy of the entire subject expression for NP$_{12}$ in (22).

*Footnotes continued*

[13] Wasow (1972) makes this point.

[14] See Meaning and Underlying Structure, SFI-1, for a discussion that is relevant to the distinction between Principles 1 and 2. Note especially §2.

[15] Jacobson (1977) has argued that the infinite number of underlying structures that the Pronominalization Hypothesis provides for (3) can be seen to represent no more than five distinct meanings.

# 83

## *New Perspectives on Meaning, Coreference, and Pronominal Anaphora*

### *1. OVERVIEW*

Difficulties with the Pronominalization Hypothesis like those discussed in sections 81 and 82 have led generative grammarians to search for new accounts of pronominal anaphora. Although several such accounts have been constructed, none has been universally accepted. Consequently, there is presently much controversy in the study of pronominal reference. In this section we will discuss the areas in which general agreement has been reached, the areas in which disagreement remains, and the major theoretical alternatives that have been developed. We will close by indicating the significance of issues involving anaphora for other rules and competing programs of research.

### *2. THE DATA: THE BASIC CONTRAST*

All theorists agree that the basic task of a theory of pronominal anaphora is to account for the contrast between sentences like those in (1) and those in (2).

(1)    a.   *Herbert bought a car before he left town.*
           b.   *The woman who hired Morton will see him tomorrow.*
           c.   *That she won the contest surprised Janet.*
           d.   *The man who loves her hinks that the guy who divorced Gracie is a fool.*
           e.   *Most people think that they are exceptional.*
           f.   *Each of the boys changed clothes before he came to dinner.*

(2)  a.  *He bought a car before **Herbert** left town.*
     b.  *Susan told **him** that **Bill** couldn't come to dinner.*
     c.  ***They** think that **most people** are exceptional.*
     d.  *He changed clothes before **each of the boys** came to dinner.*

Everyone agrees that the anaphoric possibilities in these two groups of sentences are different and that whether or not a pronoun can be understood as anaphoric or nonanaphoric with a full NP depends on the precede and command relations that hold between the two. These conditions are precisely analogous to those that were incorporated into the Pronominalization transformation. Since all theories posit essentially the same conditions, the difference between them involves the specific rules that the precede and command conditions are incorporated into.[1]

## 3. COMPETING THEORIES

### 3.1 Theories in which Anaphoric (or Nonanaphoric) Relations Are Assigned in Derived Structure

#### 3.1.1 The Main Idea

There are two major theories in which anaphoric and/or nonanaphoric relations are assigned in derived structures. According to both, all pronouns that appear in surface structure also occur in underlying structure.[2] However, anaphoric/nonanaphoric relations are not stated there. According to one theory, there are rules that assign coreference and distinct reference. According to the other, there is only a rule for assigning distinct reference. Thus, both theories abandon the assumption that information about reference is represented in underlying structure.[3]

---

[1] In footnote 9, section 74, we discussed a complication of the standard precede and command conditions necessitated by conjoined sentences. As before, we will ignore this complication here. The student who is interested in incorporating it into the theories presented in this section should consult footnote 9, Langacker's 1969 discussion, and the references of the individual theories given in §3 below.

[2] All pronouns that appear in surface structure are present in underlying structure except those that are introduced by rules like Extraposition, Left Dislocation, etc.

[3] Both theories are designed primarily to cover cases of pronominal anaphora that can be analyzed in terms of coreference and/or distinct reference—e.g., (1a–d) and (2a–b). Examples of pronominal anaphora involving quantified NPs like those in (1e–f) and (2c–d) have received less attention by these theorists. We will ignore such examples in presenting their theories.

### 3.1.2  Theory 1:  Rules for Coreference and Distinct Reference[4]

One major theory posits the following rules:[5]

(3)   *Coreference Assignment*

*Mark $NP_1$ and $NP_2$ coreferential if $NP_2$ is a pronoun that does not precede and command $NP_1$:*[6]

*(optional)*

(4)   *Distinct Reference Assignment*

*If $NP_1$ and $NP_2$ have not been marked coreferential, then mark them as referring to different things.*
*(obligatory)*

The operation of these rules can be illustrated by showing how they apply to the following underlying structure.

(5)

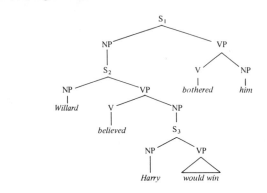

Referential information is represented in *tables of coreference* that arise from the operation of rules (3) and (4). If Coreference Assignment operates

---

[4] This theory is essentially that of Jackendoff (1972).

[5] In order to distinguish nonreflexive from reflexive pronominal anaphora, we will use examples in which $NP_1$ and $NP_2$ are in different clauses. We will not be concerned with how reflexive pronouns are marked in these theories. See Jackendoff (1972) for a discussion of a reflexivization rule designed to account for the grammaticality of examples like

(i) *Bill saw himself*

and the ungrammaticality of examples like

(ii) *\*Bill$_i$ saw him$_i$*

[6] To account for the impossibility of marking a pronoun and full NP coreferential in conjoined structures of the form

between *Harry* and *him*, followed by Distinct Reference Assignment, then

(6)   *That Willard believed that Harry would win bothered him*

will be generated with the following table of coreference.

(7)   **Willard and him** *have different referents.*
**Harry and him** *are coreferential.*
**Willard and Harry** *have different referents.*

Other tables of coreference for (6) that can be produced by rules (3) and (4) are:[7]

(8)   **Willard and him**  *are coreferential.*
**Harry and him** *have different referents.*
**Willard and Harry** *have different referents.*

and

(9)   **Willard and him** *have different referents.*
**Harry and him** *have different referents.*
**Willard and Harry** *have different referents.*

If, on the other hand, Extraposition applies to (5) on the $S_1$-cycle, then

*Footnote 6 continued*

(i)

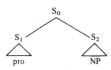

see the modification of the precede and command conditions proposed in footnote 9, section 74.

[7] In addition to (7), (8), and (9), there is nothing to prevent rules (3) and (4) from producing the following bizarre table of coreference:

(i) **Willard and him** *are coreferential.*
**Harry and him** *are coreferential.*
**Willard and Harry** *have different referents.*

Theorists who have posited (3) and (4) agree that these rules can produce (i). However, they also posit a *consistency condition,* which specifies that tables of conference like (i) are ill-formed. This condition uses the fact that coreference is a relation that is both symmetrical (if X is coreferential with Y, then Y is coreferential with X) and transitive (if X is coreferential with Y, and Y is coreferential with Z, then X is coreferential with Z). Since (i) violates these conditions, any derivation resulting in it is rejected by the grammar. See Jackendoff (1972) for further discussion of the consistency condition.

(10)

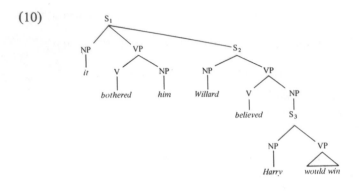

will be produced. Since the pronoun *him* both precedes and commands *Willard* and *Harry*, Coreference Assignment cannot apply. As a result the only table of coreference that can be produced for

(11)  *It bothered him that Willard believed that Harry would win*

is (9).

Examples like this show that Coreference Assignment must be prevented from applying to $S_1$ in (5) before Extraposition. (Otherwise the same tables of coreference produced for (6) would be produced for (11).) There are two main alternatives for preventing this. One is to make Coreference Assignment post-cyclical. The other is to make it a cyclical rule that applies *at the end of each cycle*. Since Extraposition is cyclical, either alternative ensures that it cannot follow Coreference Assignment on $S_1$.[8]

Sentences like those discussed in *Pronominalization and Question Movement* show that if Coreference Assignment is cyclical, then Question Movement must also be cyclical, and Distinct Reference Assignment must be postcyclical. The structure underlying

(12)  *Which of the men that Mary saw did you say she criticized?*

is (after Relativization)

---

[8] Jackendoff (1972) argues that Coreference Assignment is cyclical (applying at the end of each cycle).

(13)

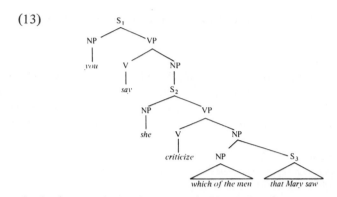

Since *she* both precedes and commands *Mary*, Coreference Assignment cannot apply on $S_2$. If Distinct Reference Assignment were cyclical, then it would obligatorily apply on the $S_2$-cycle, marking *she* and *Mary* as differing in reference. Application of Question Movement to $S_1$ would produce (12). However, since *she* and *Mary* had already been marked as having different referents, the grammar would incorrectly predict that (12) has only a nonanaphoric reading.

If, on the other hand, Distinct Reference Assignment is postcyclical, then it cannot apply at the end of the $S_2$-cycle. Making Question Movement cyclical allows (cyclical) Coreference Assignment to apply after the question phrase has been preposed, producing (14).

(14)

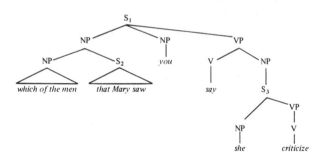

Since *she* no longer precedes and commands *Mary*, Coreference Assignment can mark them coreferential.

The same result could be achieved by making Question Movement, Coreference Assignment, and Distinct Reference Assignment postcyclical. We will not try to decide here between these alternative accounts of (12).[9]

---

[9] With Distinct Reference Assignment postcyclical, one might wonder how proponents of Theory 1 handle the data that originally led to the hypothesis of cyclic Pronominalization. First consider

### 3.1.3 Theory 2: A New Way of Characterizing the Data[10]

#### 3.1.3.1 No Ambiguities

Theory 1 and the Pronominalization Hypothesis differ in the mechanisms posited for handling pronominal anaphora. However, they agree on how the data is to be characterized. For example, both hold that the sentences in (1) are ambiguous between a reading in which the pronoun in anaphoric (coreferential)

*Footnote 9 continued*

   (i) *\*The fact that he$_i$ isn't bothered by the possibility that Tom$_i$ will lose surprises him$_i$. (§4 in the discussion of section 75)*

The conditions for Coreference Assignment are met by *he-him* and *Tom-him*. Since it is optional, the rule may either apply to these pairs or not, If it doesn't, then *(i) won't be derived. If it does, then the following table of coreference will be produced:

   (ii) *he is coreferential with **him**.*
        ***Tom** is coreferential with **him**.*

Although this might seem tantamount to deriving *(i), it isn't. The derivation is not over until *he* and *Tom* have been paired in the table of coreference. Since *he* precedes and commands *Tom,* they can't be marked coreferential. Thus, Distinct Reference Assignment obligatorily applies and we end up with

   (iii) *he and **Tom** have different referents.*
        *he is coreferential with **him**.*
        ***Tom** is coreferential with **him**.*

This table violates the consistency condition discussed in footnote 7. Thus, the derivation is rejected and *(i) is blocked by Theory 1.
    Next consider

   (iv) *\*Realizing that Tom$_i$ was unpopular didn't bother him$_i$. (§§1–3 in the discussion of section 75)*

Under the analysis we have been assuming up to now, the subject of *realizing* is deleted by Equi on the S$_1$-cycle. Since *Tom* and *he* satisfy the conditions for Coreference Assignment, it would seem that optional application of the rule would derive *(iv).
    Proponents of Theory 1 avoid this result by adopting a new analysis in which Equi is an "interpretive" rather than a deletion rule. According to this analysis, the structure underlying *(iv) is

   (v) *[Δ realizing that Tom was unpopular didn't bother him]*

Δ is a syntactic element that is phonologically null. Since it isn't pronounced, Δ doesn't have to be deleted. Rather, it is marked coreferential with **him** by interpretive Equi.

    *(iv) is then treated like *(i). Interpretive Equi marks Δ and *him* coreferential. Coreference Assignment optionally marks *Tom* and *him* coreferential, Distinct Reference Assignment obligatorily marks Δ and *Tom* distinct in reference, and the consistency condition is invoked. Thus, proponents of Theory 1 claim to be able to account for *(i) and *(iv). See Jackendoff (1972).
    [10] This theory is essentially that of Lasnik (1976).

with the underlined NP and one in which the pronoun and NP are nonanaphoric. The view that sentences like this are ambiguous is one that we have adopted up to now in characterizing data involving pronominal reference.

Theory 2 challenges this view by presenting a new way in which sentences involving pronominal anaphora can be conceived. First consider a sentence in which the pronoun has no antecedent.

(15)  *He is smart.*

What this sentence is used to assert depends on the situation in which it is uttered. In a situation in which it can be inferred that *he* refers to Mike, (15) can be used to assert that Mike is smart; in different situations it can be used to assert that Bill is smart, Jack is smart, and so on. There has been general agreement that sentences like this are not ambiguous; the *meaning* of the sentence simply does not specify who the pronoun refers to. Thus, knowing the meaning of (15) does not involve knowing all the different individuals to whom the pronoun can refer; rather it involves knowing that (15) can be used to say of a male that he is smart—which male depends on the situation.

Now consider a sentence that does contain a possible antecedent for the pronoun.

(1a)  *Herbert bought a car before he left town.*

Up to now we have characterized sentences like this as having one meaning in which *Herbert* and *he* are coreferential and another in which they are not. However, such sentences can also be viewed in another way—on the model of (15).

Like (15), (1a) can be used to assert different things in different situations. In a situation in which it can be inferred that *he* refers to Mike, (1a) can be used to assert that Herbert bought a car before Mike left town; in other situations it can be used to assert that Herbert bought a car before Bill left town, Jack left town, and so on. These are all cases in which *he* and *Herbert* refer to different individuals. In order to explain why *he* can also be used to refer to Herbert, it is not necessary to posit a separate meaning in which *he* and *Herbert* are coreferential—one may simply treat the possibility of using the pronoun to refer to Herbert on a par with the possibility of using it to refer to anyone else. Thus, in a situation in which it can be inferred that *he* refers to Herbert, (1a) can be used to assert that Herbert bought a car before Herbert left town.

As with (15), the pronoun can be used to refer to any male—which male depends on the situation in which the sentence is uttered. In the case of (15), this fact can be accounted for without making the sentence ambiguous. Proponents of Theory 2 claim that (1a) is also unambiguous; its meaning does not specify who the pronoun refers to, but rather allows it to be used to refer to any individual whose identity can be inferred from the situation in which the sentence is uttered.

How then do sentences like those in (1) contrast with sentences like those in (2)? According to proponents of Theory 2, the sentences in (1) have a single neutral meaning which allows the pronoun to refer to anyone. The sentences in (2) are also unambiguous, having only a meaning in which the pronouns and *NP*s are presumed to refer to different individuals. Thus, whereas the pronoun in (1a) can be used to refer to any male, the pronoun in

(2a)  *He bought a car before Herbert left town*

can be used to refer to any male *other* than Herbert.[11]

### 3.1.3.2 The Mechanism for Interpreting Pronouns

The way one characterizes the data involving pronominal reference affects the rules one posits to account for pronominal anaphora. Theory 1 characterizes the data in terms of anaphoric and nonanaphoric readings and posits rules to produce these readings. Theory 2 characterizes the data in terms of nonanaphoric and neutral readings and hence does not need a rule of Coreference Assignment. Like Theory 1, Theory 2 generates pronouns in underlying structure where they are not marked for either coreference or distinct reference. Unlike Theory 1, Theory 2 posits only one rule to account for the referential possibilities of different NPs.

(16)  **Distinct Reference Assignment$_2$**
      *If $NP_1$ both precedes and commands a nonpronominal $NP_2$, then mark $NP_1$ and $NP_2$ as having different referents.*
      *(obligatory)*

A sentence to which (16) does not apply is predicted to have only a neutral reading in which the pronoun can refer to any individual. A sentence to which it

---

[11] Although it has been maintained that (1a–d) have only neutral interpretations, Jacobson (1977) has shown that this cannot be the case with (1e) and (1f). For example, if

(1f)  *Each of the boys changed clothes before he came to dinner*

has a neutral meaning, then *he* can be used to refer to any individual—different individuals in different situations. In any of these situations, (1f) will be used to assert that each of the boys changed clothes before some one individual (the referent of *he* in that situation) came to dinner. However, it is clear that (1f) has a meaning that allows it to be used to make a very different assertion—namely that for each X (such that X is a boy) X changed clothes before X came to dinner. The fact that (1f) can be used to make this assertion shows that it must have a reading other than the neutral one.

does apply is predicted to have only a reading in which NP$_1$ and NP$_2$ have different referents.

For example, (16) cannot mark *him* as having a different referent from either *Willard* or *Harry* in the structure

(5)

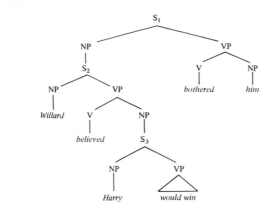

(6)    *That Willard believed that Harry could win bothered him.*

Consequently, Theory 2 predicts that (6) has only a neutral reading. This means that in some situations, *him* can be used to refer to *Harry*, in others to *Willard*, and in others to an individual not mentioned in (6).

The situation is different if Extraposition applies, producing

(10)

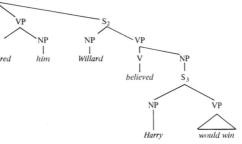

Since *him* precedes and commands the nonpronominal *Willard* and *Harry*, (16) obligatory marks *him* differing in reference from both of them. Thus, Theory 2 predicts that *him* cannot be used to refer to either Willard or Harry in

(11)    *It bothered him that Willard believed that Harry would win.*

As in the case of Theory 1, examples like

(12)    *Which of the men that Mary saw did you say she criticized?*

show that Distinct Reference Assignment must be postcyclical. Only in this way can (16) be prevented from obligatory marking *she* and *Mary* distinct in reference on the $S_2$-cycle in (13), before Question Movement applies to $S_1$ producing (12).[12,13]

(13)

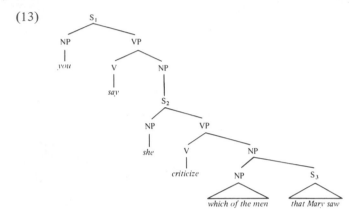

## 3.2  Theories in Which Anaphoric and Nonanaphoric Relations Are Represented in Underlying Structure

### 3.2.1  The Main Idea

Under Theories 1 and 2, pronouns are present in underlying structure, but anaphoric and nonanaphoric relations are not. According to the next two theories, pronouns are not present in underlying structure, but anaphoric and nonanaphoric relations are. These theories maintain the assumption that all aspects of meaning are represented in underlying structure. They also characterize the sentences in (1) as being ambiguous between anaphoric and nonanaphoric readings.

---

[12] Like the earlier arguments involving (12), this one depends on the assumption that Question Movement preposes the question phrase to sentence-initial position in a single movement.

[13] Theory 2 accounts for examples like

(i)  *The fact that he$_i$ isn't bothered by the possibility that Tom$_i$ will lose surprises him$_i$*

and

(ii)  *Realizing that Tom$_i$ was unpopular didn't bother him$_i$*

in essentially the same way that Theory 1 does (see footnote 9). Theory 2 does not posit a rule of Coreference Assignment or an explicit consistency condition. However, the central role of Distinct Reference Assignment and Interpretive Equi is the same as before.

### 3.2.2 Theory 3: Pronouns and Bound Variables[14]

In presenting theories (1) and (2) we did not say much about examples like (1e) and (1f) in which pronouns are anaphoric with quantified noun phrases (see footnotes 3 and 11). Theory 3 develops a mechanism to account for such sentences and extends it to cover all cases of pronominal anaphora. The paradigm cases for this theory are those like

(17) *All of the girls finished their work before they left for home.*

The anaphoric interpretation of this sentence is roughly

(18) *(All X: X is a girl) X finished Xs work before X left for home*

which can be represented syntactically as

(19)

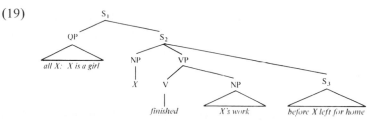

The constituent *all X: X is a girl* is called the *quantifier phrase*; the *X*s that follow are *variables* that are *bound* by the quantifier phrase. Three things happen in the derivation of (17) from (19):

(i)  *A rule of Quantifier Substitution substitutes the quantifier phrase for the first X in $S_2$.*
(ii) *The quantifier phrase is realized as **all of the girls.***
(iii) *The unsubstituted variables in $S_2$ and $S_3$ are turned into pronouns (**their** and **they**).*

The importance of precede and command conditions for sentences containing quantifier phrases and pronouns is illustrated by these examples:

(20) **QP precedes and commands pronoun**
    a.    **Some people** *think that* **they** *can get away with anything.*
    b.    *It surprised* **many taxpayers** *that* **they** *were entitled to a refund.*
(21) **Pronoun precedes but does not command QP**
    a.    *That* **they** *had to do* **their** *homework bothered* **most of the students.**

---

[14] This theory is essentially that of McCawley (1970*b*) and (1972).

b.    *The boy who disliked **them** insulted **several of the girls**.*

(22)  ***Pronoun commands but does not precede QP***
      a.    *The candidate who met **all the workers** expected **them** to vote in the election.*
      b.    *The gangster who tried to bribe **several politicians** threatened **them** with death.*

(23)  ***Pronoun precedes and commands QP***
      a.    ***They** think that **some people** can get away with anything.*
      b.    *It surprised **them** that **many taxpayers** were entitled to a refund.*

The sentences in (20–22) have anaphoric interpretations; the sentences in (23) do not. This can be accounted for by incorporating the precede and command conditions into the rule of Quantifier Substitution.

*Quantifier Substitution*

Substitute the quantifier phrase for any of its bound variables that are not both preceded and commanded by another such variable.[15]

(obligatory)

[15]In addition to the constraints we have incorporated in Quantifier Substitution (modeled on McCawley (1970*b*), other mechanisms must be posited to account for idiosyncrasies of particular quantifier phrases. For example, anaphoric interpretations are highly restricted in the case of sentences involving quantifier phrases like *each of the boys (girls)*, which take singular pronouns like *he* (*she*).

(i)  ***QP precedes and commands the pronoun***
      a.    *Each of the boys thinks that **he** will win.*
      b.    *It surprised **each of the boys** that **he** had many enemies.*

(ii)  ***Pronoun precedes but does not command QP***
      a.    *The boy who dislikes **her** insulted **each of the girls**.*
      b.    *That she had to do **her** homework bothered **each of the girls**.*

(iii)  ***Pronoun commands but does not precede QP***
      a.    *The candidate who met **each of the women** expected **her** to vote in the primary.*
      b.    *That **each of the women** is likely to lose infuriates **her**.*

Formulating the rule in this way allows it to apply in the derivations of (20–22) but not (23). For example, the structures underlying (20a,b) are (24a,b).[16]

(24) a.

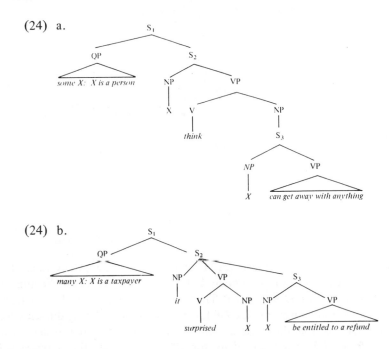

(24) b.

In each case the variable in $S_3$ is preceded and commanded by a variable in $S_2$ which is bound by the quantifier phrase. Thus, Quantifier Substitution must substitute the QP for the variable in $S_2$ rather than $S_3$. As a result, the sentences in (20) can be derived from the structures in (24), but the sentences in (23) cannot.

The structures underlying these sentences are:

*Footnote 15 continued*

    (iv) **Pronoun precedes and commands QP**
        a.   *He thinks that each of the boys will lose.*
        b.   *It surprised him that each of the boys had many enemies.*

Only the sentences in (i) have anaphoric interpretations. Since our rule of Quantifier Substitution would allow the sentences in (ii) and (iii) to be derived with anaphoric interpretations, some further constraints must be posited to prevent this.

   [16] (24b) represents the structure after Extraposition has applied to $S_2$.

(25)  a.

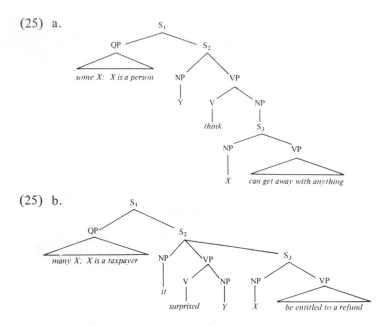

(25)  b.

These structures differ from those in (24) in that they contain the variable $Y$ in $S_2$ where the structures in (24) contain $X$. Since $Y$ is not the variable contained in the QP, it is not *bound* by the QP. This has two consequences. First, Quantifier Substitution must substitute the QP for $X$ rather than $Y$. Thus, the sentences in (23) are derived from the structures in (25), whereas the sentences in (20) are not. Second, since $Y$ is not bound by the QP, the pronoun that replaces it is understood as nonanaphoric with the QP. This analysis correctly predicts that the sentences in (20) have anaphoric readings, whereas those in (23) do not.[17]

---

[17] In addition to their anaphoric readings, the sentences in (20) also have nonanaphoric interpretations. These are derived from the underlying structures

(i)  a.

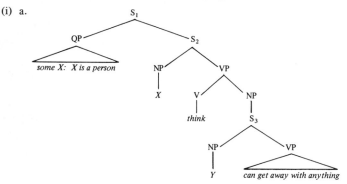

Under Theory 3, the mechanism that accounts for anaphoric relations between pronouns and quantifier phrases is extended to cover all cases of pronominal anaphora. For example, it is postulated that the structures underlying

(26) ***The fugitive bought a car before he left town***

and

(27) ***Logan bought a car before he left town***

are (on the anaphoric readings) (28) and (29).

(28)

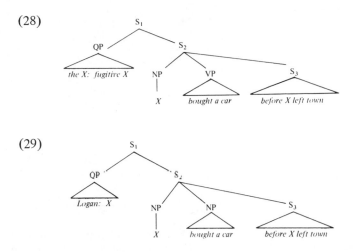

(29)

The derivations of (26) and (27) parallel those of (20a,b).[18] Thus, proponents of Theory 3 have proposed a unified account of pronominal anaphora.

*Footnote 17 continued*

b.

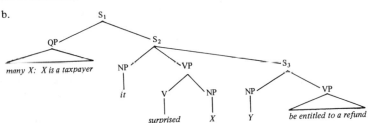

[18] According to proponents of Theory 3, (26) and (27) are ambiguous between anaphoric interpretations represented by (28) and (29) and nonanaphoric interpretations represented by (i) and (ii)

### 3.2.3 Theory 4: Quantifier Substitution and Pronominalization[19]

Theory 4 differs from Theory 3 in that it maintains that not all anaphoric pronouns arise from unsubstituted variables. Theory 4 accepts Theory 3's account of the relations between pronouns and quantifier phrases like those in (20–23). However, some pronouns that are anaphoric with proper names and definite NPs are said to arise from the operation of a Pronominalization transformation analogous to the one discussed earlier in part 8.[20] Which pronouns

*Footnote 18 continued*

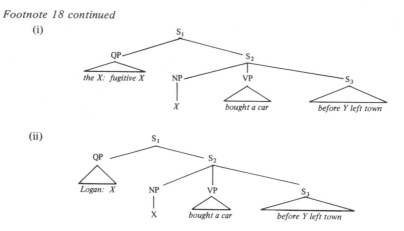

There are two possibilities open to proponents of Theory 3 regarding the semantic import of (i) and (ii). One possibility is that they represent neutral meanings. On this view, (26) and (27) are ambiguous between a reading in which the pronoun and NP are specified as co-referential and a reading in which the pronoun can be used to refer to any individual. The other possibility is that (i) and (ii) represent meanings in which the subjects of $S_2$ and $S_3$ are assumed to refer to different individuals. On this view, (26) and (27) are ambiguous between a coreferential reading and a reading in which pronouns and NPs are assumed to have different referents.

The difference between these two possibilities corresponds to an unclarity in the term "nonanaphoric" reading. One way to think of nonanaphoric readings is that they are readings in which the pronoun and NP are not anaphoric—i.e., not specified as coreferential. On this construal, neutral readings qualify as nonanaphoric (the first possibility). Another way to think of nonanaphoric readings is that they are readings in which the pronoun and NP are presumed to have distinct referents (the second possibility).

For present purposes, the difference between these two possibilities is not important. The issues they raise are discussed in greater detail in the appendix to this section.

[19] Theory 4 has been developed in greatest detail by Jacobson (1977) and Partee (1975). Some of the central ideas of this theory can also be found in Partee (1972) and Geach (1962) and (1967).

[20] Some theorists have argued that the Pronominalization transformation also derives certain pronouns with indefinite antecedents. For example, Jacobson (1977) argues that the pronouns in

arise from Pronominalization and which come from variables is a controversial matter among proponents of this theory.

## 4. RULES INVOLVING ANAPHORA

The controversy over pronominal anaphora is not an isolated one, but rather affects several of the rules discussed in this book. For example, our treatment of Reflexivization, Equi, and Super Equi assumed that anaphoric relations are marked at the stage of derivations at which these rules operate. Any change in this assumption will affect the status of these rules.

In addition, some of the data that posed problems for the Pronominalization transformation also raise questions about the status of other rules. For example, just as

(30) a. *Each of the women* thinks that *she* is the most qualified candidate

and

b. *Most people* feel sure that *they* are more intelligent than the average person

cannot be derived from the structures underlying

(31) a. *Each of the women* thinks that *each of the women* is the most qualified candidate

*Footnote 20 continued*

(i) *Every man who owns a donkey beats* ***it***

and

(ii) *The man who saw a lion shot* ***it***

cannot be derived from unsubstituted variables, but rather are produced by Pronominalization from the structures underlying

(iii) *Every man who owns a donkey beats the donkey that he owns*

and

(iv) *The man who saw a lion shot the lion that he saw.*

Similar examples are discussed in Geach (1962) and Partee (1972).

and

     b.    **Most people** *feel sure that* **most people** *are more intelligent than the average person*

in accordance with the Pronominalization Hypothesis, so

(32)  a.    *Several of the boys washed themselves*
             *(Reflexivization)*
       b.    **Most candidates** *expect to win*
             *(Equi)*

and

     c.    *It surprised* **each of the boys** *that washing* **himself** *in public irritated Eileen*
             *(Super Equi)*

cannot be derived from the structures underlying

(33)  a.    **Several of the boys** *washed* **several of the boys**
       b.    **Most candidates** *expect that* **most candidates** *will win*

and

     c.    *It surprised* **each of the boys** *that for* **each of the boys** *to wash himself in public would irritate Eileen*

without giving up the assumption that meaning is represented in underlying structure.

    Considerations like these show that pronominal anaphora is related to a variety of other grammatical phenomena. As a result, theorists who have adopted different accounts of pronominal anaphora have been led to develop alternative analyses of rules like Reflexivization, Equi, and Super Equi.

## 5. TWO RESEARCH STRATEGIES

    The theories discussed in §3 represent two different strategies for handling pronominal reference. Theories 1 and 2 give up the assumption that all aspects of meaning are represented in underlying structure. Theories 3 and 4 retain this assumption by positing underlying structures like (19), (24), (25), (28), and (29) that are further removed from (i.e., more unlike) surface structures than those posited by Theories 1 and 2.

    In recent years these two strategies have been generalized to cover more and more grammatical phenomena and have crystallized into two competing theoretical frameworks. One theory, known as *Generative Semantics*, retains the assumption that all aspects of meaning are represented in underlying structure. This theory posits underlying structures that are quite remote from surface structures and introduces new rules and other grammatical devices relating the two. The other theory, often referred to as the *Extended Standard Theory*, gives up the assumption that meaning is represented in underlying structure. This theory posits underlying structures that are closer to surface structures and introduces new rules of semantic interpretation which operate on derived structures. The dispute between theorists who work within the framework of generative semantics and those who adopt some version of the extended standard theory has expanded to cover nearly all aspects of grammatical research.[21]

[21] Although it is roughly correct to correlate Theories 1 and 2 with the Extended Standard Theory, and Theories 3 and 4 with Generative Semantics, certain complications prevent the correlations from being perfect. For example, it is possible for Extended Standard theorists to treat anaphoric pronouns as having the semantic force of bound variables. This could be done by introducing rules of semantic interpretation which operate on derived syntactic structures to produce semantic representations containing quantifiers and bound variables. Although the result would be something like Theory 3, it would be couched in an "interpretive" framework. Complications like this lie beyond the scope of this book and should not obscure the basic distinction between Generative Semantics and the Extended Standard Theory illustrated above. We wish to thank Pauline Jacobson for bringing this point to our attention.

# Appendix to
# *New Perspectives on Meaning, Coreference, and Pronominal Anaphora*

## 1. CHARACTERIZING THE DATA

In the previous section we noted three different types of readings (meanings) that linguists have used to characterize data like (1) and (2).[1]

(1)  a.  *Herbert bought a car before **he** left town.*
     b.  *The woman who hired **Morton** will see **him** tomorrow.*
     c.  *That **she** won the contest surprised **Janet**.*
     d.  *The man who loves **her** thinks that the guy who divorced **Gracie** is a fool.*
(2)  a.  *He bought a car before **Herbert** left town.*
     b.  *Susan told **him** that **Bill** couldn't come to dinner.*

The three readings are the coreferential reading, the distinct reference reading, and the neutral reading. These readings are defined roughly as follows:

### The Coreferential Reading

To say that a sentence has a coreferential reading is to say that it has a meaning in which one of its pronouns is specified as referring to the same

---

[1] In this discussion we avoid examples involving quantifier phrases like those in (1e,f) and (2c,d) of section 83 in order to simplify the presentation.

thing as one of the other NPs in the sentence. For example, to say that (1a) has a coreferential reading is to say that on one of its meanings, *Herbert* and *he* are understood as referring to the same person.

## The Distinct Reference Reading

To say that a sentence has a distinct reference reading is to say that it has a meaning in which one of its pronouns is specified as having a different reference from another NP in the sentence. For example, to say that (2a) has such a reading is to say that on one of its meanings, *Herbert* and *he* are understood to refer to different individuals.

## The Neutral Reading

To say that a sentence has a neutral reading is to say that it has a meaning in which one of its pronouns can be used to refer to any individual—the same individual that is referred to by some other NP in the sentence or anyone else.[2] The fact that different individuals may be referred to on different occasions does not show that the sentence is ambiguous—only that the meaning of the sentence does not specify the reference of the pronoun. To say that (1a) has a neutral reading is to say that on one of its meanings, *he* may be used to refer to any male.

None of the theories that we have examined posit all three readings. For example, Theory 1 characterizes the data solely in terms of coreferential and distinct reference readings.

## Position 1: Coreferential/Distinct

The sentences in (1) are ambiguous between coreferential and distinct reference readings. The sentences in (2) are unambiguous having only distinct reference readings.

This contrasts with the characterization of the data given in Theory 2.

## Position 2: Distinct/Neutral

The sentences in (1) have only neutral readings; those in (2) have only distinct reference readings.

Although these are the only characterizations we have considered thus far, there is also another possibility.

---

[2] This statement needs to be qualified slightly: on the neutral reading, *he* may be used to refer to males, *she* to females, *it* to animals, objects, etc.

### Position 3: Coreferential/Neutral

The sentences in (1) are ambiguous between coreferential and neutral readings; those in (2) have only neutral readings.[3]

If one decided that this was the correct way to characterize the data, a variety of theoretical mechanisms could be used to generate the appropriate readings. For example, the Pronominalization Hypothesis, Theory 3, and Theory 4 could each be constructed in such a way as to generate only the readings in Position 3. Alternatively, one could try to construct an analog to Theory 2, this time positing only a rule of Coreference Assignment. Whether or not any of these theories would be successful is, of course, an open question.

Positions 1–3 point up an interesting fact. Given any two of the three types of readings, a theorist can eliminate the third. If one believes that sentences have both coreferential and distinct reference readings, one can eliminate neutral readings by claiming that sentences like those in (1) are ambiguous (Position 1). If one does not think that there are coreferential readings, they can be eliminated in favor of neutral ones (Position 2). Finally, Position 3 shows how one who does not believe in distinct reference readings can dispense with them.[4]

---

[3] It is not always easy to tell whether a theorist adopts Position 3 or Position 1. One reason for this is that the readings contrasted with coreferential ones are usually referred to as "noncoreferential readings." This phrase can be interpreted to mean two quite different things. On one hand it might be taken to mean a reading in which the pronoun is not stipulated to be coreferential with another NP. On this construal, neutral readings count as noncoreferential readings. On the other hand, it can be taken to mean a reading in which the pronoun and *NP* are stipulated to have different referents. On this construal only distinct reference readings count as coreferential. Consequently, when a theorist uses the term "noncoreferential" or "nonanaphoric" one sometimes must go to some lengths to determine just what is meant.

[4] There are at least two reasons why some theorists (e.g., Wasow) have questioned the existence of distinct reference readings. The first involves sentences like

    (i) *He is Morris Fastbinder.*

As now formulated, the rules of Distinct Reference Assignment posited in Theories 1 and 2 would mark the pronoun and proper name as referring to different things. This apparently conflicts with the fact that a speaker would not normally use (i) unless he was intending to use the two expressions to refer to the same person. This problem would not arise if (i) were assigned a neutral meaning.

The second reason why some have doubted the existence of distinct reference readings involves sentences like

    (ii) *He was seen in the vicinity not long after **Jack the Ripper** had committed another murder.*

It is perfectly possible to use *he* in (ii) to refer to an individual who might turn out to be Jack the Ripper. (Imagine a detective talking about one of his suspects.) In such a situation

Each of the three positions correctly points out that there is a basic contrast between the sentences in (1) and (2). However, what is said about the contrast is different in each case. Perhaps if we were clearer about what the contrast really is, we could make progress in deciding among various characterizations of the data. One aspect of this clarification is given below.

## 2. A CRITERION OF ADEQUACY

Despite the conflict among Positions 1-3, all theorists would agree that the difference between the sentences in (1) and those in (2) affects the assertions that these sentences are used to make. What assertion a sentence can be used to make on a given occasion depends on

(3)    *the meaning(s) of the sentence*

and

(4)    *the context in which it is uttered—the physical environment, the people present, the shared knowledge of speaker and hearers, the previous discourse, and so on.*

The factors in (3) determine the range of assertions that a sentence can be used to make. Those in (4) determine which assertion in this range is made on a given occasion.

For example, one who understands

(5)    *He is tall*

knows that it can be used to assert of a male that he is taller than average. In a context in which it is clear that Morris is the referent of *he* (5) will make the assertion that Morris is tall; in different contexts it will make different asser-

---

*Footnote 4 continued*

the speaker may regard it as an open question whether the individual that he refers to is in reality Jack the Ripper. Again this apparently conflicts with the claim that (ii) has only a distinct reference reading in which *he* and *Jack the Ripper* are presumed to refer to different individuals. This problem would not arise if (ii) were characterized as having only a neutral meaning. Since (ii) is a paradigm case of a nonanaphoric relation between a pronoun and NP, it has been suggested by some theorists that nonanaphoric readings cannot be characterized correctly as distinct reference readings.

Wasow (1972, pp. 20-21) cites a discussion of examples similar to these in Postal (1971).

tions. In cases where the pronoun has no clear referent, an utterance of (5) will be bizarre and will fail to make any definite assertion.

One who understands

> (6) *Herbert likes handball, and he believes that everyone should parti-*
>      *cipate in some sport*

and

> (7) *He believes that everyone should participate in some sport, and*
>      *Herbert likes handball*

knows that they differ in the assertions they are typically used to make. In a situation in which it is clear from the context that the referent of *he* is Oscar, utterances of (6) and (7) will make the same assertion—one about Herbert's likes and Oscar's beliefs. Suppose, however, that (6) and (7) are uttered in a context that does not provide any such reference for the pronoun (e.g., at the beginning of a discourse, with no males present, with no previous understanding between speaker and hearer regarding the subject of the discourse). In such a case, an utterance of (7) will be bizarre and will fail to make any definite assertion. However, an utterance of (6) will be perfectly intelligible and will be understood as making an assertion about Herbert's likes and beliefs.

Any adequate characterization of the data involving pronominal anaphora should explain why (6) and (7) differ in this way. Such a characterization should also explain the contrast between the sentences in (1) and (2) by indicating why uttering those in (2) would be bizarre in contexts that do not provide references for the pronouns, whereas uttering those in (1) would be perfectly intelligible.

## 3. WHERE WE STAND

In this appendix and the previous section, we have not attempted to resolve the many disputes that presently characterize the study of pronominal anaphora. Our aim has been to present the major theoretical alternatives in a way that will facilitate a clear understanding of the issues. The student who has followed this discussion should be ready to read the relevant literature, evaluate existing theories, and form his or her own view regarding the proper account of pronominal anaphora.

# 84

# *Part 8: Its Place in a Wider Context*

## *1. THE PRONOMINALIZATION HYPOTHESIS*

The three classic papers on the Pronominalization Hypothesis are Lees and Klima (1963), Langacker (1969), and Ross (1969b). The initial paper by Lees and Klima was one of the first studies of pronominal anaphora within the framework of generative grammar. It covers both reflexive and nonreflexive pronouns. The Ross paper studies the conditions under which forward and backward pronominalization are possible and argues that Pronominalization is cyclical. Section 75, A Pronominalization Problem, is based on Ross's argument. Langacker's paper introduces the important notion of primacy relations (precede and command), which he uses to formulate the conditions on Pronominalization. The use of these relations to account for pronominal anaphora is one of the lasting contributions to the field, transcending the Pronominalization Hypothesis itself and finding expression in many different theoretical accounts of anaphora and other phenomena.

## *2. PARTICLE MOVEMENT, DATIVE MOVEMENT, AND PRONOMINALIZATION*

The material in section 76–78 was developed several years ago and has recently been discussed in a number of places. Wasow (1975) uses it to construct an argument against treating anaphoric pronouns as arising from bound variables. For a counterargument, see Jacobson (1977). Ross (1967) was the first to suggest handling the phenomena in section 78 with a surface structure constraint.

Perlmutter (1971) uses surface structure constraints to account for similar phenomena, primarily in Spanish and French.

## 3. THERE-*INSERTION AND PRONOMINALIZATION*

Section 79 is based on an argument due to Bresnan (1970a). The argument, originally directed against the Pronominalization Hypothesis, is adapted by Wasow (1975) for use against the view that anaphoric pronouns arise from bound variables. Counterarguments are given in Harman (1976) and Jacobson (1977).

## 4. *QUESTION MOVEMENT AND PRONOMINALIZATION*

Section 80 is based on an argument given in Postal (1971), which is a detailed study of various aspects of coreference and their interactions with a variety of grammatical rules.

## 5. *PROBLEMS WITH PRONOMINALIZATION*

As we indicated in sections 81-83, many theorists have noted problems with the Pronominalization Hypothesis. Three works surveying such problems are G. Lakoff (1968), Dougherty (1969), and Partee (1972). For more references, see the bibliographies of these works and also §§6-9 below. For a specific discussion of the point made in §3 of section 81, see Lasnik (1976).

## 6. *PARADOX LOST: THE BACH-PETERS PARADOX*

The original formulation of the paradox is found in Bach (1970). Subsequent literature includes Karttunen (1971), Fauconnier (1971), Dik (1973), Wasow (1973), and Jacobson (1977). Fauconnier (1974) contains a thorough discussion of the paradox. Although sentences with crossing coreference were originally used to construct arguments *against* a Pronominalization transformation, Jacobson (1977) uses these sentences to construct an argument *for* such a transformation.

## 7. INTERPRETIVE THEORIES OF PRONOMINAL ANAPHORA

These theories generate pronouns in underlying structure and posit rules that assign anaphoric or nonanaphoric interpretations to derived structures. Works containing arguments in favor of such theories include Dougherty (1969), Jackendoff (1972), Lasnik (1976), Reinhart (1976), and Wasow (1972, 1975).

## 8. ANAPHORIC PRONOUNS AS BOUND VARIABLES

These theories use the mechanisms of quantifiers and bound variables to handle pronominal anaphora. Arguments for such theories can be found in many works, including Bach (1968), McCawley (1970*b*, 1972), and Harman (1972, 1976). Fauconnier (1974) uses data from French in discussing this approach.

## 9. MIXED THEORIES: BOUND VARIABLES PLUS PRONOMINALIZATION

Several theorists have voiced skepticism regarding the possibility of developing a unified theory of pronominal anaphora based entirely on bound variables, coreference, interpretive rules, or syntactic pronominalization alone. For discussions of different types of pronominal anaphora, the difficulties in handling them all with the same mechanism, and proposals for blending various approaches, see Geach (1962, 1967); Karttunen (1969); Partee (1972, 1975); and Jacobson (1977).

## 10. PRONOUNS, ANAPHORA, AND BROADER CONCERNS

As was pointed out in section 83, theories of pronominal anaphora are intimately connected with accounts of rules like Reflexivization, Equi, Super Equi and others. Often the approach taken to one rule greatly influences how the others are formulated. For example, interpretive accounts of Pronominalization are often accompanied by interpretive accounts of Reflexivization, Equi, and so on. The same can be said for traditional syntactic accounts and for theories involving bound variables. Works discussing various forms of anaphora include: McCawley (1970*b*, 1972); Morgan (1970); Helke (1970); Jackendoff (1972); Wasow (1972); Partee (1975); Brame (1976); and Hankamer and Sag (1976).

Just as disputes involving pronominal anaphora are connected with broader issues involving anaphora in general, so approaches to anaphora in general have often been developed within the broader context of competing theories of grammar. Two such theories, mentioned in section 83, are Generative Semantics and the Extended Standard Theory.

Generative semantics holds that the underlying syntactic representation of a sentence is also its semantic representation. General overviews of this research program include Bach (1968), G. Lakoff (1971), Postal (1970), McCawley (1972), and Harman (1972).

Proponents of the Extended Standard Theory deny that the underlying syntactic representation of a sentence contains all of the information needed for its semantic interpretation. Thus, they posit rules of semantic interpretation that operate on derived syntactic structures. In practice this has led to treating as semantic many phenomena that were formerly handled syntactically. General overviews of this research program include Chomsky (1970, 1972*a*, 1972*b*, 1973); Jackendoff (1972); and Fiengo (1974).

# Discussions of Problems

## Discussion of Section 10, Activization vs. Passivization

### 1. SOLUTION TO THE PROBLEM

#### 1.1 Hypothesis A

Under Hypothesis A, the structure underlying (1), (3), and (4) is

(8)  *[everyone took advantage of their inexperience]*

In (8), *advantage* occurs in the expression *take advantage of*. If we assume that the restriction on the distribution of *advantage* is stated in underlying structure, then the constraint can be formulated as follows:

(9)  ***Advantage** can occur without an article or modifier only in the expression **take advantage of**.*

Since (8) satisfies (9), it is a possible underlying structure. The fact that *advantage* can occur on the surface in (1), (3), and (4) follows automatically from the fact that these sentences are derived from (8). The ungrammaticality of (*5b-*7b) is accounted for by the fact that none of these sentences is derived from an underlying structure containing the expression *take advantage of*. Thus, Hypothesis A allows us to account for all of the data in the problem by positing a single restriction on *advantage*.

#### 1.2 Hypothesis B

According to Hypothesis B, there are two underlying structures for (1).

(i)  *[advantage was taken of their inexperience by everyone]*
(ii)  *[their inexperience was taken advantage of by everyone]*

There is no stage in the derivation of (3) and (4) at which they have the same structure. Therefore, two separate restrictions are needed.

(10) *Advantage can occur without an article or modifier if it is the sub-ject of the verbal expression* **be taken of***.*

(11) *Advantage can occur without an article or modifier in the expression* **be taken advantage of***.*

Postulating (10) and (11) allows Hypothesis B to account for all of the data in the problem. However, the fact that Hypothesis B requires two constraints on *advantage* while Hypothesis A requires only one is an argument against Hypothesis B in favor of Hypothesis A.

## 2. POST MORTEM

The above argument in favor of Hypothesis A is based on the fact that under Hypothesis A there is only one structure underlying (1), (3), and (4). Hypothesis B, on the other hand, posits both (i) and (ii) as underlying structures and therefore needs two restrictions on *advantage*.

It might be thought that Hypothesis B can be saved by replacing Assumption 2 by Assumption 2'. Hypothesis B then would posit a single underlying structure for (1), (3), and (4). We will now show that even under Assumption 2', Hypothesis B must be rejected.

If (i) is the structure underlying (1), (3), and (4), then one constraint on *advantage* is needed—(10). However, both (1) and (4) must be derived from (i). Since (4) is a passive sentence, the rule that derives it from (i) must be distinct from the Activization rule that derives (1) from (i). Thus, Hypothesis B needs two rules to account for the data, whereas Hypothesis A needs only one. Therefore, even if Hypothesis B posits (i) as the only underlying structure for (1), (3), and (4), we must still select Hypothesis A.

An analogous argument can be made if Hypothesis B posits (ii) as the only structure underlying (1), (3), and (4).

## 3. ANOTHER ARGUMENT FOR THE PASSIVE AS A TRANSFORMATION

In section 8 we gave an argument for deriving an active sentence and its corresponding passive from the same underlying structure. That argument consisted of showing that otherwise, separate selectional restrictions would have to be stated on active and passive verbs, causing unnecessary duplication in the grammar. A similar argument can be constructed based on the distribution of *advantage* without an article or other modifier: If passive sentences are derived from underlying active structures, the restriction on *advantage* can be stated by means of a single statement—(8). If active and passive sentences had different underlying structures, three separate restrictions would be needed—(8), (9), and (10). The passive transformation allows us to avoid this duplication.

# Discussion of Section 22, Missing Subjects

## 1. AN ARGUMENT AGAINST HYPOTHESIS B

Hypotheses A and B maintain that *want* takes a sentential complement in the structure underlying (4). They differ as to whether or not the complement has a subject. To construct an argument for Hypothesis A, one must find an element in the embedded sentence that depends upon the complement having a subject at some stage of derivation. Reflexivization can be used to construct such an argument.

## 2. AN ARGUMENT AGAINST HYPOTHESES B AND C

The argument based on Reflexivization applies only against Hypothesis B. However, a similar argument can be constructed that works against both B and C. Passive is a transformation that requires a subject in order to operate. Thus, if you can find sentences that are like (4) except for the fact Passive has applied in the complement of *want*, then you will have shown that these complements must have had subjects at earlier stages of derivation before they were deleted by Equi.

## 3. MEANING AND UNDERLYING STRUCTURE

The arguments in §§1 and 2 should have led you to posit

(11)

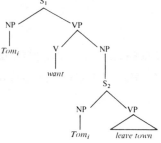

as the underlying structure of

(4)    *Tom wants to leave town.*

Now notice that (11) is precisely the structure that is needed to give the meaning (4). A speaker of English recognizes that the semantic relation between *Tom* and *want* is the same as the relation between *Tom* and *leave* i.e., the person doing the wanting is also the person whose departure is desired. This fact is accounted for automatically if the meaning of a sentence is represented in underlying structure. Thus, the arguments given in support of Hypothesis A also support our tentative hypothesis about meaning.

# Discussion of Section 24,
## *LIKELY: Equi vs. Subject-to-Subject Raising*

### *1. SURFACE SUBJECTS THAT ARE NOT UNDERLYING SUBJECTS*

Two noun phrases that cannot be subjects in underlying structure are *there* of THERE-Insertion and *advantage* in *take advantage of*. Since the Equi Hypothesis makes the claims in (13), it predicts that these noun phrases cannot occur as surface structure subjects of *likely* in sentences of the form (12). The Subject-to-Subject Raising Hypothesis predicts that they can. These predictions allow us to construct two arguments in favor of Subject-to-Subject Raising.

### 1.1 Argument One: Fixed Expressions

(14) *Advantage is likely to be taken of their inexperience by everyone.*

Under the Subject-to-Subject Raising Hypothesis, (14) is derived from

(15)

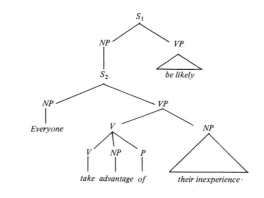

Application of Passive to $S_2$ produces

(16)

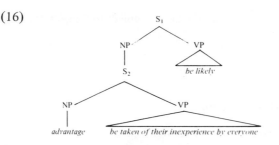

Application of Subject-to-Subject Raising produces (14).

Under the Equi Hypothesis, (14) cannot be derived. Since this hypothesis predicts that the surface structure subject of *likely* is also its underlying subject, the underlying structure of (14) would have to have *advantage* as subject.

(17)

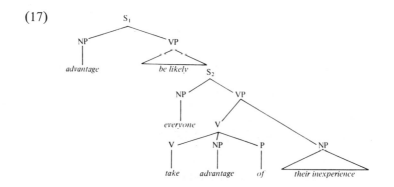

However, this violates the following constraint on *advantage* (described in the discussion of section 10):

(18) *Advantage can occur in underlying structure without an article or other modifier only in the fixed expression* **take advantage of.**

Since (17) violates this constraint, it is not a well-formed underlying structure.

We have shown that the Subject-to-Subject Raising Hypothesis is capable of deriving (14) automatically whereas the Equi Hypothesis is not. The same point holds for sentences involving other fixed expressions—e.g., the expressions *pay heed to* and *pay attention to*.

(19) a. *Heed is likely to be paid to that proposal by everyone who hears of it.*

b.    *Attention is likely to be paid to that proposal by everyone who hears of it.*

Sentences like these show that *likely* takes Subject-to-Subject Raising rather than Equi.

## 1.2  Argument Two: THERE-Insertion

Another argument is provided by sentences like

(20)  *There is likely to be a pile of dirt under the rug.*

The Subject-to-Subject Raising Hypothesis derives (20) from

(21)

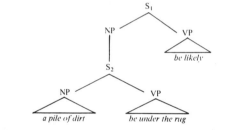

Application of THERE-Insertion in $S_2$ produces

(22)

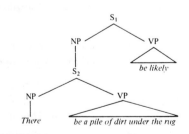

Application of Subject-to-Subject Raising produces (20).

The Equi Hypothesis incorrectly predicts that (20) cannot be derived. According to it, the structure underlying (20) must be

(23)

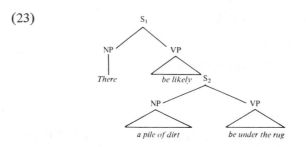

But this can't be. The unstressed *there* of THERE-Insertion is never present in underlying structure, but rather is introduced transformationally. Thus, (23) is not a well-formed underlying structure, and the Equi hypothesis cannot derive (20).

Note, this conclusion cannot be avoided by positing

(24)

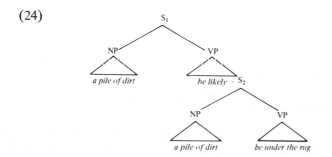

as the underlying structure of (20). Although Equi can apply to (24) producing

(25)

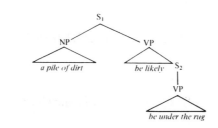

(20) cannot be derived by applying THERE-Insertion to (25).

There are two reasons for this. First, THERE-Insertion applies to structures of the form

(26)  *NP, Verb of Existence, X*

to produce structures of the form

(27)  *There, Verb of Existence, NP, X.*

The structure of (25) is

(28)  *A pile of dirt, be, likely, . . .*

Thus, applying THERE-Insertion to (28) would not produce (20), but rather would produce

(29) ?*There is a pile of dirt likely to be under the rug.*

Second, the verb that determines whether or not a sentence of the form

(30)  *There, be, likely,* $\underset{[+infinitive]}{V}$ *NP, . . .*

is grammatical is not the *be* immediately following *there,* but rather is the infinitive in the complement of *likely.*

(31)  a.    *A copy of that book exists.*
      b.    *There exists a copy of that book.*
      c.    *There is likely to exist a copy of that book.*
(32)  a.    *A copy of that book disappeared.*
      b.    *\*There disappears a copy of that book.*
      c.    *\*There is likely to disappear a copy of that book.*

The comparison between (31) and (32) indicates that in the derivation of sentences like (20), THERE-Insertion applies in the complement of *likely.* Thus, (20) cannot be derived from (24), but rather must be derived from (21) in accordance with the Subject-to-Subject Raising Hypothesis.


## 2. SUPPLEMENTARY ARGUMENTS

### 2.1  How's the Weather?

An additional argument is provided by sentences like

(33)  *It's raining.*

The *it* in (33) is a "dummy subject" that does not refer to anything. The distribution of these subjects is highly restricted. For example, the sentences

(34)  a.    *\*It's singing*

b.  *\*It's happy*
c.  *\*It's larger than a bread box*

are acceptable if *it* is referential, and deviant if it is not.

Dummy subjects like the one in (33) also appear as surface structure subjects of *likely*.

(35)  *It is likely to rain.*

By deriving (35) from

(36)

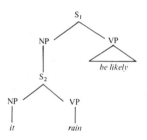

Subject-to-Subject Raising accounts for this automatically without any additional devices. The Equi Hypothesis does not.

(37)

Since the *it* in $S_2$ is nonreferential, Equi cannot apply, and (35) cannot be derived.[1]

## 2.2 Extra NPs

So far all the arguments against the Equi Hypothesis have been based on grammatical sentences that it cannot derive. It is also possible to use ungrammatical sentences to construct an argument against this hypothesis.

---

[1] Note also that in order to derive (37) as an underlying structure, the Equi Hypothesis would have to complicate restrictions on the distribution of dummy subjects in underlying structure.

Consider the ungrammatical sentence[2]

(38) *\*Martha is likely (for) Tom to be intelligent.*

Under the Equi Hypothesis, sentences with *likely* are derived from structures of the form

(39)

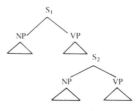

Unless special restrictions are adopted, the Equi Hypothesis will make it possible to generate the underlying structure

(40)

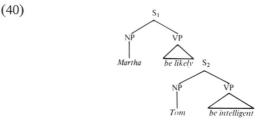

Since (40) does not satisfy the structural description of Equi, *Tom* will not be deleted, and *\*(38) will be derived.

The Subject-to-Subject Raising Hypothesis does not have this problem. *\*(38) could be generated only if both the matrix and the complement sentences could have subjects after the operation of Subject-to-Subject Raising. Since this is impossible, the Subject-to-Subject Raising Hypothesis automatically accounts for its ungrammaticality. This means that the Equi Hypothesis requires an extra constraint to block *\*(40) that is not required by the Subject-to-Subject Raising Hypothesis.[3]

---

[2] The parentheses around *for* indicate that *\*(38) is ungrammatical whether or not *for* occurs.

[3] For purposes of this argument, it does not matter how the additional constraint required by the Equi Hypothesis would be stated. The crucial point is that the Subject-to-Subject Raising Hypothesis requires no additional mechanism to block *\*(38).

## 3. MEANING AND UNDERLYING STRUCTURE

On the basis of the arguments in §§1 and 2, we adopt the Subject-to-Subject Raising Hypothesis. In this subsection, we examine the consequences of this hypothesis for the thesis that the meaning of a sentence is represented in underlying structure.

### 3.1 Semantic Relations

In §2 of the problem we said that *Martha* is understood to be the semantic subject of *intelligent* in

(5)   *Martha is likely to be intelligent.*

In other words, it is Martha whose intelligence is in question. This is reflected by the fact that *Martha* is the subject of *intelligent* in underlying structure.

(4)

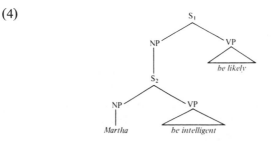

We can make a similar point about *likely*. What is likely in (5) is not Martha, but Martha's being intelligent. Thus, *Martha to be intelligent* is understood to be the semantic subject of *likely*. Hence, the understood (or semantic) subject of *likely* is also its underlying subject. This fact provides further support for the thesis that meaning is represented in underlying structure.

### 3.2 Synonymy

#### 3.2.1 Extraposition and Subject-to-Subject Raising

Additional support for the thesis is provided by sentences like

(2)   *That Martha is intelligent is likely*
(3)   *It is likely that Martha is intelligent*
(5)   *Martha is likely to be intelligent.*

Under the Subject-to-Subject Raising Hypothesis, each of these sentences is derived from (4). The thesis that meaning is represented in underlying structure correctly predicts that these sentences are synonymous.

### 3.2.2 Downstairs Passive

Our final example of synonymy involves application of Passive to the complement of *likely*.

(41)  *CBS is likely to interview Martha.*
(42)  *Martha is likely to be interviewed by CBS.*

Both of these sentences come from

(43)

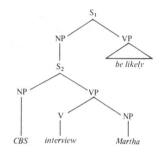

In (41), only Subject-to-Subject Raising applies. In (42) Subject-to-Subject Raising follows Passive. Since both sentences are derived from the same underlying structure, they are synonymous.

Sentences like these in which Subject-to-Subject Raising applies differ from sentences like

(44)  *CBS wants to interview Martha*
(45)  *Martha wants to be interviewed by CBS*

in which Equi applies. (44) and (45) are nonsynonymous and come from different underlying structures. (44) is derived from

(46)

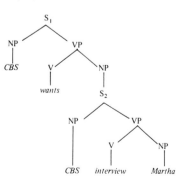

by the application of Equi. (45) is derived from

(47)

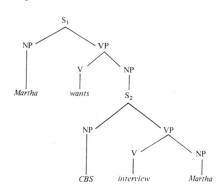

by Passive followed by Equi. The fact that (41) and (42) are synonymous whereas (44) and (45) are not illustrates an important difference between verbals that trigger Subject-to-Subject Raising and those that trigger Equi.

## 4. THE IMPORT OF THESE ARGUMENTS

The arguments showing that *likely* triggers Subject-to-Subject Raising rather than Equi are important for several reasons. First, they show that there is a rule of Subject-to-Subject Raising in English. Second, each argument shows one way in which Subject-to-Subject Raising triggers like *likely* are different from Equi triggers like *want*. These arguments provide diagnostic tests for determining whether other verbals trigger Subject-to-Subject Raising or Equi. You will need to know these arguments well in order to be able to do problems and exercises that come later.

# Discussion of Section 34, Evidence for the Cycle in a Theory with the Frustrated Characterization of Obligatory Rules-1

## 1. SUBJECT-TO-OBJECT RAISING AND REFLEXIVIZATION

The underlying structure

(1)

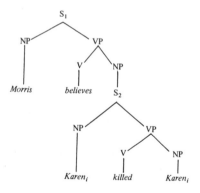

satisfies the structural descriptions of both Subject-to-Object Raising and Reflexivization.[1] According to the Anywhere Theory, rules can apply in any order so long as a derivation is not terminated leaving the structural description of an

---

[1] For simplicity, we ignore the question of how complementizers and tense are represented in underlying structure. Thus, we represent as *killed* what is realized in surface structure (after Subject-to-Object Raising) as *has killed*. In general, when $S_2$ is infinitival, the past tense of the embedded verb appears in surface structure with *have*. This *have* is systematically absent from the tree structures given here.

obligatory rule satisfied. If Reflexivization applies first, followed by Subject-to-Object Raising, then

(2)   *Morris believes Karen to have killed herself*

is derived. However, if Subject-to-Object Raising applies first, the result is

(3)

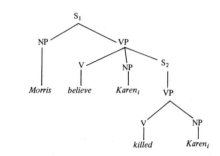

In (3), the two occurrences of *Karen* are in different clauses. Since the structural description of Reflexivization is no longer satisfied it cannot apply. Instead, Pronominalization produces

(4)   *\*Morris believes Karen$_i$ to have killed her$_i$.*[2]

Thus, the Anywhere Theory incorrectly predicts that *Karen* and *her* are coreferential.

The Cyclical Theory allows the derivation of (2) while preventing the derivation of \*(4). Rules apply to (1) first on the $S_2$-cycle. Since Reflexivization is obligatory, rule application on $S_2$ cannot terminate until Reflexivization has applied, producing

(5)

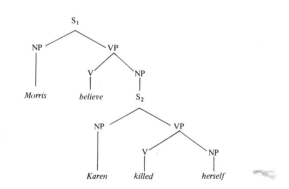

---

[2] The asterisk on (4) indicates that *Karen* and *her* cannot be coreferential.

Application of Subject-to-Object Raising on $S_1$ results in (2). Note, Reflexivization has already operated before Subject-to-Object Raising gets a chance to
apply. Thus, (3) cannot be produced, and *(4) cannot be derived.[3] This result is
an argument in favor of the Cyclical Theory and against the Anywhere Theory.
The arguments for parts B and C of the problem are exactly analogous.

---

[3] Although *(4) cannot be derived on the coreferential interpretation, it can be derived
if *Karen* and *her* are noncoreferential. The noncoreferential reading is derived from

(i)  MS 81

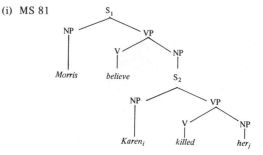

# Discussion of Section 35, Evidence for the Cycle in a Theory with the Frustrated Characterization of Obligatory Rules-2

## 1. THE DERIVATION OF (3)

The structure underlying (3) is roughly

(5)

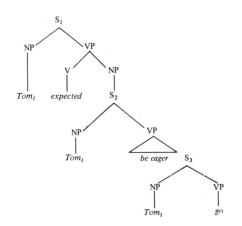

Both the Cyclical Theory and the Anywhere Theory allow (3) to be derived by first applying Equi to delete the subject of $S_3$ and then applying it to delete the subject of $S_2$.

## 2. A PROBLEM FOR THE ANYWHERE THEORY

Under the Anywhere Theory, it is also possible for Equi to delete the subject of $S_2$ before the subject of $S_3$ has been deleted. This results in

(6)

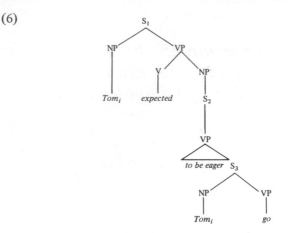

*Tom* in $S_1$ is not a constituent of the sentence immediately above *Tom* in $S_3$; it is two sentences up. Therefore, the structural description of Equi is not satisfied in (6) and the subject of $S_3$ cannot be deleted. Instead, Pronominalization produces

(7) *\*Tom_i expected to be eager for him_i to go.*[1]

Since the Anywhere Theory predicts that *Tom* and *him* are coreferential, it must be rejected.

## 3. THE CYCLICAL THEORY

The Cyclical Theory correctly blocks \*(7). No rules apply on the $S_3$-cycle. On the $S_2$-cycle, the structural description of Equi is met. Since Equi is obligatory with *eager*, it must delete the subject of $S_3$ before any rules apply on the $S_1$-cycle.

---

[1] The asterisk indicates that *Tom* cannot be coreferential with *him*. The presence of *for* in (7) is irrelevant to this problem.

(8)

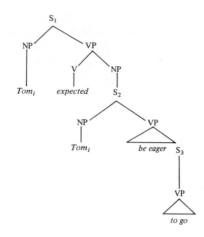

Since Equi cannot apply on the $S_1$-cycle before it applies on the $S_2$-cycle, (6) cannot be produced, and *(7) cannot be derived.[2] This result is a further indication of the superiority of the Cyclical Theory over the Anywhere Theory.

## 4. ADDITIONAL ARGUMENTS: AN EXERCISE

The argument just given is exactly analogous to the one we asked you to construct in (2B) of the previous problem (section 34). Both arguments show that the cycle is needed to ensure that applying Equi in $S_1$ cannot prevent an

---

[2] Note, under the Cyclical Theory (7) can be derived on the noncoreferential reading from

(i)

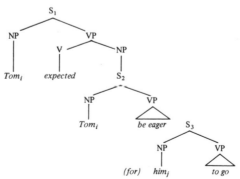

obligatory rule from applying in $S_2$. The only difference is that in (2B) of section 34 the obligatory rule in $S_2$ is Reflexivization, whereas here it is Equi. This suggests that analogous arguments paralleling (2A) and (2C) of (34) can also be constructed. Do this for yourself, first considering the interaction of Subject-to-Object Raising with Equi and then considering Subject-to-Subject Raising and Equi.

# Discussion of Section 38, Evidence for the Cycle in a Theory with the Immediate Characterization of Obligatory Rules

## 1. THE FORM OF ARGUMENT: THE IMMEDIATE CHARACTERIZATION

Arguments against the Anywhere Theory involve the interaction of an obligatory two-story rule $R_1$ with an optional one-story rule $R_2$[1] in a structure of the form

(1)
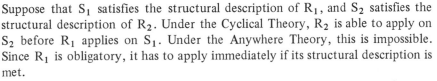

Suppose that $S_1$ satisfies the structural description of $R_1$, and $S_2$ satisfies the structural description of $R_2$. Under the Cyclical Theory, $R_2$ is able to apply on $S_2$ before $R_1$ applies on $S_1$. Under the Anywhere Theory, this is impossible. Since $R_1$ is obligatory, it has to apply immediately if its structural description is met.

To decide between these two theories, we must find a sentence that can only be derived by allowing $R_2$ to apply on $S_2$ before $R_1$ applies on $S_1$. The Cyclical Theory predicts that such a sentence will be grammatical. The Anywhere Theory predicts that it will be ungrammatical.

[1] It is not essential for $R_2$ to be one-story or for it to be optional. However, it is simpler to begin with cases in which it is both. The more complicated cases will be discussed in §§2.3 and 3.

## 2. FOUR ARGUMENTS FOR THE CYCLE

Each of the arguments in §2 involves the interaction of an optional rule in $S_2$ with an obligatory instance of Subject-to-Subject Raising in $S_1$. Two verbals for which Subject-to-Subject Raising is obligatory are *apt* and *bound.* The fact that Subject-to-Subject Raising applies with these verbals is demonstrated by the grammaticality of

(2)   a.   *Advantage is* $\left\{ \begin{array}{l} apt \\ bound \end{array} \right\}$ *to be taken of their inexperience by everyone.*

   b.   *There is* $\left\{ \begin{array}{l} apt \\ bound \end{array} \right\}$ *to be a mouse in the bathtub.*

   c.   *It is* $\left\{ \begin{array}{l} apt \\ bound \end{array} \right\}$ *to rain tomorrow.*

The fact that Subject-to-Subject Raising is obligatory with *apt*[2] and *bound* is demonstrated by the ungrammaticality of

(3)   a.   **For advantage to be taken of their inexperience by everyone*
         *is* $\left\{ \begin{array}{l} apt \\ bound \end{array} \right\}$

   b.   **That advantage will be taken of their inexperience by everyone*
         *is* $\left\{ \begin{array}{l} apt \\ bound \end{array} \right\}$

   c.   **It is* $\left\{ \begin{array}{l} apt \\ bound \end{array} \right\}$ *that advantage will be taken of the inexperience*
         *by everyone.*

Examples analogous to *(3) can easily be constructed for the other sentences in (2).

### 2.1  Subject-to-Subject Raising and Passive

The structure underlying

(4)   *Ali is* $\left\{ \begin{array}{l} apt \\ bound \end{array} \right\}$ *to be interviewed by CBS*

is

---

[2] *Apt* is ambiguous. The reading we are concerned with is one in which it triggers Subject-to-Subject Raising and means something like *likely.* On this reading *(3a–c) are ungrammatical. On the reading in which it means *appropriate,* (3a–c) are grammatical. However, on this reading, *apt* does not trigger Subject-to-Subject Raising.

(5)

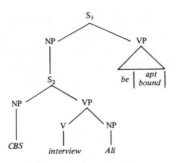

To derive (4), Passive must apply on $S_2$ followed by Subject-to-Subject Raising on $S_1$. Under the Anywhere Theory, this is impossible. Since Subject-to-Subject Raising is obligatory with *apt* and *bound*, it must apply immediately, producing

(6)

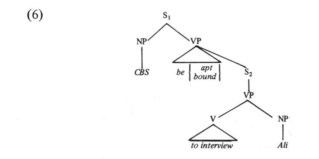

(6) does not satisfy the structural description of Passive. Thus, (4) cannot be derived, and the Anywhere Theory must be rejected.

The Cyclical Theory allows (4) to be derived. Although Subject-to-Subject Raising is obligatory, it does not get a chance to apply until the $S_1$-cycle. Consequently, there is nothing to prevent Passive from applying on the $S_2$-cycle to produce

(7)

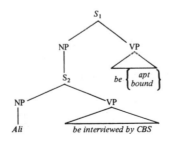

Subsequent application of Subject-to-Subject Raising produces (4).

Note, under the Frustrated Characterization of obligatory rules, arguments against the Anywhere Theory come from ungrammatical sentences that the theory derives. Under the Immediate Characterization, arguments come from grammatical sentences that the theory cannot derive.

## 2.2 Subject-to-Subject Raising and THERE-Insertion

A parallel argument involves the rule of THERE-Insertion. The structure underlying

(8)  *There is* $\begin{Bmatrix} apt \\ bound \end{Bmatrix}$ *to be a policeman on the corner*

is

(9)

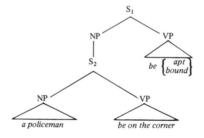

To derive (9), THERE-Insertion must apply on $S_2$, followed by Subject-to-Subject Raising on $S_1$. The Anywhere Theory does not allow this. Since Subject-to-Subject Raising is obligatory with *apt* and *bound,* it must apply immediately, producing

(10)

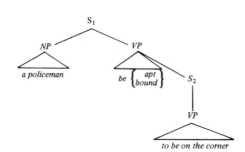

Since (8) cannot be derived from (10), the Anywhere Theory is incorrect.[3]

As before, the Cyclical Theory allows (8) to be derived. Although Subject-to-Subject Raising is obligatory with *apt* and *bound,* it cannot apply until the $S_1$ cycle. Thus, there is nothing to prevent *there* from being inserted on the $S_2$ cycle and raised to matrix subject on the $S_1$ cycle.

## 2.3 Subject-to-Subject Raising and Equi

Another argument against the Anywhere Theory can be based on the interaction of Subject-to-Subject Raising and Equi in the derivation of

(11) *The President is* $\begin{Bmatrix} apt \\ bound \end{Bmatrix}$ *to expect to be re-elected by the people.*

The structure underlying (11) is

(12)

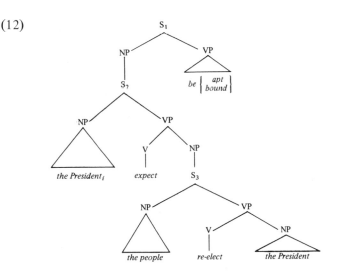

In the derivation of (11), Passive applies on $S_3$, followed by Equi on $S_2$, and Subject-to-Subject Raising on $S_1$. The Cyclical Theory makes this possible. The Anywhere Theory does not.

With *expect,* Equi is optional, as is Passive in $S_3$. Since Subject-to-Subject Raising is obligatory with *apt* and *bound,* the Anywhere Theory predicts that it must apply first, producing

[3] For a discussion of why sentences like (8) cannot be derived from structures like (10) see §1.2 of the discussion of section 24.

(13)

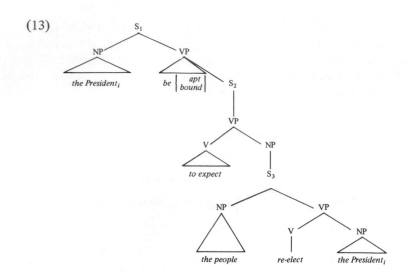

Passive can now apply on $S_3$, producing

(14)

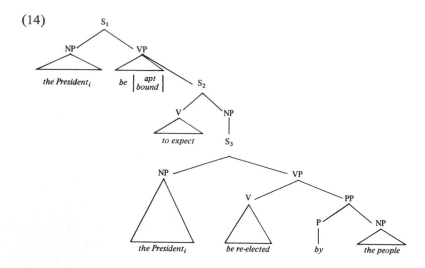

However, Equi can no longer apply since the subject to be deleted is not in the first S below the Equi trigger. As a result, the Anywhere Theory cannot generate (11). Thus, the assumption that Equi deletes the subject of the *first* S below the matrix subject provides us with an additional argument against the Anywhere Theory.

## 2.4 Subject-to-Subject Raising and Extraposition

One final argument involves Extraposition. The structure underlying

(15)  *It is* $\begin{Bmatrix} apt \\ bound \end{Bmatrix}$ *to be illegal for stores to open on Sunday*

is

(16)

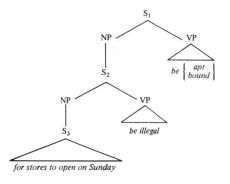

To derive (15), Extraposition must apply on $S_2$ followed by Subject-to-Subject Raising on $S_1$. Under the Cyclical Theory, this is unproblematic. Under the Anywhere Theory, it is impossible.

The problem is that Subject-to-Subject Raising must apply immediately, producing

(17)

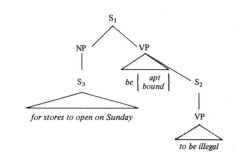

(18)  *For stores to open on Sunday is* $\begin{Bmatrix} apt \\ bound \end{Bmatrix}$ *to be illegal.*

(18) is grammatical. However, since *apt* and *bound* do not trigger Extra-

position,[4] (15) cannot be derived from it. Thus, the interaction of Subject-to-Subject Raising and Extraposition provides a further example of a grammatical sentence that can be derived by the Cyclical Theory, but not by the Anywhere Theory.

## 3. A VARIANT OF THE BASIC ARGUMENT

Each of the arguments in §2 was based on the application of an optional rule in $S_2$. Suppose the rule were obligatory. If the Immediate Characterization requires two obligatory rules that are satisfied by the same structure to apply simultaneously, then a further argument can be constructed. For example, the structure

(19)

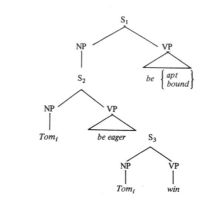

---

[4] The fact that *apt* and *bound* do not trigger Extraposition is illustrated by

(i)  a.  *For the President to be re-elected is $\begin{Bmatrix} apt \\ bound \end{Bmatrix}$

b.  *It is $\begin{Bmatrix} apt \\ bound \end{Bmatrix}$ for the President to be re-elected

c.  *That the President will be re-elected is $\begin{Bmatrix} apt \\ bound \end{Bmatrix}$

d.  *It is $\begin{Bmatrix} apt \\ bound \end{Bmatrix}$ that the President will be re-elected

e.  The President is $\begin{Bmatrix} apt \\ bound \end{Bmatrix}$ to be re-elected.

For further examples, see *(3a–c) in the text. In the discussion of section 48, What is the Cycle-Type of Extraposition, we give an independent argument that sentences like (15) cannot be derived from structures like (16) by first applying Subject-to-Subject Raising on $S_1$ and then applying Extraposition.

satisfies the structural descriptions of obligatory Equi on $S_2$ and obligatory Subject-to-Subject Raising on $S_1$. Applying these rules simultaneously would produce

(20)  *Tom is* $\begin{Bmatrix} apt \\ bound \end{Bmatrix}$ *to be eager to win.*

In other cases, however, it is impossible for rules to apply simultaneously. For example,

(21)

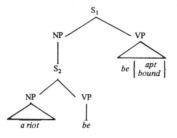

satisfies the structural description of obligatory There-Insertion on $S_2$ and obligatory Subject-to-Subject Raising on $S_1$. In this structure, these rules perform incompatible operations. Application of THERE-Insertion to (21) would introduce *There* and move *a riot* to the right of *be*. Application of Subject-to-Subject Raising to (21) would make a *a riot* the matrix subject. Since these rules cannot be applied simultaneously, the Anywhere Theory taken together with the Immediate Characterization incorrectly predicts that no grammatical sentence can be derived from (21).

In response to this argument, one might modify the Immediate Characterization of obligatory rules to allow two obligatory rules to apply in either order when their structural descriptions are satisfied by the same structure. This would make it possible for the Anywhere Theory to derive

(22)  *There is* $\begin{Bmatrix} apt \\ bound \end{Bmatrix}$ *to be a riot*

from (21) by first applying THERE-Insertion and then applying Subject-to-Subject Raising. However, it would also make it possible for Subject-to-Subject Raising to apply first, destroying the environment for THERE-Insertion. Thus, the Anywhere Theory would generate

(23) \**A riot is likely to be.*

Since the Cyclical Theory blocks the derivation of \*(23), the above modification of the Immediate Characterization would still allow us to construct an argument in favor of the cycle.

# Discussion of Section 39, Strict Cyclicity

## 1. ARGUMENT 1: MULTIPLE APPLICATIONS OF SUBJECT-TO-OBJECT RAISING

Consider the underlying structure:[1]

(4)

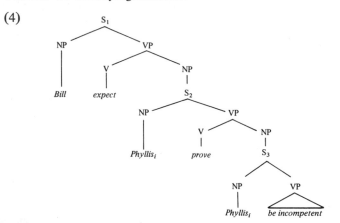

Since *expect* and *prove* trigger Subject-to-Object Raising, the structural description of this rule is met on both $S_1$ and $S_2$. Since Subject-to-Object Raising is optional, it is free either to apply or not to apply on each of these cycles. If it does not apply on either cycle, the result is

---

[1] We ignore here the question of how the future tense is represented in underlying structure. With *that*-clauses it shows up on the surface as *will* (see [5] and [6] below). With infinitival clauses it does not show up on the surface (see [7] and [8]).

(5)   *Bill expects that Phyllis$_i$ will prove that she$_i$ is incompetent.*[2]

If it applies on $S_2$ followed by obligatory Reflexivization, the result is

(6)   *Bill expects that Phyllis will prove herself to be incompetent.*

On the other hand, it may apply only with *expect.*

(7)   *Bill expects Phyllis$_i$ to prove that she$_i$ is incompetent.*

Finally, applying Subject-to-Object Raising on $S_2$ followed by Reflexivization on $S_2$ and Subject-to-Object Raising on $S_1$ results in

(8)   *Bill expects Phyllis to prove herself to be incompetent.*

All of these derivations are consistent with the Principle of Strict Cyclicity; however, none require it. To demonstrate the need for adopting this principle, one must show that certain derivations violating it lead to ungrammatical sentences.

The underlying structure (4) provides us with the starting point for such a derivation. No rules are applied on the $S_3$ cycle. On $S_2$, Subject-to-Object Raising is allowed not to apply. Thus, we move to $S_1$ without having applied any transformations on lower cycles. On $S_1$ we first apply Subject-to-Object Raising with *expect,* producing

(9)

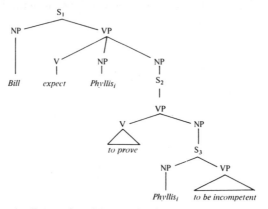

Next we violate the Principle of Strict Cyclicity by applying Subject-to-Object Raising with *prove.*[3] This produces

---

[2] We assume, for concreteness, that the nonreflexive pronouns that occur on the surface in (5), and the sentences that follow, are produced by Pronominalization. It should be noted, however, that none of the arguments presented in this section depend crucially on this assumption.

[3] Subject-to-Object Raising requires information about the matrix verb (in this case *prove*) in order to operate. However, it does not require any information about the matrix

(10)

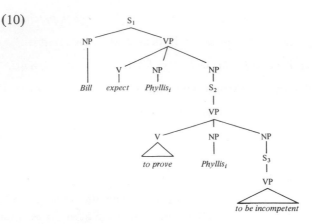

Since the two occurrences of *Phyllis* are still in different clauses, Reflexivization cannot apply. Instead, Pronominalization operates and

(11) **Bill expects Phyllis$_i$ to prove her$_i$ to be incompetent*[4]

is derived.

The ungrammaticality of *(11) is a direct result of the violation of Strict Cyclicity. Without this principle it would be possible to apply Subject-to-Object Raising twice without ever satisfying the structural description of Reflexivization.

(12)

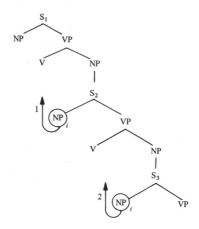

*Footnote 3 continued*

subject. For this reason, we assume that the structural description of Subject-to-Object Raising is satisfied by S$_2$ in (9).

[4] The asterisk on *(11) indicates that *Phyllis* and *her* cannot be coreferential.

With Strict Cyclicity this is impossible. If Subject-to-Object Raising applies with *prove,* then it must do so on the $S_2$ cycle. At this point the structural description of Reflexivization will be satisfied. No matter what characterization of obligatory rules is adopted, Reflexivization must apply on the $S_2$ cycle before Subject-to-Object Raising on $S_1$ has a chance to destroy the environment for its operation. Thus, by preventing rules from applying as in (12), the Principle of Strict Cyclicity blocks the derivation of *(11). For this reason, Strict Cyclicity must be adopted.

## 2. ARGUMENT 2: EQUI AND SUBJECT-TO-OBJECT RAISING

A parallel argument can be constructed involving single applications of Subject-to-Object Raising and Equi. For example, the structure underlying

(13)  a.    *Betty$_i$ expects that she$_i$ will prove that she$_i$ is electable*
     b.    *Betty$_i$ expects that she$_i$ will prove herself to be electable*
     c.    *Betty$_i$ expects to prove that she$_i$ is electable*
     d.    *Betty$_i$ expects to prove herself to be electable*

is

(14)

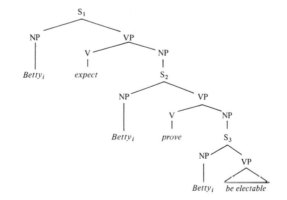

If neither Subject-to-Object Raising nor Equi applies, then (13a) is derived. (13b) results from applying Subject-to-Object Raising on $S_2$ followed by Reflexivization. Application of Equi on $S_1$ produces (13c). Subject-to-Object Raising, Reflexivization, and Equi each apply in deriving (13d).

Strict Cyclicity is needed to block

(15) *\*Betty$_i$ expects to prove her$_i$ to be electable.*[5]

Without this principle, *(15) would be derived by applying no rules on the S$_3$ and S$_2$ cycles, and then applying Equi with *expect* followed by Subject-to-Object Raising with *prove.*

(16)

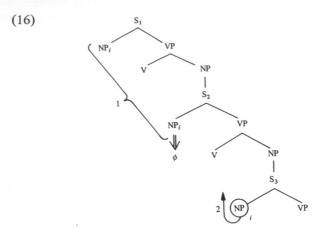

In such a derivation, the structural description of Reflexivization would never be satisfied. Instead, Pronominalization would apply, and *(15) would be generated. Strict Cyclicity prevents this by requiring Subject-to-Object Raising to apply on the S$_2$ cycle if it is to apply with *prove* at all.

### 3. ARGUMENT 3: SUBJECT-TO-SUBJECT AND SUBJECT-TO-OBJECT RAISING

The structure underlying

(17)   a.    *Bill$_i$ seems to believe that he$_i$ is flawless*

and

      b.    *Bill$_i$ seems to believe himself$_i$ to be flawless*

---

[5] The asterisk on *(15) indicates that *Betty* and *her* cannot be coreferential.

is

(18)

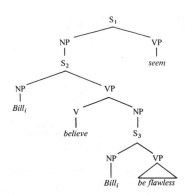

(17a) is derived by applying Subject-to-Subject Raising on $S_1$. (17b) is derived by applying Subject-to-Object Raising and Reflexivization on $S_2$ followed by Subject-to-Subject Raising on $S_1$.

Strict Cyclicity is needed to block

(19) *$Bill_i$ seems to believe $him_i$ to be flawless.

Without this principle, *(19) would be derived by applying no rules on the $S_3$ and $S_2$ cycles, applying Subject-to-Subject Raising with *seem* to produce

(20)

and then applying Subject-to-Object Raising with *believe* to produce

(21)

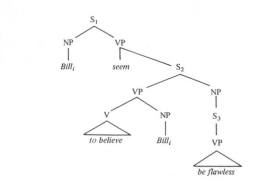

In such a derivation the structural description of Reflexivization would never be met, Pronominalization would apply, and *(19) would be generated. Strict Cyclicity prevents this.


## 4. ELIMINATING THE DEPENDENCE ON ASSUMPTION 2

### 4.1 A Possible Objection

One of the assumptions on which the arguments in §1-3 are based is Assumption 2.

*Assumption 2*

Rules of grammar are not ordered. Within each cycle, each rule is free to apply whenever its structural description is met.

It might be objected that if this assumption were rejected, then there would be no need to adopt the principle of Strict Cyclicity.

Consider again the arguments in §§2–3 involving Equi and Subject-to-Subject Raising. In both cases it was shown that an ungrammatical sentence results from applying rules on the $S_1$ cycle in the order

(22)

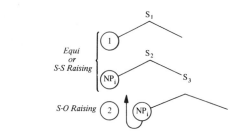

If rules are unordered and are free to apply whenever their structural descriptions are met, then the principle of Strict Cyclicity is needed to prevent the rule application represented in (22). However, if the grammar orders its rules as in [6]

(23)                  ⋮

*Subject-to-Object Raising*

⋮

*Equi*

*Subject-to-Subject Raising*

⋮

then the rule application illustrated in (22) cannot occur on the $S_1$ cycle. Consequently, *(15) and *(19) could be blocked by a grammar that imposed rule ordering without Strict Cyclicity.

A similar objection might be made against the argument in §1. That argument involves multiple applications of Subject-to-Object Raising on the $S_1$ cycle in the order

(24)

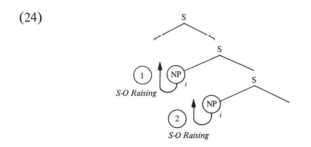

If the rules of the grammar are ordered, and if each rule can apply only once each time its turn comes up in the ordering, then Subject-to-Object Raising can apply only once on the $S_1$ cycle. Consequently, *(11) could be blocked by a grammar that imposed rule ordering without Strict Cyclicity.

### 4.2 A Further Challenge

Answer the objection in §4.1 by showing that the principle of Strict Cyclicity is required even if all rules of a grammar are ordered. Hint: consider the effects of embedding *(11), *(15), and *(19) in higher sentences. Try to do this yourself before reading the solution in §5.

---

[6] The relative order of Equi and Subject-to-Subject Raising is irrelevant.

## 5. HIGHER CYCLES

The rule ordering suggested in §4 prevents rules from applying on the $S_1$ cycle in the order

(25)

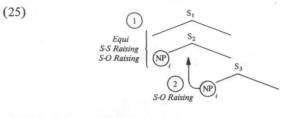

Suppose, however, that we add a higher cycle.

(26)

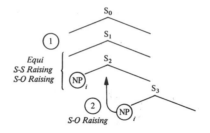

Rule ordering affects only the order of application *within* cycles. Consequently, without Strict Cyclicity, nothing prevents ① from occuring on the $S_1$ cycle followed by ② on the $S_0$ cycle. Since the situation in (26) can occur if ① and ② apply in different cycles, Strict Cyclicity is needed to block the sentences in (27).[7]

(27)  a.   *Harry said that Bill expects Phyllis$_i$ to prove her$_i$ to be incompetent.*

  b.   *Harry said that Betty$_i$ expects to prove her$_i$ to be electable.*

  c.   *Mary said that Bill$_i$ seems to believe him$_i$ to be flawless.*

This shows that an argument for Strict Cyclicity can be constructed which is independent of any assumptions about rule ordering.

---

[7] The asterisks in (27) indicate the impossibility of the coreferential interpretations.

## 6. *STRICT CYCLICITY IS AN EMPIRICAL PRINCIPLE*

The arguments in this discussion show that Strict Cyclicity is not a logical consequence of the Cycle, but rather is an empirical principle that is motivated by linguistic data. A priori, a grammar incorporating the Cycle could either include Strict Cyclicity or exclude it. Thus, each of the following grammars is conceptually possible.

*Grammar A*

The Cycle and Strict Cyclicity are both adopted.

*Grammar B*

The Cycle is adopted but Strict Cyclicity is not.

If sentences like *(11), *(15), *(19), and *(27) had been grammatical, then Grammar B would have been adopted. The fact that these sentences are ungrammatical supports Grammar A.

It should be noted that there is one way in which the Cycle and Strict Cyclicity are logically connected. Since the notion of Strict Cyclicity presupposes the Cycle, one could not have a grammar that incorporated Strict Cyclicity without the Cycle. Thus, each of our arguments for Strict Cyclicity is also a new argument for the Cycle.

# Discussion of Section 45, Cycle-Types

## 1. STEP 1: HOW TO SHOW THAT TWO RULES ARE OF THE SAME CYCLE-TYPE

To show that two rules $R_1$ and $R_2$ are of the same cycle-type, it is sufficient to show that some applications of $R_1$ must precede some applications of $R_2$ and vice versa. If one of these rules were cyclical and the other post-cyclical, then this would be impossible. For example, if $R_1$ were cyclical and $R_2$ postcyclical, then $R_2$ could never apply before $R_1$.

One way of showing that two rules have the same cycle-type is to find a grammatical sentence that can be derived only by applying rules in the order $R_1$, $R_2$, $R_1$. Since $R_1$ is applied both before and after $R_2$, the two rules must be of the same cycle-type.

Another way of showing the same thing is to find one grammatical sentence that can only be derived by applying $R_1$ before $R_2$ and another grammatical sentence that can only be derived by applying $R_2$ before $R_1$. In such a case, either both rules must by cyclical or both must be postcyclical.

Use these techniques in working Step 1. One way to proceed is to first show that Subject-to-Object Raising and Passive are of the same cycle-type; then show that Subject-to-Object Raising and Reflexive are, too; finally show that Subject-to-Subject Raising is of the same cycle-type as the other three.

Your argument for this conclusion should be independent of any assumptions about the characterization of obligatory rules. As a result, no matter what assumption one uses to construct an argument for the cycle, each of the four rules in this problem must have the same cycle-type. Consequently, any argument that establishes the cycle-type of one of them will automatically establish the cycle-type of all of them.

## 2. STEP 2: THE FRUSTRATED CHARACTERIZATION

In the discussion of section 34 we used Reflexivization and Subject-to-Object Raising to construct an argument for the cycle. Use this argument to show that if the Frustrated Characterization of obligatory rules is adopted, then Reflexivization must be cyclical. The results of Step 1 will then allow you to conclude that all four rules are cyclical.

## 3. STEP 3: THE IMMEDIATE CHARACTERIZATION

Adapt the argument in the discussion of section 38 to show that if the Immediate Characterization of obligatory rules is adopted, then Passive must be cyclical. Step 1 can then be used as before.

## 4. SUPPLEMENTARY ARGUMENTS

The results of Step 1 allow one to use *any* cycle argument involving Reflexivization, Passive, and the two Raisings to show that all four rules are cyclical. Consequently, those who assumed in part 3 that the rules of a grammar are strictly ordered can use the argument in section 31 to show that Reflexivization and Subject-to-Object Raising are cyclical. From this it follows that Passive and Subject-to-Subject Raising are, too.

A similar argument can be constructed involving the principle of Strict Cyclicity. In section 39 we showed that Subject-to-Object Raising obeys this principle. Since any rule that obeys Strict Cyclicity is cyclical, Subject-to-Object Raising is a cyclical rule. Thus, the other three rules in this problem are cyclical as well.

# Discussion of Section 48, What Cycle-Type is Extraposition?

## 1. AN ARGUMENT FOR CYCLICAL EXTRAPOSITION

In the discussion of section 45 we showed that Subject-to-Subject Raising is cyclical. To show that Extraposition is cyclical, it is sufficient to find a grammatical sentence that can only be derived by applying Extraposition before Subject-to-Subject Raising. One such sentence is

(1)   *It seems to be obvious to everyone that Martin was right.*

The structure underlying (1) is

(2)

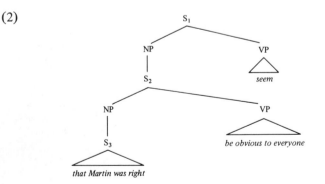

To derive (1) we first apply Extraposition in $S_2$, producing

(3)

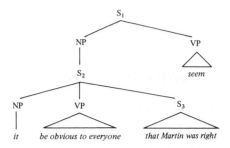

Next, we apply Subject-to-Subject Raising to (3), producing (1). Since Extraposition applies before a cyclical rule, it must be cyclical, too.

## 2. A POSSIBLE OBJECTION: DELAYED EXTRAPOSITION

The argument in §1 shows that (1) can be derived if Extraposition is cyclical. It *assumes* that (1) cannot be derived if Extraposition is postcyclical. However, it might be objected that this assumption is incorrect.

Both Extraposition and Subject-to-Subject Raising must apply in the derivation of (1). If Extraposition is postcyclical, then it cannot apply until after Subject-to-Subject Raising has operated on $S_1$ to produce

(4)

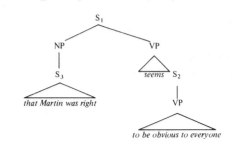

If Extraposition can apply to (4), it will produce

(5)

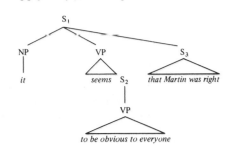

Consequently, it might be claimed that (1) can be derived even if Extraposition is postcyclical.[1]

### 3. TWO CONFLICTING HYPOTHESES

We can now construct two hypotheses regarding the derivation of sentences of the form

(6)   *It seems [ to be _____ ] $_{VP}$ that S*[2]

from structures of the form

(7)

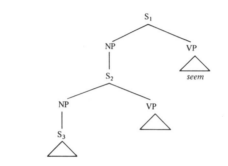

### Hypothesis A: Downstairs Extraposition

Sentences of the form (6) can be derived *only* by applying Extraposition on $S_2$ followed by Subject-to-Subject Raising on $S_1$.

---

[1] Note, if Extraposition applies in $S_2$, the derived constituent structure of (1) is

(i)

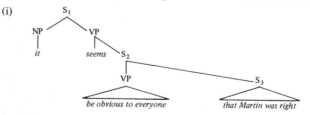

However, if Extraposition applies after Subject-to-Subject Raising in $S_1$, then the derived constituent structure of (1) is (5). We will not attempt to evaluate these derived constituent structures directly.

[2] "[   ] $_{VP}$" indicates that the structure with brackets is a verb phrase.

*Hypothesis B: Delayed Extraposition*

Sentences of the form (6) can be derived by applying Extraposition to $S_1$ after Subject-to-Subject Raising has applied to produce

(8)

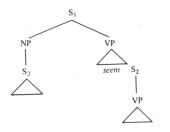

If Hypothesis A is correct, then Extraposition must be cyclical.[3] If Hypothesis B is correct, then sentences like (1) provide no argument for cyclical Extraposition.[4]

## 4. HOW TO DECIDE BETWEEN THE TWO HYPOTHESES: THE CRUCIAL PREDICTIONS

According to Hypothesis A, Extraposition applies on $S_2$ in the derivation of sentences of the form (6). In those cases in which Extraposition can apply on $S_2$, Hypothesis A predicts that the corresponding sentences of the form (6) will be grammatical. In those cases in which Extraposition cannot apply on $S_2$, Hypothesis A predicts that the corresponding sentences of the form (6) will be ungrammatical.

Hypothesis B, on the other hand, predicts that sentences of the form (6) can always be derived from structures of the form (7). According to this hypothesis, Extraposition applies to structures of the form (8). Thus, sentences of the form (6) can always be derived by first applying Subject-to-Subject Raising and then applying Extraposition to $S_1$.

Hypotheses A and B make different predictions in precisely those cases in which Extraposition cannot apply to $S_2$ in structures of the form (7). Hypo-

---

[3] Under Hypothesis A, some mechanism is needed to prevent delayed Extraposition. We will not be concerned here with the nature of this mechanism.

[4] Hypothesis B is compatible with either cyclical or postcyclical Extraposition. If Extraposition is postcyclical, then (1) can be derived only by delayed Extraposition. If Extraposition is cyclical, then Hypothesis B predicts that (1) can be derived by applying Extraposition either before or after Subject-to-Subject Raising.

thesis A predicts that sentences of the form (6) cannot be derived from these structures. Hypothesis B predicts that they can.

## 5. *CYCLICAL EXTRAPOSITION*

For many speakers of English, Extraposition cannot apply in sentences like the following:

(9)   a.   *That arithmetic is incomplete undermines the work of many logicians.*

   b.   *\*It undermines the work of many logicians that arithmetic is incomplete.*

(10)  a.   *That light is a wave contradicts all of the professor's assumptions.*

   b.   *\*It contradicts all of the professor's assumptions that light is a wave.* [5]

(11)  a.   *That there is no largest natural number shows that the set of natural numbers is inifinte.*

   b.   *\*It shows that the set of natural numbers is infinite that there is no largest natural number.*

The ungrammaticality of the (b)-sentences shows that Extraposition does not apply in these cases.

Now consider the structure

(12)

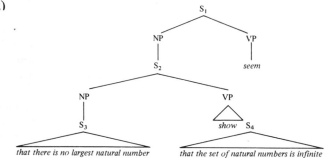

---

[5] The asterisk indicates that \*(10b) is ungrammatical on the reading in which it is derived from (10a). \*(10b) has another reading in which *it* is referential, and *the professor's assumptions that light is a wave* is a relative clause. On this reading \*(10b) is grammatical, but it is not derived by Extraposition.

(12) underlies the grammatical sentence

(13) *That there is no largest natural number seems to show that the set of natural numbers is infinite.* [6]

Extraposition cannot apply to $S_2$ in (12). Thus, Hypothesis A correctly predicts the ungrammaticality of

(14) *\*It seems to show that the set of natural numbers is infinite that there is no largest natural number.*

Hypothesis B, on the other hand, allows \*(14) to be derived by the application of Subject-to-Subject Raising and Extraposition on $S_1$. Application of Subject-to-Subject Raising to (12) produces

(15)

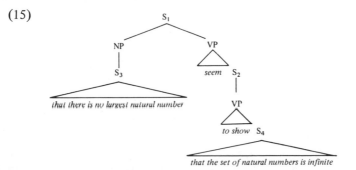

Application of Extraposition to (15) produces \*(14). Since Hypothesis B incorrectly predicts that \*(14) is grammatical, it must be rejected in favor of Hypothesis A. [7]

---

[6] (13) is derived under both hypotheses by applying Subject-to-Subject Raising on $S_1$.

[7] Under Hypothesis B, this result cannot be avoided by preventing Extraposition from applying to structures of the form

(i)

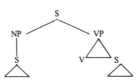

since these are the structures that are routinely required for delayed Extraposition. One might try to save Hypothesis B by adding a constraint preventing Extraposition from applying to structures of the form

Similar arguments can be constructed involving

(16) *\*It seems to undermine the work of many logicians that arithmetic is
incomplete*

which is the counterpart of \*(9b) and

(17) *\*It seems to contradict all of the professor's assumptions that light is
a wave*

*Footnote 7 continued*

(ii)

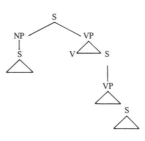

thereby blocking \*(14). However, there are two difficulties with this. First, if under this
hypothesis Extraposition is to be postcyclical, then it must apply to at least some structures
of the form (ii). For example, in order to derive

(iii) *It is certain to appear to many sports fans to be obvious that the Yankees can't
keep winning forever*

by postcyclical, delayed Extraposition, the rule would have to apply to

(iv)

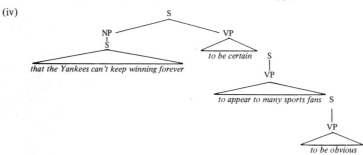

It is not clear how Extraposition could be formulated under Hypothesis B so as to apply to
(iv), but not (15). Second, under Hypothesis A the ungrammaticality of \*(14) follows
automatically from whatever constraint is needed independently to prevent Extraposition
from producing \*(11b). Unless the same can be demonstrated for Hypothesis B, it must be
rejected in favor of Hypothesis A.

which is the counterpart of *(10b). Thus, the objection in §2 is undermined, and Extraposition is cyclical.[8]

---

[8] Exactly the same form of argument can be used to establish the impossibility of delayed Subject-to-Subject Raising. This result involves the derivation of sentences like

(i) *John seems to be likely to win*

from structures like

(ii)

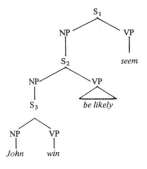

(i) is derived by applying Subject-to-Subject Raising first to $S_2$ and then to $S_1$. It cannot be derived by delaying Subject-to-Subject Raising until the $S_1$-cycle, applying it to produce

(iii)

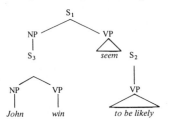

and then applying it again to produce

(iv)

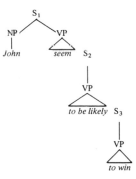

An additional argument for the cyclicity of Extraposition is given in part 5 in the section on Super Equi-NP Deletion.[9]

*Footnote 8 continued*

This is shown by comparing (i) with sentences like

(v)     *That John will win the race is probable*
(vi)    *\*John is probable to win the race*
(vii)   *That John will win the race seems to be probable*
(viii)  *\*John seems to be probable to win the race.*

If the verbal in $S_2$ triggers Subject-to-Subject Raising, then sentences of the form

(ix)    *John seems to be **Verbal** to win*

are grammatical. If the verbal in $S_2$ does not trigger Subject-to-Subject Raising, these sentences are ungrammatical. This shows that sentences of the form (ix) can only be derived by applying Subject-to-Subject Raising in both $S_1$ and $S_2$.

[9] For further arguments for the cyclicity of Extraposition, see Jacobson and Neubauer (1976).

# Appendix to the Cycle-Type of Extraposition

*Appendix to the Cycle-Type of Extraposition*

In §1 of the previous Discussion we showed that sentences like

(1)  *It seems to be obvious to everyone that Martin was right*

can be derived from structures like

(2)

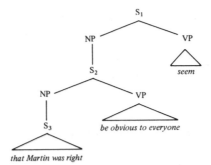

by applying Extraposition on $S_2$ followed by Subject-to-Subject Raising on $S_1$. In §§2–5 we argued that this is the only way that sentences like (1) can be derived. Thus, we concluded that Extraposition is cyclical.

In working this problem, a somewhat different argument may have occurred to you. A sentence like

(3)  *It is* $\begin{Bmatrix} apt \\ bound \end{Bmatrix}$ *to be illegal for stores to be open on Sunday*

can be derived from a structure like

(4)

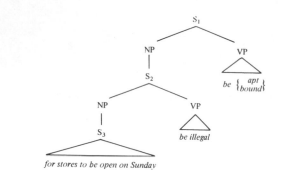

by applying Extraposition on $S_2$ followed by Subject-to-Subject Raising on $S_1$. To show that this is the only way that (3) can be derived, you may have appealed to the assumption

(5)   ***Apt* and *bound* do not trigger Extraposition.**

If (5) is correct, then (3) cannot be derived by first applying Subject-to-Subject Raising to produce

(6)

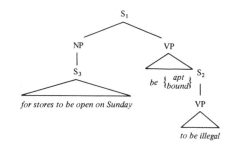

and then applying Extraposition with *apt* or *bound* to produce (3). Consequently, Extraposition must be cyclical.

Given (5), this a good argument. The reason we did not present it earlier is that we wanted to free the argument for the cyclicity of Extraposition from assumptions about particular verbals. (5) is motivated by examples like

(7)   a.   *\*It is* $\begin{Bmatrix} apt \\ bound \end{Bmatrix}$ *for the President to be re-elected*

      b.   *\*It is* $\begin{Bmatrix} apt \\ bound \end{Bmatrix}$ *that the President will be re-elected*

However, it has sometimes been suggested that the way to handle cases like these is not to adopt (5), but rather to adopt the constraint

(8)    *Subject-to-Subject Raising must apply with **apt** and **bound**.*

*(7a–b) violate (8). Thus, if (8) is adopted, then (5) is not needed to account for these examples.[1]

It might be thought that if (8) is adopted rather than (5), then (3) could be derived from (4) by first applying Subject-to-Subject Raising (thus satisfying [8]) and then applying Extraposition. The argument in §§2–5 shows that this is incorrect. Thus, it is possible to construct an argument for the cyclicity of Extraposition no matter what principle one adopts to account for examples like *(7a–b).[2]

---

[1] It should be noted that (8) is not necessarily equivalent to

(i)    *Subject-to-Subject Raising is obligatory with **apt** and **bound**.*

Under the Frustrated Characterization of obligatory rules, (i) is not enough to characterize *(7a–b) as ungrammatical; either (5) or (8) is also needed. Under the Immediate Characterization, all that is needed is (i). Whether or not some special statement like (5) or (8) is required depends upon what characterization of obligatory rules is adopted.

[2] The question of how to account for examples like *(7a–b) is one that we will leave open. In §2.4 of the discussion of section 38 we used (5) to argue that (3) cannot be derived from (4) by applying Extraposition after Subject-to-Subject Raising. The argument just presented shows that (5) is not essential to establish this conclusion.

# Discussion of Section 51,
# FORCE and EXPECT

## 1. UNDERLYING OBJECTS AND DERIVED OBJECTS

### 1.1 Strategy

Hypothesis A claims that sentences of the form

(7)    *NP expect NP[ to−]* $_{VP}$

are derived from underlying structures of the form

(3)

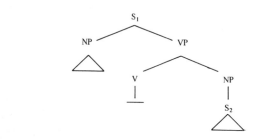

by Subject-to-Object Raising. This means that any *NP* that becomes the subject of $S_2$ during the course of derivation can become the derived object of *expect*.

Hypothesis B makes a different claim. Under this hypothesis, sentences of the form

(8)   *NP force NP [ to– ]* $_{NP}$

are derived from underlying structures of the form

(5)

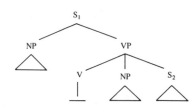

by object-controlled Equi. This means that only those NPs that can be underlying objects of *force* can be surface structure objects of *force*.

In §1 we will use these claims to construct three arguments for Hypotheses A and B.

## 1.2  Fixed Expressions

(9)  a.    *I expected advantage to be taken of their inexperience by
           everyone.*

     b.    *I expected heed to be paid to that proposal by all of the
           legislators.*

(10) a.    *\*I forced advantage to be taken of their inexperience by
           everyone.*

     b.    *\*I forced heed to be paid to that proposal by all of the
           legislators.*

The distribution of *advantage* and *heed* is limited by restrictions (11) and
(12). (See the discussion of section 10.)

(11)  *Advantage can occur in underlying structures without an article or
      other modifier only in the context of the fixed expression* **take
      advantage of.**

(12)  *Heed can occur in underlying structures only in the context of the
      fixed expressions* **take heed of** *and* **pay heed to.**

According to these restrictions

(13)  a.

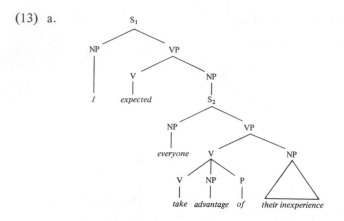

and

(13)  b.

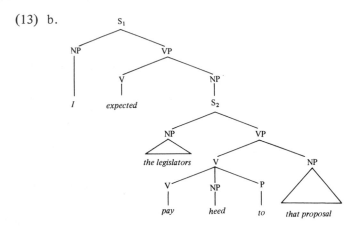

are well-formed underlying structures, but

(14)  a.

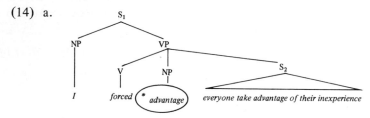

and

(14) b.

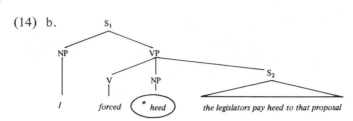

are not.

Under Hypothesis A, (9a) and (9b) are derived from (13a) and (13b) by first applying Passive to produce

(15) a.

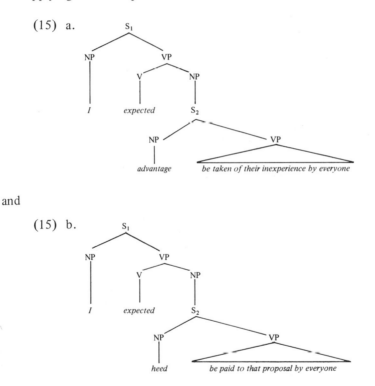

and

(15) b.

and then applying Subject-to-Object Raising. Thus, Hypothesis A correctly predicts that (9a) and (9b) are grammatical.

Hypothesis B also makes the right predictions. Under this hypothesis, the structures underlying *(10a) and *(10b) are (14a) and (14b). Since these are not well-formed underlying structures, Hypothesis B accounts for the fact that *(10a) and *(10b) are deviant.

The correct predictions made by these two hypotheses contrast with the incorrect predictions made by alternative hypotheses in which *force*-sentences are derived from structures like (3) and *expect*-sentences are derived from structures like (5). These alternatives incorrectly characterize *(10a–b) as grammatical and (9a–b) as ungrammatical. (9) and *(10) provide an argument for rejecting these alternatives in favor of Hypotheses A and B.

## 1.3 THERE

Another argument is provided by sentences like

(16)  *I expected there to be a man behind the counter*
(17) *I forced there to be a man behind the counter.*

Under Hypothesis A, (16) is derived from

(18)

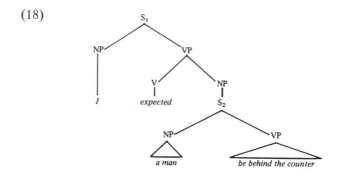

by applying THERE-Insertion of $S_2$ followed by Subject-to-Object Raising on $S_1$. Under Hypothesis B, the surface object of *force* is also its underlying object. Since *there* does not occur in underlying structure, but rather is introduced by THERE-Insertion, the structure

(19)

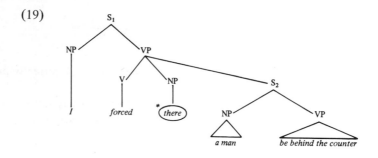

is not a well-formed underlying structure. Thus, *(17) cannot be derived.
Note also that *(17) cannot be derived from

(20)

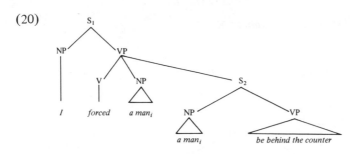

If THERE-Insertion applies on $S_2$ producing

(21)

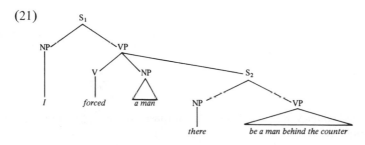

then Equi cannot apply and no grammatical sentence results. If Equi applies to
(20), then

(22)

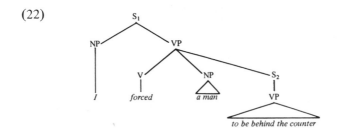

is produced. Since THERE-Insertion cannot apply to (22), *(17) cannot be
generated.[1]

---

[1] Two things are needed to account for examples like *(17).

  (i) *Hypothesis B*
  (ii) *The assumption that THERE-Insertion cannot apply to (22)*

Examples like *(17) simultaneously provide arguments for both (i) and (ii).

## 1.4 Dummy Subjects

A third argument involves examples like

(23)  *I expected it to rain in March*

and

(24) *\*I forced it to rain in March.*

Under Hypothesis A, (23) is derived from

(25)

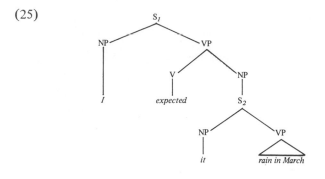

by Subject-to-Object Raising. Under Hypothesis B, the structure underlying *(24) would have to be

(26)

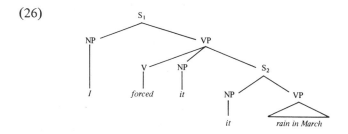

In (26), the subject of $S_2$ is a nonreferential dummy that cannot occur as the object of *force.*[2] Since the two occurrences of *it* are not coreferential, Equi cannot apply and *(24) cannot be derived. Thus, Hypotheses A and B account for the fact that (23) is grammatical and *(24) is not.

---

[2] Note that *force* can take *it* as an underlying object, provided that *it* is referential. Thus, in talking about a being from outer space, one might say,

(i)   *I don't know what it was, but I forced it to retreat.*

Nonreferential *its,* on the other hand, cannot be objects of **force**. Such dummies do not

## 2. *MEANING AND SELECTIONAL RESTRICTIONS*

### 2.1 Strategy

In this section we will be concerned with the connection between the following hypotheses.

(27) a. *Hypotheses A and B*
  b. *The hypothesis that the meaning of a sentence is represented in underlying structure.*
  c. *The hypothesis that selectional restrictions are stated on underlying structure.*

In §2.2 we will look for evidence bearing on (a) and (b). In §2.3 we will look for evidence bearing on (a) and (c).

### 2.2 Embedded Passives

Consider the following sentences.

(28) a. *I expected the doctor to examine Mark.*
  b. *I expected Mark to be examined by the doctor.*
(29) a. *I forced the doctor to examine Mark.*
  b. *I forced Mark to be examined by the doctor.*

The sentences in (28) are synonymous. Under Hypothesis **A**, (28a) is derived from

(30)

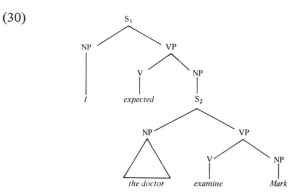

*Footnote 2 continued*
occur freely in underlying structure, but rather occur as subjects with a highly restricted class of verbals.

by Subject-to-Object Raising. (28b) is derived from the same underlying structure by applying Passive on $S_2$ followed by Subject-to-Object Raising on $S_1$.

The sentences in (29) are nonsynonymous. Under Hypothesis B, (29a) is
derived from

(31) a.

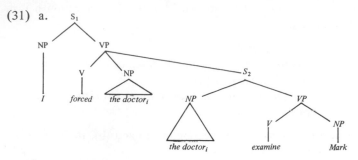

by Equi; (29b) is derived from

(31) b.

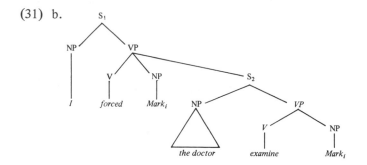

by applying Passive on $S_2$ followed by Equi on $S_1$.

Given Hypotheses A and B, we can use (28) and (29) to provide further
support for the hypothesis that the meaning of a sentence is represented in
underlying structure. Under Hypothesis A, synonymous sentences ([28a-b]) are
derived from the same underlying structure. Under Hypothesis B, nonsynonymous sentences ([29a-b]) are derived from different underlying structures.[3]
Since we have found independent evidence that Hypotheses A and B are correct,
(28) and (29) provide further confirmation of the thesis that meaning is represented in underlying structure.

---

[3] Note that the difference between the underlying structures (31a) and (31b) reflects
the difference in meaning between (29a) and (29b). In each case the underlying object of
*force* indicates the person I prevailed upon to ensure that the examination took place.

We have just shown that Hypotheses A and B support our tentative thesis about meaning.

(32)  *Hypotheses A and B* $\xrightarrow{support}$ *Meaning in Underlying Structure*

However, one can also argue in the other direction—i.e., one can show that the thesis that meaning is represented in underlying structure provides further support for Hypotheses A and B.

(33)  *Meaning in Underlying Structure* $\xrightarrow{supports}$ *Hypotheses A and B.*

The argument for Hypothesis A is that it automatically accounts for the synonymy of (28a) and (28b) by deriving them from the same underlying structure. Thus, *expect*-sentences are derived from structures like (3) rather than structures like (5). The argument for Hypothesis B is that, given our thesis about meaning, we cannot derive nonsynonymous sentences ([29a-b]) from the same underlying structures. Thus, *force*-sentences cannot be derived from structures like (3), but rather must come from structures like (5). Since we have previously found independent evidence that meaning is represented in underlying structure, (28) and (29) provide further evidence for Hypotheses A and B.

These results show that Hypothesis A, Hypothesis B, and the hypothesis that meaning is represented in underlying structure support one another.

(34)  *Hypotheses A and B* $\xleftrightarrow{support}$ *Meaning in Underlying Structure*

Each is needed to account for (28) and (29). Thus, (28) and (29) simultaneously provide arguments for all three hypotheses.

## 2.3  Selectional Restrictions

A slightly different point is illustrated by

(35)  a.   *I expected Sam's proposal to be rejected by the committee.*
      b.   *I expected the earthquake to destroy the city.*
      c.   *I expected the election to be a landslide.*

and

(36)  a.   *\*I forced Sam's proposal to be rejected by the committee.*
      b.   *\*I forced the earthquake to destroy the city.*
      c.   *\*I forced the election to be a landslide.*

There are no selectional restrictions on the surface objects of *expect*; any NP that become the subject of the complement during the derivation can be raised to become the derived object of *expect.* However, there are selectional restrictions on the surface objects of *force*; only those NPs that are capable of denoting animate beings can be objects of *force*.

This difference between *force* and *expect* follows automatically if we accept the following hypotheses.

(37)  a.    *Hypothesis A*
      b.    *Hypothesis B*
      c.    *The hypothesis that selectional restrictions are stated on underlying structures.*
      d.    *The hypothesis that selectional restrictions involve only members of the same clause (e.g., subjects and objects of verbs).*

Under Hypothesis A, the derived object of *expect* is not its underlying object, but rather is a constituent of the complement clause. Thus, there can be no selectional restrictions on what can become the derived object of *expect*. Under Hypothesis B, the derived object of *force* is also its underlying object. Thus, there can be selectional restrictions on the objects of *force*.

## 3.  SUPPLEMENTARY ARGUMENTS

### 3.1  Extraposition

In §1.3 we used THERE-Insertion to argue for Hypotheses A and B. Extraposition can be used in exactly the same way.

(38)  *I expected it to be obvious to everyone that the earth is round.*
(39)  *\*I forced it to be obvious to everyone that the earth is round.*

Under Hypothesis A, (38) is derived from

(40)

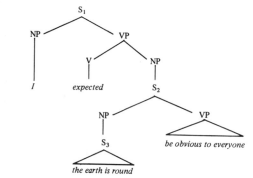

by applying Extraposition on $S_2$ followed by Subject-to-Object Raising on $S_1$. Thus, Hypothesis A correctly characterizes (38) as grammatical.

Under Hypothesis B, the surface object of *force* is also its underlying object. Since the nonreferential *it* of Extraposition does not occur in underlying structure, *(39) cannot be derived. Thus, Hypothesis B correctly characterizes *(39) as ungrammatical.[4]

## 3.2 Sentence Idioms

Another difference between *force* and *expect* is illustrated by the following sentences.

(41) a.  *I expected the cat to be out of the bag.*
  b.  *I expected all hell to break loose.*
  c.  *I expected the shoe to be on the other foot.*

[4] Note also that *(39) cannot be derived from

(i)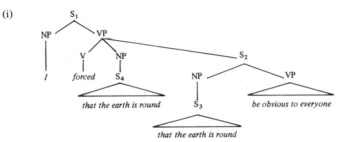

There are three reasons for this. First, (i) violates selectional restrictions that require that the object of *force* be capable of designating an animate being. Thus, (i) is not a well-formed underlying structure. Second, since sentential NPs are not referential, Equi cannot operate on (i) to produce

(ii)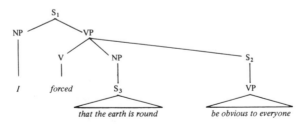

Third, even if (ii) could be produced, given the way we have formulated Extraposition, we could not apply it to (ii) to produce *(39). Thus, Hypothesis B accounts for the fact that *(39) cannot be derived.

(42)  a.  *\*I forced the cat to be out of the bag.*
      b.  *\*I forced all hell to break loose.*
      c.  *\*I forced the shoe to be on the other foot.*

When the embedded sentence is a sentence idiom, *expect*-sentences are grammatical; *force*-sentences are not.

Hypothesis B accounts for the ungrammaticality of the sentences in \*(42). According to this hypothesis, the structure underlying \*(42a) is

(43)

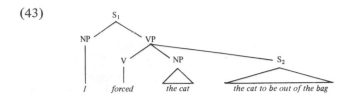

The occurrence of *the cat* in the matrix sentence refers to an animal; the occurrence of *the cat* in $S_2$ does not. Thus, Equi cannot apply, and \*(42) cannot be derived.

Unlike Equi, Subject-to-Object Raising does not require coreference. Consequently, if *force*-sentences were derived from structures like (3) by Subject-to-Object Raising, then nothing would prevent the sentences in \*(42) from being derived. This is another reason for rejecting the hypothesis that *force*-sentences are derived from structures like (3) and accepting Hypothesis B.

We can also construct an argument for Hypothesis A. Since the sentences in (41) are grammatical, they cannot be derived from structures like (5) by the application of Equi. Rather, they are derived from structures like (3) by Subject-to-Object Raising. Thus, sentence idioms also provide us with another argument for Hypothesis A.

### 3.3  Independent Evidence that EXPECT Takes Sentential Objects

(44)  a.  *Everyone expected that war would break out.*
      b.  *That war would break out was expected by everyone.*
      c.  *It was expected by everyone that war would break out.*
(45)  a.  *\*Everyone forced that war would break out.*
      b.  *\*That war would break out was forced by everyone.*
      c.  *\*It was forced by everyone that war would break out.*

The sentences in (44) are derived from

(46)

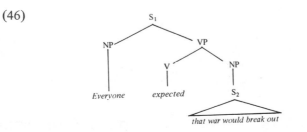

Thus, the grammaticality of (44) constitutes independent evidence that *expect* occurs in underlying structures of the form (3).[5] The ungrammaticality of the sentences in *(45) is a result of the fact that *force* does not occur in underlying structures of this form.[6]

---

[5] Note also that (44a–c) are synonymous with (i).

   (i) *Everyone expected war to break out.*

This is automatically accounted for by Hypothesis A together with the hypothesis that meaning is represented in underlying structure.

  [6] Note that *want* occurs in underlying structures of the form (3) even though

   (i)  a.   *\*Everyone wants that war will break out*
        b.   *\*That war will break out is wanted by everyone*
        c.   *\*It is wanted by everyone that war will break out*

are ungrammatical. Thus, the ungrammaticality of *(45) does not, by itself, constitute conclusive evidence that *force* fails to occur in structures like (3). This means that although Hypothesis B correctly predicts the ungrammaticality of the sentences in *(45), these sentences do not provide an additional argument for Hypothesis B that is independent of the arguments in the foregoing sections.

# Discussion of Section 55, THERE-Insertion and Verb Agreement

Arguments can be based on each of the following sets of data.

(1)  a.  *That some mice are in the bathtub is likely.*
   b.  *Some mice are likely to be in the bathtub.*
   c.  *There are likely to be some mice in the bathtub.*
   d.  *That a mouse is in the bathtub is likely.*
   e.  *A mouse is likely to be in the bathtub.*
   f.  *There is likely to be a mouse in the bathtub.*

(2)  a.  *The police chief **believes** that many criminals are still at large.*
   b.  *Many criminals **are** believed by the police chief to be still at large.*
   c.  *There **are** believed by the police chief to be many criminals still at large.*
   d.  *The police chief **believes** that a criminal is still at large.*
   e.  *A criminal **is** believed by the police chief to be still at large.*
   f.  *There **is** believed by the police chief to be a criminal still at large.*

Make these arguments explicit.

# Discussion of Section 57, Super Equi-NP Deletion

## 1. THE CONSTRAINTS ON SUPER EQUI

### 1.1 Potential Triggers: Sentences (5) and (6)

Hypothesis 1 accounts for the derivation of (5b) from (5a). However, it incorrectly predicts that *(6b) can be derived from (6a).

(6)  a.

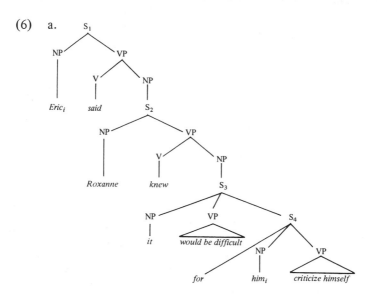

*Eric* both precedes and unilaterally commands *him*. However, in this case there is another NP–*Roxanne*–which also precedes and unilaterally commands *him*. Further, *Roxanne* is between *Eric* and *him* in left-to-right order in the string. It may be this that prevents *Eric* from deleting *him*. This suggests a modification of the initial hypothesis.

Hypothesis 2

Super Equi may delete the subject of an embedded sentence (the victim) under coreferentiality with another NP (the trigger) if and only if

(i)  *the trigger precedes the victim*

and

(ii)  *the trigger unilaterally commands the victim*

and

(iii)  *no potential trigger intervenes between the trigger and the victim in left-to-right order in the string.*

## 1.2  The Importance of Command:  Sentences (7) and (8)

Consider first the sentences in (7).

(7)    a.

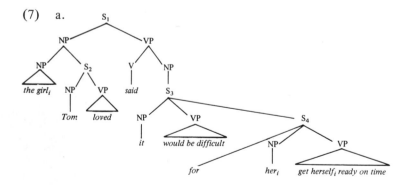

(7b) is derived from (7a) by deleting *her* under coreferentiality with *the girl*. Although *Tom* intervenes between the trigger and the victim, it does not command the victim and therefore it is not a potential trigger. Thus, Hypothesis 2 correctly predicts that deletion is possible.

Next, consider the sentences in (8).

(8)    a.

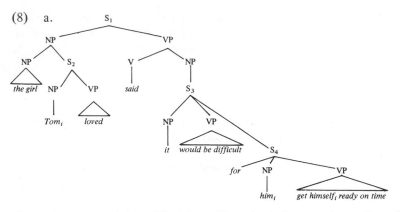

*Tom* does not command *him*. Therefore, Hypothesis 2 correctly predicts that *him* cannot be deleted.

## 1.3  Deletion and Linear Order:  Sentences (9), (10) and (11)

(9)

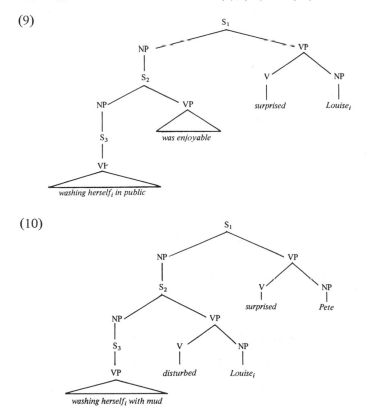

(10)

In both (9) and (10), the fact that *herself* in $S_3$ is coreferential with *Louise* shows that *Louise* must have triggered the delection of the subject of $S_3$. Thus, deletion is possible even when the victim precedes the trigger. Therefore, Hypothesis 2 must be modified.

*Hypothesis 3*

Super Equi may delete the subject of an embedded sentence (the victim) under coreferentiality with another *NP* (the trigger) if and only if

     (i)   *the trigger unilaterally commands the victim*

and

     (ii)   *no potential trigger intervenes between the trigger and the victim in left-to-right order in the string.*

In addition to accounting for all of the data considered so far, Hypothesis 3 correctly predicts the ungrammaticality of *(11).

(11)

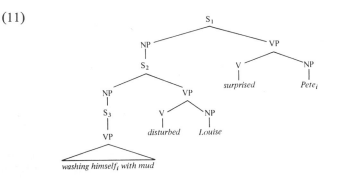

*(11) could be derived only if *Pete* were allowed to trigger the deletion of the subject of $S_3$. However, since *Louise* intervenes between trigger and victim in left-to-right order, no deletion is possible.

## 1.4  More Work for Command:  Sentences (12) and (13)

Hypothesis 3 correctly predicts that *Louise* is able to trigger the deletion of the subject of $S_3$ in the derivation of (12).

(12)

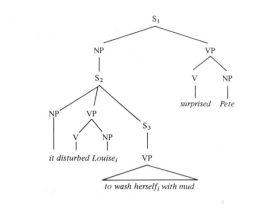

However, Hypothesis 3 incorrectly predicts that *Pete* should also be able to trigger the deletion of the subject of S₃ in the derivation of *(13).

(13)

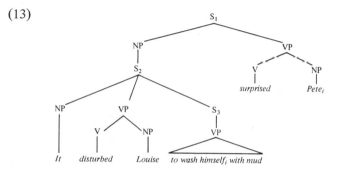

In the derivation of *(13) *Pete* unilaterally commands the subject of S₃. Further, although *Louise* is a potential trigger, it is not located between *Pete* and the subject of S₃. Thus, Hypothesis 3 does not explain why deletion is blocked.[1]

The condition that no potential trigger can intervene between trigger and victim in left-to-right order is inadequate. Notice that in *(13) the potential trigger—*Louise*—is unilaterally commanded by the trigger—*Pete*. Looking back, we find that this is also the case in the other two examples in which a potential trigger blocks deletion [*(6b) and *(11)]. This suggests that we replace condition (ii) in Hypothesis 3 by the following condition:

---

[1] If Super Equi were cyclical and Extraposition were postcyclical, then *(13) could be accounted for without abandoning Hypothesis 3. We will see in §2.2, however, that this assignment of cycle-types is impossible.

(ii)   *There is no potential trigger that is unilaterally commanded by the trigger.*

This gives us Hypothesis 4.

*Hypothesis 4*

Super Equi may delete the subject of an embedded sentence (the victim) under coreferentiality with another *NP* (the trigger) if and only if

(i)   *the trigger unilaterally commands the victim*

and

(ii)   *there is no potential trigger that is unilaterally commanded by the trigger.*

This hypothesis accounts for all of the data considered so far.

### 1.5  The Importance of Precedence:  Sentences (14) and (15)

Hypothesis 4 correctly predicts that *Louise* can delete the subject of $S_3$ in the derivation of (14).

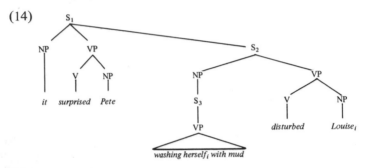

However, Hypothesis 4 incorrectly predicts that *Pete* should be unable to trigger deletion in (15).

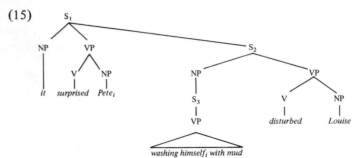

In the derivation of (15), both *Pete* and *Louise* unilaterally command the subject of $S_3$. Further, since *Pete* unilaterally commands *Louise*, clause (ii) of Hypothesis 4 is not met. Thus, Hypothesis 4 incorrectly predicts that deletion should be blocked.

The key sentences to compare are *(13) and (15). In *(13), the potential trigger—*Louise*—precedes the victim, but the trigger does not. Here deletion is blocked. In (15), the trigger precedes the victim, but the potential trigger does not. Here deletion is possible. This shows that the relation *precedes in left-to-right order* is relevant to stating the constraints on Super Equi.

In the data considered so far there have been three cases in which deletion is blocked by a potential trigger—*(6b), *(11), and *(13). In all three cases the trigger unilaterally commands the potential trigger. However, the relative order of the trigger and potential trigger with respect to the victim is different in each case. In *(6b), both trigger and potential trigger precede the victim. In *(11), neither trigger nor potential trigger precedes the victim. In *(13), the potential trigger precedes the victim, but the trigger doesn't. We can represent these cases in the following way:

(24) a.

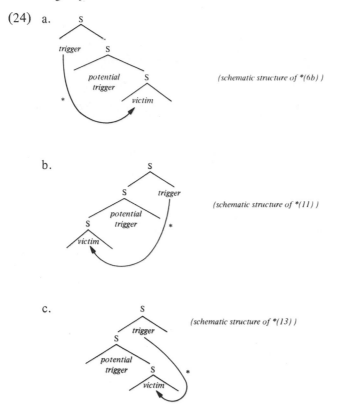

(schematic structure of *(6b) )

b.

(schematic structure of *(11) )

c.

(schematic structure of *(13) )

What we need is a hypothesis that blocks the deletions represented in (24), but allows the deletion represented in (25).

(25)

*(schematic structure of 15)*

Since deletion is sensitive to both *command* and *precedence,* we can use Langacker's notion of primacy relations to formulate a new hypothesis.

*Hypothesis 5*

Super Equi may delete the subject of an embedded sentence (the victim) under coreferentiality with another NP (the trigger) if and only if

    (i)    *the trigger unilaterally commands the victim*

and

    (ii)   *there is no potential trigger which*

        (a)    *is unilaterally commanded by the trigger*

        and

        (b)    *bears at least as many primacy relations to the victim as the trigger does.*

By definition, a potential trigger must command the victim. Thus, both trigger and potential trigger will always bear one primacy relation to the victim. Where they may differ is in whether or not they precede the victim. The effect of clause (iib) in Hypothesis 5 is to allow a potential trigger that is unilaterally commanded by the trigger to prevent deletion in all cases except those in which the trigger alone precedes the victim. Thus, Hypothesis 5 correctly blocks deletion in the cases represented in (24) while allowing deletion in the case represented in (25). As a result, Hypothesis 5 correctly accounts for all of the facts that we have encountered so far.

## 1.6 Further Confirmation of Hypothesis 5: Sentences (16) and (17)

From the point of view of Hypothesis 5, (16a) is just like (14), and (16b) is just like (15). (14) and (16a) exhibit the pattern represented in (26).

(26)

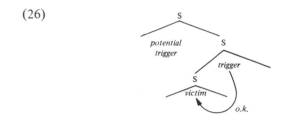

Deletion is permitted since the potential trigger is not commanded by the trigger. (15) and (16b) exhibit the pattern represented in (25). Deletion is permitted because the trigger precedes the victim but the potential trigger does not.

(17a-*b) are just like (6a-*b). (6a) and (17a) exhibit the pattern represented in

(27)

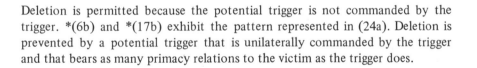

Deletion is permitted because the potential trigger is not commanded by the trigger. *(6b) and *(17b) exhibit the pattern represented in (24a). Deletion is prevented by a potential trigger that is unilaterally commanded by the trigger and that bears as many primacy relations to the victim as the trigger does.

## 1.7  When the Trigger and the Potential Trigger Command Each Other:  Sentences (18) and (19)

The sentences in (18) and (19) allow us to test one part of Hypothesis 5 that we have not yet investigated. Clause (ii) of Hypothesis 5 says that a potential trigger will *block* deletion if and only if

(28)  a.  *the potential trigger is unilaterally commanded by the trigger*

and

b.  *the potential trigger bears at least as many primacy relations to the victim as the trigger does.*

One question that might be asked is whether it is necessary that the potential trigger be *unilaterally* commanded by the trigger in order to prevent deletion. Perhaps what is necessary is only that the potential trigger be commanded by the trigger. Perhaps, that is, clause (ii) should say that a potential trigger will block deletion if and only if

(29)   a.    *the potential trigger is commanded by the trigger*

and

b.    *the potential trigger bears at least as many primacy relations to the victim as the trigger does.*

These two versions of clause (ii) make different predictions about structures in which the trigger and potential trigger are in the same clause. In such cases, the trigger and the potential trigger command each other.

(18a)

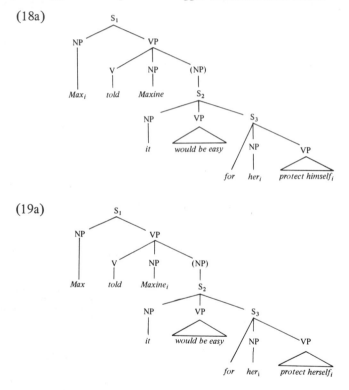

(19a)

In (18a), *Max* is the trigger, and *Maxine* is the potential trigger. In (19a) the situation is reversed. In both cases, the trigger and the potential trigger command each other.

Since *Max* and *Maxine* command each other in (18a) and (19a), (29) predicts that neither should be able to trigger deletion. Thus, (29) incorrectly predicts that (18b) and (19b) are ungrammatical. (28), on the other hand, allows these sentences to be produced. Since neither *Max* nor *Maxine* unilaterally commands the other, both can trigger deletion. Therefore, Hypothesis 5 correctly accounts for (18) and (19).

## 2. THE ANSWERS TO SUBSIDIARY QUESTIONS 1 AND 2

### 2.1 The Derived Constituent Structure of Subject-to-Subject Raising: The Answer to Subsidiary Question 1

The structure underlying (20a) (after Reflexivization in $S_4$) is (30).

(30)

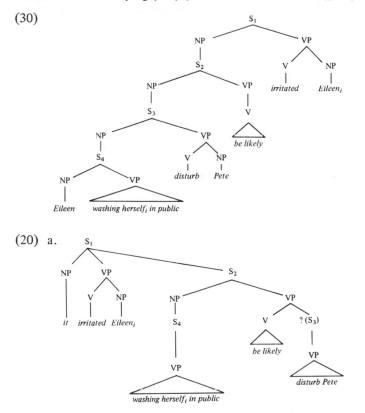

In order to derive (20a) from (30) three things must happen.

(i) *Subject-to-Subject Raising must apply in $S_2$, making* **Eileen washing herself in public** *the subject of* **be likely** *and moving* **disturb Pete** *to the right.*

(ii) *Extraposition must apply in $S_1$, making **it** the subject of **irritate Eileen** and moving $S_2$ to the right.*

(iii) *Super Equi must apply, deleting the subject of $S_4$ under coreferentiality with **Eileen** in $S_1$.*

"?($S_3$)" in (20a) indicates that, so far, it is an open question whether or not the $S_3$-node remains after the application of Subject-to-Subject Raising. If it does remain, then *Pete* will no longer command the subject of $S_4$. If the *S*-node does not remain, then *Pete* will continue to command the subject of $S_4$. Either way, Hypothesis 5 correctly predicts that *Eileen* is able to trigger the deletion of the subject of $S_4$. The reason for this is that *Eileen* both precedes and unilaterally commands the victim. Even if *Pete* continues to command the victim, it won't block deletion since it bears fewer primacy relations to the victim than *Eileen* does.

The crucial sentence is (20b). It is derived from (30) by first applying Subject-to-Subject Raising to $S_2$ and then applying Super Equi in $S_1$. We know that Subject-to-Subject Raising must apply first, since before it operates the relationship between *Eileen, Pete,* and the subject of $S_4$ is represented in (24b).

(24) b.

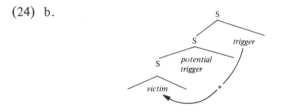

If Super Equi attempts to apply to this structure, no deletion will take place.

Suppose, then, that Subject-to-Subject Raising applies to (30). What will be the resulting structure? Consider the following two alternatives.

(31)

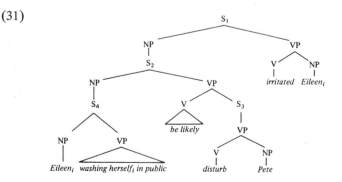

(32)

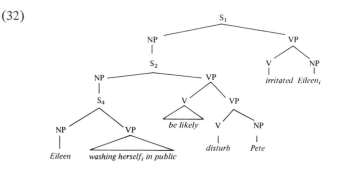

The only difference between (31) and (32) is that in (32) the $S_3$-node is no longer present. We can use the constraints on Super Equi to decide which of these two structures is the one that is produced by applying Subject-to-Subject Raising to (30).

In order to derive (20b), *Eileen* must trigger the deletion of the subject of $S_4$. If (31) is the structure that is produced by Subject-to-Subject Raising, then this deletion can take place. Since *Pete* no longer commands the subject of $S_4$, it is not a potential trigger and cannot prevent *Eileen* from triggering deletion. If, on the other hand, (32) were the structure that was produced by applying Subject-to-Subject Raising to (30), then *Pete* would still command the victim and deletion would be blocked. Since deletion must take place in the derivation of (20b), (31) is the structure that is produced by applying Subject-to-Subject Raising to (30).

From this we can draw a general conclusion about the derived constituent structure produced by Subject-to-Subject Raising. When Subject-to-Subject Raising applies to a structure of the form

(33)

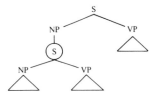

the circled *S*-node is retained and a structure of the form (34) is produced.

(34)

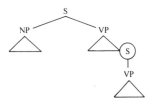

Only by formulating Subject-to-Subject Raising in this way can we ensure that it will produce the structures that are required by Super Equi.

## 2.2 Cycle-Types: The Answer to Subsidiary Question 2

### 2.2.1 The Cycle-Type of Super Equi

The structure underlying (21) is

(35)

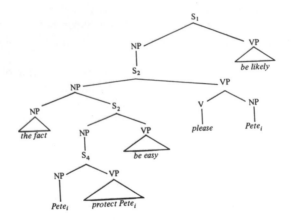

In order for (21) to be derived, three things must happen: Reflexivization must apply in $S_4$; Super Equi must delete the subject of $S_4$[2]: and Subject-to-Subject Raising must apply in $S_1$. Since Reflexivization is cyclical, it must apply first. The question that we will be concerned with is whether it makes a difference in which order Super Equi and Subject-to-Subject Raising apply. We can use our conclusion about the derived constituent structure produced by Subject-to-Subject Raising to answer this question.

The first thing to notice is that (21) can be derived by allowing deletion to take place before Subject-to-Subject Raising operates. Under this alternative, Super Equi applies directly to

---

[2] Since the victim is embedded two sentences below the trigger, the deletion must be the result of Super Equi rather than ordinary Equi.

(36)

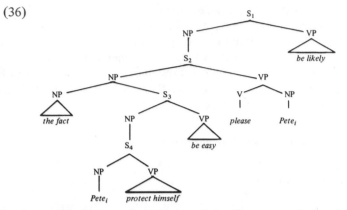

Deletion is possible because the trigger unilaterally commands the victim and no potential trigger intervenes. After this occurs, Subject-to-Subject Raising can apply in $S_1$ to produce

(21)

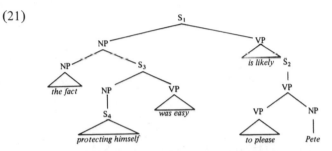

Suppose, however, that Subject-to-Subject Raising were applied before *Pete* triggered the deletion of the subject of $S_4$. Then Subject-to-Subject Raising would apply to (36), producing

(37)

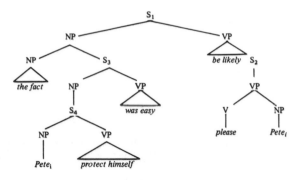

The key fact here is that the $S_2$-node remains in (37). This means that *Pete* no longer commands the subject of $S_4$, and therefore can no longer trigger deletion. Thus, if Subject-to-Subject Raising were applied to (36) before Super Equi had deleted the subject of $S_4$, then (21) would not be generated.

We conclude from this that Super Equi must be able to apply in $S_2$ before Subject-to-Subject Raising applies in $S_1$. Since Subject-to-Subject Raising is cyclical, this means that Super Equi is also cyclical.[3,4]

### 2.2.2 The Cycle-Type of Extraposition

#### 2.2.2.1 Argument 1

Since Super Equi is cyclical, we can show that Extraposition is also cyclical by finding an example in which it must apply before Super Equi. One such example is (15).

(15)

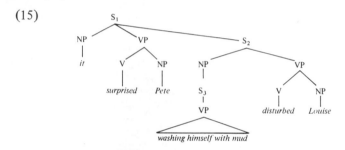

The structure underlying (15) (after Reflexivization in $S_3$) is

(38)

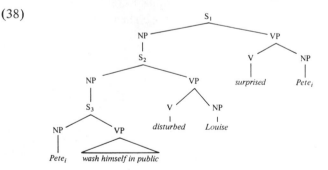

[3] It is not necessary to order Super Equi before Subject-to-Subject Raising. Since both rules are cyclical, Super Equi will apply on the $S_2$-cycle in (36) before Subject-to-Subject Raising has a chance to apply on the $S_1$-cycle.

[4] If you assume that all deletions in which the victim is embedded in the sentence immediately beneath the trigger are produced by ordinary (rather than Super) Equi, then ordinary Equi can be shown to be cyclical by an argument based on

In order for (38) to be derived, Extraposition must apply on $S_1$, and Super Equi must delete the subject of $S_3$.

Extraposition must apply first. Before it applies, deletion is blocked by the potential trigger *Louise*, as is shown by the ungrammatical sentence *(11).

(11)  *That washing himself with mud disturbed Louise surprised Pete.*

However, after Extraposition has produced

(39)

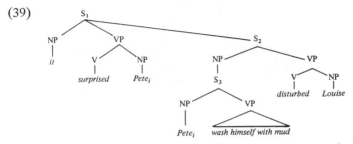

deletion is possible, since the trigger *Pete* bears more primacy relations to the victim than the potential trigger *Louise* does. The fact that Extraposition must apply before Super Equi in the derivation of (15) shows that Extraposition must also be cyclical.

### 2.2.2.2 The Cycle, Strict Cyclicity and Extraposition

The argument just given depends on the cyclicity of Super Equi, which in turn depends on the assumption (established in section 45) that Subject-to-Subject Raising is cyclical. Sentences (22) and *(23) provide an argument for the cyclicity of Extraposition that does not depend on these assumptions.

The structure underlying (22) (after Reflexivization in $S_3$) is

(40)

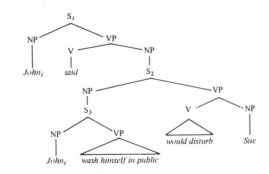

*Footnote 4 continued*

  (i)  *Protecting himself is likely to please Pete.*

The argument involving ordinary Equi is exactly parallel to the argument involving Super Equi presented above.

This structure exhibits the pattern

(25)

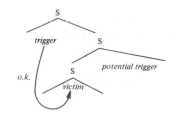

Thus, Super Equi can apply in $S_1$, producing (22). However, if Extraposition could apply in $S_2$ *after* Super Equi applies in $S_1$, then *(23) would be generated. An adequate grammar of English must prevent this.

Now consider the following two hypotheses.

*Hypothesis A*

Extraposition is cyclical and the principle of Strict Cyclicity is adopted.

*Hypothesis B*

Extraposition is postcyclical. (Note, if this is the case, then Super Equi must also be postcyclical.)

Under Hypothesis A, Extraposition must apply on the $S_2$-cycle of (40), if it is to apply at all. (Since Extraposition is cyclical, it *can* apply on the $S_2$-cycle. Given Strict Cyclicity, it can *only* apply on the $S_2$-cycle.) Thus, Extraposition cannot apply after Super Equi operates in $S_1$, and *(23) cannot be derived.

Hypothesis B does not have this consequence. As a result, this hypothesis has to posit an additional constraint prohibiting Extraposition from applying after Super Equi. Since Hypothesis B requires an extra constraint not needed by Hypothesis A, we reject Hypothesis B in favor of Hypothesis A.

The argument just presented is a new argument for the Cycle and Strict Cyclicity. Like Hypothesis B, the Anywhere Theory would have to posit an additional constraint preventing Extraposition from applying in $S_2$ after Super Equi has applied in $S_1$. The Cyclical Theory, together with Strict Cyclicity does not require any such constraint.[5]

---

[5] (i) shows that Super Equi and Extraposition are optional in their application to (40).

   (i) *John$_i$ said that for him$_i$ to make a fool of himself in public would disturb Sue.*

Thus, the argument just constructed for the cycle and Strict Cyclicity is independent of any assumptions about obligatory rules.

## 3. *SUMMARY OF CONCLUSIONS*

### 3.1 The Constraints on Super Equi

Super Equi may delete the subject of an embedded sentence (the victim) under coreferentiality with another NP (the trigger) if and only if

   (i)   *the trigger unilaterally commands the victim*

and

   (ii)   *there is no potential trigger which*

       (a)   *is unilaterally commanded by the trigger*

     and

       (b)   *bears at least as many primacy relations to the victim as the trigger does.*

### 3.2 The Derived Constituent Structure of Subject-to-Subject Raising

When Subject-to-Subject Raising applies to a structure of the form

(39)

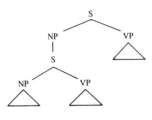

a structure of the form

(40)

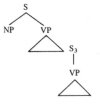

is produced

### 3.3 Cycle Types

   (i)   *Super Equi and Extraposition are cyclical.*
   (ii)   *The interaction of Super Equi and Extraposition provides a new argument for the Cycle and Strict Cyclicity.*

### 3.4 Alternative Formulations

There are, of course, different ways of stating essentially the same constraints on Super Equi. If your solution is stated differently from ours, you can
check it by making sure that it correctly accounts for the following paradigms.

(43)  a.

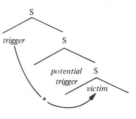

b.

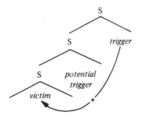

c.

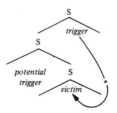

(44)  a.

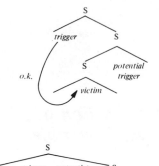

b.

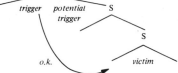

# Discussion of Section 61, Nonsubject Deletion vs. Nonsubject Raising

## 1. THE CRUCIAL SENTENCE

(23) *Getting herself arrested on purpose is hard for me to imagine Betsy being willing to consider.*

In (23) *Betsy* is understood as being the subject of *getting herself arrested on purpose.* Note also that *Betsy* must have been present at some stage of the derivation in order to trigger Reflexivization, which produces the reflexive pronoun *herself.*

## 2. THE STRUCTURES UNDERLYING (23) UNDER EACH HYPOTHESIS

### 2.1 The Nonsubject Deletion Hypothesis

(24)

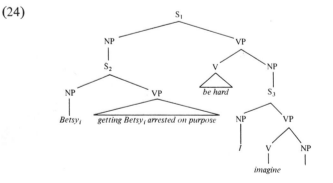

(24) continued

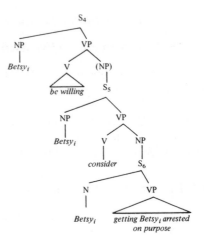

## 2.2 The Nonsubject Raising Hypothesis

(25)

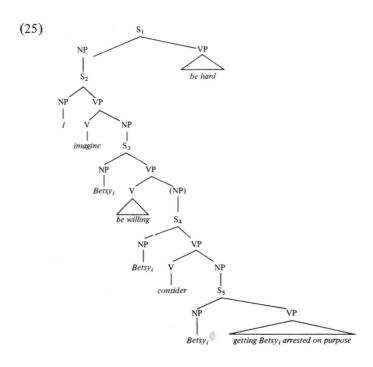

## 3. THE DERIVATIONS UNDER EACH HYPOTHESIS

### 3.1 The Nonsubject Raising Hypothesis

In the derivation of (23), Reflexivization applies on the $S_5$-cycle, followed by Equi on $S_4$ and $S_3$. Next, Nonsubject Raising makes what remains of $S_5$, (which is still dominated by an *NP*-node) the subject of $S_1$ and moves the rest of $S_2$ to the right. Note, Nonsubject Raising cannot apply until the $S_1$-cycle has been reached. Thus, by the time it operates, the subject of $S_5$ will already have been deleted and (23) will be produced.

### 3.2 The Nonsubject Deletion Hypothesis

As before, Reflexivization and Equi apply on the bottom three cycles (in this case, $S_6$, $S_5$, and $S_4$). This produces

(26)

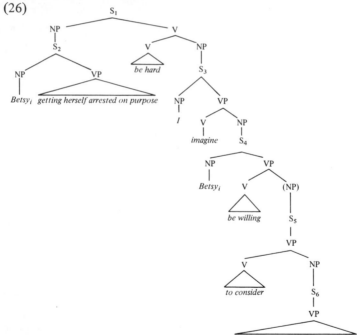

In order for (23) to be derived from (26), two things must happen.

    (i)   *The subject of $S_2$ must be deleted under coreference with the subject of $S_4$.*

(ii)   *$S_6$ must be deleted under identity with $S_2$ by Nonsubject Deletion.*

The problem is that we have no way of accomplishing the deletion in (i). Neither Equi or Super Equi can do it since there is no coreferential NP that commands the subject of $S_2$. Thus, the Nonsubject Deletion Hypothesis would have to posit a new rule that deletes the subject of $S_2$ under coreference with the subject of $S_4$. Unless this rule can be shown to be needed independently, the fact that it is required by the Deletion Hypothesis constitutes an argument against deletion and for movement.[1]

## 4. SUBSIDIARY ARGUMENTS

### 4.1  A Theory-Internal Argument Against the Deletion Hypothesis

Under the Deletion Hypothesis, the structure underlying (1) is

(27)

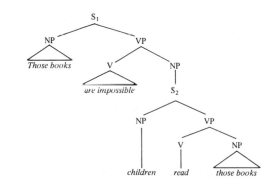

In this case the matrix subject is identical with the object of the complement. Hence, deletion can apply, and (1) can be derived. However, there is nothing to prevent (28) or (29) from being generated as underlying structures.

(28)

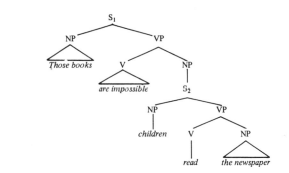

[1] This argument is due to Postal and Ross (1971).

(29)

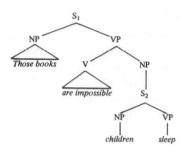

As a result, the Deletion Hypothesis would have to posit a constraint ensuring that Nonsubject Deletion actually applies to all structures of the form

(30)

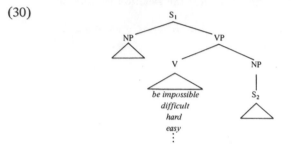

Since Nonsubject Deletion cannot apply to (28) and (29), this constraint would characterize

(31) *Those books are impossible for children to read the newspaper.*

and

(32) *Those books are impossible for children to sleep.*

as ungrammatical.[2]

⸜The fact that the Deletion Hypothesis requires this constraint whereas the Movement Hypothesis does not constitutes another argument for movement rather than deletion. Note, we are not arguing against the *type* of constraint required by the Deletion Hypothesis. We saw that this kind of constraint is needed with *force*. However, if we have two hypotheses only one of which requires this additional constraint, then, all other things being equal, we choose the hypothesis that does not require it.

---

[2] Note, since (28) and (29) do not satisfy the structural description of Nonsubject Raising, it is not enough to say that this rule is obligatory. The constraint in question must require that Nonsubject Deletion actually apply.

## 4.2 Semantics

If we ask what is easy in

(33)  *The manuscript will be easy for me to arrange for you to see.*

it is not the manuscript that is easy, but rather my arranging for you to see it. This suggests that the structure underlying (33) is

(34)

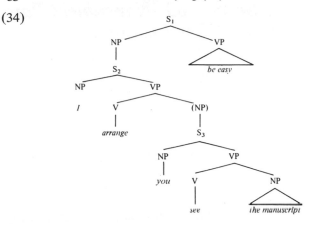

Note also that, except for a difference in focus and emphasis, (33) is synonymous with

(35)  *It will be easy for me to arrange for you to see the manuscript.*

If the meaning of a sentence is represented in underlying structure, then the Movement Hypothesis accounts for this fact automatically by deriving (33) and (35) from the underlying structure (34). Under the Deletion Hypothesis, each of these sentences is derived from a different underlying structure. Thus, the assumption that meaning is represented in underlying structure provides a further argument in favor of movement over deletion.[3]

---

[3] For further discussion of arguments involving movement vs. deletion (particularly the argument based on [23]), see SFI-8.

# Discussion of Section 63, Nonsubject Raising and FOR-*Phrases*

## *1. NONSUBJECT RAISING AND EMBEDDED SENTENCES: ANSWER TO (A)*

According to Assumption 2, the sentences in (3) and (4) are derived from underlying structures of the form

(15)

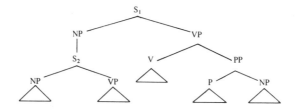

If Nonsubject Raising could apply to structures of this form, then *(8) and *(9) could be derived from the structures underlying (3) and (4). Since *(8) and *(9) are ungrammatical, we conclude that Nonsubject Raising cannot apply to such structures.

What is it about these structures that prevents Nonsubject Raising from applying? In *(8) and *(9), where Nonsubject Raising does not apply, there are two *for*-phrases—one in the matrix and the other that is the subject of the embedded clause. In (1c–d), (2c–d), (6d), (7d), (12d), (13d), and (14d), where Nonsubject Raising does apply, there are either no *for*-phrases or only one. Thus, it might seem that what prevents Nonsubject Raising from applying to structures of the form (15) is the presence of two *for*-phrases.

However, this does not account for the ungrammaticality of *(10c) and *(11c–d). Nonsubject Raising cannot apply to the structures underlying (10a–b) and (11a–b) even though they contain only one *for*-phrase. To see why this is so we must determine what the underlying structures of these sentences are.

In (10), the NP in the *for*-phrase is a nonreferential dummy—*it*; in (11) the NP is *there*. The structure underlying (10) is

(16)

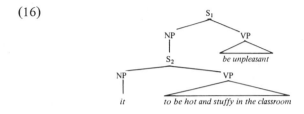

The structure underlying (11) is

(17)

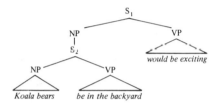

In the derivation of the sentences in (11), THERE-Insertion applies on the $S_2$-cycle, producing

(18)

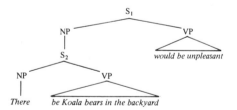

If Nonsubject Raising could apply to (16) and (18), then *(10c), *(11c), and *(11d) could be derived. Since these sentences are ungrammatical, we conclude that Nonsubject Raising cannot apply to these structures.

Structures like (16) and (18) have something in common with structures of the form (15); they each contain a *for*-phrase involving the subject of the embedded S. Perhaps it is the presence of this subject that keeps Nonsubject Raising from applying. If so, then the constraint we are looking for is:

(19)  *Nonsubject Raising cannot apply if the embedded clause contains a subject.*

According to this constraint, Nonsubject Raising cannot apply to structures of the form[1]

(20)

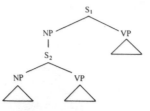

This constraint accounts for the ungrammaticality of the Nonsubject Raising sentences in the first two sets of data.

Now consider the sentences in the third set of data. Nonsubject Raising applies in the derivation of (12d). If (19) is correct, then the *for*-phrase in (12d) originates in the matrix, and the structure to which Nonsubject Raising applies is

(21)

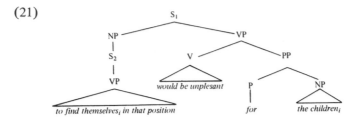

The reflexive pronoun in $S_2$ indicates that the embedded clause contained an underlying subject coreferential with *the children* which was deleted (by Equi) in the course of derivation. Thus, the structure underlying (12d) is

(22)

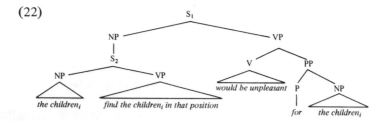

[1] This constitutes a modification of the assumption made in §2.3 of section 61 regarding the kind of structures to which Nonsubject Raising applies.

(12d) is derived from (22) by applying Reflexivization on $S_2$ followed by Equi and Nonsubject Raising on $S_1$.[2,3]

## 2. MEANING AND UNDERLYING STRUCTURE: ANSWER TO (B)

The structure underlying (14a) is

(23)

The structure underlying (14b) is

(24)

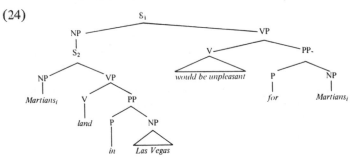

Equi deletes the subject of $S_2$ in the derivation of (14b).

If the meaning of a sentence is represented in underlying structure, then the difference in meaning between (14a) and (14b) is accounted for automatically. In (24) *Martians* is a constituent of the matrix verb phrase. Thus, Martians are understood to be the ones who would experience unpleasantness. In (23), the matrix verb is simply *would be unpleasant*; it is not specified who would experience unpleasantness.

---

[2] Because of constraint (19), Nonsubject Raising cannot apply until after the subject of $S_2$ has been deleted. Thus, it is not necessary to posit a rule-ordering constraint ordering Nonsubject Raising after Equi.

[3] Analogous remarks apply to the sentences in (13).

Next consider (14c). This sentence can be derived from both (23) and (24). Application of Extraposition to (23) produces

(25)

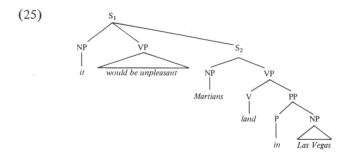

Application of Equi and Extraposition to (24) produces

(26)

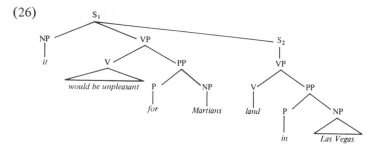

The ambiguity of (14c) is accounted for by the fact that it can be derived from both the structure underlying (14a) and the structure underlying (14b).[4]

Constraint (19) has an important consequence for the analysis of sentences in which Nonsubject Raising applies: the *for*-phrase in such a sentence must originate in the matrix sentence in underlying structure. Since there is no *for*-phrase in the matrix of (23), the subject of $S_2$ cannot be deleted, and Nonsubject Raising cannot apply. Thus, (14d) cannot be derived from the structure underlying (14a). Rather it is derived from the structure underlying (14b) by first applying Equi and then applying Nonsubject Raising. Thus, constraint (19) automatically accounts for the fact that (14d) is unambiguous. The ability of (19) to account for the differences in meaning exhibited by the sentences in (14) is a further argument in its favor. (Analogous remarks hold for the sentences in (6), (7), (12), and (13).)

---

[4] Note that (14c) has two different surface structures as well as two different underlying structures.

## 3. *MORE ON NONSUBJECT RAISING AND* FOR-*PHRASES*

### 3.1 PRO

In this problem we have focused on sentences that have one or more *for*-phrases in surface structure. However, there are other sentences that must also be accounted for. Consider the sentences in (2).

(2)  a.  *To talk to Mark about politics is exciting.*
     b.  *It is exciting to talk to Mark about politics.*
     c.  *Mark is exciting to talk to about politics.*
     d.  *Politics is exciting to talk to Mark about.*

These sentences do not contain *for*-phrases indicating who will be excited. However, it is understood that the ones who will be excited are those who will talk to Mark about politics.

This fact can be accounted for by deriving the sentences in (2) from the underlying structure[5]

(27)

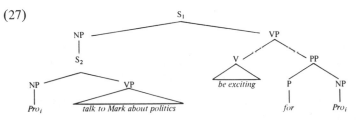

The element *pro* in this structure is an unspecified noun phrase that has roughly the meaning *one* and that is automatically deleted in surface structure. This element is also posited as the trigger of Reflexivization in the structure underlying (28).

(28)  *To find oneself in that position would be exciting.*

(29)

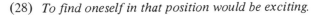
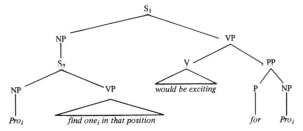

[5] A similar analysis can be used to account for the sentences in (1).

## 3.2 Differences Among Verbals

Our argument for constraint (19) was based on three properties of verbals like *unpleasant* and *exciting.*

### Property 1

These verbals can occur with *for*-phrases in both the matrix and the embedded sentence (examples [3] and [4]). However, Nonsubject Raising cannot apply to structures that contain *for*-phrases in both places (examples *[8] and *[9]).

### Property 2

These verbals can occur with elements like *it* and *there* as embedded subjects (examples [10a–b] and [11a–b]). However, Nonsubject Raising cannot apply to structures in which these subjects appear (examples *[10c] and *[11c–d]).

### Property 3

The meaning of sentences containing these verbals depends on the location of the *for*-phrase (examples [6a–b], [7a–b] and [14a–b]). Nonsubject Raising sentences have only the meaning in which the *for*-phrase originates in the matrix (examples [6d], [7d], and [14d]).

Not all Nonsubject Raising verbals have these properties. For example, *easy* does not. First consider

(30) a.   *For his children to get good grades would be easy for Frank.*
     b.   *It would be easy for Frank for his children to get good grades.*

Since *easy* cannot occur with *for*-phrases in both the matrix and embedded S, it does not have Property 1. Next consider

(31) a.   *For it to be cold in July would be easy.*
     b.   *It would be easy for it to be cold in July.*
(32) a.   *For there to be dirt under the rug would be easy.*
     b.   *It would be easy for there to be dirt under the rug.*

Since easy cannot occur with elements like *it* and *there* as embedded subjects, it does not have Property 2. Finally, consider

(33) a.   *For the children to get good grades would be easy.*
     b.   *To get good grades would be easy for the children.*
     c.   *It would be easy for the children to get good grades.*
     d.   *Good grades would be easy for the children to get.*

The sentences in (33) are all synonymous, having only the meaning of (33b) in which the children are the ones for whom getting good grades is easy. Since (33a) and (33b) have the same meaning, even though the *for*-phrase originates in different clauses in these sentences, *easy* does not have Property 3.

There are two important points to notice about the differences between *unpleasant* and *exciting* on one hand and *easy* on the other. First, different Nonsubject Raising verbals place different restrictions on the possible occurrences of *for*-phrases.[6] These restrictions vary somewhat from verbal to verbal; it is an open question how such restrictions ought to be accounted for. Second, the differences between *unpleasant* and *exciting* on one hand and *easy* on the other are independent of constraint (19). Since *easy* does not have Properties 1–3, sentences with *easy* do not provide additional evidence for the constraint. However, these sentences also do not contradict it.[7] Thus, (19) can be posited as a general constraint on Nonsubject Raising that does not have to be limited to particular verbals.

## 3.3 Nonsubject Raising and Subjects

Constraint (19) prevents Nonsubject Raising from applying to structures of the form

[6] It is tempting to postulate that

    (i) *easy requires identical for-phrases in the matrix and embedded Ss in underlying structure*

and

    (ii) *When no for-phrase occurs in the surface structure of the matrix, the underlying structure contains Pro.*

This would account for the ungrammaticality of \*(30)-\*(32). Unfortunately, sentences like (33a) pose a problem for this analysis.

[7] To find data contradicting (19) it would be sufficient to find at least one of the following three kinds of verbals.

    (i) *A verbal that can appear with for-phrases in both the matrix and embedded sentences (as in [3] and [4]), but which also allows Nonsubject Raising to apply to such structures.*

    (ii) *A verbal that can occur with it or **there** as embedded subjects (as in [10a-b] and [11a-b]), but which also allows Nonsubject Raising to apply to such structures.*

    (iii) *A verbal for which the meanings of sentences depend on the location of for-phrases (as in [6a-b], [7a-b], or [14a-b]), and for which the relevant Nonsubject Raising sentences are synonymous with sentences in which the for-phrase originates in the embedded sentence.*

(34)

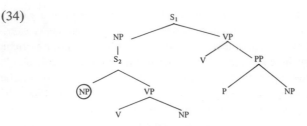

in which the subject of $S_2$ is present. It does not prevent Nonsubject Raising from applying to structures containing more deeply embedded subjects. For example, if the subject of $S_2$ has been deleted, it is possible for Nonsubject Raising to apply to the boxed NP in

(35)

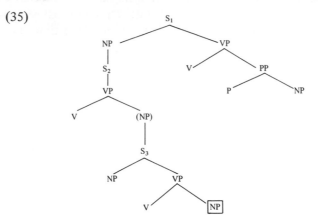

One sentence that is derived in this way is

(36)  *The President will be easy for me to arrange for you to see.*

The structure underlying (36) is

(37)

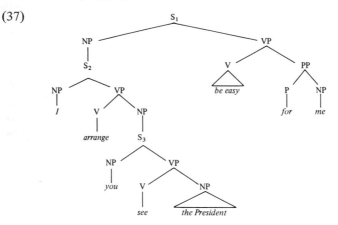

In the derivation of (36), Equi first deletes the subject of $S_2$, producing a structure of the form (35).[8] Nonsubject Raising then applies producing (36). Examples like this show that the subject mentioned in constraint (19) must be the subject of the *first* S embedded immediately beneath the Nonsubject Raising trigger.

## 4. CONCLUSION

On the basis of the above discussion we conclude that Nonsubject Raising applies only to Equi-derived structures of the form

(38)

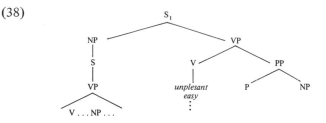

This rule makes an NP in the embedded verb phrase the subject of the upstairs sentence, moving the rest of the embedded VP to the right. If the subject of the sentence immediately beneath the Nonsubject Raising trigger is present, the rule cannot operate.

[8] We assume, on the basis of examples like

    (i) *I arranged to go*

and

    (ii) *\*I arranged for myself to go*

that *arrange* governs Equi rather than Subject-to-Object Raising. Since Subject-to-Object Raising does not apply with *arrange, you* in (37) remains as the subject of $S_3$.

# Discussion of Section 65, Two Hypotheses About Question Movement

## 1. STRANDED PREPOSITIONS: THE ARGUMENT BASED ON (4)

### 1.1 The Key Fact

(4) shows that when Question Movement applies to a question word that is preceded by a preposition, it may optionally move the preposition along with the question word.

### 1.2 Implications for the Successive Cyclic Hypothesis

Under this hypothesis, Question Movement applies twice in the derivations of (4a) and (4b). In the derivation of (4a) from

(7)

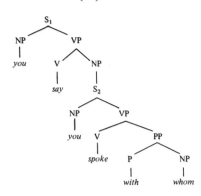

*whom* is first moved to initial position in $S_2$.

(8)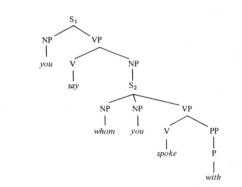

Question Movement applies again in the $S_1$-cycle to produce (4a).[1] In the deriva-tion of (4b), *with* is optionally moved together with *whom* to initial position in $S_2$.

(9)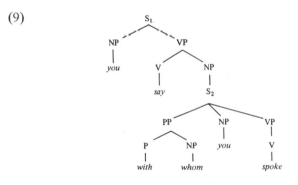

Question Movement applies again on the $S_1$-cycle. If it again takes the option of moving *with* along with *whom*, (4b) is derived. However, the rule is also free to move *whom* by itself, leaving *with* stranded in mid-sentence. Since this would produce

(10) *Whom did you say with you spoke?*

the Successive Cyclic Hypothesis incorrectly predicts *(10) to be grammatical.

---

[1] Strictly speaking, the rule that inverts subjects and auxiliaries also applies in (4a) and in all of the other sentences on the problem sheet. However, this rule is irrelevant to the issues raised by this problem and therefore may be safely omitted in the discussion that follows.

### 1.3  Implications for the Single Movement Hypothesis

Under this hypothesis (4b) is derived if Question Movement preposes *with* together with *whom*; otherwise (4a) is derived. Since Question Movement applies only once in these derivations, it cannot strand a preposition in mid-sentence.

### 1.4  Comparison

In order to block the derivation of ungrammatical sentences like *(10), the Successive Cyclic Hypothesis requires an extra constraint.

(11)  *If a preposition has been moved along with a question word on a lower cycle, it cannot be left behind on a higher cycle.*

The fact that the Single Movement requires no such constraint is an argument in its favor.

## 2. *NONSUBJECT RAISING:  THE ARGUMENT BASED ON (5) AND (6)*

### 2.1  The Relevant Rules

The structure underlying both (5) and (6) is

(12)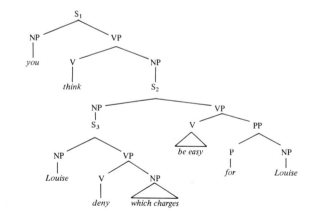

(5) is derived by preposing the question phrase and applying Equi and Extraposition in $S_2$. The order in which these operations occur is irrelevant.

Question Movement and Equi also apply in the derivation of (6); Extraposition does not. (6) differs from (5) in two respects:

(i)    *(6) does not contain it.*
(ii)   *In (6),* **be easy** *agrees with the plural* **which charges.** *In (5),* **be easy** *is singular.*

These facts show that Nonsubject Raising applies in the derivation of (6), producing the derived structure

(13)

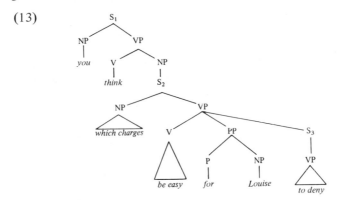

Here *deny* has been moved to the right of the VP in $S_2$, *which charges* has been made the subject of *easy* (and hence can trigger agreement), and *it* has not been introduced. Application of Question Movement produces (6).

## 2.2  The Successive Cyclic Hypothesis

Since Question Movement is assumed to be both obligatory and successive cyclic, it must apply on the $S_3$-cycle to (12), producing

(14)

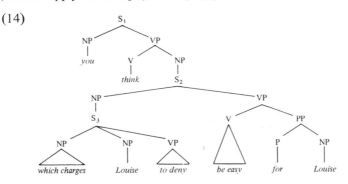

If Equi and Extraposition apply on $S_2$, followed by further applications of Question Movement, (5) will be derived. To derive (6), Equi and Nonsubject

Raising must apply on $S_2$. However, the Successive Cyclic Hypothesis has made this impossible. Equi can apply, producing

(15)

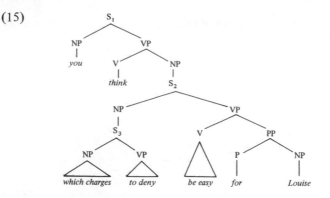

However, the structural description of Nonsubject Raising stipulates that it applies to an NP following the verb in a clause embedded immediately below a verb phrase like *be easy*.[2] Since there is no longer any NP following *deny* in (14) or (15), Nonsubject Raising cannot apply, and (6) cannot be derived.

## 2.3  The Single Movement Hypothesis

Under this hypothesis, (5) and (6) can be derived without difficulty. In the derivation of (5), Equi and Extraposition apply on $S_2$ followed by Question Movement. In the derivation of (6), Equi and Nonsubject Raising apply on the $S_2$-cycle, producing (13). Question Movement applies to (13) to derive (6).

## 2.4  Comparison

Since there is a grammatical sentence that can be generated by the Single Movement Hypothesis, but not by the Successive Cyclic Hypothesis, the latter hypothesis must be rejected.[3]

---

[2] See §4 of the discussion of section 63, Nonsubject Raising and FOR-Phrases.

[3] The argument in this section was based on the interaction of Question Movement and Nonsubject Raising. Check for yourself to see that an analogous argument could be constructed even if we had posited Nonsubject Deletion instead of Nonsubject Raising.

## 3. FURTHER ISSUES

### 3.1 An Unexplained Fact

In working through the argument in §2, you may have noticed that there is an ungrammatical sentence that can be generated under both the Successive Cyclic and the Single Movement Hypothesis.

(16) *Which charges do you think for Louise to deny was easy?*

This sentence is derived by applying Equi and Question Movement and by failing to apply Nonsubject Raising and Extraposition. This is possible since both Nonsubject Raising and Extraposition are optional. Although nothing we have said thus far accounts for *(16), its ungrammaticality follows automatically from a general constraint that we will present in part 7. Keep this example in mind for future reference.

### 3.2 Cyclicity, Postcyclicity, and the Formulation of Question Movement

It might seem that rejecting the Successive Cyclic Hypothesis is the same. as rejecting the hypothesis that Question Movement is cyclical. Whether or not it is depends on how Question Movement is formulated. If it is formulated roughly as

(17)   X - question phrase - Y ⇒ 2, 1, 3
       1      2      3

then Cyclicity entails Successive Cyclicity.

(18)

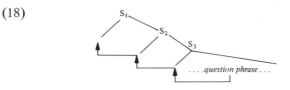

Since the structural description of (17) is met on all three cycles, making it cyclical would result in successive applications all the way up the tree. We have seen that this is undesirable. Consequently, if Question Movement is formulated as in (17), it must be postcyclical.

However, there is another way in which Question Movement might be formulated. Many linguists have posited an abstract element $Q$ in the structures underlying questions. One of the functions of this element is to mark the ultimate destination of the question phrase.

(19)  a.

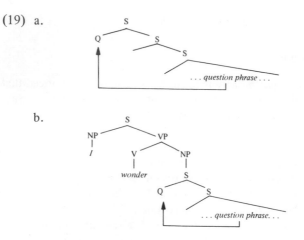

b.

If Question Movement is formulated roughly as

(20)  Q - X – question phrase – Y ⇒ 1, 3, 2, 4
     1   2        3          4

then its structural description will be met only once in structures like (19), no matter whether it is cyclical or postcyclical.[4] Thus, with this formulation Question Movement can be either cyclical or postcyclical.

    We will not attempt to decide between these alternatives here, but rather will leave the cycle-type of Question Movement open.

---

[4] Strictly speaking, if $Q$ is posited and Question Movement is postcyclical, it must be formulated (roughly) as

(i)  X  –  Q  –  Y  – question phrase –  Z  ⇒  1, 2, 4, 3, 5
    1    2    3         4         5

in order to account for examples like (19b).

# Discussion of Section 75,
# A Pronominalization Problem

## *1. STRATEGY*

The surface structure of *(4) is

(6)

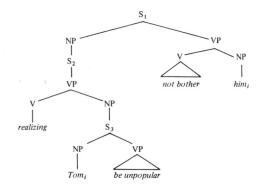

What must be explained is why (6) is not derived from

(7)

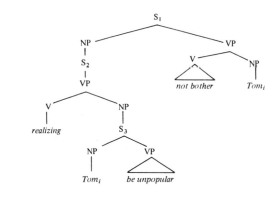

by forward pronominalization. Since Assumption 1 has the consequence that forward pronominalization is always possible, the only way to save this assumption is to show that Pronominalization never gets a chance to apply to (7). We will do this by constructing an account that prevents (7) from being produced.

## 2. THE MISSING SUBJECT

The subject of the complement is missing in both *(4) and (5). Assumption 3 indicates that Equi deletes complement subjects. Since Equi applies with *realize,* the structure underlying (5) according to Assumptions 1–3 is

(8)

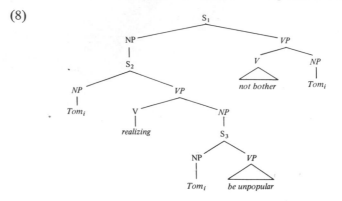

What must be explained is why (5) can be derived from (8), but *(4) cannot.

## 3. THE CYCLE-TYPE OF PRONOMINALIZATION

### 3.1 Pronominalization is not Postcyclical

If Pronominalization were postcyclical, then it could not apply until after all cyclical rules had operated. Since Equi is cyclical, this means that Pronominalization could not apply until after Equi had deleted the subject of $S_2$ in (8), producing (7). But then there would be no way to prevent Pronominalization from deriving (6) (i.e., *[4]). Thus, if Assumptions 1–3 are correct, Pronominalization cannot be postcyclical.

### 3.2 Cyclical Pronominalization

If pronominalization is cyclical, then its structural description is met on the $S_2$-cycle. Since it is obligatory, it must apply to $S_2$ in (8), producing

(9)

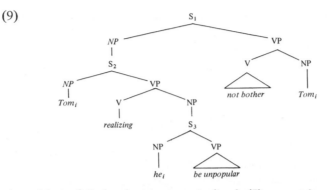

Since the subject of $S_3$ has been pronominalized, (7) cannot be produced, and *(4) cannot be derived. Instead, application of Equi on the $S_1$-cycle produces

(10)

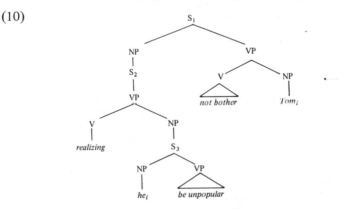

which is the surface structure of (5). Thus, *(4) and (5) do not show that Assumptions 1–3 are false; rather they show that if these assumptions are true, Pronominalization must be cyclical.

## 4. ANOTHER ARGUMENT

A parallel argument for the cyclicity of Pronominalization that does not depend on Equi is provided by the following sentences:

(11) a. *The fact that he$_i$ isn't bothered by the possibility that he$_i$ will lose surprises Tom$_i$.*

b. *The fact that Tom$_i$ isn't bothered by the possibility that he$_i$ will lose surprises him$_i$.*

c. *\*The fact that he$_i$ isn't bothered by the possibility that Tom$_i$ will lose surprises him$_i$.*

Under Assumption 1, the structure underlying these sentences is

(12)

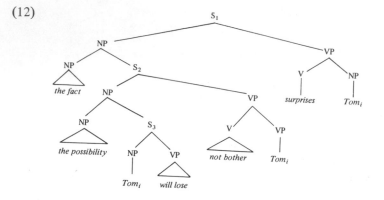

After Passive applies to $S_2$, the resulting structure is

(13)

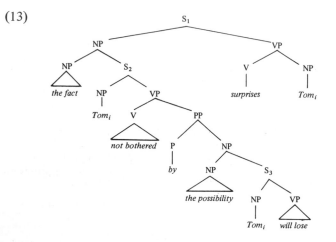

    If Pronominalization were postcyclical, there would be nothing to prevent *Tom* in $S_1$ from pronominalizing the subject of $S_2$, leaving the subject of $S_3$ to pronominalize *Tom* in $S_1$. Since this would produce *(11c), Pronominalization cannot be postcyclical.

    However, if Pronominalization is cyclical, then the subject of $S_2$ obligatorily pronominalizes the subject of $S_3$ on the $S_2$-cycle.

(14)

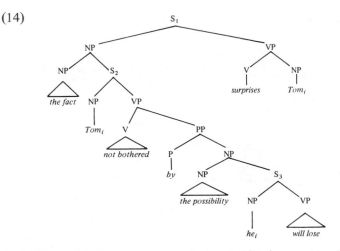

Since the subject of $S_3$ has been pronominalized, *(11c) cannot be derived.[1] On the $S_1$-cycle, Pronominalization can apply forward to produce (11b) or backward to produce (11a). Thus, if Assumptions 1 and 2 are correct, then Pronominalization is cyclical.

---

[1] We saw in *Pronominalization* that the grammar must contain a mechanism preventing Passive from applying after Pronominalization (on a given cycle). Thus, *(11c) cannot be derived by applying Pronominalization forward on the $S_2$-cycle in (12), producing

(i)

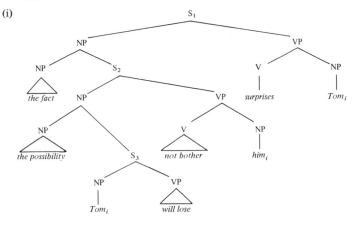

and then applying Passive on $S_2$ to produce

*Footnote 1 continued*

(ii)

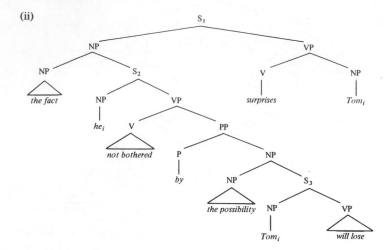

If this derivation were possible, then *(11c) could be derived by forward pronominalization on the $S_1$-cycle. This is prevented by the constraint that ensures that Passive cannot apply after Pronominalization (on a given cycle).

Note that this constraint also correctly prevents application of Passive to (11b) to produce:

(iii)  *$He_i$ is surprised by the fact that $Tom_i$ isn't bothered by the possibility that $he_i$ will lose.*

# Discussion of Section 80, Question Movement and Pronominalization

## 1. THE EFFECTS OF MOVEMENT

According to Assumption 1, the possibility of applying Pronominalization depends on precede and command relationships. Since Question Movement can move whole phrases to sentence-initial position, it can change the precede and command relationships between coreferential NPs.

(2)

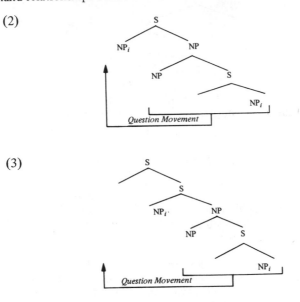

(3)

What must be determined is how this movement affects pronominalization possibilities.

## 2. PROBLEM 1

First consider sentence

(4)   *Which of the men that she$_i$ saw did Mary criticize?*

which is derived from the underlying structure:[1]

(5)

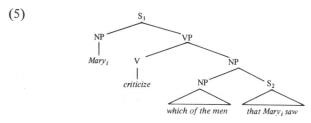

Under Assumptions 1–3, Pronominalization applies on the $S_1$-cycle, producing

(6)

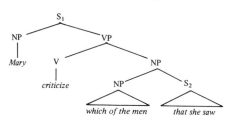

followed by postcyclical Question Movement that produces (4).

Although (4) can be derived in accordance with Assumptions 1–3, (7) cannot.

(7)   *Which of the men that Mary$_i$ saw did she$_i$ criticize?*

To derive (7), *Mary* in $S_1$ must be pronominalized by *Mary* in $S_2$. Under Assumption 1, this is impossible unless Pronominalization is allowed to operate after Question Movement has applied to (5) to produce

---

[1] (5) is a structure produced after Relativization has applied. The order in which Relativization and Question Movement apply is irrelevant to this problem. For convenience we will present only structures to which Relativization has applied.

(8)

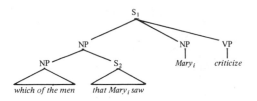

However, Assumptions 2 and 3 stipulate that Pronominalization is cyclical and Question Movement is postcyclical. Thus, Pronominalization cannot follow Question Movement and (7) cannot be derived. Since Assumptions 1–3 prevent us from deriving a grammatical sentence, these assumptions cannot all be correct.

## 3. PROBLEM 2

If Question Movement is cyclical, then the fact that Pronominalization must follow it in the derivation of (7) is unproblematic. Since both rules apply on the same cycle, nothing prevents this order of application. However, suppose we had a structure like (3).

(3)

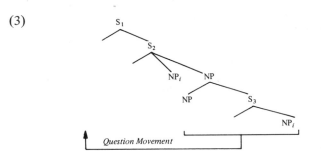

Under Assumptions 4 and 5, Pronominalization is obligatory and Question Movement operates in a single movement. Thus, $NP_i$ in $S_3$ must be pronominalized on the $S_2$-cycle before Question Movement applies on $S_1$.

One such structure is

(9)

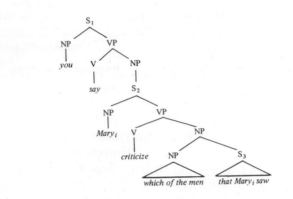

Under Assumptions 1, 2, 4, and 5, Pronominalization must apply on the $S_2$-cycle, producing

(10)

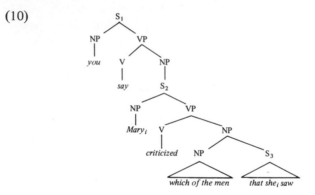

before Question Movement applies to $S_1$, producing

(11)  *Which of the men that she$_i$ saw did you say Mary$_i$ criticized?*

Since *Mary* in $S_3$ must be pronominalized on the $S_2$-cycle, Question Movement never gets a chance to apply to (9). As a result

(12)

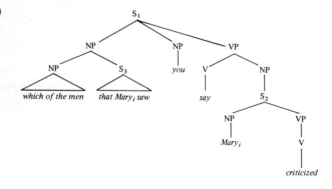

cannot be produced, and

(13)  *Which of the men that Mary$_i$ saw did you say she$_i$ criticized?*

cannot be derived. Since Assumptions 1, 2, 4, and 5 incorrectly predict that (12) is ungrammatical,[2] these assumptions cannot all be correct.

[2] Assumptions 1, 2, 4, and 5 predict that

(i)  *Which of the men that Mary saw did you say she criticized*

is ungrammatical on the interpretation in which *Mary* and *she* are coreferential—i.e., these assumptions predict that *Mary* and *she* cannot be understood to be coreferential in (i).

# Some Further Issues

This part of the book deals with issues that may arise in discussing material in the main text. Although what is included here is not prerequisite to anything else in the book, it will be of interest to those who wish to pursue specific issues more deeply.

# SFI — 1: Meaning and Underlying Structure

1. In section 8 we compared a grammar that derives actives and passives from the same underlying structures with a grammar that derives them from different underlying structures. Selectional restrictions provided an argument in favor of the former grammar and against the latter. Since actives and passives are synonymous, the argument in 8 lends further support to Hypothesis (1).

(1)   *The meaning of a sentence is represented in underlying structure.*

Two general points are illustrated by this example.

a.   To determine what structure underlies a sentence, one compares grammars that derive the sentence from different sources. One then looks for reasons to prefer one grammar over the others.

b.   Having found the underlying structure, one then asks if it correctly represents the meaning of the sentence. If it does, then (1) is partially confirmed. If it does not, (1) is falsified.

These points were applied in our investigation of imperatives, reflexives, and active-passive pairs. In each case, the evidence supported (1).

## 2. INTERPRETING 1

Having found some reasons to adopt (1), we now must clarify precisely what it entails. Consider the following two claims:

(2)   *If two stentences have the same underlying structure, then they must be synonymous.*

(3)    *If two sentences are synonymous, then they must have the same underlying structure.*

(1) clearly entails (2). If two sentences S and S' are derived from a single underlying structure U, then, according to (1), U represents the meaning of both sentences—i.e., they are synonymous.

(4)

Thus, if (1) is true, then (2) must also be true.

Now consider the relationship between (1) and (3). Suppose we have two synonymous sentences P and P'. Suppose also that P and P' have different but semantically equivalent underlying structures.

(5)

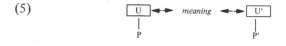

If there are cases like this in English, then (3) is false. However, such cases would not necessarily falsify (1). If U and U' are semantically equivalent, then (1) will correctly predict that P and P' are synonymous. Since it is theoretically possible for (1) to be true while (3) is false, (1) does not entail (3).

Thus, in adopting (1) as a working hypothesis, we are implicitly committing ourselves to (2), but not (3). For example, in adopting (1), we are not claiming that the synonymous (a) and (b) sentences in (6–8) must necessarily be derived from the same underlying structure.

(6)   a.    *John owns a car.*
      b.    *John owns an automobile.*
(7)   a.    *Martha bought skis from Bill.*
      b.    *Bill sold skis to Martha.*
(8)   a.    *John and Bill are friends.*
      b.    *Bill and John are friends.*

Whenever synonymous sentences are found, one must determine whether or not the grammar would be simplified by assuming that they have the same underlying structure. If simplification results, then the assumption should be adopted. If it leads to unnecessary complexity, it should be rejected. Either result is compatible with (1).

What would conflict with (1) would be evidence leading us to derive nonsynonymous sentences from the same underlying structure. If such evidence is found, then (1) must be given up. If not, then (1) may be retained.

## 3. MEANING AND EMPHASIS

Although actives and passives like (9) and (10) are synonymous, they differ in emphasis.

(9)  *Columbus discovered America.*
(10)  *America was discovered by Columbus.*

(9) emphasizes *Columbus*. (10) emphasizes *America*. Because of this, there are contexts in which it would be stylistically preferable to use one of these sentences rather than the other. We follow the usual practice of linguists in regarding such differences in emphasis as being irrelevant to synonymy.

# SFI – 2: Two Formulations of Passive

We have stated the structural description of Passive as

(1)   X – NP – V – NP – Y

However, there are grammatical passive sentences that cannot be derived if Passive is formulated in this way. Consider, for example,

(2)   *That bed was slept in by George Washington.*

(2) presumably has the same underlying structure as

(3)   *George Washington slept in that bed.*

a structure roughly like

(4)

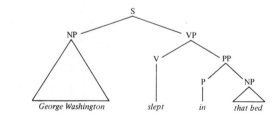

If Passive is formulated as in (1), it will not apply to (4) because the preposition *in* intervenes between the verb and the following noun phrase.

The grammaticality of (2) suggests that perhaps Passive should be formulated as

(5)   X – NP – V – (Prep) – NP – Y

The inclusion of (*Prep*) in (5) would make it possible for Passive to apply even when there is a preposition intervening between the verb and the following noun phrase, as in (4). At the same time, the fact that *Prep* is enclosed between parentheses would make it possible for Passive to apply to structures in which no preposition intervenes, as in the derivation of[1]

(6)   *America was discovered by Columbus.*

The problem with the formulation of Passive in (1) was that there are grammatical sentences, such as (2), which it cannot generate. The problem with the formulation of Passive in (5) is that it will generate sentences that are not grammatical. For example, from the structure underlying

(7)   *George Washington slept near that tree.*

(5) will generate

(8)   **That tree was slept near by George Washington.*

Similarly, from the structure underlying

(9)   *George Washington slept in Philadelphia.*

(5) will generate

(10) **Philadelphia was slept in by George Washington.*

In some cases, the differences between strings of the form (5) that have grammatical passives and those that do not are minimal.

(11)   *Some of the best orchestras in Europe have played in that hall.*
(12)   *Some of the most appreciative audiences in Europe have applauded in that hall.*

Corresponding to (11) there is a grammatical passive.

(13)   *That hall has been played in by some of the best orchestras in Europe.*

---

[1] If *Prep* were *not* enclosed in parentheses in (5), then *only* structures with a preposition between the verb and the following noun phrase would satisfy the structural description in (5).

However, the passive that corresponds to (12) is ungrammatical.

> (14) *\*That hall has been applauded in by some of the most appreciative audiences in Europe.*

Neither formulation of Passive—(1) or (5)—accounts for all of the data—(2), (13), *(8), *(10), and *(14). The question of how such examples are to be accounted for remains controversial. The only conclusion that can be drawn at present is that neither formulation of Passive succeeds in accounting for the full range of data concerning passive sentences in English.

# SFI − 3: Is the Complement of PROVE a Noun Phrase?

## 1. THE PROBLEM

In section 15 (Recursion) we claimed that the structure underlying the sentences

(1)  *Magellan proved that the world is round.*

and

(2)  *That the world is round was proved by Magellan.*

is[1]

(3)

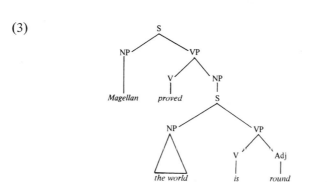

Here we will be concerned with justifying the presence of an *NP*-node above the complement S.

---

[1] Here again we ignore the complementizer *that.*

We will contrast two grammars of English—Grammar A, in which the structure underlying (1–2) is (3), and Grammar B, in which the structure underlying (1–2) is

(4)
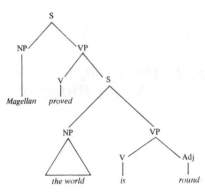

## 2. ARGUMENT ONE: THE DISTRIBUTION OF PROVE

Consider the kind of underlying structures in which the verb *prove* can occur. The fact that there are grammatical sentences like

(5)    *Magellan proved amazing things.*

shows that *prove* takes direct objects. Thus, both Grammar Λ and Grammar B must include the following statement:

(6)    **Prove** *occurs in structures of the form*

Because it postulates that the structure underlying (1–2) is (4) rather than (3), Grammar B must also include both:

(7)    **Prove** *occurs in structures of the form*

(8)    ***Prove*** *cannot occur in structures of the form*

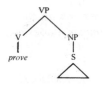

Grammar A does not need these statements, but rather accounts for the data by means of (6) alone. This fact constitutes an argument in favor of Grammar A over Grammar B.

## 3. ARGUMENT TWO: PASSIVE

We have seen that Passive applies to structures of the form

(9)   X – NP – V – NP – Y

Under Grammar A, the complement sentence in (3) is dominated by *NP*. Thus, (3) has the structure (9) and Passive can apply to produce (2). Since complement sentences are dominated by *NP*, Grammar A explains why structures with complements can be passivized.

Under Grammar B, the complement sentence is not dominated by *NP*. Thus, in order to derive (2), the Passive rule would have to be reformulated as (10).[2]

(10)   $X - NP - V - \begin{Bmatrix} NP \\ S \end{Bmatrix} - Y$

Note, under Grammar B, the fact that Passive applies to structures containing a complement sentence does not follow from anything else, but rather must be stated separately in the rule itself. As a result, Grammar B fails to explain why structures with sentential components can be passivized.

There are two ways of viewing this argument for Grammar A.

---

[2] (10) says that Passive can apply to structures of the form

(i)  X – NP – V – NP – Y

and

(ii)  X – NP – V – S – Y

(11) a.   *Grammar A explains why Passive applies to Ss while Grammar B does not.*

     b.   *Grammar B requires an additional complication in the Passive rule that Grammar A does not.*

## 4. EXERCISE

Show that the form of argument in 2 can be used to construct an argument for the *NP*-node dominating sentential subjects in structures like

(12)  *That he is guilty is obvious.*

# SFI − 4: A Quandary

Extraposition must be an optional rule if the grammaticality of sentence pairs like (1a–b) is to be accounted for.

(1)  a.    *That Suzie bought a polar bear is true.*
     b.    *It is true that Suzie bought a polar bear.*

Now consider the underlying structure

(2)

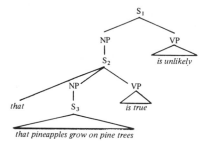

If Extraposition does not apply to (2), then

(3)  *?That that pineapples grow on pine trees is true is unlikely.*

will be generated. Applying Extraposition to $S_1$ (but not $S_2$) produces

(4)  *?It is unlikely that that pineapples grow on pine trees is true.*

Although these examples are deviant in some way, applying Extraposition to both $S_1$ and $S_2$, or to $S_2$ alone, produces sentences that are fully acceptable.

(5)   *It is unlikely that it is true that pineapples grow on pine trees.*
(6)   *That it is true that pineapples grow on pine trees is unlikely.*

Since Extraposition is an optional rule, it would seem that ?(3), ?(4), (5), and (6) should all have the same status. The fact that they don't raises a problem. Some linguists claim that an adequate grammar should characterize the difference between these sentences by generating (5) and (6) and not generating ?(3) and ?(4). Others claim that all of these sentences are grammatical and should therefore be generated by the grammar. On this view, ?(3) and ?(4) are deviant for the grammatically irrelevant reason that their structure is hard to process. Which of these views is correct is an open question that we will not try to resolve.

## SOME SUGGESTIONS FOR FURTHER READING

The quandary discussed here has led to a literature of its own. See Ross (1967, chapter 3), Ross (1973), Kuno (1973), Tanenhaus and Carroll (1975), and Grosu and Thompson (1977). For an important discussion of the general relation between grammaticality and acceptability, see chapter 1, §2 of Chomsky (1965).

# SFI — 5: THAT and Infinitives in Complements of BELIEVE

## 1. OUTLINE

In this section we compare two different formulations of Subject-to-Object Raising. We test these formulations by determining how they interact with the Passive transformation.

## 2. TWO CONFLICTING HYPOTHESES

*Hypothesis A*

The structure

(1)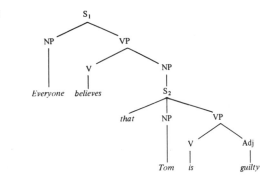

underlies not only the sentence

(2)    *Everyone believes that Tom is guilty.*

but also the sentence

(3)    *Everyone believes Tom to be guilty.*

Application of Subject-to-Object Raising to (1) produces the derived structure

(4)

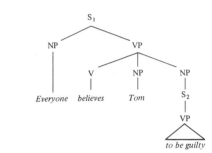

which is ultimately realized as (3). Subject-to-Object Raising not only makes the subject of $S_2$ the direct object of $S_1$, it also results in deletion of *that* and reduction of the complement verb to an infinitive.[1] Subject-to-Object Raising is the only source of infinitives with *believe*. Since both (2) and (3) are grammatical, Subject-to-Object Raising is an optional rule.

*Hypothesis B*

The structure underlying (2) is (1). However, the structure underlying (3) is

(5)

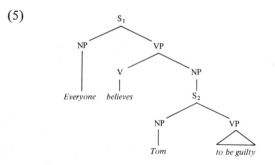

Sentences with infinitival complements and sentences with *that*-complements are different in underlying structure. Subject-to-Object Rais-

---

[1] It is not relevant for our purposes whether deletion of *that* and infinitivalization are part of Subject-to-Object Raising itself, or follow as a result of the application of Subject-to-Object Raising.

ing applies only to sentences with infinitival complements. Thus, it applies to (5), but not (1). Furthermore, since the sentence

(6) *Tom$_i$ believes himself$_i$ to be guilty.*

is grammatical, while the sentence

(7) *\*Tom$_i$ believes him$_i$ to be guilty.*[2]

is not, Subject-to-Object Raising must obligatorily apply to sentences with infinitival complements in underlying structure. Thus, Hypothesis B entails that Subject-to-Object Raising is an obligatory rule.

## 3. EXERCISE

Check for yourself to see that both hypotheses account for the following data:

(6) *Tom believes himself to be guilty.*
(7) *\*Tom$_i$ believes him$_i$ to be guilty.*
(8) *Tom$_i$ believes that he$_i$ is guilty.*
(9) *\*Tom believes that himself is guilty.*

## 4. AN UNGRAMMATICAL PASSIVE

The crucial sentences for choosing between Hypotheses A and B are:

(10) *That Tom is guilty is believed by everyone.*
(11) *Tom is believed by everyone to be guilty.*
(12) *\*Tom to be guilty is believed by everyone.*

Under Hypothesis A, both (10) and (11) are derived from the underlying structure (1).

(1)

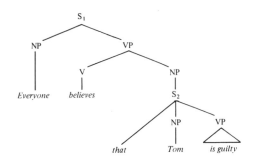

---

[2] \*(7) is ungrammatical on the reading in which *Tom* and *him* are coreferential.

This structure satisfies the structural description of both Subject-to-Object Raising and Passive—where the object NP is *that Tom is guilty*. Applying Passive produces (10). Applying Subject-to-Object Raising produces (4).

(4)   IN

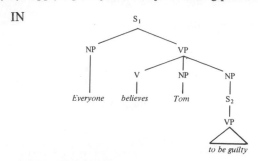

In (4), *Tom* is the object of *believe*. This means that the structural description of Passive is again satisfied, although in a different way. Since there is nothing to prevent Passive from applying now, it may apply to produce (11).

Note that under Hypothesis A there is no way to generate *(12). Since infinitives in these structures come from the operation of Subject-to-Object Raising, the infinitive in *(12) could only arise from the application of this rule. However, after Subject-to-Object Raising has applied to produce (4), *Tom to be guilty* is not even a constituent, let alone an NP. Thus, it cannot undergo Passive, and *(12) cannot be generated. This shows that Hypothesis A automatically accounts for (10), (11), and *(12) without having to postulate any additional grammatical devices.

Under Hypothesis B, (10) is derived in exactly the same way it was derived under Hypothesis A. However, the derivation of (11) is slightly different; the structure underlying (11) is (5), in which the infinitive is already present.

(5)

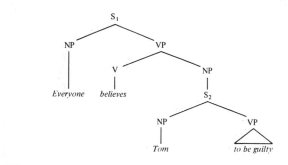

(11) is derived by first applying Subject-to-Object Raising (to produce [4]) and then applying Passive. Notice, however, that Passive need not wait until (4) is produced in order to apply. Its structural description is also satisfied by (5),

where the object NP is *Tom to be guilty*. Thus, applying Passive directly to (5) produces *(12). Since nothing in Hypothesis B prevents us from doing this, it is inadequate as it now stands.[3]

In order to save Hypothesis B, it would be necessary to add a constraint to the grammar to prevent Passive from applying before Subject-to-Object Raising. The fact that there is no independent motivation of this additional constraint constitutes an argument against Hypothesis B and for Hypothesis A.

## 5. THE STATUS OF RULE ORDERING

In considering this argument, some readers may have been surprised that we did not simply assume that the grammar of English contains constraints fixing the order in which rules can apply. The reason we did not make this assumption is that the postulation of rule ordering constraints, like the postulation of any other grammatical devices, must be justified by showing that they are needed to account for linguistic data. Since (10), (11), and *(12) can be accounted for by allowing rules to apply freely, rule ordering constraints are not needed for this data. To posit such constraints in this case would be to complicate the grammar needlessly by adding unnecessary devices.

This point can be made more general. To justify positing rule ordering constraints, one must show that allowing rules to apply freely either leads to the generation of an ungrammatical sentence or makes it impossible to generate some grammatical sentence. In the absence of such a demonstration, rule ordering constraints cannot be adopted. This issue is discussed in greater detail in section 30 of part 3 where we consider the logical status of rule ordering arguments and their historical role in the development of transformational grammar.

---

[3] It might be objected that an obligatory rule is a rule that must apply immediately if its structural description is satisfied at some stage of the derivation. According to this objection, since Subject-to-Object Raising is an obligatory rule whose structural description is satisfied by (5), application of Passive to (5) is impossible because it would destroy the environment for application of Subject-to-Object Raising.

This objection is based on one particular assumption about how obligatory rules are to be characterized. In part 3 we discuss alternative assumptions about the characterization of obligatory rules.

# SFI — 6: A Note on Section 28

Throughout the discussion of Equi and Subject-to-Subject Raising we have not made any assumptions about the following two questions.

(1)    a.    *Which complementizers occur with which verbals?*

        b.    *Do Subject-to-Subject Raising and Equi apply to structures with the **that**-complementizer, causing infinitivalization in the complement (as we argued in the case of Subject-to-Object Raising), or are the infinitives that occur in Equi and Subject-to-Subject Raising sentences present in the underlying structure?*

These two questions are interrelated. For example, with the adjective *certain* we find the following paradigms:

(2)    a.    *That Joe will win is certain.*

        b.    *It is certain that Joe will win.*

(3)    a.    *\*For Joe to win is certain.*

        b.    *\*It is certain for Joe to win.*

(4)         *Joe is certain to win.*

There are two ways that this paradigm could be accounted for.

(5)    a.    *Subject-to-Subject Raising optionally converts a **that**-clause into an infinitival clause. **Certain** does not take infinitival complements in underlying structure; Subject-to-Subject Raising is the only source of infinitival complements with **certain**.*

b.     *Certain takes both **that**-complements and infinitival comple-*
        *ments in underlying structure. Subject-to-Subject Raising*
        *applies only in sentences in which the complement of **certain***
        *is infinitival. In these cases, Subject-to-Subject Raising is oblig-*
        *atory.*

In this way, a decision about whether a verbal takes a particular complementizer in underlying structure may determine whether that verbal triggers a given rule optionally or obligatorily. We do not take any position on questions (5a–b).

In some cases, however, the question of which verbals take which complementizers does not affect the optionality or obligatoriness of the rules they trigger. For example, this is the case with *apt* and *bound,* which will play an important role in the arguments in part 3. You should be able to answer Question 3 of section 28 without worrying about questions (5a–b).

# SFI — 7: Selectional Restrictions and the Status of the Passive Transformation

## 1. IS PASSIVE A TRANSFORMATION?
### THE ARGUMENT BASED ON SELECTIONAL RESTRICTIONS

In *Actives and Passives,* we considered two ways of accounting for active and passive sentence pairs like

(1)    *Columbus discovered America.*

and

(2)    *America was discovered by Columbus.*

*Hypothesis A (The Phrase Structure Hypothesis)*

Active and passive sentences are derived from different underlying structures. The structure underlying each is essentially the same as its surface structure.

*Hypothesis B (The Transformational Hypothesis)*

Active and passive sentences are derived from the same underlying structures. Either there is a transformation deriving passives from active underlying structures or there is a transformation deriving actives from passive underlying structures.

We argued that a grammar incorporating Hypothesis A has to posit selectional restrictions that are not required by a grammar incorporating Hypothesis B. For example, the direct object of the verb *reapportion* must refer to a legislative body or a geographical entity on the basis of which members of such a body are chosen. The same constraint applies to the subject of the passive form *be reapportioned.* Since Hypothesis B states selectional restrictions on underlying structures, only one restriction is needed to characterize examples like

(3)  *The court reapportioned the explosion.

and

(4)  *The explosion was reapportioned by the court.

as deviant. Under Hypothesis A, however, it is necessary to posit two selectional restrictions—one specifying the possible objects of *reapportion* and the other specifying the possible subjects of *be reapportioned.* Since Hypothesis A states two selectional restrictions where only one is needed, we rejected Hypothesis A in favor of Hypothesis B.

In section 10, Activization vs. Passivization, we showed that a grammar in which passives are derived from actives is preferable to a grammar in which actives are derived from passives. We also noted that the phenomena discussed in that section provided an additional argument for Hypothesis B.

## 2.  *A POSSIBLE OBJECTION*

### 2.1  A Weakness in the Argument

Our rejection of Hypothesis A was motivated by a desire to avoid duplicating selectional restrictions. However, it might be objected that there are other ways to avoid such duplication that do not involve positing a transformation. Here we consider one such alternative.

### 2.2  Redundancy Rules

*Hypothesis C (The Redundancy Rule Hypothesis)*

Active and passive sentences are derived from different underlying structures; the underlying structure of each is essentially the same as its surface structure. As in Hypothesis B, selectional restrictions are stated on active underlying structures. However, there is no transformation relating actives and passives. Instead, selectional restrictions for passive structures are specified by the *redundancy rule* informally stated in (5).

(5)  *If an NP can be the object of an active verb in underlying structure, it can be the subject of the corresponding passive*

*verb in underlying structure; if it can be the subject of an*
*active verb in underlying structure, then it can occur in the*
*by-phrase in the corresponding passive underlying structure.*

Redundancy rules are part of the machinery for lexical insertion and so help determine which underlying structures various expressions can be inserted into. To indicate how these rules work requires a brief explanation of lexical insertion in general. For this purpose it is useful to think of the generation of underlying structures as a two-stage process; first, phrase structure rules generate a tree—e.g.,

(6)

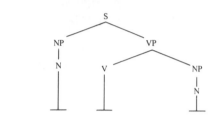

Then, lexical insertion rules insert lexical items into the tree under "lexical category symbols"—*N, V, Adj, Prep,* etc.[1]

In placing lexical items in trees, lexical insertion rules are subject to at least three types of constraints: category restrictions, strict subcategorizational restrictions, and selectional restrictions. Category restrictions simply require that verbs be placed under *V*-nodes in trees, nouns under *N*-nodes, and so on. Strict subcategorizational restrictions (on verbs) place structural constraints on what kind of verb phrases individual expressions can be placed in. For example, the verb *sleep* is intransitive and so cannot be inserted into (6). The verb *grab,* on the other hand, is subcategorized as taking an object and so can be inserted into (6). Selectional restrictions place constraints on what types of subjects and objects individual verbs may take. For example, selectional restrictions on *grab* require that its subject be animate and its object concrete (as opposed to abstract). Thus, it cannot be inserted into either

---

[1] Different proposals have been made concerning the formal nature of lexical insertion. Under one such proposal, the symbol "Δ" is generated under lexical category symbols, and lexical items are substituted for "Δ." Issues involving the formal nature of lexical insertion have no bearing on our argument and so are ignored here.

The explanation of lexical insertion that follows is a highly simplified and incomplete version of the standard treatment in transformational grammar, which is given in greater detail in Chomsky (1965, chapters 2 and 4).

(7)

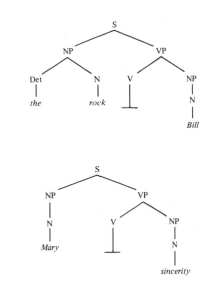

or

(8)

In order for lexical insertion rules to operate, they must be able to compare information present in a tree with information about particular lexical items. This, in turn, assumes that the grammar contains a *lexicon* in which individual words are associated with categorical, strict subcategorizational and selectional information. For example, the lexical entries for the verbs *sleep* and *grab* can be thought of along roughly the following lines:[2]

(9)  a.   (*sleep*, [+V, – ____ NP, + [+Animate] ____ , . . .])
     b.   (*grab*, [+V, + ____ NP, + [+Animate] ____ , + ____ [+Concrete], . . .])

"+V" indicates that the expression is a verb. "± ____ NP" indicates whether or not it can occur in a VP in which it is immediately followed by an NP (i.e., whether or not it is transitive). "+ [+Animate] ____ " indicates that *sleep* and *grab* take animate subjects and "+ ____ [+Concrete]" indicates that *grab* takes concrete objects. Lexical entries for nouns can be thought of roughly as follows:

(10)  a.   (*John*, [+N, – Det ____ , [+Human], . . .])
      b.   (*boy*, [+N, + Det ____ , [+Human], . . .])
      c.   (*monkey*, [+N, + Det ____ , [– Human], [+Animate], . . .])
      d.   (*rock*, [+N, + Det ____ , [–Animate], [+Concrete], . . .])
      e.   (*sincerity*, [+N, – Det ____ , [+Abstract], . . .])

---

[2] There are various possible conventions for representing category, strict subcategorizational, and selectional features in lexical entries. For a discussion of these possibilities, see Chomsky (1965), especially chapter 2, §3, and chapter 4, §2.1.

('± Det        ' indicates whether or not the noun takes a determiner—'the,' 'a,' etc.)

Lexical insertion into a structure like

(11)

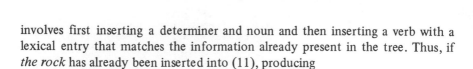

involves first inserting a determiner and noun and then inserting a verb with a lexical entry that matches the information already present in the tree. Thus, if *the rock* has already been inserted into (11), producing

(12)

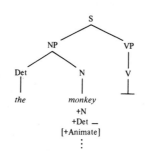

then *sleep* cannot be inserted under the *V*-node. However, if *the monkey* has been inserted into (11), producing

(13)

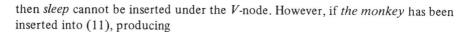

then *sleep* can be inserted.

Now consider

(14)

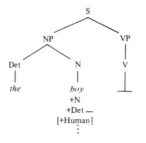

*Sleep* can be inserted only into structures whose subjects have the feature '[+Animate]'. So far, our entry for *boy* does not include this feature. To ensure that *sleep* is substitutable in (14), we must see to it that *boy* contains the feature '[+Animate]' when it is inserted into (14).[3]

One way to do this would simply be to add '[+Animate]' to the entry for *boy* in the lexicon. However, to do this would be to miss the generalization that all nouns that are '[+Human]' are also '[+Animate]'. Rather than complicating the lexicon by adding '[+Animate]' to the entry for each such noun, we may simply posit rule (15), which applies prior to lexical insertion.

(15) *If the entry for a noun contains the feature '[+Human]', then mark it '[+Animate]'.*

Rules like (15) are known as *redundancy rules.* They were originally introduced into syntax to simplify the lexicon by taking advantage of the hierarchical relationships that hold among various syntactic features. Such rules make it possible to state general relationships among such features and to eliminate from lexical entries all information that is predictable.

Although several types of redundancy rules have been posited for this purpose, such rules were not originally intended to do the work of the Passive transformation. Thus, Hypothesis C represents an extension of the original notion of a redundancy rule. Under this hypothesis, actives and passives would

---

[3] There are alternative conventions for lexical insertion. For example, one might permit *sleep* to be inserted into any structure in which the object is *not* marked '[−Animate]'. This would eliminate the need for ensuring that when *boy* is inserted into (14), it is marked '[+Animate]'. Rather *boy* could remain unmarked for animacy.

However, the problem of having to introduce features would still arise in other cases. For example, our lexical entry for *rock* includes the features '[−Animate]', but not either '[+Human]' or '[−Human]'. Nevertheless, a construction requiring a human noun will not take *rock*. Thus, some mechanism would be needed to add '[−Human]' to its entry.

be generated in underlying structures and the lexicon would contain entries for both active and passive verbs. Lexical entries for passive verbs would be devoid of selectional and strict subcategorizational features, which would be filled in by a redundancy rule that copied the selectional restrictions on active objects as restrictions on passive subjects, the restrictions on active subjects as restrictions on the *by*-phrase, and so on.

For our purposes it is not important how such a rule would be formalized. What is important is that under Hypothesis C, both

(16)

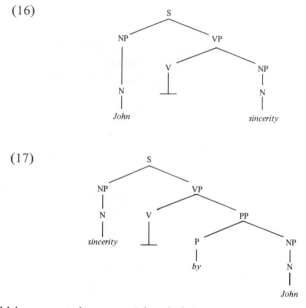

and

(17)

as an ill-formed underlying structure. The passive redundancy rule posited by Hypothesis C would allow the same selectional restrictions to block the insertion of *be grabbed* into (17). Thus,

would be generated as potential underlying structures. Selectional restrictions on the active verb *grab* would prevent it from being inserted into (16) and thus would characterize

(18)

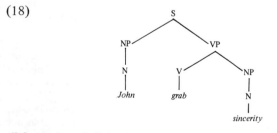

(19)

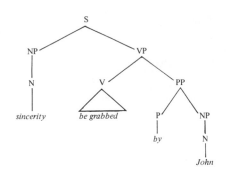

would be characterized as ill-formed.

The Passive transformation of Hypothesis B and the Passive redundancy rule of Hypothesis C both account for actives and passives without duplicating selectional restrictions. However, there is an important difference between them. The Passive transformation takes one tree structure as input and produces a new structure as output. Redundancy rules do not do this. Strictly speaking, they operate on lexical entries. However, their effect (when combined with the rest of the mechanism for lexical insertion) is to characterize one underlying structure (e.g., [19]) as well- (or ill-) formed if and only if another underlying structure (e.g., [18]) is well- (or ill-) formed. In light of this, it will be convenient for the discussion that follows to take the Passive redundancy rule of Hypothesis C as saying, in effect:

(20)  *A passive underlying structure is well-formed if and only if the corresponding active underlying structure is well-formed.*


## 3.  RULE INTERACTION


### 3.1  A Difference Between Hypotheses B and C

In order to decide between the two hypotheses, one must look at complex sentences involving the interaction of several rules. Under Hypothesis B, Passive is a transformation and hence can apply both before and after other transformations. Under Hypothesis C, passive forms are produced in underlying structure before any transformations have applied. Thus, an important difference between Hypotheses B and C is the following:

(21)  *Under Hypothesis B, some passive forms are produced after other transformations have applied. Under Hypothesis C, passive forms are produced before the application of any transformations.*

## 3.2 Extending Hypothesis C

### 3.2.1 Compound Sentences

The difference in (21) has important consequences for cyclical rules like those in (22).

(22)  *Subject-to-Object Raising*
      *Subject-to-Subject Raising*
      *Equi*
      *THERE-Insertion*

Under Hypothesis B, certain sentences can be derived only by applying Passive after these cyclical rules.

(23) a.   *The court is expected by everyone to reapportion the*
          *legislature.*
          *(Passive follows Subject-to-Object Raising)*

     b.   *The court is expected by everyone to be likely to reapportion*
          *the legislature.*
          *(Passive follows Subject-to-Subject and Subject-to-Object*
          *Raising)*

     c.   *The court is expected by everyone to be eager to reapportion*
          *the legislature.*
          *(Passive follows Equi and Subject-to-Object Raising)*

     d.   *There are believed by the authorities to be many criminals still*
          *at large.*
          *(Passive follows THERE-Insertion and Subject-to-Object*
          *Raising)*

Under Hypothesis C, the derivations in (23) are impossible. According to this hypothesis, there is no Passive transformation and passive forms are generated by phrase structure rules in underlying structure. Since transformations cannot apply until after underlying structures have been produced, the transformations in (22) cannot be involved in the derivation of the sentences in (23). Under Hypothesis C, the structures underlying these sentences must be essentially the same as their surface structures.

(24)  a.

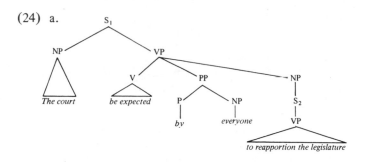

b.

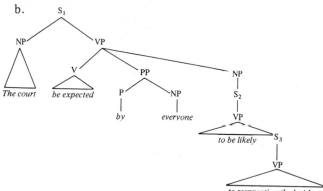

c.

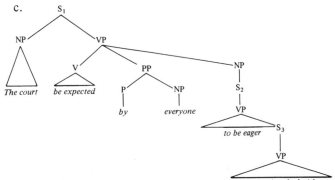

d.

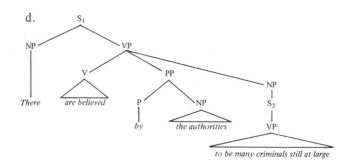

This result has important consequences for the status of the rules in (22) under Hypothesis C. The active structures corresponding to the passive structures in (24) are:

(25)  a.

b.

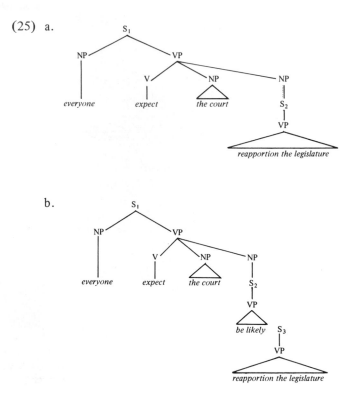

c.

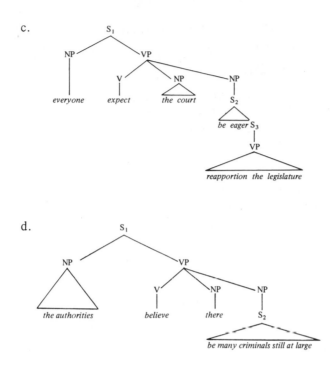

d.

According to redundancy rule (20), the passive underlying structures in (24) are well-formed iff their corresponding active underlying structures are well-formed. Thus, the well-formedness of the structures in (24) will follow from the well-formedness of the structures in (25), only if the latter are also *underlying* structures. Given (20) and the general characterization of redundancy rules as part of the mechanism for lexial insertion, we have no other choice; (24a–d) and (25a–d) must be underlying structures. Only in this way can Hypothesis C distinguish grammatical sentences like (23a–d) from deviant examples like (26a–d).

(26) a.  *The rainbow is expected by everyone to reapportion the legislature.*

b.  *The rainbow is expected by everyone to be likely to reapportion the legislature.*

c.  *The rainbow is expected by everyone to be eager to reapportion the legislature.*

d.　*There are believed by the authorities to be most of the criminals still at large.*[4]

### 3.2.2 The Hypothesis Extended

We have seen that Hypothesis C must generate both (24) and (25) as underlying structures. Under this hypothesis, the transformations in (22) play no role in deriving such structures and hence need not be posited. Just as the Passive transformation is replaced by a redundancy rule, so Hypothesis C must replace the transformations in (22) by rules stating well-formedness constraints on underlying structures. Again the precise formalization of these rules under Hypothesis C is not important for our argument. What is important is that such rules would have roughly the effect of (27–30).[5]

(27)　*S-O-R Well-Formedness Rule*
　　　An underlying structure of the form

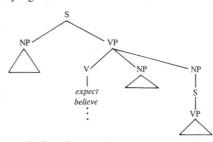

　　　is well-formed if and only if the corresponding underlying structure of the form

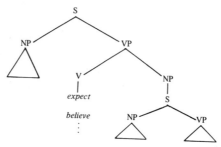

　　　is well-formed.

----

[4] *(26a–c) are deviant because *the rainbow* violates selectional restrictions on *reapportion.* *(26d) is deviant because *most of the criminals* is a definite rather than indefinite NP. The mechanisms by which Hypothesis C characterizes the difference between (23) and *(26) are explained in §3.2.2.

[5] Rules (27–30) go far beyond the original notion of redundancy rule. What they have in common with the proposed Passive redundancy rule of Hypothesis C is that their effect is to state well-formedness constraints on one set of underlying structures in terms of the constraints on another set of underlying structures.

(28) *S-S-R Well-Formedness Rule*
An underlying structure of the form

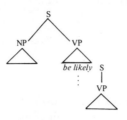

is well-formed if and only if the corresponding underlying structure
of the form

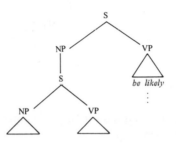

is well-formed.

(29) *Equi Well-Formedness Rule*
An underlying structure of the form

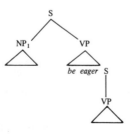

is well formed if and only if the corresponding underlying structure
of the form

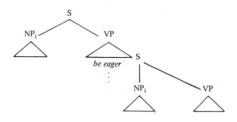

is well formed.[6]

(30) *THERE-Insertion Well-Formedness Rule*
An underlying structure of the form

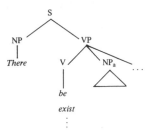

is well-formed if and only if $NP_a$ is indefinite and the corresponding underlying structure of the form

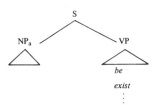

is well-formed.

As in the case of the treatment of actives and passives under Hypothesis C, each of the structures mentioned in rules (27–30) is an underlying structure generated by the phrase structure rules. The function of rules (27–30) is to show

---

[6] Special problems arise when we try to replace obligatory transformations like Equi with redundancy rules. These problems will be illustrated in our discussion of Reflexivization. For the present you may simply assume that under Hypothesis C, something with roughly the effect of (29) replaces Equi.

how constraints on the well-formedness of certain complex structures follow from the constraints on the well-formedness of simpler structures.

This point can be illustrated by showing how rules (20), (27), and (28) can be used to characterize (23b) as grammatical. We begin with structure (31).

(31)

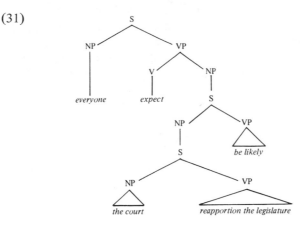

As in Hypothesis B, selectional restrictions are stated on simple underlying forms. Since (31) satisfies these restrictions, it is well-formed. (28) tells us that

(32)

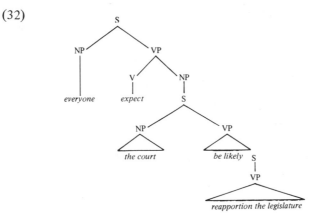

is well-formed iff (31) is. Hence, (32) is also a well-formed underlying structure. The well-formedness of (25b) follows by rule (27). Finally, (20) characterizes (24b) as well-formed, and sentence (23b) is correctly characterized as grammatical. (The deviance of *(26b) is accounted for in analogous fashion.)

### 3.2.3 The Heart of the Argument

The argument in §§3.2.1–3.2.2 shows that if Passive is a redundancy rule, then the rules in (22) must also be rules stating well-formedness constraints on underlying structures. The argument is based on the fact that whatever rule accounts for passives must be able to interact with other cyclical rules. The characterization of redundancy rules in §2.2 makes it impossible for the hypothesized Passive redundancy rule to interact with transformations. Thus, either all the rules discussed above have the effect of relating underlying structures, or none do. The extended redundancy rule hypothesis opts for the former alternative.

## 4. PHRASE STRUCTURE RULES

An important difference between Hypothesis B and Hypothesis C involves the different roles played by the rules they posit. Transformations perform the following functions:

(i)   *They create new structures from underlying structures.*
(ii)  *They ensure that constraints stated on simple sentences carry over to more complicated (derived) structures.*

Hypothesis C separates these two functions. Structures previously produced by transformations must now be generated directly by phrase structure rules. Rules whose effect is to state well-formedness conditions on underlying structures accomplish only the second of the two functions listed above.

This difference suggests one way of evaluating the two hypotheses. Let's compare what each must posit in order to account for the data presented so far. For each transformation countenanced by Hypothesis B there is a corresponding well-formedness rule adopted by Hypothesis C. Presumably all phrase structure rules posited by Hypothesis B must also be posited by Hypothesis C. However, Hypothesis C may require additional phrase structure rules that Hypothesis B does not. Structures like (24) and (25), which are produced by transformations under Hypothesis B, are underlying structures under Hypothesis C. Unless the phrase structure rules needed to generate these structures can be independently motivated, the need to posit them constitutes an argument against Hypothesis C in favor of Hypothesis B.[7]

---

[7] We will not try to resolve the question of which phrase structure rules required by Hypothesis C are independently motivated. The point is more general; in order to defend Hypothesis C, one must show that phrase structure rules generating structures like (24) and (25) are needed independently elsewhere in the grammar. One rule that poses particular

## 5. REFLEXIVIZATION

### 5.1 Overview

Another argument against Hypothesis C is provided by Reflexivization. So far we have shown

(33) *If Passive is a redundancy rule, then Passive and the rules in (22) (Subject-to-Object Raising, Subject-to-Subject Raising, Equi, and THERE-Insertion) have the effect of relating underlying structures.*

We will now argue that

(34) *If Passive and the rules in (22) have the effect of relating underlying structures, then certain crucial facts involving Reflexivization cannot be accounted for.*

From (33) and (34) we will conclude

(35) *Passive and the rules in (22) do not have the effect of relating underlying structures. In particular, Passive is not a redundancy rule.*

Thus, if (34) can be established, it will follow that Hypothesis C is false.

*Footnote 7 continued*
problems is

(i)  S → VP

If structures (24) and (25) are correct, then Hypothesis C must include (i). If (i) cannot be independently motivated, then either Hypothesis C must be given up or some way of reanalyzing (24) and (25) must be found so as not to include the structure

(ii)

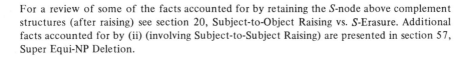

For a review of some of the facts accounted for by retaining the *S*-node above complement structures (after raising) see section 20, Subject-to-Object Raising vs. *S*-Erasure. Additional facts accounted for by (ii) (involving Subject-to-Subject Raising) are presented in section 57, Super Equi-NP Deletion.

## 5.2 Establishing (34)

### 5.2.1 Strategy

(34) is the result of two observations:

(i)  *Given (33), Hypothesis C has the consequence that Reflexivization operates on underlying structures. (Since Passive and the rules in [22] do not create derived structures, the only structures available for Reflexivization are underlying structures.)*

(ii)  *Constraints on Reflexivization cannot be stated solely at the level of underlying structure*

We will show that these points hold regardless of whether Reflexivization is conceived of as a transformation, an interpretive rule, or a well-formedness device on the model of (27–30). Thus, no matter how Reflexivization is formulated, the extended Hypothesis C must be rejected.

### 5.2.2 Reflexivization as a Transformation: A Problem for Hypothesis C

Suppose that Passive is a redundancy rule. Then by (33), Passive and Subject-to-Object Raising have the effect of relating underlying structures. Suppose also that Reflexivization is a transformation. Given all of this, the following will be generated as underlying structures:

(36)

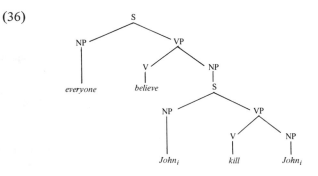

(37)

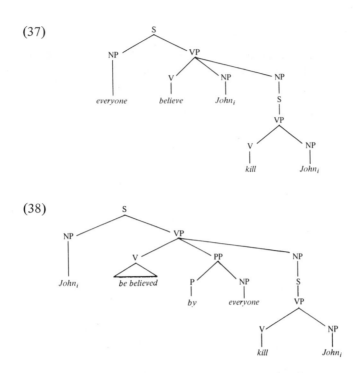

(38)

Since the two occurrences of *John<sub>i</sub>* are in the same clause in (36), Reflexiviza-tion will apply, producing

(39) *Everyone believed that John killed himself.*

However, in (37) and (38), the two occurrences of *John<sub>i</sub>* are in different clauses. Thus, Reflexivization cannot apply and

(40) *Everyone believed John to have killed himself.*

and

(41) *John was believed by everyone to have killed himself.*

cannot be derived. Instead,

(42) *Everyone believed John<sub>i</sub> to have killed him<sub>i</sub>.*

and

(43) *John_i was believed by everyone to have killed him_i.

will be produced. For this reason, we must reject a theory in which Passive is a redundancy rule, and Reflexivization is a transformation.[8]

[8] Such a theory cannot be saved by claiming that the structures underlying (40) and (41) are not (37) and (38), but rather are

(i)

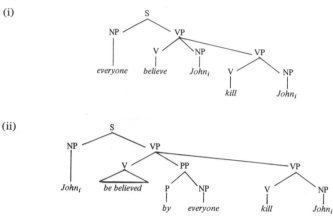

and

(ii)

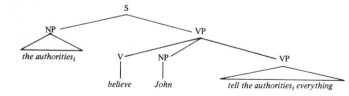

In (i) and (ii) there are no *NP* and *S*-nodes dominating the complement. Thus, the two occurrences of *John_i* are in the same clause and Reflexivization can apply, producing (40) and (41). Since Reflexivization is obligatory, *(42) and *(43) cannot be derived.

However, now there is no way to produce

(iii) a.   *The authorities_i believe John to have told them_i everything*

and

b.   *John was believed by the authorities_i to have told them_i everything.*

There is also no way to block

(iv) a.   **The authorities_i believe John to have told themselves_i everything*

and

b.   **John was believed by the authorities_i to have told themselves_i everything.*

If there is no *S*-node above the complement, then the structure underlying the (a)-sentences is

(v)

### 5.2.3 Reflexivization as an Interpretive Rule: Déjà Vu

Exactly the same argument can be used against a theory in which Passive is a redundancy rule and Reflexivization is an interpretive rule. On this account, reflexive pronouns are generated freely in underlying structure, but coreference relations aren't. Rather, they are assigned by an obligatory rule of Relfexive Coreference Assignment that marks a reflexive pronoun as coreferential with a preceding NP in the same clause. If there is no such NP, the reflexive pronoun

*Footnote 8 continued*
and the structure underlying the (b)-sentences is

(vi)

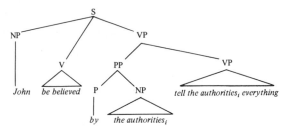

Since the two occurrences of the *authorities*$_i$ are in the same clause, Reflexivization will obligatorily produce *(iva) and *(ivb) and block (iiia) and (iiib). Thus, positing underlying structures in which the complement is not dominated by an *S*-node will not save a theory in which Passive and Subject-to-Object Raising have the effect of relating underlying structures whereas Reflexivization is a transformation. No matter which decision is made about the complement, such a theory must be rejected.

Similar arguments involving the interaction of Subject-to-Subject Raising and Equi with Passive, Subject-to-Object Raising, and Reflexivization are provided by the sentences in (vii) and (viii).

(vii) a.  *Everyone believes John to be likely to make a fool of himself.*
    b.  *John is believed by everyone to be likely to make a fool of himself.*
    c.  *\*Everyone believes John$_i$ to be likely to make a fool of him$_i$.*
    d.  *\*John$_i$ is believed by everyone to be likely to make a fool of him$_i$.*
    e.  *The authorities$_i$ believe John to be likely to tell them$_i$ everything.*
    f.  *John is believed by the authorities$_i$ to be likely to tell them$_i$ everything.*
    g.  *\*The authorities believe John to be likely to tell themselves everything.*
    h.  *\*John is believed by the authorities to be likely to tell themselves everything.*
(viii) a.  *Everyone believes John to be eager to improve himself.*
    b.  *John is believed by everyone to be eager to improve himself.*
    c.  *\*Everyone believes John$_i$ to be eager to improve him$_i$.*
    d.  *\*John$_i$ is believed by everyone to be eager to improve him$_i$.*
    e.  *The authorities$_i$ believe John to be eager to tell them$_i$ everything.*
    f.  *John is believed by the authorities$_i$ to be eager to tell them$_i$ everything.*
    g.  *\*The authorities believe John to be eager to tell themselves everything.*
    h.  *\*John is believed by the authorities to be eager to tell themselves everything.*

cannot be marked for coreference, and the sentence is characterized as ungrammatical.[9]

Although the mechanism for reflexivization is different, the argument against this theory precedes exactly as before. If Passive is a redundancy rule, then both Passive and Subject-to-Object Raising have the effect of relating underlying structures. Thus,

(44)

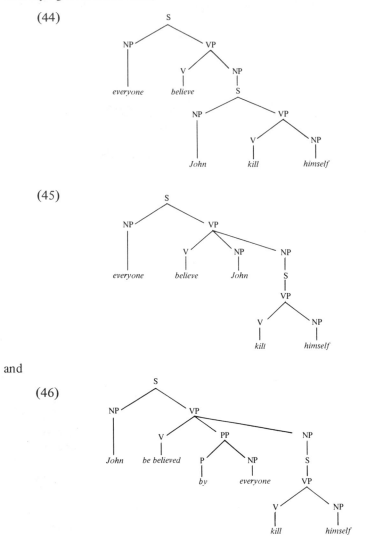

(45)

and

(46)

[9] For more on interpretive theories of pronominal anaphora, see section 83 and Jackendoff (1972). Jackendoff does not claim that Passive is a redundancy rule.

will be generated as underlying structures. Since *John* and *himself* are in the same clause in (44), Reflexive Coreference Assignment will apply, producing the grammatical

(47)  *Everyone believes that John$_i$ killed himself$_i$.*

However, in (45) and (46), there is no other NP in the same clause with *himself.* Thus, Reflexive Coreference Assignment cannot apply and

(48)  *Everyone believed John to have killed himself.*

and

(49)  *John was believed by everyone to have killed himself.*

will be characterized as ungrammatical. Consequently, we must reject a theory in which Passive is a redundancy rule and Reflexivization is interpretive.[10]

### 5.4.2  Reflexivization on the Model of (27–30): No Way Out

Finally, suppose that reflexive and nonreflexive pronouns are generated freely in underlying structure, and that Reflexivization is understood on the model of (27–30). Under this alternative, Reflexivization does not produce new derived structures from input structures, but rather marks certain underlying structures as well- or ill-formed. It is not necessary for our purposes to specify how Reflexivization would be formulated under this alternative. It is sufficient to assume that it characterizes underlying structures like (50) as ill-formed, and underlying structures like (51) as well-formed.

(50)  a.

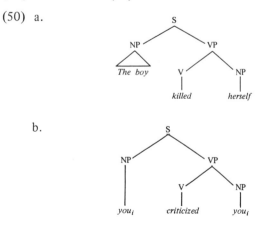

b.

---

[10] The considerations mentioned in footnote 8 apply here as well.

c.

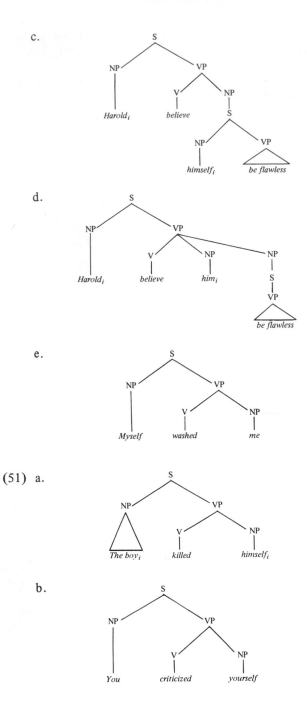

d.

e.

(51) a.

b.

c.

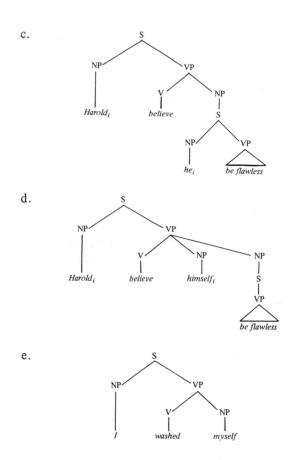

d.

e.

We must now determine whether or not such a rule of Reflexivization can be successfully integrated with the other rules posited by the extended Hypothesis C—e.g., with the S-O-R redundancy rule (27). According to (27), an underlying structure of the form

(52)

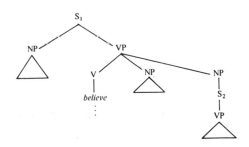

is well-formed if and only if the corresponding underlying structure of the form

(53)

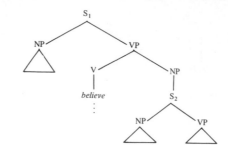

is well-formed. However, this raises a question: Does the well-formedness mentioned in (27) include constraints on Reflexivization or doesn't it? If it does, then a structure must satisfy constraints on Reflexivization to be well-formed in the sense of (27). If it does not, then this is not necessary.

Neither alternative is satisfactory. If well-formedness in (27) includes constraints on Reflexivization, then

(54)  *John believes himself to be flawless.*
       *(which is of the form [52])*

will be incorrectly characterized as deviant because the corresponding structure

(55)  *John believes that himself is flawless.*
       *(which is of the form [53])*

fails to satisfy constraints on Reflexivization. On the other hand, if well-formedness in (27) does not include constraints on Reflexivization, then the fact that

(56)

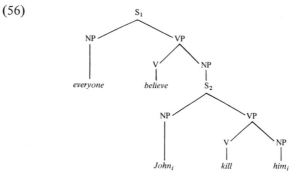

fails to satisfy constraints on Reflexivization will not prevent

(57) *Everyone believed John$_i$ to have killed him$_i$.*

and

(58) *\*John$_i$ was believed by everyone to have killed him$_i$.*

from being incorrectly characterized as well-formed.[11],[12] Thus, no matter what decision is made about the notion of well-formedness in rules like (27), certain data involving reflexive and nonreflexive pronouns will not be accounted for. If Subject-to-Object Raising, Passive, and Reflexivization are to interact correctly, they cannot all have the effect of relating underlying structures.

[11] *\*(57) has the structure

(i)

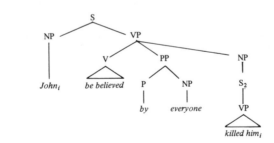

and *\*(58) has the structure

(ii)

Since *John* and *him* are in different clauses, applying the Reflexivization rule directly to these structures does not result in their being characterized as deviant. The only way in which they could be marked as deviant would be on the basis of the deviance of (56). But this cannot be done if well-formedness in (27) does not include constraints on Reflexivization.

[12] If there were no *S*-node above the complement, then

(i) *\*The authorities$_i$ expected John to tell themselves$_i$ everything*

and

(ii) *\*John was expected by the authorities$_i$ to tell themselves$_i$ everything*

would be problematic. These examples would be incorrectly characterized as grammatical if well-formedness in (27) did not include constraints on Reflexivization.

## 6. *CONCLUSION*

This completes the argument for a Passive transformation and against a Passive redundancy rule. First we argued that

(i)   *If Passive were a redundancy rule, then Passive, Subject-to-Object Raising, Subject-to-Subject Raising, Equi, and THERE-Insertion would be rules that have the effect of relating underlying structures.*

Next we showed that

(ii)  *If all these were rules that have the effect of relating underlying structures, then certain facts involving reflexive and nonreflexive pronouns could not be accounted for.*

From this we conclude that

(iii) *Passive and the other cyclical rules mentioned in (i) do not have the effect of relating underlying structures. In particular, Passive is not a redundancy rule.*

In addition to strengthening the original argument for the Passive transformation, the present argument makes it possible to make a more general point. The set of transformations that we have postulated constitutes a highly interconnected system. In certain cases, questions about the status of one rule in the system can only be resolved by considering the impact of different alternatives on the entire system. In the case discussed in this section, the crucial facts involve a complex chain of rule interaction. By making these facts explicit, we were able to decide in favor of the transformational approach against the redundancy rule hypothesis.

# SFI — 8: TOO-Deletion

## 1. THE PHENOMENON

English has pairs of sentences like the following:

(1)  a.   *This rock is too heavy for me to pick it up.*
     b.   *This rock is too heavy for me to pick up.*
(2)  a.   *Susie is too crazy for me to understand her.*
     b.   *Susie is too crazy for me to understand.*
(3)  a.   *Those things are too complicated for me to talk about them.*
     b.   *Those things are too complicated for me to talk about.*
(4)  a.   *That merchandise is too shoddy for you to spend good money on it.*
     b.   *That merchandise is too shoddy for you to spend good money on.*

## 2. A DIFFERENCE BETWEEN TOO-SENTENCES AND NONSUBJECT RAISING SENTENCES

In addition to the obvious difference that TOO-sentences contain *too* while Nonsubject Raising sentences do not, TOO-sentences may contain a pronoun coreferential with the surface subject (as in [1a], [2a], [3a] and [4a]); Nonsubject Raising sentences cannot.

(5)  a.   *\*These books are impossible for the children to read them.*
     b.   *These books are impossible for the children to read.*

## 3. THE SEMANTICS OF TOO-SENTENCES AND
## NONSUBJECT RAISING SENTENCES

If we ask what it is that is crazy in (2), it is not my understanding Susie
that is crazy, but rather Susie herself. This suggests an underlying structure in
which *Susie* is the subject of *crazy*. (We ignore here the question of how *too* is
represented in underlying structure, assuming without argument that *too crazy* is
the predicate.)

(6)

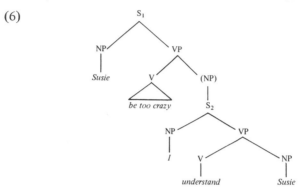

In the Nonsubject Raising sentence (5b), it is not the books but rather the
children's reading the books that is impossible. This suggests the underlying
structure:

(7)

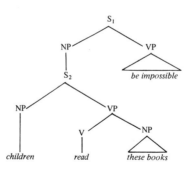

## 4. A HYPOTHESIS TO ACCOUNT FOR TOO-SENTENCES

It is possible to derive (2a–b) from (6) if the grammar contains a rule that
we will call *TOO-Deletion*, which optionally deletes an NP to the right of the
verb in $S_2$ if it is coreferential with the subject of $S_1$. Application of TOO-
Deletion to (6) produces (2b). TOO-Deletion does not apply in the derivation of
sentence (2a).

## 5. TOO-DELETION AND EQUI

One of the arguments in the Discussion of section 61 for Nonsubject Raising over Nonsubject Deletion was provided by the sentence

(8)     *Getting herself arrested on purpose is hard for me to imagine Betsy being willing to consider.*

The argument was based on the assumption that in order to derive (8), the Deletion Hypothesis would have to posit an unnecessary rule that is not independently motivated. If the account of TOO-sentences sketched above is right, then this assumption is incorrect.

Consider the sentences

(9)     a.     *Getting herself arrested on purpose is too crazy for me to imagine Betsy being willing to consider it.*

        b.     *Getting herself arrested on purpose is too crazy for me to imagine Betsy being willing to consider.*

(9a) and (9b) are derived from:[1]

[1] This assumes that the *it* in (9a) arises from the Pronominalization of $S_6$ by $S_2$. Whether or not this assumption is correct is irrelevant to the argument. The argument goes through even if the underlying structure of (9a) is

(i)

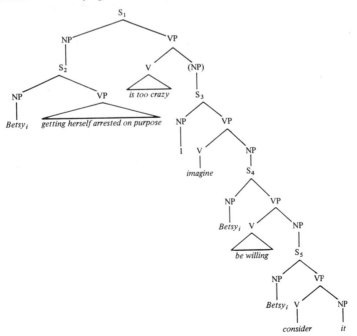

(10)

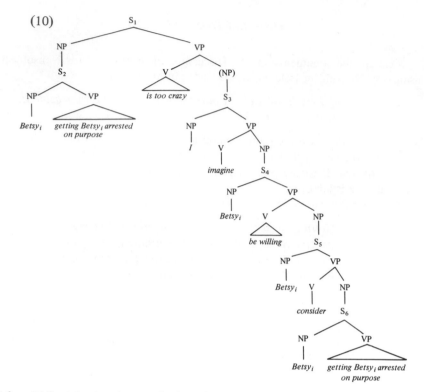

After Reflexivization has applied on $S_6$ and $S_2$, and Equi has deleted the subjects of $S_5$ and $S_6$, the resulting structure is

(11)

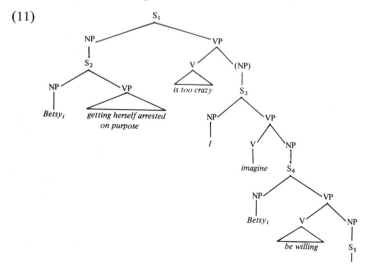

(11) continued

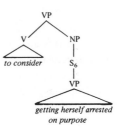

In order to derive (9a) and (b) from (11), two things must happen:

(i) *The subject of $S_2$ must be deleted under coreference with the subject of $S_4$.*

(ii) *TOO-Deletion must delete $S_6$.*

Whatever rule performs the deletion in (i) could presumably be used by the Nonsubject Deletion Hypothesis to derive (8). Since sentences like (9a) and (9b) provide independent motivation for this rule, the argument against Nonsubject Deletion based on (8) is nullified.[2]

## 6. *NONSUBJECT RAISING VS. NONSUBJECT DELETION AGAIN*

Even though TOO-sentences undermine one of our arguments for the rule of Nonsubject Raising, several differences between Nonsubject Raising sentences and TOO-sentences provide reasons for positing this rule. As we pointed out in §3, the semantic relations in the two kinds of sentences are different. In addition, Nonsubject Raising constructions can occur with sentential subjects (or extraposed sentential subjects) in surface structure whereas TOO-constructions cannot.

(12) a. *For the children to read these books is impossible.*
b. *It is impossible for the children to read these books.*
(13) a. *\*For me to pick up this rock is too heavy.*
b. *\*It is too heavy for me to pick up this rock.*
(14) a. *\*For you to spend good money on that merchandise is too shoddy.*
b. *\*It is too shoddy for you to spend good money on that merchandise.*

---

[2] This counterargument is due to Akmajian (1972).

These semantic and syntactic differences can be accounted for if sentences like (5b) are derived from structures like (7) by a rule of Nonsubject Raising, while sentences like (2b) are derived from structures like (6) by a rule of TOO-Deletion. On this analysis, the structures underlying the two kinds of sentences correctly represent their different semantic relations, and the contrast between sentences like (12) and sentences like *(13) and *(14) is automatically explained. For these reasons we posit both a rule of Nonsubject Raising and a rule of TOO-Deletion.

# SFI — 9: Movement in Questions

(1)   *What will Jojo bring _____ for Sue?*
(2)   *Who did Sidney expect Mary Lou to invite _____?*
(3)   *Where did Curtis see Nate _____ yesterday?*
(4)   *When will the doctor arrive _____?*
(5)   *Which team do you think _____ is likely to win?*

In section 64 we mentioned that the arguments that were used to show that topicalized sentences are not generated directly by phrase structure rules, with an NP in initial position and a gap elsewhere, can also be used to show that questions are not generated directly by phrase structure rules. Rather, a transformation is needed to produce the gap in questions.

Generative grammarians have assumed that questions like (1–5) are derived by a rule of Question Movement which moves question phrases to sentence-initial position, thereby creating a gap. However, one might wonder why linguists have assumed that the gap is created by movement rather than deletion.

(6)   a.

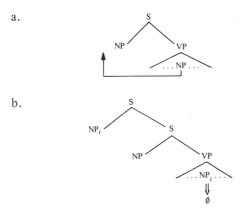

The strongest arguments for movement over deletion are patterned after the argument based on

(7)   *Myself I can't stand* _____ .

which was used to show that Topicalization is a movement rather than a deletion rule. In (7), the topicalized NP must originate elsewhere in the sentence in order to undergo Reflexivization. Thus, (7) must be derived from

(8)

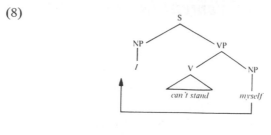

rather than

(9)

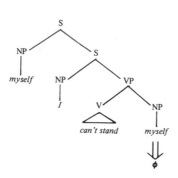

Since question phrases are not reflexive, this argument does not carry over directly to questions. However, if question phrases show other signs of having originated elsewhere in the sentence, then analogous arguments can be used to show that questions like (1–5) are produced by movement rather than deletion. Such arguments are forthcoming in languages which have extensive case marking systems. In these languages, subjects and objects typically display different case markings. If the case marking system extends to question phrases, and if these phrases are required to appear in sentence-initial position, then an argument for Question Movement can be constructed. In such languages, the question phrase appears with the case marking that it would have had if it were in the gap. This fact can be accounted for if the question phrase originates inside the sentence, receives appropriate case marking depending on its position in the sentence, and then is moved to initial position by Question Movement.

The ability to construct this kind of argument for English is limited by the fact that in most dialects of English, case marking of question words is either extremely restricted or nonexistent. There are, however, some dialects in which such case marking does show up.

(10) a.   *With **whom** did you speak_____?*
     b.   **With **who** did you speak_____?*

(11) a.   *With **whom** did you say you spoke_____?*
     b.   **With **who** did you say you spoke_____?*

(12) a.   ***Whom** did you see_____?*
     b.   ***Who** did you see_____?*

(13) a.   ***Whom** did Sue say she saw_____?*
     b.   ***Who** did Sue say she saw_____?*

(14) a.   ***Who** is coming tonight?*
     b.   ***Whom** is coming tonight?*

(15) a.   ***Who** did Sue say_____is coming tonight?*
     b.   ***Whom** did Sue Say_____is coming tonight?*

It would be desirable to show that the distribution of *who* and *whom* in (10–15) follows automatically from something that is needed independently in the grammar of these dialects.

There is a class of questions in English called *echo questions* or *incredulity questions,* in which the question word is not in initial position and is pronounced with extra emphasis and rising intonation. In the varieties of English with which we are concerned, the distribution of *who* and *whom* in these questions is as follows.

(16) a.   *You spoke with **whom**?*
     b.   **You spoke with **who**?*

(17) a.   *You saw **whom**?*
     b.   **You saw **who**?*

(18) a.   *She said she saw **whom**?*
     b.   **She said she saw **who**?*

(19) a.   *Who is coming tonight?*
     b.   **Whom is coming tonight?*

(20) a.   *She said **who** is coming tonight?*
     b.   **She said **whom** is coming tonight?*

Some rule is needed to account for the distribution of *who* and *whom* in (16–20). If the grammar has a rule of Question Movement that applies after the rule needed for (16–20), then the distribution of *who* and *whom* in (10–15) will follow automatically. If, on the other hand, a grammar generated question words directly in initial position, then we would need one rule to account for the distribution of *who* and *whom* in (10-15) and another rule to account for their distribution in (16-20). In such a grammar there would be no way of making (10-15) follow automatically from (16-20). Positing a rule of Question Movement allows us to do this.

It should be pointed out that this argument works only if the grammar has some way of ensuring that Question Movement does not apply until after the case marking rule that accounts for the distribution of *who* and *whom*. There are at least two ways that a grammar might do this. It could include a special rule ordering statement preventing Question Movement from applying before Case Marking or it could make Case Marking cyclical and Question Movement post-cyclical. We will not try to decide between these alternatives here.

It should also be pointed out that the above argument is not applicable to all varieties of English. Many speakers do not use *whom* at all; others use it only immediately following a preposition. In these dialects, the distribution of *who* and *whom* provides no evidence either for or against deriving questions by movement rather than deletion. Nevertheless, we follow the great majority of generative grammarians in positing a rule of Question Movement for all dialects of English.

# Bibliography

Aissen, J. (1974a) "Verb Raising," *Linguistic Inquiry* 5, 325-366.

_____. (1974b) "The Syntax of Causative Constructions." Doctoral dissertation, Harvard.

Aissen, J., and D. M. Perlmutter. (1976) "Clause Reduction in Spanish," in *Proceedings of the Second Annual Meeting of the Berkeley Linguistics Society*, Dept. of Linguistics, University of California at Berkeley.

Akmajian, A. (1972) "Getting Tough," *Linguistic Inquiry* 3, 373-377.

_____. (1975) "More Evidence for the NP Cycle," *Linguistic Inquiry* 6, 115-129.

Anderson, S. A., and P. Kiparsky, eds. (1973) *A Festschrift for Morris Halle.* Holt, Rinehard & Winston, New York.

Bach, E. (1968) "Nouns and Noun Phrases," in Bach and Harms (1968).

_____. (1970) "Problominalization," *Linguistic Inquiry* 1, 121-122.

_____. (1971) "Questions," *Linguistic Inquiry* 2, 153-166.

_____. (1974) *Syntactic Theory.* Holt, Rinehart & Winston, New York.

Bach, E., and R. Harms, eds. (1968) *Universals in Linguistic Theory.* Holt, Rinehart & Winston, New York.

Bach, E., and G. Horn. (1976) "Remarks on 'Conditions on Transformations,' " *Linguistic Inquiry* 7, 265-299.

Baker, C. L. (1970) "Notes on the Description of English Questions: The Role of an Abstract Question Morpheme," *Foundations of Language* 6, 197-219.

Berman, A. (1973) "Adjectives and Adjective Complement Constructions in English." Doctoral dissertation, Harvard University.

_____. (1974) "On the VSO Hypothesis," *Linguistic Inquiry* 5, 1-38.

Berman, A., and M. Szamosi. (1972) "Observations on Sentential Stress," *Language* 48, 304-325.

Bolinger, D. L. (1967) "The Imperative in English," in *To Honor Roman Jakobson.* Mouton, The Hague.

————. (1972) "What did John keep the car that was in?" *Linguistic Inquiry* 3, 109–114.

Brame, M. K. (1976) *Conjectures and Refutations in Syntax and Semantics.* Elsevier, Amsterdam and New York.

Breckenridge, J. (1975) "The Post-Cyclicity of ES-Insertion in German," *Papers from the Eleventh Regional Meeting of the Chicago Linguistic Society,* University of Chicago, Chicago, Illinois.

Bresnan, J. (1970a) "An Argument Against Pronominalization," *Linguistic Inquiry* 1, 122–123.

————. (1970b) "On Complementizers: Toward a Syntactic Theory of Complement Types," *Foundations of Language* 6, 297–321.

————. (1971) "On Sentence Stress and Syntactic Transformations," *Language* 47, 257–281.

————. (1972) "Theory of Complementation in English Syntax." Doctoral dissertation, M.I.T.

————. (1975) "Comparative Deletion and Constraints on Transformations," *Linguistic Analysis* 1, 25–74.

————. (1976a) "Evidence for a Theory of Unbounded Transformations," *Linguistic Analysis* 2, 353–393.

————. (1976b) "Nonarguments for Raising," *Linguistic Inquiry* 7, 485–501.

————. (1976c) "On the Form and Functioning of Transformational Rules," *Linguistic Inquiry* 7, 3–40.

————. (1977) "Variables in a Theory of Transformations," in Culicover, Akmajian, and Wasow (1977).

————. (1978) "A Realistic Transformational Grammar," in M. Halle, J. Bresnan, and G. Miller, eds. *Linguistic Theory and Psychological Reality.* M.I.T. Press, Cambridge, Mass.

Cattell, R. (1976) "Constraints on Movement Rules," *Language* 52, 18–50.

Chomsky, N. (1956) *The Logical Structure of Linguistic Theory.* Mimeographed. Published by Plenum, New York, 1975.

————. (1957) *Syntactic Structures.* Mouton, The Hague.

————. (1961) "On the Notion 'Rule of Grammar,'" in R. Jakobson, ed. *Structure of Language and its Mathematical Aspects,* Proceedings of Symposia in Applied Mathematics, vol. 12, American Mathematical Society, Providence, R.I. Reprinted in Fodor and Katz (1964).

————. (1962) "A Transformational Approach to Syntax," in A. Hill, ed., *Third Texas Conference on Problems of Linguistic Analysis in English,* University of Texas, Austin. Reprinted in Fodor and Katz (1964).

————. (1963) "Formal Properties of Grammars," in Luce, Bush, and Galanter (1963).

————. (1964) *Current Issues in Linguistic Theory.* Mouton, The Hague.

————. (1965) *Aspects of the Theory of Syntax.* M.I.T. Press, Cambridge, Mass.

————. (1966) "The Current Scene in Linguistics: Present Directions," *College English,* 27, 587–595. Reprinted in Reibel and Schane (1969).

————. (1968) *Language and Mind.* Harcourt Brace & World, New York. Second edition, 1972.

————. (1970) "Remarks on Nominalization," in Jacobs and Rosenbaum (1970). Also reprinted in Chomsky (1972*c*).

————. (1972*a*) "Deep Structure, Surface Structure, and Semantic Interpretation," in Chomsky (1972*c*).

————. (1972*b*) "Empirical Issues in the Theory of Transformational Grammar," in Peters (1972). Also reprinted in Chomsky (1972*c*).

————. (1972*c*) *Studies on Semantics in Generative Grammar.* Mouton, The Hague.

————. (1973) "Conditions on Transformations," in Anderson and Kiparsky (1973).

————. (1976) "Conditions on Rules of Grammar," *Linguistic Analysis* 2, 303–350.

————. (1977) "On WH-Movement," in Culicover, Akmajian, and Wasow (1977).

Chomsky, N., and H. Lasnik. (1977) "Filters and Control," *Linguistic Inquiry* 8, 425–504.

Chomsky, N., and G. Miller. (1963) "Introduction to the Formal Analysis of Natural Languages," in Luce, Bush, and Galanter (1963).

Clark, H. H., and E. V. Clark (1977) *Psychology and Language.* Harcourt Brace Jovanovich, New York.

Clements, G. N. (1975) "Super-Equi and the Intervention Constraint," in Kaisse and Hankamer (1975).

Cole, P., and J. L. Morgan, eds. (1975) *Syntax and Semantics 3: Speech Acts.* Academic Press, New York.

Cole, P., W. Harbert, S. Sridhar, S. Hashimoto, C. Nelson, and D. Smietana. (1977) "Noun Phrase Accessibility and Island Constraints," in P. Cole and J. Sadock, eds., *Syntax and Semantics 8: Grammatical Relations.* Academic Press, New York.

Culicover, P., A. Akmajian, and T. Wasow. (1977) *Formal Syntax.* Academic Press, New York.

Culicover, P., and K. Wexler (1977) "Some Syntactic Implications of a Theory of Language Learnability," in Culicover, Wasow, and Akmajian (1977).

Davidson, D., and G. Harman, eds. (1972) *Semantics of Natural Language.* Reidel, Boston, Mass.

Dik, S. (1973) "Crossing Coreference Again," *Foundations of Language* 9, 306–325.

————. (1978) *Functional Grammar.* North-Holland Publishing, Amsterdam and New York.

Dougherty, R. (1969) "An Interpretive Theory of Pronominal Reference," *Foundations of Language* 5, 488–519.

Downing, B. T. (1969) "Vocatives and Third-Person Imperatives in English," *Papers in Linguistics* 1, 570–592.

Eckman, F. (1974) "Optional Rules and Inclusion Relations." Available from Indiana University Linguistics Club.

Emonds, J. E. (1972) "A Reformulation of Certain Syntactic Transformations," in Peters (1972).

—————. (1976) *A Transformational Approach to English Syntax: Root, Structure-Preserving, and Local Transformations.* Academic Press, New York.

Erteschik, N. (1973) "On the Nature of Island Constraints." Doctoral dissertation, M.I.T.

Evers, A. (1975) "The Transformational Cycle in Dutch and German." Doctoral dissertation, Rijksuniversiteit te Utrecht.

Fauconnier, G. (1971) "Theoretical Implications of Some Global Phenomena in Syntax." Doctoral dissertation, University of California at San Diego.

—————. (1974) *La Coréférence: Syntaxe ou sémantique?* Editions du Seuil, Paris.

Fiengo, R. (1974) "Semantic Conditions on Surface Structure." Doctoral dissertation, M.I.T.

—————. (1977) "On Trace Theory," *Linguistic Inquiry* 8, 35–61.

Fillmore, C. J. (1963) "The Position of Embedding Transformations in a Grammar," *Word* 19, 208–231.

—————. (1968) "The Case for Case," in Bach and Harms (1968).

Fodor, J. A., T. G. Bever, and M. F. Garrett. (1974), *The Psychology of Language.* McGraw-Hill, New York.

Fodor, J. A., and J. J. Katz, eds., (1964) *The Structure of Language.* Prentice-Hall, Englewood Cliffs, New Jersey.

Fodor, J. D. (1967) "Noun Phrase Complementation in English and German." Paper, M.I.T., Cambridge, Mass.

Freidin, R. (1975) "The Analysis of Passives," *Language* 51, 384–405.

Geach, P. T. (1962) *Reference and Generality.* Cornell University Press, Ithaca, New York.

—————. (1967) "Intentional Identity," *Journal of Philosophy* 64, 627–632.

Green, G. M. (1975) "How to Get People to Do Things with Words," in Cole and Morgan (1975).

Grinder, J. (1970) "Super Equi-NP Deletion," in *Papers from the Sixth Regional Meeting of the Chicago Linguistic Society.* University of Chicago, Chicago, Illinois.

—————. (1971) "A Reply to 'Super Equi-NP Deletion as Dative Deletion,' " in *Papers from the Seventh Regional Meeting of the Chicago Linguistic Society.* University of Chicago, Chicago, Illinois.

—————. (1972) "Cyclic and Linear Grammars," in Kimball (1972b).

Grinder, J., and P. M. Postal. (1971) "Missing Antecedents." *Linguistic Inquiry* 2, 269–312.

Gross, M. (1972) *Mathematical Models in Linguistics.* Prentice-Hall, Englewood Cliffs, New Jersey.

Gross, M., and A Lentin. (1970) *Introduction to Formal Grammars.* Springer-Verlag, New York and Berlin.

Grosu, A. (1972) *The Strategic Content of Island Constraints.* Ohio State University Working Papers in Linguistics 13.

_____. (1973*a*) "On the Nonunitary Nature of the Coordinate Structure Constraint," *Linguistic Inquiry* 4, 88–92.

_____. (1973*b*) "On the Status of the So-called Right Roof Constraint," *Language* 49, 294–311.

_____. (1974*a*) "On the Nature of the Left Branch Condition," *Linguistic Inquiry* 5, 308–319.

_____. (1974*b*) "On Reordering Elements of Clause-Nonfinal Constituents," *Papers from the Tenth Regional Meeting of the Chicago Linguistic Society,* University of Chicago, Chicago, Illinois.

_____. (1974*c*) "On Self-embedding and Double Function," *Linguistic Inquiry* 3, 464–469.

_____. (1975) "On the Inherent Difficulty of Center-embedding Constructions," *Die Sprache* 21, 1.

Grosu, A., and S. A. Thompson. (1977), "Constraints on the Distribution of NP Clauses," *Language* 53, 104–151.

Hankamer, J. (1974) "On the Non-cyclic Nature of Wh-Clefting," *Papers from the Tenth Regional Meeting of the Chicago Linguistic Society,* University of Chicago, Chicago, Illinois.

Hankamer, J. and I. Sag. (1976), "Deep and Surface Anaphora," *Linguistic Inquiry* 7, 391–428.

Harman, G. (1972) "Deep Structure as Logical Form," in Davidson and Harman (1972).

_____. ed. (1974) *On Noam Chomsky: Critical Essays.* Anchor, Garden City, New York.

_____. (1976) "Anaphoric Pronouns as Bound Variables: Syntax or Semantics," *Language* 52, 78–81.

Harris, F. W. (1976) "Reflexivization," in McCawley (1976).

Harris, Z. (1946) "From Morpheme to Utterance," *Language.* Reprinted in M. Joos, ed. *Readings in Linguistics 1.*

_____. (1956) "Introduction to Transformations," reprinted in Z. Harris, *Papers in Structural and Transformational Linguistics.* Reidel, Dordrecht, Holland (1970).

_____. (1957) "Co-occurrence and Transformation in Linguistic Structure," reprinted in Fodor and Katz (1964).

Hasegawa, K. (1965) "English Imperatives," in *Festschrift for Professor Nakajima.* Kenkyusha, Tokyo, 20–28.

_____. (1968) "The Passive Construction in English," *Language* 44, 230–243.

Hastings, A. J. (1976) "On the Obligatory-Optional Principle," in Koutsoudas (1976*a*).

Hayes, B. (1976) "The Semantic Nature of the Intervention Constraint," *Linguistic Inquiry* 7, 371–376.

Helke, M. (1970) "The Grammar of English Reflexives." Doctoral dissertation, M.I.T.

Higgins, R. (1973) "On J. Emonds' Analysis of Extraposition," in J. Kimball, ed., *Syntax and Semantics 2.* Academic Press, New York.

Hooper, J., and S. A. Thompson. (1973) "On the Applicability of Root Transformations," *Linguistic Inquiry* 4, 465–498.

Horn, G. (1974) "The Noun Phrase Constraints." Doctoral dissertation, University of Massachusetts, Amherst.

Jackendoff, R. S. (1972) *Semantic Interpretation in Generative Grammar.* M.I.T. Press, Cambridge, Mass.

————. (1975) "*Tough* and the Trace Theory of Movement Rules," *Linguistic Inquiry* 6, 437–446.

————. (1977) $\overline{X}$ *Syntax: A Study of Phrase Structure,* Linguistic Inquiry Monograph No. 2, M.I.T. Press, Cambridge, Mass.

Jacobs, R., and P. Rosenbaum. (1968) *English Transformational Grammar.* Blaisdell, Waltham, Mass.

————. eds. (1970) *Readings in English Transformational Grammar.* Blaisdell, Waltham, Mass.

Jacobson, P. (1977) "The Syntax of Crossing Coreference Sentences." Doctoral dissertation, University of California, Berkeley.

Jacobson, P., and P. Neubauer. (1976) "Rule Cyclicity: Evidence from the Intervention Constraint," *Linguistic Inquiry* 7, 429–461.

Jenkins, L. (1975) *The English Existential.* Max Niemeyer Verlag, Tübingen.

Jespersen, O. (1965) *The Philosophy of Grammar.* Norton, New York.

Joseph, B. (1976) "Raising in Modern Greek: A Copy Process?" in J. Hankamer and J. Aissen, eds., *Harvard Studies in Syntax and Semantics,* vol. 2, 290r.

————. (1978) "On the Role of Morphology in Syntactic Change." Doctoral dissertation, Harvard.

Joseph, B., and D. M. Perlmutter (to appear) "On the Empirical Content of the Cyclical Theory of Grammar: A Study of Modern Greek."

Kaisse, E., and J. Hankamer, (1975) *Papers from the Fifth Annual Meeting of the North East Linguistic Society,* Dept. of Linguistics, Harvard University, Cambridge, Mass.

Kajita, M. (1968) *A Generative-Transformational Study of Semi-Auxiliaries in Present-Day American English.* Sanseido, Tokyo.

Karttunen, L. (1969) "Pronouns and Variables," in *Papers from the Fifth Regional Meeting of the Chicago Linguistic Society,* University of Chicago, Chicago, Illinois.

————. (1971) "Definite Descriptions with Crossing Coreference," *Foundations of Language* 7, 157–182.

Katz, J. J., and P. M. Postal. (1964) *An Integrated Theory of Linguistic Descriptions.* M.I.T. Press, Cambridge, Mass.

Kaufman, E. (1974) "Navajo Spatial Enclitics: A Case for Unbounded Rightward Movement," *Linguistic Inquiry* 5, 507–533.

Kayne, R. S. (1975) *French Syntax: The Transformational Cycle,* M.I.T. Press, Cambridge, Mass.

Keenan, E., ed. (1975) *Formal Semantics of Natural Language,* Cambridge University Press, Cambridge, England.

Keyser, S. J., and P. M. Postal. (1976) *Beginning English Grammar,* Harper & Row, New York.

Kimball, J. P. (1971) "Super Equi-NP Deletion as Dative Deletion," in *Papers from the Seventh Regional Meeting of the Chicago Linguistic Society,* University of Chicago, Chicago, Illinois.

————. (1972*a*) "Cyclic and Noncyclic Grammars," in Kimball (1972*b*).

————. ed. (1972*b*) *Syntax and Semantics 1.* Seminar Press, New York.

————. (1973*a*) *The Formal Theory of Grammar.* Prentice-Hall, Englewood Cliffs, New Jersey.

————. (1973*b*) "Seven Principles of Surface Structure Parsing," *Cognition* 2, 15–47.

Kiparsky, P., and C. Kiparsky. (1970) "Fact," in M. Bierwisch and K. Heidolph, eds., *Progress in Linguistics,* Mouton, The Hague.

Klima, E. S. (1964*a*) "Negation in English," in Fodor and Katz (1964).

————. (1964*b*) "Relatedness between Grammatical Systems," *Language* 40, 1–20.

Kohrt, M. (1975) "A Note on Bounding," *Linguistic Inquiry* 6, 167–171.

Koutsoudas, A. (1972) "The Strict Order Fallacy," *Language* 48, 88–96.

————. (1973) "Extrinsic Order and the Complex NP Constraint," *Linguistic Inquiry* 4, 69–81.

————. ed. (1976*a*) *The Application and Ordering of Grammatical Rules.* Mouton, The Hague and Paris.

————. (1976*b*) "Unordered Rule Hypotheses," In Koutsoudas (1976*a*).

Koutsoudas, A., G. A. Sanders, and C. Noll. (1974) "On the Application of Phonological Rules," *Language* 50, 1–28.

Kuno, S. (1973) "Constraints on Internal Clauses and Sentential Subjects," *Linguistic Inquiry* 4, 363–385.

————. (1975*a*) "Super Equi-NP Deletion is a Pseudo-Transformation," in Kaisse and Hankamer (1975). Revised version published in *Studies in English Linguistics,* Vol. 4 (1976), Asahi Press, Tokyo.

————. (1975*b*) "Three Perspectives in the Functional Approach to Syntax," in *Papers from the Parasession on Functionalism,* Chicago Linguistic Society.

————. (1976) "Subject, Theme, and the Speaker's Empathy—A Reexamination of Relativization Phenomena," in C. Li, ed. *Subject and Topic.* Academic Press, New York.

Kuno, S., and E. Kaburaki. (1977) "Empathy and Syntax," *Linguistic Inquiry* 8, 627–672.

Kuroda, S. Y. (1968) "English Relativization and Certain Related Problems," *Language* 44, 244–266. Reprinted in Reibel and Schane (1969).

Lakoff, G. (1966) "Deep and Surface Grammar." Paper, Harvard. Available from Indiana University Linguistics Club.

————. (1968) *Pronouns and Reference.* Available from Indiana University Linguistics Club.

————. (1971) "On Generative Semantics," in D. Steinberg and L. A. Jakobovits, eds., *Semantics: An Interdisciplinary Reader in Philosophy, Linguistics, and Psychology.* Cambridge University Press, Cambridge.

Lakoff, R. (1968) *Abstract Syntax and Latin Complementation.* M.I.T. Press, Cambridge, Mass.

————. (1971) "Passive Resistance," *Papers from the Seventh Regional Meeting of the Chicago Linguistic Society,* University of Chicago, Chicago, Illinois.

Langacker, R. (1969) "Pronominalization and the Chain of Command," in Reibel and Schane (1969).

————. (1974) "The Question of Q," *Foundations of Language* 11, 1-37.

Langacker, R., and P. Munro. (1975) "Passives and their Meaning," *Language* 51, 789-830.

Lasnik, H. (1976) "Remarks on Coreference," *Linguistic Analysis* 2, 1-22.

Lasnik, H., and R. Fiengo. (1974) "Complement Object Deletion," *Linguistic Inquiry* 5, 535-571.

Lees, R. B. (1960) *The Grammar of English Nominalizations.* Mouton, The Hague.

Lees, R. B., and E. S. Klima. (1963) "Rules for English Pronominalization," *Language* 39, 17-28. Reprinted in Reibel and Schane (1969).

Lehmann, T. (1972) "Some Arguments against Ordered Rules," *Language* 48, 541-550.

Levelt, W. (1974) *Formal Grammars in Linguistics and Psycholinguistics.* Mouton, The Hague.

Luce, R. D., R. R. Bush, and E. Galanter, eds. (1963) *Handbook of Mathematical Psychology,* Vol. II, Wiley, New York.

Maling, J. (1978) "An Asymmetry with respect to WH-Islands," *Linguistic Inquiry* 9, 75-89.

Matthews, P. (1970) "A Note on the Ordering of Transformations," *Journal of Linguistics* 6, 115-117.

McCawley, J. D. (1970a) "English as a VSO Language," *Language* 46, 286-299.

————. (1970b) "Where Do Noun Phrases Come From?" in Jacobs and Rosenbaum (1970).

————. (1972) "A Program for Logic," in Davidson and Harman (1972).

————. ed. (1976) *Syntax and Semantics 7: Notes from the Linguistic Underground.* Academic Press, New York.

Miller, G. A., E. Galanter, and K. H. Pribram. (1960) *Plans and the Structure of Behavior.* Holt, Rinehart, & Winston, New York.

Milsark, G. L. (1977) "Toward an Explanation of Certain Peculiarities of the Existential Construction in English," *Linguistic Analysis* 3, 1-29.

Morgan, J. L. (1970) "On the Criterion of Identity for Noun Phrase Deletion," in *Papers from the Sixth Regional Meeting of the Chicago Linguistic Society,* University of Chicago, Chicago, Illinois.

Morgan, J. L., and G. M. Green. (1977) "More Evidence for a Cycle of Transformations?" in McCawley (1976).

Morin, J. Y. (1976) "Rule Ordering and the Cyclic Principle in Syntax," in Koutsoudas (1976a).

Moyne, J., and G. Carden. (1974) "Subject Reduplication in Persian," *Linguistic Inquiry* 5, 205-249.

Neeld, R. (1976) "On Some Non-evidence for the Cycle in Syntax," *Language* 52, 51-60.

Neubauer, P. (1972) "Super Equi Revisited," in *Papers from the Eighth Regional Meeting of the Chicago Linguistic Society,* University of Chicago, Chicago, Illinois.

Newmeyer, F. J. (1969) "The Underlying Structure of the *Begin*-class Verbs," *Papers from the Fifth Annual Meeting of the Chicago Linguistic Society,* University of Chicago, Chicago, Illinois.

————. (1971) "The Source of Derived Nominals in English," *Language* 47, 786–796.

————. (1975) "The Position of Incorporation Transformations in the Grammar," *Proceedings of the First Annual Meeting of the Berkeley Linguistics Society,* Dept. of Linguistics, University of California at Berkeley.

————. (1976) "The Precyclic Nature of Predicate Raising," in M. Shibatani, ed., *Syntax and Semantics 6: The Grammar of Causative Constructions.* Academic Press, New York.

Nida, E. A. (1943) "A Synopsis of English Syntax." Doctoral dissertation, University of Michigan. Published, revised, by Mouton, The Hague, 1966.

Noll, C. (1976) "Arguments for the Noncyclicity of Transformations," in Koutsoudas (1976*a*).

Partee, B. (1972) "Opacity, Coreference, and Pronouns," in Davidson and Harman (1972).

————. (1975) "Deletion and Variable Binding," in Keenan (1975).

Peranteau, P., J. Levi, and G. Phares. (1972) *The Chicago Which Hunt.* Chicago Linguistic Society, University of Chicago.

Perlmutter, D. M. (1970) "The Two Verbs 'Begin,' " in Jacobs and Rosenbaum (1970).

————. (1971) *Deep and Surface Structure Constraints in Syntax.* Holt, Rinehart & Winston, New York.

————. (1972) "Evidence for Shadow Pronouns in French Relativization," in Peranteau, Levi, and Phares (1972).

Perlmutter, D. M., and P. M. Postal. (1977) "Toward a Universal Characterization of Passivization," *Proceedings of the Third Annual Meeting of the Berkeley Linguistics Society,* Dept. of Linguistics, University of California at Berkeley.

Peters, S. (1972) *Goals of Linguistic Theory,* Prentice-Hall, Englewood Cliffs, New Jersey.

Peters, S., and R. Ritchie. (1973) "On the Generative Power of Transformational Grammars," *Information Sciences* 6, 49–83.

Postal, P. M. (1963) "Mohawk Prefix Generation," in H. Lunt, ed., *Proceedings of the Ninth International Congress of Linguists* Mouton, The Hague.

————. (1964*a*) *Constituent Structure: A Study of Contemporary Models of Syntactic Description,* Publication 30 of the Indiana University Research Center in Anthropology, Folklore, and Linguistics. Reprinted by Mouton, The Hague.

————. (1964*b*) "Underlying and Superficial Linguistic Structure," *Harvard Educational Review* 34, 246–266. Reprinted in Reibel and Schane (1969).

————. (1968) Epilogue to Jacobs and Rosenbaum (1968).

————. (1969) Review of A. McIntosh and M. A. K. Halliday, *Patterns of Language,* in *Foundations of Language* 5, 409–426.

————. (1970) "On the Surface Verb 'Remind,' " *Linguistic Inquiry* 1, 37–20.

————. (1971) *Crossover Phenomena,* Holt, Rinehart & Winston, New York.

————. (1972a) "The Best Theory," in Peters (1972).

————. (1972b) "On Some Rules That Are Not Successive Cyclic," *Linguistic Inquiry* 3, 211–222.

————. (1974) *On Raising.* M.I.T. Press, Cambridge, Mass.

————. (1977) "About a 'Nonargument' for Raising," *Linguistic Inquiry* 8, 141–154.

Postal, P. M., and J. R. Ross. (1971) "Tough Movement Sí, Tough Deletion No!" *Linguistic Inquiry* 2, 544–546.

Pullum, G. K. (1976) "Rule Interaction and the Organization of a Grammar." Doctoral dissertation, University of London. To be published by Garland, New York.

Quícoli, C. (1976) "On Portuguese Impersonal Verbs," in J. Schmidt-Radefeldt, ed., *Readings in Portuguese Linguistics.* North-Holland Publishing, Amsterdam and New York.

Reibel, D. A., and S. A. Schane, eds. (1969) *Modern Studies in English.* Prentice-Hall, Englewood Cliffs, New Jersey.

Reinhart, T. (1976) "The Syntactic Domain of Anaphora." Doctoral dissertation, M.I.T.

Ringen, C. (1972) "On Arguments for Rule Ordering," *Foundations of Language* 8, 266–273.

————. (1974) "Obligatory-Optional Precedence," *Foundations of Language* 11, 565–570.

Rizzi, L. (1976) "La Montée du sujet, le *si* impersonnel, et une règle de restructuration dans la syntaxe italienne." Paper, Scuola Normale Superiore, Pisa.

Rosenbaum, P. (1967a) *The Grammar of English Predicate Complement Constructions.* M.I.T. Press, Cambridge, Mass.

————. (1967b) "Phrase Structure Principles of English Complex Sentence Formation," *Journal of Linguistics* 3, 103–118. Reprinted in Reibel and Schane (1969).

————. (1970) "A Principle Governing Deletion in English Sentential Complementation," in Jacobs and Rosenbaum (1970).

Ross, J. R. (1967) "Constraints on Variables in Syntax." Doctoral dissertation, M.I.T., Cambridge, Mass. Available from Indiana University Linguistics Club.

————. (1969a) "A Proposed Rule of Tree-Pruning," in Reibel and Schane (1969).

————. (1969b) "The Cyclical Nature of English Pronominalization," in Reibel and Schane (1969).

————. (1970) "*Whether*-Deletion," *Linguistic Inquiry* 1, 146.

————. (1973) "Nouniness," in O. Fujimura, ed., *Three Dimensions of Linguistic Theory.* TEC, Tokyo.

_____. (1974) "Three Batons for Cognitive Psychology," in W. B. Weimer and D. S. Palermo, eds., *Cognition and the Symbolic Processes,* Lawrence Erlbaum Associates.

Rouveret, A. (1977) "Les consécutives: Forme et interprétation," *Linguisticae Investigationes* 1, 197-234.

Ruwet, N. (1972) *Théorie syntaxique et syntaxe du français.* Éditions du Seuil, Paris.

_____. (1976) "Subject-Raising and Extraposition," in M. Luján and F. Hensey, eds., *Current Studies in Romance Linguistics,* Georgetown University Press, Washington, D.C.

Sanders, G. A. (1974a) "Precedence Relations in Language," *Foundations of Language* 11, 361-400.

_____. (1974b) "On the Notions 'Optional' and 'Obligatory' in Linguistics," *Minnesota Working Papers in Linguistics and the Philosophy of Language* 2, 145-186.

_____. (1976) "On the Exclusion of Extrinsic Ordering Constraints," in Koutsoudas (1976a).

Schachter, P. (1973) "Focus and Relativization," *Language* 49, 19-46.

Schmerling, S. (1975) "Imperative Subject Deletion and Some Related Matters," *Linguistic Inquiry* 6, 501-510.

_____. (1977) "The Syntax of English Imperatives." Paper, University of Texas, Austin.

Schwartz, A. (1972) "Constraints on Movement Transformations," *Journal of Linguistics* 8, 35-85.

Smith, C. S. (1961) "A Class of Complex Modifiers in English," *Language* 37, 342-365.

_____. (1964) "Determiners and Relative Clauses in a Generative Grammar of English," *Language* 40, 37-52. Reprinted in Reibel and Schane (1969).

Soames, S. (1974) "Rule Orderings, Obligatory Transformations, and Derivational Constraints," *Theoretical Linguistics* 1, 116-138.

Stockwell, R., P. Schachter, and B. Partee. (1973) *The Major Syntactic Structures of English.* Holt, Rinehart & Winston, New York.

Szamosi, M. (1973) "On the Unity of Subject Raising," in *Papers from the Ninth Regional Meeting of the Chicago Linguistic Society,* University of Chicago, Chicago, Illinois.

Tanenhaus, M. K., and J. M. Carroll (1975) "The Clausal Processing Hierarchy and Nouniness," in *Papers from the Parasession on Functionalism,* 499-511, Chicago Linguistic Society, Department of Linguistics, University of Chicago, Chicago, Illinois.

Thorne, J. P. (1966) "English Imperative Sentences," *Journal of Linguistics* 2, 69-78.

Vergnaud, J. R. (1974) "French Relative Clauses." Doctoral dissertation, M.I.T.

Wall, R (1972) *Introduction to Mathematical Linguistics,* Prentice-Hall, Englewood Cliffs, New Jersey.

Wasow, T. (1972) "Anaphoric Relations in English." Doctoral dissertation, M.I.T.

———. (1973) "More Migs and Pilots," *Foundations of Language* 9, 297-305.

———. (1975) "Anaphoric Pronouns as Bound Variables," *Language* 51, 368-384.

———. (1977) "Transformations and the Lexicon," in Culicover, Akmajian and Wasow (1977).

Zwicky, A. M. (1971) "In a Manner of Speaking," *Linguistic Inquiry* 2, 223-233.